An Abolitionist in
the Appalachian South

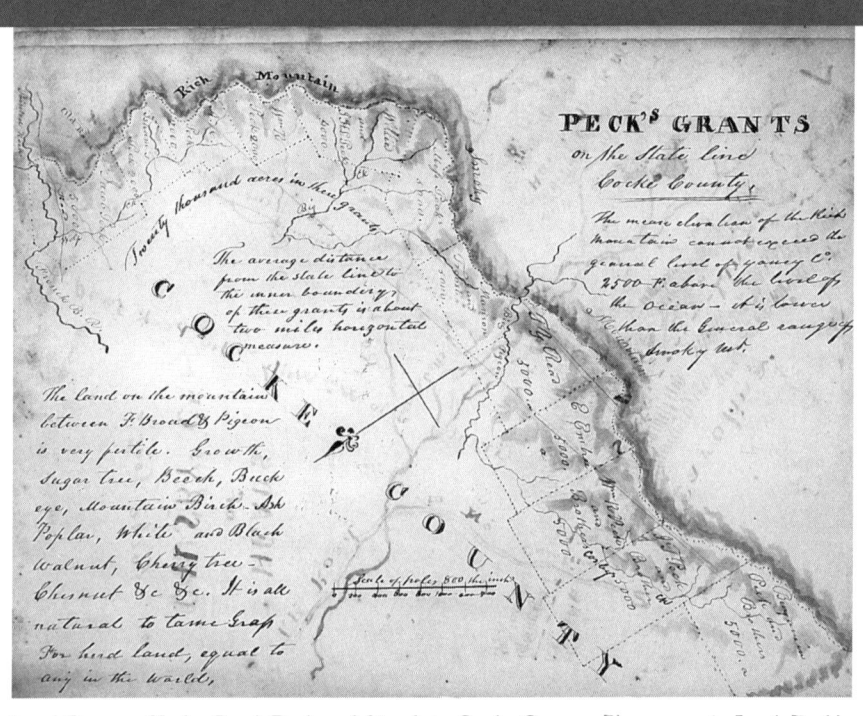

Land Grants of Judge Jacob Peck and friends in Cocke County, Tennessee, in Jacob Peck's Notes. Courtesy of McClung Historical Collection, Knox County Public Library System, Knoxville, Tennessee.

An Abolitionist in the Appalachian South

Ezekiel Birdseye on Slavery, Capitalism, and Separate Statehood in East Tennessee, 1841–1846

Durwood Dunn

The University of Tennessee Press / Knoxville

Copyright © 1997 by The University of Tennessee Press / Knoxville.
All Rights Reserved. Manufactured in the United States of America.
First Edition.

The paper in this book meets the minimum requirements of the American National Standard for Permanence of Paper for Printed Library Materials. ∞ The binding materials have been chosen for strength and durability. ♻ Printed on recycled paper.

Library of Congress Cataloging-in-Publication Data

Birdseye, Ezekiel, 1796-1861.
  An abolitionist in the Appalachian South : Ezekiel Birdseye on slavery, capitalism, and separate statehood in East Tennessee, 1841-1846 / Durwood Dunn.—1st ed.
    p. cm.
  Includes bibliographical references and index.
  ISBN 0-87049-964-5 (cloth: alk. paper)
  1. Slavery—Tennessee, East—History—19th century—Sources.
  2. Tennessee, East—History—Autonomy and independence movements—Sources.
  3. Capitalism—Tennessee, East—History—19th century—Sources.
  4. Birdseye, Ezekiel, 1796-1861—Correspondence.
I. Dunn, Durwood, 1943-   . II. Title.
E445.T3B57 1997
306.3'62'09768—dc20   96-25271
                                      CIP

Dedicated to the memory of Dr. Leroy P. Graf (1915–1993), scholar, mentor, and friend, who, like Ezekiel Birdseye, hated bigotry and loved East Tennessee

Contents

	Preface	ix
	Abbreviations	xiii
Part I.	**Ezekiel Birdseye's Life and Times in East Tennessee, 1838–1861**	
Chapter 1.	Political Abolitionism and Separatism	3
Chapter 2.	Ezekiel Birdseye	26
Chapter 3.	Entrepreneurship, Capitalism, Economic Progress, and Abolitionism	44
Chapter 4.	The Legal Status and Actual Treatment of Slaves	67
	Epilogue	87
	Notes	89
Part II.	**Ezekiel Birdseye's Letters**	127
	Bibliography	273
	Index	295

Preface

For over a hundred years, historians have tried to analyze the sources of East Tennessee's distinctiveness, and the basis for her continuing efforts to separate from the rest of the state. These political aspirations toward separation seem to have begun with the lost State of Franklin in the eighteenth century, long before Tennessee became a state in 1796. They continued with the movement for separation from the state in the early 1840s, which failed due to a lack of support in Tennessee's legislature. In the secession crisis of 1861, delegates from East Tennessee counties, meeting in two conventions in Knoxville and Greeneville in May and June of that year, tried to separate from Tennessee rather than to be taken out of the federal Union against the wishes of a majority of the section's citizens. After the Civil War, separatism long manifested itself politically in a solidly Republican majority in the eastern section of a state otherwise uniformly part of the Democratic South.

Almost all the participants in Tennessee's secession crisis in 1861 denied that slavery or abolition had anything to do with the section's unwillingness to remain part of a Tennessee leaving the Union; but previous analyses in terms of political loyalties, regional variations in geography and economy, and even specific trade links to the Lower South, do not satisfactorily answer all our questions about why East Tennessee remained distinct. Doubtless the majority of East Tennesseans by 1861 viewed abolitionism as a type of irresponsible extremism associated with fanatics in the North. But an earlier history of active antislavery activity and organized manumission societies in this section during the 1820s and 1830s indicates that East Tennessee indeed was more susceptible to feeling guilty about the institution of slavery than other sections of the South. Certainly, as the letters of Ezekiel Birdseye testify, an open discussion of the questions of slavery and abolition continued during the 1840s, and most casual observers noted that slaves seemed, in general, to have been much better treated in this section than in the rest of the South. Could a subterranean stream of antislavery sentiment have persisted into the 1860s, especially among East Tennesseans born before 1800?

I first discovered some of Ezekiel Birdseye's letters, edited by W. Freeman Galpin and originally published in 1931, in the *East Tennessee Historical Society's Publications*. These were so fascinating that eventually I sought to obtain the other letters in the Gerrit Smith Collection in the library of Syracuse University. The handwriting in these letters proved extremely difficult to decipher; Birdseye used the double *es* sign, ß, throughout his writing and often wrote diagonally across the same page. My labors were rewarded, however, when I discovered that twenty-eight letters, written between 1841 and 1846, contained an intense description of both slavery and abolitionism in East Tennessee. I later discovered three additional Birdseye letters: one from 1837, published in the *New York Emancipator and Republican*; another in the *Christian Freeman* from 1843; and a brief letter written to Andrew Johnson in February 1861. I have included them here with the letters to Gerrit Smith because they seem to mesh perfectly with Birdseye's central arguments and offer a perspective not otherwise afforded.

Birdseye's contribution to our understanding of East Tennessee seems greatly enhanced by his tolerance of individual slaveholders while at the same time he was condemning the peculiar institution itself. His letters frequently were published in various northern antislavery papers and provided an experiential basis of evidence for his audience from one actually living in the South and daily witnessing the horrors of slavery. Because he mentioned so many specific places and events in these letters to Smith, it was necessary to track down as many of these references as possible. In this effort, the work of local historians and genealogists has proven invaluable. Faye A. Axford, for example, compiled the tombstone inscriptions in the cemetery of Athens, Alabama, where I located the grave of Birdseye's beloved first wife, Lucinda. When Birdseye mentioned the murder of a Mrs. McMahan and her daughter by a slave in Athens in 1842, I was able to verify this incident from Reba Bayless Boyer's *Wills and Estate Records of McMinn County, Tennessee, 1820–1870*. Because these details are verifiable in nearly all instances, collectively they tend to corroborate Birdseye's testimony on other matters. My interpretation of Birdseye's correspondence in four separate chapters dealing with slavery and abolitionism in East Tennessee will, I hope, quickly be superseded by the value of the actual letters themselves, as historians continue to probe these complex issues.

The connection made by Birdseye's friends in East Tennessee between abolitionism and entrepreneurial capitalism—or, more particularly, the search for minerals of commercial value—seems to be the most important discovery. Next in historical significance is the discovery that large numbers of lawyers and judges, particularly on the Tennessee Supreme Court, rendered decisions unequivocally indicating deep sympathy for the slaves, and a concurrent determination to recognize their basic human rights in both procedural guarantees and protections in the substantive law. Finally, Birdseye's repeated observation of what he termed a "prevailing public sentiment" among East Tennesseans which discountenanced both cruelty toward slaves and their continuing condition of servitude offers insight into values and attitudes of the community during the early 1840s.

I have reproduced Birdseye's letters exactly as they were written, with original spelling and punctuation intact, with two important exceptions. I have removed the author's ubiquitous dashes, and I have capitalized the first word beginning each sentence and placed a period after the last. These changes, I believe, are justified, as they make the letters much more readable to a general audience. I have attempted to identify every person to whom Birdseye refers, but some simply were not to be located, particularly when he used only the last name. I also have removed the ß that Birdseye used throughout and replaced it with *ss*, as is the current practice.

The many sources of help throughout the preparation of this manuscript are too numerous to mention here, although I have tried to give them due credit in my notes and bibliography. The work of Arthur F. Howington, *What Sayeth the Law: The Treatment of Slaves and Free Blacks in the State and Local Courts of Tennessee* (1986), has been particularly valuable in determining the involvement of various members of Tennessee's judiciary in the antislavery movement. Terrance Keenan, special collections librarian at the Syracuse University Library, has been unfailingly kind and helpful in allowing me access to Gerrit Smith's letters and papers. I am particularly indebted to Steve Cotham, head of the McClung Historical Collection, Knox County Public Library, Knoxville, Tennessee, for acquiring, at my request, the valuable notebook of Judge Jacob Peck. The McClung Historical Collection has been a gold mine of materials useful in identifying Birdseye's references. I also would like to thank the staff of the Special Collections Library, University of Tennessee, Knoxville; and the staff, particularly Marylin Bell Hughes, at the Tennessee State Library and Archives, Nashville. I am appreciative of the unfailing courtesy and helpfulness of Julie Adams, librarian at Tennessee Wesleyan College, for obtaining many interlibrary loans of obscure materials often difficult to locate.

I am greatly indebted to both John C. Inscoe and Merton L. Dillon, who read this manuscript and offered invaluable criticisms and suggestions for improvement. Any remaining errors or mistakes in either fact or interpretation are solely my responsibility. Finally, I am grateful to the Andrew W. Mellon Foundation for providing me a Mellon Appalachian Fellowship in the Humanities and Social Sciences for the 1994–95 academic year, which enabled me to complete this research. I also am grateful for the consistent good will and cooperation of Fellowship Coordinator Dorothy Graddy. Dr. C. W. Minkel, vice provost and dean of the Graduate School, University of Tennessee at Knoxville, kindly provided parking and a library card, enabling me to utilize the resources of that institution.

Durwood Dunn
Tennessee Wesleyan College

Abbreviations

BDAC	*Biographical Directory of the American Congress, 1774-1971* (Washington, D.C.: U.S. Government Printing Office, 1971)
BDTGA	Robert M. McBride and Dan M. Robison, eds., *Biographical Directory of the Tennessee General Assembly, 1791–1861*, 2 vols. (Nashville: Tennessee State Library and Archives and Tennessee Historical Commission, 1975)
DAB	*Dictionary of American Biography*
EB/GS	Ezekiel Birdseye's letters to Gerrit Smith, in the Gerrit Smith Collection, George Arents Research Library for Special Collections, Syracuse University, Syracuse, New York
Petitions	*Petitions to the Tennessee General Assembly,* Rolls 1-20, Tennessee State Library and Archives, Nashville
Tennessee Acts	Tennessee General Assembly, *Private Acts*

Part I
**Ezekiel Birdseye's
Life and Times in
East Tennessee, 1838–1861**

1.
Political Abolitionism and Separatism

"Thousands of first rate citizens, men remarkable for their piety and virtue, have within 20 years past, removed from this and other slave states, to Ohio, Indiana, and Illinois," Elihu Embree lamented in April 1820, "that their eyes may be hid from seeing the cruel oppressor lacerate the backs of his slaves, and that their ears may not hear the bitter cries of the oppressed." In this single prescient observation, made nine months before his own untimely death added to antislavery's losses in the state, Embree summed up the single most important reason why abolitionism failed to achieve its basic political objective—ending slavery by law in Tennessee. Elihu Embree wondered what the outcome would have been for the state if these talented and energetic antislavery leaders had remained, since the afterglow of their efforts to emancipate all slaves was still apparent to Ezekiel Birdseye in the early 1840s.[1]

There are uncorroborated accounts of a great struggle to abolish slavery in Tennessee's first constitutional convention in 1796. One source indicates that petitions signed by nearly two thousand citizens to abolish slavery by 1864 were sent to this convention, but no documentary evidence now exists to support this assertion. Horace Maynard, a famous Unionist in East Tennessee at the outbreak of the Civil War, said in an 1863 speech in Nashville that a proposition to make Tennessee enter the federal Union as a free state had been defeated by only one vote in the 1796 constitutional convention, but this story is likewise apocryphal, as documentation is lacking. All we really know from written sources is that Tennessee's 1796 constitution was silent on slavery, except in regard to taxation, and that North Carolina's statutes regulating the institution remained in effect and became the basis upon which Tennessee erected its own slave code thereafter. Tennessee's first constitution also enfranchised free blacks; not until 1834 would their right to vote be revoked.[2]

The earliest efforts at organizing antislavery societies in East Tennessee lie hidden in obscurity, but it is almost certain that Quakers, always generic abolitionists, were among those in the vanguard. As early as 1797, a Pennsylvania Quaker, Thomas Embree, father of Elihu, published a letter in the *Knoxville Gazette* calling on "the public spirited citizens of every denomination whose patriotic zeal is not limited to those of their own color" to join in an effort to effect "a gradual abolition of slavery of every kind" in the state. The legislature was admonished to make no laws nor suffer any to exist which might compel a citizen to "keep mankind in slavery . . . when he is so far enlightened as to see the injustice of holding them." John Caldwell, Birdseye's friend, later wrote that emancipation societies had been organized in East Tennessee as early as 1809, but Elihu Embree said in 1820 that the first such society was formed in 1815 at Lost Creek Meeting House, Jefferson County, by Charles Osborn and seven others.[3]

On November 21, 1815, the first general convention of the newly organized Manumission Society of Tennessee was held at the Lick Creek Meeting House of Friends in Greene County. Soon after the first society had been formed in Jefferson County on February 25, 1815, new societies were formed in Blount, Cocke, Grainger, Greene, Knox, Sullivan, and Washington counties. By the time of the eighth annual convention, August 12 and 13, 1822, sixteen societies had been formed in East Tennessee, with a total membership of 474. Almost from the beginning, the major aim of these manumission societies was to effect the abolition of slavery by political means—primarily through numerous petitions to the state and national governments. Typical were two impassioned memorials, probably written by Elihu Embree, that were sent to the state legislature in 1817:

> We most cordially appraise the declaration of independence; and hold these truths to be self evident, "that all men are created equal; that they are endowed by their Creator with certain unalienable rights; and among these are life, liberty, and the pursuit of happiness." We believe that God has made of one blood all conditions of men to dwell upon the face of the earth; that he looks down with an equal eye upon them all; that he is pleased when they do to others as they would be done unto in similar circumstances; and that

he may be displeased when any disregard this rule. We cannot suppose that having given to all men rational and immortal minds, he intended the difference of colour in our species, either as the brand of Slavery, or the title to Oppression: we rather view it as a providential trial of our hearts; to prove what is in us. When, therefore, we consider the depressed condition of many in our land, we fully agree with the remark of one of our late Presidents in his notes on Virginia. "We tremble to reflect that God is just; and that in a more than possible extremity we know not what Attribute of his nature could take part with us." We are confident that nations, states, and individuals prosper by righteousness, as they cannot by any other means; and that their unrighteousness, only brings down the judgments of God upon them with unfailing certainty. We are persuaded, that to bring up children in the expectation of possessing as property the servants who wait upon them, is to train them to oppression and tyranny; to indolence and vice; and to prevent the eternal principles of justice, benevolence, and mercy from taking proper hold on their hearts. We believe also, that slavery tends, on the one hand, to debase the minds of its subjects; and unfits the rational creatures of God for the noble duties that He requires at their hands. In this enlightened age these obvious facts are generally admitted with expressions of lamentation that they exist.[4]

By 1817, however, only two years after its formal establishment, the Tennessee Manumission Society already had lost two critically important and influential leaders—Charles Osborn and the Presbyterian minister John Rankin. Born of Quaker parents in North Carolina, Charles Osborn (1775–1850), removed to East Tennessee in 1794, where he became a Quaker minister. Between 1814 and 1816, he devoted his considerable abilities and time exclusively to organizing antislavery societies in the region, both in Tennessee and North Carolina. In 1816, however, Osborn's aversion to slavery caused him to leave East Tennessee for Mount Pleasant in southeastern Ohio, where in 1817 he began publishing the *Philanthropist,* a weekly newspaper devoted in part to the antislavery cause. In 1818, he removed to Indiana, where he spent the remainder of his life as an ardent and effective spokesman for emancipation. His exhortations resulted in the formation of the Free Produce Association of Indiana, a movement to boycott goods made with slave labor, and in the establishment in 1842 of a propagandist newspaper, the *Free Labor Advocate and Anti-Slavery Chronicle.*[5]

John Rankin was born in Jefferson County, East Tennessee, in 1793, and was educated under Samuel Doak (1749–1830), Princeton graduate and founder of Washington and Tusculum colleges. Although not formally associated with abolitionist societies, Doak fervently opposed slavery and, like Isaac Anderson at Maryville College, trained a host of young preachers with similar views. After marrying Samuel Doak's daughter and becoming licensed to preach, Rankin, unwilling to raise a family in a state "polluted" by slavery, left East Tennessee in 1817. Thereafter, he was probably the leading Presbyterian abolitionist in the United States, called by some during the 1830s the "father of abolitionism" and "the Martin Luther of the cause." A series of letters Rankin wrote to his brother protesting against ownership of slaves was first published in 1823 as *Letters on American Slavery, Addressed to Mr. Thomas Rankin, Merchant at Middlebrook, Augusta County, Virginia*; it quickly became a classic bestseller and remains one of the most important antislavery books ever written. His most important contribution, however, was in leading the antislavery battle in the Presbyterian General Assemblies until the schism of 1837.[6]

Dr. David Nelson (1793–1844) was another famous abolitionist, also educated by Samuel Doak, who at the age of sixteen, after graduating from Washington College, left his native East Tennessee to study medicine. In 1830, Nelson went to Palmyra, Missouri, where he founded Marion College, a theological school modeled after the Oneida Institute and Lane Theological Seminary in Cincinnati, both famous abolitionist institutions. As a college president and Presbyterian minister, he boldly preached the antislavery gospel to often hostile audiences; in 1836, he was driven out of Missouri by an "infuriated blood-thirsty mob of pro-slavery men" after calling on the slaveholders in his congregation to repent of their sins and free their slaves. He ended his life as an agent for the American Anti-Slavery Society, eventually becoming a vice-president of that organization, and as an antislavery lecturer in western Illinois. Dr. Nelson was responsible for converting to the antislavery cause Elijah P. Lovejoy, a famous abolitionist editor who was martyred in 1837 by a proslavery mob in Alton, Illinois. Both Rankin and Nelson are excellent examples of men born, raised, and educated through college in East Tennessee, who later became famous in the national crusade against slavery; contemporaries considered both men to be radicals and fearless, uncompromising advocates.[7]

With important leaders such as Charles Osborn, John Rankin, and David Nelson, as well as a host of minor leaders such as Jesse Willis and Jesse Lockhart, all leaving East Tennessee between 1816 and 1825, it is difficult to measure the continuing strength of antislavery sentiment there during the 1820s. Conflicting evidence comes from two leading abolitionist editors, Elihu Embree and Benjamin Lundy, both Quakers. Embree (1782–1820), a leading iron manufacturer, established a paper, the *Manumission Intelligencer,* in 1819, and continued with the *Emancipator* in 1820 until his untimely death in December of that year. Benjamin Lundy (1789–1839) moved his antislavery paper, *The Genius of Universal Emancipation,* from Ohio to Greeneville, Tennessee, in 1822, where it continued to gain a national readership before Lundy removed to Baltimore in 1824. An ongoing historiographical debate over the nature of southern antislavery leaders and how they influenced the later abolitionist movement in the North, associated with William Lloyd Garrison, recently has moved toward rehabilitating the reputations of individual southern antislavery leaders such as Embree and Lundy, while denying the strength of the abolitionist movement in the Upper South generally. The consensus now is that the antislavery movement in the Upper South before 1831 was an amalgamation of a tiny number of immediatists, larger numbers who advocated gradual emancipation combined with expatriation of all blacks, and a much larger group associated with the American Colonization Society, who sought the elimination of free blacks as a means of strengthening slavery. In a very perceptive recent study of abolitionists in the South, moreover, historian Stanley Harrold argues persuasively that a causal relationship existed between southern antislavery action and the Civil War.[8]

Even if Embree and Lundy did not advocate immediate abolition, their rhetoric nevertheless was harsh and fundamentally critical of slavery. As Merton Dillon observes, they made "no effort to conciliate slaveholders or spare their feelings," and their untempered condemnation of slavery was "scarcely exceeded in severity by that of their successors of the 1830s." It is indeed difficult not to infer from the dire jeremiads in these papers some sense that immediate action should be taken to save the state and nation from moral bankruptcy or the certain visitations of an offended Providence. Yet Lundy continued to lament in the pages of *The Genius of Universal Emancipation* the declining support for organized antislavery societies in East Tennessee. Continuing losses of key leaders persisted into the 1830s; in 1830, James Jones, president of the Tennessee Manumission Society, died. Lundy extravagantly eulogized Jones, emphasizing his irreplaceability at the very moment when astute leadership was most needed.[9]

As late as 1827, East Tennessee alone contained nearly one-fifth of all the antislavery societies in the United States and nearly one-sixth of the total membership, according to Benjamin Lundy. By 1830, however, these societies were largely moribund, owing primarily to apathy and a large migration of the antislavery rank and file from East Tennessee to the West.

An important ancillary stream of antislavery sentiment within the Methodist church seems increasingly to have been neutralized after 1824. Between 1784 and 1824, the Methodists, second only to the Quakers and Presbyterians in antislavery zeal, had tried to legislate slavery out of their church. From 1819 to 1822, one presiding elder, James Axley, a prominent East Tennessee preacher, employing a rigid antislavery policy, refused to license slaveholders to preach, to exhort, or even to lead a public prayer meeting. From 1824 until 1844, however, when the Methodist church divided over slavery, these same rules remained unchanged, but increasingly they simply were not enforced. After 1824, the Tennessee Conference, located in Middle and West Tennessee, became increasingly proslavery. In 1824, Methodist churches in East Tennessee were organized into the Holston Conference, which adopted a rigorous stance against slavery until 1843, when it rejected a proposal by the Genesee and New York conferences demanding abolition of slaves in all states and territories where the law would permit. Like their Quaker and Presbyterian antislavery brethren, Methodists emigrated in large numbers from East Tennessee to the Northwest during the 1820s on account of slavery, further weakening the antislavery forces within the Holston Conference.[10]

Other than the newspapers of Embree and Lundy, the chief form of protest among organized antislavery societies were numerous petitions to the state legislature, signed by as many citizens as could be persuaded within a particular county. Only by examining virtually all petitions submitted to the Tennessee legislature between 1799 and 1861 can these antislavery petitions be placed in proper perspective. First, most of these antislavery petitions clearly seem to have been sponsored by various organized manumission societies, mainly in the eastern part of the state. The same names tend to appear over and over; the petitions were sporadic but tended to cluster around occasions like the 1834 constitutional convention. Second, usually the petitioners sought gradual emancipation, to become effective at some future date—1866, for instance—or to be in effect for children born to slaves after a particular date. Provisions for religious training and some basic education for these future citizens were also requested, but all too often even the petitioners most sympathetic to the plight of slaves sought their expatriation through colonization or removal from the state as a condition for emancipation. Finally, the language of the majority of these petitions is suspiciously repetitious; evidently the same formula was repeated over and over. Often a printed version of the same petition was used; throughout the period of the greatest number of antislavery petitions, 1818–34, there is little variety in either expression or sentiment.[11]

Compared to petitions on other topics, antislavery petitions were always in a very small minority and usually were signed by only a limited number of stalwarts. The vast majority of petitions to the legislature had to do with economic issues, such as obtaining bridges, roads, railroads, or banks, or political problems at the local level, like forming new counties or civil districts. These sorts of petitions, in contrast to the antislavery ones, often were signed by hundreds of citizens. Between 1818 and 1834, antislavery petitions peaked; thereafter, during the later 1830s and 1840s, entire years passed when none appeared. Petitions to free *individual* slaves occasionally were received after 1837, but petitions seeking abolition of all slavery in the state were exceedingly rare. Petitions seeking a license for disabled white men to "hawk," or peddle goods, were far more numerous even than petitions to free individual slaves. After 1837, the social reform eliciting the largest number of petitions was the temperance crusade. Except for a rare petition in the 1840s, bearing language identical to that of earlier antislavery memorials, the abolitionist movement in Tennessee, even in East Tennessee, was politically inactive after 1837.[12]

Although antislavery petitions *per se* decreased rapidly after 1836, East Tennesseans did continue to protest various restrictions on slaves that were thought to limit the civil liberties of the entire citizenry. One notable example was an 1837 protest by citizens of Meigs and Rhea counties against a "very bloody and tyrannical" law passed in February 1836 by the Tennessee General Assembly, making it a felony to circulate any printed matter among slaves or free blacks which might incite discontent or rebellion among them:

> Be pleased to apply this law too and execute it upon the maker, and publishers of our Bill of Rights the immortal Franklin and others who wrote and published to the world to the whole world that they held these truths to be self-evident, That all men are created equal[,] that they are endowed by their creator with certain unalienable rights[, and] that among these are life[,] liberty and the pursuit of happiness. Give them according to the letter of this law their just deserts for publishing such language as this for the world could say nothing more and they would be ranked among thieves false swearers and all abominable characters which your petitioners are not willing should be done neither are we willing to be ranked as such for having reading publishing or circulating that sacred instrument. We your petitioners are of opinion that to take the law in its strict sense it is highly probable provided it should be vigorously enforced according to its true meaning that those who circulate aid or abet in circulating the Holy Bible would in all probability incur the penalties named in the law for that book certainly does teach that all men are equal in point of birth and that we should do no wrong

one towards another, and we strongly appeal to your reason and Judgment to decide impartially upon this matter and say whether or no the reading of this book would not create discontent in the black population.[13]

It should also be pointed out that many other Tennesseans who were by no means abolitionists themselves periodically made rational expostulation against Tennessee's increasingly restrictive slave laws. After Tennessee passed a law in 1831 requiring that all slaves who were emancipated thereafter must leave the state, considerable debate erupted in the legislature, and many strongly urged its repeal. One of the most rational, incisive arguments was presented in October 1833 by a state senator, Jacob F. Foute, representative of Blount, Monroe, and McMinn counties in East Tennessee. Foute ridiculed the supposedly preemptive expulsion law, saying that it had been passed only out of the fear of insurrection occasioned by the Nat Turner revolt in neighboring Virginia. He also bitterly challenged the growing belief that Tennessee's free blacks threatened insurrection or were capable of exerting a pernicious influence out of all proportion to their numbers. "The slaves will long for freedom if there are no free Negroes," Foute persuasively argued. "Flatter not yourselves that by the removal of every free person of color, you will remove all causes of discontent and restlessness to your slaves; or that by limiting to a very few, or preventing entirely the emancipation of slaves, that discontent will cease, and all will be quietude and repose." The best means of alleviating slave anxiety, he continued, was to hold out some reasonable hope of possible future freedom, not to cut that hope off entirely.[14]

During the 1820s, the thorny issue of colonizing both free blacks and former slaves to Liberia further complicated matters for the weakening antislavery movement. Even many staunch abolitionists could not envision a biracial society, and removing blacks to Africa at first seemed a logical solution. As early as 1816, the Tennessee Manumission Society endorsed colonization; in 1818, Andrew Jackson was elected a vice-president of the national American Colonization Society. In 1823, the state legislature authorized Tennessee's congressional delegation to seek federal assistance to procure a colony in Africa for this purpose; earlier, the Tennessee Manumission Society had lobbied for Haiti as a rendezvous for free blacks. In 1829, the Tennessee Colonization Society was formally organized, and the movement seems to have enjoyed widespread support throughout Tennessee. In 1833, Tennessee's legislature passed two resolutions requesting a committee to investigate the expediency of asking Congress for an annual appropriation of $100,000 for colonization, and also requesting $5,000 for the same purpose from the state. In that same year, 1833, the state authorized paying $10 to assist every free black transported to Liberia; the total appropriation, however, could not exceed $500 in any one year.[15]

Yet colonization ultimately failed in Tennessee, due both to the prohibitive cost per freedman ($180), and the disinclination of most free blacks voluntarily to leave their homes. It also failed because proslavery advocates, who initially had seen colonization as a means of eliminating free blacks and thereby strengthening slavery, by the 1830s had become suspicious that the whole effort was inextricably linked to universal emancipation. The successful efforts of former Tennessee slaves who now were prominent citizens of Liberia, such as Sion Harris, challenged prevailing notions concerning the racial inferiority of blacks, as Ezekiel Birdseye reported in 1841. Yet at the same time, ironically, abolitionists such as Birdseye, James G. Birney, Gerrit Smith, and others were becoming completely disillusioned with colonization as an effective means toward the ultimate goal of universal freedom for all slaves. John Caldwell and other Tennessee abolitionist friends of Birdseye did continue to support the movement into the 1840s. Others, such as Dr. Isaac Anderson of Maryville College, agreed with Birdseye's reservations. In any event, no accurate figures exist on how many former Tennessee slaves were sent to Liberia, but one scholar estimates the number could not have exceeded two thousand. After 1833, colonization effectively was dead in the state, having failed as a means of abolitionism and as a way of improving the status and lives of free blacks in Tennessee.[16]

Antislavery forces in East Tennessee were still strong enough, however, to wage their single greatest political effort to abolish slavery in Tennessee's 1834 convention to revise the state constitution. Part of the struggle clearly involved East Tennessee's growing awareness that the balance of power, in terms of both population and wealth, had shifted to the middle and western parts of the state, where the terrain permitted creation of large plantations worked by numerous slaves in a pattern typical of the Lower South. The opening salvo in this last great constitutional battle consisted of thirty petitions to the convention calling for the gradual abolition of slavery in sixteen counties—eleven in East Tennessee, five in Middle Tennessee, and none in West Tennessee. Only 1,804 citizens, out of an estimated 550,000 total white population, had signed these memorials; 651, or more than one-third of the total number of signers, were from Washington and Greene counties alone. Of the 105 slaveholders in East Tennessee who signed, all together owned fewer than 500 slaves, probably far fewer.[17]

Bitter political infighting and recriminations quickly erupted over the slavery issue. The convention did not wish to, and ultimately never did, debate the issue of slavery in the committee of the whole. Instead, the antislavery memorials were referred to a special committee composed of one delegate from each of the state's three grand divisions. This committee was created *only* to draft formal reasons for the convention's refusal even to consider abolition. John A. McKinney, a distinguished lawyer, a native of Ireland, and a delegate from Hawkins County, was named committee chair. In the meantime, all additional petitions concerning slavery were to be tabled until January 1, 1835. None of the previously submitted petitions called for immediate abolition of all slaves. Various proposals for gradual emancipation were offered; one memorial recommended that all children born after 1835 be free; others sought to have all slaves free in 1855, with the understanding that they would be removed from the state. The remaining petitions wanted all slaves free by 1866 and freedmen subsequently expatriated and colonized to Africa.[18]

The McKinney report, when called up and read before the entire convention on June 24, caused a firestorm of debate among East Tennessee antislavery forces. Basically, McKinney offered an apology for slavery, with several specious propositions attached to justify continuing the institution as it existed. Slavery was an admitted but necessary evil, because the matter of race precluded any viable alternative: "To prove it to be a great evil is an easy task, but to tell how that evil can be removed, is a question that the wisest heads and the most benevolent hearts have not been able to answer in a satisfactory manner." McKinney then proceeded to paint an idyllic portrait of slavery as a sort of cradle-to-grave social security system for blacks. Blacks were better off as slaves than as free blacks in a racist society; the life and status of free blacks he portrayed in the most dismal tones. Emancipating slaves, far from conferring freedom upon them, actually enslaved them in another form of misery and degradation, from which no escape or relief was possible. If all Tennessee's slaves were freed and allowed to remain, he concluded, internecine strife between the races would become inevitable.[19]

Angry antislavery delegates protested that the McKinney report's outrageous propositions ignored public opinion in the state. Joseph Kincaid, a physician from Bedford County, at length extolled the rights and privileges enjoyed by free blacks and moved to strike out that part of the McKinney report denigrating the condition of free blacks. Terry H. Cahal defended the report, taking umbrage particularly at Kincaid's insinuation that the signers of the Declaration of Independence had mediated a revolution in the social system. Kincaid's motion was defeated, 42 to 12; McKinney's report finally was adopted,

44 to 10. Yet, despite the fact that they clearly were outnumbered, the antislavery group, composed mainly of East Tennesseans, continued to wage savage parliamentary guerrilla warfare. Led by Matthew Stephenson of Washington County, they demanded to attach their written protest to the McKinney report in the journal of the convention. The number and respectability of the memorialists merited more consideration than a mere three-man report, they argued. Arguments used and principles assumed in this meretricious report were "in their tendency subversive to the true principles of Republicanism," against the Declaration of Independence, and at variance with the Gospel! The protesters further asserted that they could never subscribe to the rule that would "assign to men their rights according to different shades of colour" and that they were convinced that all the evils of freemen applied in equal force to slaves, "unless indeed slavery gives dignity to man."[20]

The indefatigable antislavery delegates continued their protests to the limits of parliamentary procedure. On June 28, Gray Garrett, a native of Cocke County who now represented Claiborne County, moved that the antislavery petitions be returned to the McKinney committee for further and more complete consideration. A new report from this committee on July 9 simply justified earlier arguments; they had kindly refused to offend the antislavery petitioners' sensibilities earlier by pointing out that slaveholders who signed these petitions ought to free their own slaves before presuming to ask others to do so. Nonslaveholders had no fear from the "sin" of slaveholding, the second report continued, since they themselves were not involved in the folly of others. This particular argument was bitterly contested by the "abolition" protesters. "Great mischief" might be done by unrealistically raising the expectations of slaves, the report concluded, and there was something very questionable in the motives of the antislavery protesters who were attempting to impose on their neighbors their own notions of morality. On July 21, Stephenson's group lodged a second protest, now charging that, since slavery had not been denounced, the committee merely had given "countenance to slavery in its worst form." Even after their final defeat on July 30, Joseph Kincaid delivered a blistering diatribe against slavery and slaveholders on August 5. The small group leading the antislavery protest in this convention displayed quite remarkable energy and capacity, despite its ultimate defeat.[21]

The final vote, on July 30, on the provision that "the General Assembly shall have no power to pass laws for the emancipation of slaves without the consent of their owner or owners," passed by a surprisingly narrow margin, 30 to 27. Fourteen of the dissenters were from East Tennessee, but they were joined by ten negative votes from Middle Tennessee and three from West Tennessee. What had occurred in the 1834 constitutional convention was, in a certain sense, a microcosm of the whole antislavery movement in Tennessee: a small number of highly motivated, capable, and extremely dedicated abolitionists, mainly from East Tennessee had, through sheer determination, exercised an influence completely out of all proportion to their representative numbers, and they almost succeeded in carrying the day. Among the East Tennesseans voting against the final amendment were two later friends of Ezekiel Birdseye: Robert J. McKinney of Greene County and William C. Roadman of Cocke County.[22]

The most important piece of evidence concerning this last great political battle to end slavery in Tennessee is recorded not in the journal of the 1834 constitutional convention but rather in a late memorial from Jefferson County, dated July 28, 1834, only two days before the final vote. Signed and possibly written by John Caldwell, this petition contains the most specific and incisive condemnation of slavery to be found among all such antislavery petitions addressed to the convention. The "very instrument, by which we are about to be secured in the possession of our liberties," the new state constitution, unfortunately would "contain the seed" for the overthrow of those liberties, the signers lamented. "For the very toleration of slavery, according to the inevitable results of human events, if not removed, will ultimately end in anarchy, ruin, & bloodshed." In stirring language they warned that, "unless the united wisdom and virtue of the American people impel them to action" to abolish slavery, "it will be said in after times, America is fallen."[23]

The real significance of this Jefferson County petition of July 28, 1834, however, lies in its conclusive evidence that each action of the convention in Nashville was being meticulously monitored in East Tennessee, and that the antislavery delegates to the convention there were being carefully coordinated by the parent organization. The specious arguments in both McKinney reports were all dissected and demolished through a blaze of sarcasm in this petition. If the committee *admitted* that slavery was a great evil but could not remove it, they argued, Tennesseans were doomed to live under the name of republican government without enjoying the substantive benefits of democracy. They ridiculed the committee's maudlin picture of free blacks neglected in their old age, "for we assert without fear of successful contradiction, that the free people of colour, according to their numbers and the length of time they have enjoyed their freedom, are as well prepared for the ills of life, as the white population." Particularly vituperative sarcasm was reserved for the committee's comments on colonization of former slaves to Africa:

> The committee in the third place tell the community, that the colonization of the black population is a scheme beyond the resources of the state; at least they infer that opinion from the questions they propound. Yet in winding up this report, the committee tell us the friends of humanity need not despair; that providence has already opened a door of hope; that is every day becoming wider and wider. That the foundation of a mighty empire, is already laid on the coast of Africa, and that slavery will be removed from our highly favoured country, by colonizing the black population on the African coast by funds raised by the benevolent. Thus we are to be told that the state of Tennessee is not able to colonize, her portion of the slave population, and at the same time slavery is to be banished from the country, by the individual efforts of the benevolent; is an inconsistency too glaring to be palmed [off] on this enlightened community.[24]

Finally, these Jefferson County petitioners excoriated the committee "in their second effort" for assuming "the position that the voice of the nonslaveholder shall not be heard on the subject." They inquired: "From whom (whence?) we would ask your honorable body does the slaveholder derive this exclusive privilege?" The Constitution? The Bible? "Is the nonslaveholder not a member of the same community, is he not endowed with the same natural rights, is he not guaranteed of the possession of the same civil rights, or has he no interest in the welfare of the community," these memorialists respectfully further begged to inquire. The rhetoric is so sardonic, even vitriolic, that it reminds one of the later writings of "Parson" William G. Brownlow, outspoken editor, Unionist leader, and Reconstruction governor of Tennessee. Perhaps Parson Brownlow did assist in the composition of this compelling document; in any event, he was one of its prominent signers. Their closing blast pretermits summary or adequate characterization:

> We look upon the doctrines of the second report, as being more completely at war with the genuine principles, of a free government, than any production, we have ever seen from the pen of an American. We therefore present this humble petition, for a reconsideration. We come with the constitution of our country in one hand in it we are recognized, as having equal rights and priviledges; in the other we hold the volume of inspiration, whose lan-

guage your committee have misquoted, and whose doctrines they have misrepresented. The doctrines of the new testament are heaven bound; they stand in opposition to oppression of every grade, and when universally received and practiced; will convert this earth into a paradise.[25]

Robert J. McKinney (1803–1875), who represented Greene County at this convention, was a well-known opponent of slavery who earlier had freed all his own slaves. He was the nephew of John A. McKinney, author of the infamous report on slavery. Later he would serve as a justice on the Tennessee Supreme Court from 1847 to 1861, where his opinions inevitably betrayed deep sympathy for the plight of the slaves. Oliver P. Temple asserted in 1899 that Robert J. McKinney was second only to Matthew Stephenson during the convention as a leader of the antislavery group. In October 1842 McKinney told Ezekiel Birdseye that "it would be difficult to imagine the excitement produced in the convention when he presented the petitions for the gradual abolition of slavery." He further told Birdseye at this point that "it was unfortunate that they were presented at all as it led to restrictions in the constitution that would not have been thought of." In the summer of 1834, however, protest against slavery's continuation in Tennessee was a moral imperative which the East Tennessee dissenters responded to with courage, zeal, and great determination. And, although they were narrowly defeated, it is difficult to suppose that such moral fervor quickly dissipated in East Tennessee.[26]

If the proslavery forces throughout the rest of Tennessee had won their point in the 1834 constitutional convention, however, they nevertheless were increasingly alarmed by both antislavery sentiment in the eastern part of the state and in the North. This anxiety was both reflected and fueled by an incident which occurred in Nashville the following summer of 1835. Amos Dresser, a student at Lane Theological Seminary in Cincinnati, a well-known abolitionist institution, came to Nashville in July of that year to sell "Cottage Bibles" in order to pay for his education. Among his possessions were some antislavery tracts and papers, which, once discovered, caused an immediate outcry in that city. Dresser was summoned before a "Committee of Vigilance and Safety," comprised of some of Nashville's most prominent citizens, and accused of distributing incendiary propaganda to persuade slaves and free blacks to rebel. Dresser denied all such charges of inciting blacks to insurrection but did admit earlier having sold a copy of John Rankin's *Letters on Slavery* to a white man in Sumner County. The vigilante committee finally sentenced Dresser to twenty lashes on his bare back, after which he fled Nashville as soon as possible, leaving all his merchandise behind. The Amos

Dresser case quickly became a *cause célèbre* among abolitionists throughout the nation, and Dresser's own account of the incident promptly joined the ranks of antislavery tracts. Birdseye made reference to this case several times, citing it as an example of growing proslavery opinion in Middle Tennessee. Ironically, John Rankin, author of the incendiary volume, had been a native of East Tennessee.[27]

By the time of Birdseye's arrival in East Tennessee in 1838, the residual effect of the earlier antislavery movement still was readily apparent throughout the region. Birdseye time and again in his correspondence discussed the continuation in this section of free and open discussion of both abolitionism and the evils of slavery, and the free circulation of abolitionist tracts and newspapers, although distribution of such "incendiary" antislavery literature by this time was expressly forbidden by state law. In April 1842 Birdseye reported that a public debate had occurred at Newport as to whether slavery or intemperance was the greatest national evil. Earlier he had reported that free discussion of slavery and abolition was widespread in Blount County. Some postmasters, such as Birdseye's friend William C. Roadman in Newport, were sympathetic to the cause and circulated antislavery newspapers among their friends, but others were hostile. In December 1841 Birdseye warned Gerrit Smith to send any letters for Judge Jacob Peck directly to him at Newport, since the postmasters at Mossy Creek and New Market were proslavery and likely to intercept any correspondence from him.[28]

Birdseye in addition frequently commented on the continuing diminution of the antislavery ranks in East Tennessee both by the deaths of important leaders and by emigration of those hostile to slavery from the region to the free states. On October 1841 he noted the death during the previous year of his good friend the Reverend L. F. Clark, professor at the University of Tennessee in Knoxville, "one of the most ardent abolitionists" he had encountered. "His labors among the colored population of Knoxville were successful and placed him so high in their affections," Birdseye noted, "that they yet speak of him with warm affections and lament his death." Birdseye also mentioned specific individuals, like Mr. Patterson, president of the Jefferson County Manumission Society, and Colonel Bradford in Athens, both of whom were planning to move west to escape slavery.[29]

It would be a serious error, however, to attribute the wildly popular idea of separate statehood for East Tennessee in 1842 to a preponderance of antislavery feeling in this section. Overwhelming evidence shows that separatism was the direct result of economic grievances, real or imagined, over Middle Tennessee's allegedly unfair distribution of state funds for internal improvements. After great expectations were raised by the passage of internal improvements legislation in 1836 and 1838, the depression following the Panic of 1837 caused the repeal of state aid laws by 1840. The 1836 and 1838 acts were passed largely by votes from East and West Tennessee, over the strenuous opposition of legislators from the middle part of the state. Yet, ironically, only Middle Tennessee received any substantive benefit from this legislation, in the form of a number of completed turnpikes, before repeal in 1840. This fact only intensified and exacerbated already strong sectional jealousy and antagonism in East Tennessee.[30]

The crux of the matter involved the Hiwassee Railroad in East Tennessee, whose funding had collapsed due to the depression. Two conventions were held in Knoxville on November 22–23 and December 13–14, 1841, attended by delegates from Bradley, Cocke, Hamilton, Jefferson, Knox, McMinn, and Washington counties; Ezekiel Birdseye was the delegate representing Cocke County at both these conventions. They memorialized the state legislature to award to East Tennessee the $650,000 previously appropriated in 1838 for the construction of the now defunct Louisville, Cincinnati, and Charleston Railroad. The money was to be used to construct a graded, macadamized turnpike from the Virginia line near Abingdon to Knoxville; to complete the Hiwassee Railroad from Knoxville to the Georgia line; and for various improvements to aid navigation on the Tennessee River. A proposal to establish a bank in East Tennessee was, by a narrow margin, excluded from this memorial, but it became the subject of numerous other petitions during the next two years. When the state in effect denied this request, canceling the state subscription by filing a lawsuit against the Louisville, Cincinnati, and Charleston Railroad Company to recover any state money invested therein, sectional anger in East Tennessee reached a fever pitch.[31]

This anger manifested itself during the 1841–42 session of the legislature, when Andrew Johnson in the Senate and Samuel Milligan in the House introduced resolutions to form a separate state of Frankland from East Tennessee and adjacent portions of Virginia, North Carolina, and Georgia. Although great enthusiasm was shown in the press throughout East Tennessee, where conventions were held in the summer of 1842 in Jonesboro, Greeneville, and other towns advocating separation, the bill was rejected in the House, 29 to 41. Ezekiel Birdseye was very hopeful that this new state of Frankland would enter the Union as a free state, but there is virtually no evidence that antislavery played any role in these negotiations or in the public debate over separate statehood. An examination of the petitions to the legislature during the years 1840–43 reveals no mention of slavery, but numerous protests involving charges of unfair sectional distribution of state aid for internal improvements. Also, West Tennessee, where antislavery sentiment was practically nonexistent, showed its irritation with Middle Tennessee by introducing at the same time a motion to form a new state, Jacksoniana.[32]

Birdseye optimistically had anticipated that, if widespread discontent over economic issues was harnessed to allow the formation of a new state in East Tennessee, the new state legislature would be more willing to invest public funds in better transportation facilities. Railroads would improve both the prospects for manufacturing in East Tennessee, he argued, and at the same time increase the value of his own lands there. He told Gerrit Smith that the antislavery objectives within the separatist movement were being downplayed temporarily, so as not to arouse the suspicions or hostility of slaveowners before separate statehood could be effected. Sectional antipathy and intrastate jealousy were means to abolitionist ends in his mind, but no evidence exists that antislavery sentiment was a significant factor in the debate over separation during this period. By January 1841, the Hiwassee Railroad already had completed the grading of a sixty-five-mile span between the Georgia state line and Blair's Ferry (Loudon) on the Tennessee River. The legislature's refusal to fund or support its extension meant that East Tennessee unfortunately had to wait until 1855 for completion of the road by its successor company, the East Tennessee and Georgia.[33]

Between the 1834 constitutional convention and the outbreak of the Civil War in 1861, massive changes occurred in East Tennessee's economy, particularly during the 1850s, which made the section's prosperity increasingly dependent upon growing commerce with the Lower South. Some earlier antislavery stalwarts remained faithful to the cause throughout these changes. One was John Caldwell, Birdseye's good friend who had removed to Sevier County after selling his farm in Jefferson County in 1842. Other antislavery advocates, however, experienced a radical transformation in their outlook regarding the peculiar institution. No such apostate made this astounding change with more publicity or zeal than "Parson" William G. Brownlow. After signing what was surely the single most denunciatory petition damning slavery in 1834, Brownlow emerged in the 1840s and 1850s, during his tenure as editor of the *Knoxville Whig*, as the most forceful proslavery spokesman in the region. His attacks on abolitionists would surpass in vituperation and political hyperbole most southern proslavery rhetoric of his age. Although he became the de facto Unionist leader of East Tennessee before and during the war, he stated categorically that if abolition were the true goal of Lincoln Republicanism, he would be the first to leave the Union. Repeatedly, Brownlow argued in 1861 and 1862 in the pages of the *Knoxville Whig* that remaining in the Union was the best way to *preserve* the institution of slavery.[34]

So radical and outspoken was Brownlow in his defense of slavery that, before my discovery of his signature in the 1834 petition from Jefferson County, no scholar had previously even *suspected* him of such heresy. Yet, when compared to other samples of his writing, this signature unmistakably is the parson's; and the virulent and uncompromising tone and language of the petition indicate that, in 1834, he was no lukewarm fellow traveler in the East Tennessee antislavery vanguard. If Parson Brownlow—the leading apologist of slavery, an advocate so enthusiastic that he would debate the issue publicly in the North with antislavery spokesmen in the 1850s— once had believed in freeing the slaves, how many other East Tennesseans likewise changed their opinions in the 1840s and 1850s? This remains an intriguing but largely unanswered question.[35]

One other such famous apostate whom Birdseye knew was the prominent Presbyterian clergyman, Frederick Augustus Ross (1796–1883). Born into a wealthy Virginia family, Ross established his home, Rotherwood, in 1818, in Sullivan County, twenty-five miles north of Rogersville, in northeastern Tennessee, on land inherited from his father. Despite his great wealth and luxurious lifestyle, he was ordained at Rogersville in October 1825. Possibly due in part to his friendship with Dr. David Nelson and the Reverend Isaac Anderson, both strong abolitionists, he was converted to the antislavery cause and subsequently freed all his own slaves in 1830. When Ezekiel Birdseye met Ross in June 1841, he was greatly impressed with his antislavery zeal; "his heart is much in the cause," Birdseye commented. Ross also expressed his expectation that raising silkworms, a cause in which he had invested heavily, would promote antislavery by giving employment to poor whites.[36]

Unfortunately for Reverend Ross, his investment in the silk culture deprived him of his entire fortune. Whether economic ruin affected his views on slavery is difficult to ascertain, but by the 1850s he had become a leading defender of slavery. In 1857 in Philadelphia, he published a book entitled *Slavery Ordained of God*, in which he claimed divine sanction for the peculiar institution. That same year he published a pamphlet, *Position of the Southern Church in Relation to Slavery*, which continued his proslavery argument upon similar grounds. Ross's arguments were largely unoriginal; he seems to have subscribed to all the commonplace proslavery arguments circulating throughout the South during the 1850s. Numerous other examples could be given of less well-known men who earlier had held antislavery views but became strongly proslavery by the 1840s. One such man, Gen. William Brazelton, of New Market, Jefferson County, was mentioned by Birdseye in 1841 as a "despotic slaveholder." In 1817, however, Brazelton had been one of the signers of an antislavery petition from Jefferson County written by Elihu Embree.[37]

The ultimate question regarding East Tennessee's antislavery movement is to what extent such sentiment influenced separatism throughout this region in the tumultuous political crisis of 1861. Although Tennessee voted almost four to one against secession in February 1861, in a second referendum on June 8, after Fort Sumter had fallen, Tennesseans voted by a substantial majority, 104,913 to 47,238, in favor of leaving the Union. East Tennessee, however, in this second referendum on June 8, voted overwhelmingly, 32,923 to 14,780 (68 to 23 percent), against separation. An East Tennessee Convention, specially called by Unionist leaders, met in Knoxville on May 30 and later in Greeneville on June 17 to debate the momentous question of whether East Tennessee should secede from the state. Unionist delegates from most counties in the section attended these meetings; old friends of Birdseye—Spencer Henry, representing Blount County, and John Caldwell, representing Sevier County—were present. At the Greeneville meeting, a committee consisting of John Netherland, Oliver P. Temple, and James P. McDowell prepared and presented to the legislature a declaration of grievances and a petition asking permission for the dissident East Tennessee counties to form a separate state. Subsequently East Tennessee was refused permission to secede from the state and failed to effect such a move through revolution or force of arms, as West Virginia did. This failure was due primarily to East Tennessee's geographical location, surrounded by strong Confederate forces, and its strategic possession of a vital railroad link between Virginia and Georgia.[38]

Later historians, including Oliver P. Temple, a leader of East Tennessee's Unionist separatist movement, tried to identify political or economic reasons why some people remained Unionist and others supported the new Confederacy. Temple identified old Whigs, among them many of Birdseye's friends, who remained loyal. There are so many exceptions to every generalization about these defining characteristics, however, that virtually any hypothesis is fraught with hazard. Historian Todd Groce, in a recent study, illuminated the economic reorientation of East Tennessee's economy toward the Lower South during the 1850s, and found a clear correlation between new merchants in towns and cities and Confederate sympathy. He also discovered a significant age difference between East Tennessee Unionists and Confederates; the Confederates tended to be much younger men. Indeed, many prominent Unionist leaders, such as T. A. R. Nelson, Thomas Arnold, W. C. Kyle, Seth J. W.

Lucky, and Fred Heiskell, had sons who joined the Confederate army or government. This generational difference was reflected in the experience of many of Birdseye's antislavery friends; Judge Jacob Peck, John Caldwell, and David A. Deaderick all had sons who joined the Confederate army. Judge Peck's son, William Raine Peck, actually became a brigadier general in the Confederate army.[39]

Oliver P. Temple was quite adamant in his assertion that abolitionism had played no role in East Tennessee's Unionist stance in 1861, and subsequent historians confirm that nearly all the section's Unionist leaders, like Parson Brownlow, condemned abolitionism as a form of irresponsible extremism. Most East Tennesseans viewed slaves much as Andrew Johnson did: as tools of the planter aristocracy, the invidious means of creating a privileged elite in the South which epitomized all that prevailing doctrines of republican egalitarianism denounced. Antislavery sentiment certainly never was mentioned in the elaborate political rhetoric East Tennesseans used both to confirm and to justify their deep estrangement from, and distrust of, Middle and West Tennessee. The high correlation of votes against secession in the June 8 referendum in counties where earlier antislavery activity had been strongest—Claiborne (83 percent), Blount (81 percent), Greene (78 percent), Jefferson (77 percent), Knox (72 percent), and Cocke (70 percent)—is an intriguing coincidence. No corroborating evidence, however, justifies assuming a definite connection. Part of the problem lies in the lack of any evidence to measure how earlier political antislavery agitation by a few prominent leaders percolated down into the mass rank and file of voters, or withstood the potent proslavery counterpropaganda which utilized racist attitudes shared almost universally by whites in the South as a whole.[40]

The only evidence of a body of opinion consistently hostile to slavery, or at least hostile to the effects of slavery, spanning the period of time between the constitutional convention of 1834 and the Civil War, resides in the judicial opinions of two East Tennesseans appointed to the state supreme court. Robert J. McKinney (1803–1875) and William B. Reese (1793–1859) both were antislavery advocates who freely expressed their convictions to Ezekiel Birdseye in the 1840s. Following Judge Jacob Peck's tenure on the court (1822–34), Reese served from 1835 to 1847; McKinney was elected in his place in 1847 and served until 1861. In numerous cases involving slaves, both these justices consistently ruled in favor of "humanity and reason," rather than merely upholding the letter of the law. In an 1845 case, Justice Reese refused to allow what he termed the "monstrous" sale, to satisfy creditors, of a free black's wife and child; he insisted that the court would "look at the substance of things, ... and will not suffer mere legal forms, the dress and drapery of a transaction, to alter the nature of things, and baffle the end aimed at." In like manner, Justice McKinney upheld the rights of slaves accused of various crimes, particularly insisting on their entitlement to the guarantees of procedural due process, up to the outbreak of the Civil War.[41]

The decision to give allegiance to the Confederacy was no indication of proslavery or antislavery sentiment, however. Justice McKinney, for example, with a clear record of antislavery belief and action both in the constitutional convention of 1834 and thereafter on the Tennessee Supreme Court, nevertheless elected to remain with Tennessee and join the Confederacy in 1861. Nor, it should be added, was antislavery sentiment limited, however veiled, to East Tennessee justices on the state supreme court. But most other notable justices who defended the rights of slaves, at least occasionally, were East Tennesseans. Among the latter were Nathan Green (1792–1866), who served on the court between 1831 and 1852; and R. L. Caruthers (1800–1882), who succeeded Green and served on the court between 1852 and 1861. Finally, Arthur F. Howington finds pronounced intrastate regional differences in trials in the lower circuit and criminal courts involving slave defendants accused of capital crimes; 82 percent of East Tennessee slaves on trial for their lives were acquitted, compared to 59 percent in Middle Tennessee and 49 percent in West Tennessee.[42]

Ezekiel Birdseye's testimony concerning slavery and abolitionism between 1838 and 1846 thus occurs at an opportune time—in 1842, during the last great effort to form a separate state in East Tennessee, amid an ongoing economic depression which seemed to cause doubts among many slaveholders in the region about the economic viability of their peculiar institution. Other observers, too, left a record of their impressions of East Tennessee during this period. George W. Featherstonhaugh in 1844 traveled from Virginia to Knoxville, where he stopped for only a few hours to pronounce that city "a poor neglected-looking place," notwithstanding "some tolerable dwelling-houses." A decade later, in 1854, Frederick Law Olmsted—like Ezekiel Birdseye a native of Connecticut who hated slavery—visited East Tennessee, where he found the region generally more prosperous than the plantation South, and its inhabitants "more cheerful, more amiable, more sociable, more liberal." Due primarily to the absence of large numbers of slaves, Olmsted also pronounced those southern highlanders he encountered "more hopeful, more ambitious, more intelligent, more provident, and more comfortable" than southerners living in the Lower South.[43]

Olmsted's specific indictments mirror many of Birdseye's own observations about slavery—the detrimental effect of slavery upon southern whites, the inefficiency of slave labor, and the blighting effect of the whole system upon the southern economy generally. The critical difference between the testimony of men like Olmsted and Featherstonhaugh lies in the brevity of their visits to East Tennessee. In contrast, Birdseye lived and worked in the region, actively cultivating friends among slaves, slaveholders, and nonslaveholders, and gaining insight into the mentality of the folk community in a manner impossible to accomplish during a brief visit. Thus he was able to formulate his own answers to the all-important question of how East Tennesseans viewed themselves in comparison with their neighbors in other southern states and in other parts of their own state.[44]

Seeking to discover why East Tennessee remained overwhelmingly Unionist at the outbreak of the Civil War, historian John C. Inscoe has examined western North Carolina and East Tennessee, two regions in the South which, on the basis of antebellum demographic, economic, and political characteristics, appeared remarkably similar. According to the 1860 census, Tennessee's thirty easternmost counties contained only 12.5 percent of slaves in the total population, while, in North Carolina's 15 westernmost counties, slaves made up 10.2 percent of the population. Inscoe concludes that the critical difference between the two regions actually lay in their respective self-images—"that is, the way in which the residents of each section perceived themselves and their region in relation to their respective states and to the South."[45]

Ezekiel Birdseye's correspondence time and again corroborates, among all classes and occupations, East Tennessee's distinct self-image. In one particularly revealing incident in Jefferson County in 1841, a planter-aristocrat from South Carolina adopted a particularly brutal method of disciplining his slaves which shocked the community and brought immediate condemnation from other slaveowners in the neighborhood. According to Birdseye, several planters called on William Moore, the transplanted South Carolinian in question, and "told him that it must be discontinued." So, in this instance, even East Tennessee slaveholders had distinctive norms of proper behavior in treating slaves, according to Birdseye, and they refused to tolerate alien South Carolina patterns of slave management or discipline in their midst.[46]

East Tennessee's sense of separateness further was defined by geography and by a fear of being continually displaced, economically and politically, by the faster-growing and more prosperous middle section of the state. On the east, the section was bordered by the high Unaka chain of the Appalachian Mountains separating Tennessee from North Carolina.

On the western boundary of East Tennessee was the crest of the rugged Cumberland Plateau, a subregion of sandy, thin, porous, and generally unproductive soil. Few transportation links existed among the state's three divisions in the nineteenth century; even the advent of the railroad in the 1850s saw little effort before the Civil War to link the regions of the state together on an east-west axis. For example, when finally completed in 1858, the East Tennessee and Virginia Railroad, which linked the region's major cities of Knoxville and Chattanooga, connected East Tennessee with Georgia on the southwest and Virginia on the northwest.[47]

Although East Tennessee had been the dominant section in terms of size and political power in the first quarter of the nineteenth century, by 1860 it contained only 298,881 inhabitants, or 26 percent of the state's total population. Political representation was beginning to decline in proportion to the population shift. As the plantation economy rapidly expanded into West Tennessee, East Tennessee by mid-century had come to possess the least fertile soil of the three grand divisions, and the section produced no large quantities of specialized cash crops. Only in manufacturing was there anything like parity with Middle Tennessee, which in 1860 had a capital investment in manufacturing of $6,329,000 (45 percent of the state's total); East Tennessee was not far behind with $5,870,000 (41 percent). The most striking difference between East Tennessee and the other sections of the state, of course, involved the number of slaves. East Tennessee's population in 1860 contained only 9.2 percent of slaves, compared to 29 percent in Middle Tennessee and 33.5 percent in West Tennessee.[48]

How Ezekiel Birdseye happened to come to East Tennessee in 1838 is a question never answered in his correspondence. Yet almost from the moment of his arrival in this region, he often asserts, he sensed among the people there attitudes toward slavery and abolition very different from those prevalent in other parts of the South where he had lived previously. Birdseye's explanation of this East Tennessee distinctiveness emerges from a wealth of descriptive detail of various people, places, and events in his letters to Gerrit Smith. These letters, judged collectively, offer perhaps the most compelling and comprehensive examination of East Tennessee by an outside observer during the 1840s. If the veracity of these observations can be judged in part by examining the character of Birdseye himself, then his life history, the subject of the next chapter, may offer the most important key to corroborating his narrative description of East Tennessee and his analysis of why the region remained so self-consciously separate, or distinct, from both the rest of Tennessee and the other antebellum southern states.

2.
Ezekiel Birdseye

A chance fitness lies in the dates of Ezekiel Birdseye's birth and death—1796 and 1861—since these were the identical years of Tennessee's birth and symbolic death as a state within the federal Union. His own character was rooted deeply in the rocky soil of New England Puritanism. His great-great-great-grandfather, Deacon John Birdsey, came to America in 1636 from Reading, Berkshire, England, and settled at Wethersfield, Connecticut, where he married Phillipa, the daughter of the Reverend Henry Smith. In 1649, he moved to Stratford, Connecticut, where he died at the age of seventy-four.[1]

By the time of the deacon's great-grandson, the Reverend Nathan Birdseye (1714–1818), the family had become both numerous and generally prosperous. Nathan was a 1736 graduate of Yale who became a noted Congregational minister in Stratford, Connecticut. At his death in 1818, at the age of 103, Nathan Birdseye left 206 living descendants. It was a singular fact, his obituary noted, "that of all the branches of this numerous family, not one of them has been reduced to want."[2]

From the Birdseye family, which had been firmly established in Connecticut for 160 years by the time of his own birth on March 17, 1796, Ezekiel inherited several traits of character which remained evident throughout his life. First, deep Christian piety, together with "a retentive memory, sound judgment, and a good heart," qualities enumerated in his grandfather Nathan's

1818 obituary, also characterized Ezekiel. Like the Reverend Nathan, also, he would be widely hailed as "an honest man and a real Christian," even by those otherwise hostile slaveholders who later were so impressed with his obvious sincerity, humility, and civility.[3]

Second, it was not the way of the Birdseyes to be poor and honest; the family motto seemed rather to prescribe honesty together with a spirit of energetic acquisitiveness which pushed its members to become as prosperous as possible. Ezekiel would devote an enormous amount of time and energy to acquiring wealth; if he was not always successful in his numerous ventures, that never was due to any lack of entrepreneurial zeal on his part. Nor was there ever any conscious conflict between piety and vigorous pursuit of wealth by personal industry in Ezekiel's correspondence. Like other Puritans, he seemed to regard wealth as a providential reward for continued exertion, and always viewed any idleness, such as the perceived leisure of slaveholders in the South, as a species of sin in itself.

Birdseye's letters are in fact replete with condemnations of just such "idleness" among the sons of the planter class whom he encountered in the South. He believed this sloth to be directly responsible for the venereal disease widespread among those young men, which "cut off thousands in the morning of life, or leave them with a broken constitution." Thus, "from long habits of ease, they become unfitted for active labor." At the deaths of their parents, these licentious slaveholding sons soon exhausted their patrimony and then were forced to live "like drones in society, unfitted to be useful members of it or the heads of households."[4]

Although Birdseye's entrepreneurial zeal forced him to live practically all his adult life away from his native home in Cornwall, Litchfield County, Connecticut, he nevertheless would demonstrate time and again a third basic characteristic—an intense love of New England and his extended family there. He always was something of a visitor or temporary resident wherever else he lived, regardless of the number of years spent in one location. He lived perhaps for the longest period of his life in East Tennessee, from 1838 until his death in Knoxville in 1861, but his name never appeared on any census of that state, and in his business transactions, Cornwall, Connecticut, always was given as his permanent residence. Both his wives were natives of Connecticut, and his second wife remained at the home of her father throughout their marriage.[5] Ezekiel Birdseye never established his own household in any location, but always boarded with a local family which kept, in his language, a "public" house. Clearly he always hoped to return to Connecticut at the end of his career; like so many seafaring sons of New England, he remained emotionally and spiritually rooted in the land of his childhood, regardless of how widely he traveled throughout the southern states.[6]

Further insight into Ezekiel's background may be gleaned from the will of his father, Ebenezer Birdseye (1757–1829), who outlived two wives, leaving nine children at the time of his death in 1829. Settling in Cornwall as a young man, Ebenezer industriously accumulated small tracts of land in Litchfield County throughout his life, leaving an estate valued at $4,006. Skill in appraising land values, as well as some knowledge of commercial law, were passed on to Ezekiel, who would speculate similarly in land on a much larger scale later in his career. Ebenezer also owned a small store, evident from his store account book, and such training must have been Ezekiel's first mercantile experience.[7]

Very significantly, the Cornwall records also reveal that Ebenezer set free his only Negro slave, named Obed, in 1805, when Ezekiel was nine years old. The fact that his own father owned a slave and voluntarily freed him indicates that, within his own family and New England community, attitudes toward slavery and blacks were undergoing rapid transformation in Ezekiel's childhood. Obed's existence also clearly shows that the institution of slavery was not totally foreign to a Connecticut abolitionist who later came to reside in the slaveholding South. What Ebenezer's reasons were for freeing his slave are nowhere made explicit, but the changing social climate in the northern states, as well as his membership in the Cornwall First Congregational Church, offer the most logical explanations.[8]

In terms of his later career, Ezekiel's most important sibling was his eldest half-brother, Victory Birdseye (1782–1853), who, after graduating from Williams College in 1804, studied law and became a prominent attorney in Pompey Hill, Onondaga County, New York. Victory was elected to the Fourteenth Congress (1815–17); served as postmaster of Pompey Hill between 1817 and 1838; was district attorney of Onondaga County in 1818–33; worked as master of chancery of Onondaga County in 1818–22; and served in both the New York state senate (1827) and assembly (1823, 1838–40). He ended his political career as a Whig representative to the Twenty-seventh Congress (1841–43) and afterwards resumed the practice of law in Onondaga County, New York, until his death in 1853. Victory Birdseye offered financial, moral, and legal support for his brother's widespread entrepreneurial ventures, particularly those in East Tennessee.[9]

In 1818, Ezekiel Birdseye went to Union County, South Carolina, to pursue his fortune. There is no record of his business transactions there, but presumably he was in the mercantile business or served as clerk in some such enterprise. The brutality of slavery in the Palmetto State left an indelible impression; nothing ever exceeded in his mind the horror of seeing slaves burned alive in public executions for crimes of widely varying degrees of severity. Observing such atrocities in Union, Laurens, Abbeville, and Newberry counties (or districts, as they were then called) gave Ezekiel the basis for accurately comparing the treatment and conditions of slaves in other parts of the South, however.[10]

Two important friendships were formed during his residence in South Carolina between 1818 and 1824. James Henderson Irby (1793–1860), son of Birdseye's landlord, William Irby, became an intimate friend and remained so for many years. James H. Irby, after graduating from South Carolina College in 1816, became an important attorney and state legislator, representing Laurens District in the state's house of representatives (1826–30, 1832–40, 1848–52) and in its senate (1854–60). He was brigade major of the militia in 1822 and served as lieutenant governor of the state in 1852–54, in addition to numerous other prestigious state appointments. In 1842, he told Birdseye that he owned over one hundred slaves and a plantation "about 4 miles square" that produced an annual cotton crop selling for seven thousand dollars. At his death in 1860, Irby was one of the wealthiest planters in the northern part of the state, leaving an estate valued at nearly half a million dollars.[11]

Birdseye reported that he and Irby conversed freely about slavery and abolitionism on a visit to Laurens District in June 1842. Irby had always deplored cruelty toward slaves and earlier had threatened his own brother-in-law "who had whipped a woman so as to endanger her life." Birdseye's continued friendship with a pillar of the South Carolina planter aristocracy is amazing, considering the universal censure of all abolitionists in this stronghold of proslavery advocacy. That James H. Irby, within the shadow of John C. Calhoun's territory, would frankly discuss the evils of the peculiar institution with his old friend represents a remarkable tribute to Birdseye's character. This same friend, interestingly, was a member of the Southern Rights Convention which met in 1851 to consider South Carolina's secession from the Union. Irby strongly opposed disunion; to what degree he was influenced by his old friend Birdseye is unknown. He did share Birdseye's vision of the importance of commerce and industry to the southern economy, however; between 1853 and 1855 he was president of Laurens Railroad Company, and earlier, in 1839, he was a commissioner to represent South Carolina at stockholders' meetings of the South-Western Railroad Bank and the Louisville, Cincinnati, and Charleston Railroad Company.[12]

Birdseye's ability to discover and appreciate merit in an individual planter aristocrat whose social class he otherwise collectively despised is also evident in his regard for John Belton O'Neall (1793–1863), distinguished justice of the South Carolina Court of Appeals. In a letter condemning South Carolina's planter class and the brutal suppression of dissent by individuals of "great moral worth" there who feared "being even suspected of heresy" on the subject of abolition, Birdseye singled O'Neall out for special praise. "If there is a redeeming spirit in all that state I should suppose it to be John B. O[']Neal[l]," he wrote, indicating some private sympathy for the plight of slaves on the part of this "pious man well acquainted throughout the state."[13]

Was the man who, in 1859, on the eve of the Civil War, became chief justice of South Carolina's Supreme Court actually a closet abolitionist? O'Neall's Quaker ancestry makes Birdseye's assertion plausible, but there were other intellectual affinities as well between the two men. Both were ardent advocates of temperance; O'Neall exerted a profound influence on behalf of that crusade and in 1852 was elected president of the Sons of Temperance of North America. Like Birdseye, he strongly supported scientific agriculture and railroads in South Carolina. In 1835, O'Neall incurred the hostility of the secessionists by declaring unconstitutional the test oath devised by nullifiers. Vigorously opposed to secession and nullification at every opportunity, he also was a prolific writer whose longer works include *The Negro Law of South Carolina* (1848). In this book, O'Neall expresses disapproval of some of the laws regulating slavery and advocates reforms such as allowing owners the regulated right to manumit slaves and leave bequests to them. He also objected to the prohibition against teaching slaves to read or write and argued that kindness towards them should inform all legislation regulating slave behavior. All his proposals for ameliorating the lot of slaves were rejected by the South Carolina Committee of the Judiciary, but O'Neall's recommendations clearly indicate where his true sentiments lay in regard to slavery. As a leader of the Upcountry Unionist faction and president of the Greenville and Columbia Railroad, O'Neall combined an energetic zeal for social reform with an entrepreneurial zest for material progress—a mix closely resembling Birdseye's own moral chemistry.[14]

Leaving South Carolina in 1824, Ezekiel moved to Limestone County in northern Alabama, where he remained until 1828. These Alabama years represented something of a crucible in his personal life, since it was here that his young wife of less than two years died. On October 5, 1826, he had married Lucinda Pierce in the First Congregational Church in Cornwall. They moved to Athens, Alabama, where Ezekiel was in business, but in the spring of 1828, Lucinda became gravely ill. Five days before her death on May 27, 1828, she made her last will and testament, leaving the bulk of her estate to "my beloved, and ever affectionate husband." Writing fifteen years later to a friend who had lost his wife, Ezekiel recalled poignantly "a time when my heart bled from the same stroke," when "my lovely and beloved L. was taken away—How severe the trial, none can tell, who are not called to endure the same bereavement." After all these years, Lucinda's death remained vivid in his mind. "All those afflictions appear to me, as though they were of yesterday," he lamented to his friend in 1843.[15]

During the next ten years, 1828–38, Ezekiel traveled widely, but there are only a few clues to his specific whereabouts at any given moment. Within this period, he spent part of two years in Georgia; the exact location is nowhere mentioned in his correspondence. "In the fall of 1828 I was in Nashville," he notes in one letter. "During the time that nullification was rife I was in South Carolina," he notes elsewhere, indicating that he spent at least part of 1832 or 1833 in that state. An inventory of Birdseye's estate in 1862 enumerated 204,345 acres of "wild lands" in his possession in North Carolina, Tennessee, Indiana, and New York—lands presumably acquired during his travels in the 1830s. In another letter, Birdseye relates overhearing, while traveling "in the stage in company with slaveholders between Maysville & Lexington," talk of a plot to kill James G. Birney, with whom he had become acquainted earlier in Alabama. These slaveholders were angry over a rumor that Birney planned to publish an antislavery paper in Danville, Kentucky, and they threatened in Birdseye's presence that "he should never survive the second number if he did the first." These events place Birdseye in Kentucky in 1835, where it seems likely, from other evidence, he remained until 1838.[16]

In 1834, Ezekiel married Mary M. Stone, daughter of the Reverend Timothy Stone of the First Congregational Church of Cornwall. Reverend Stone had performed the ceremony when he married his first wife, Lucinda, so the family evidently had been known to him for some time. Whether this second wife ever moved from Connecticut to be with her husband in the 1830s is uncertain, but after Birdseye moved to East Tennessee in 1838, Mary remained at the home of her father. In 1838, his only daughter, Irene Lucinda, was born. This daughter, named after his first wife, eventually became a schoolteacher but died on February 25, 1858, just before she was to have been married.[17] So, twice in his life, Birdseye suffered the loss of his closest family member, wife and daughter, who bore the same name.

Greater insight may be gained into Birdseye's personal attachments by examining the chief beneficiaries listed in his will. In his original will, dated November 13, 1856, he left ten thousand dollars each to his wife, Mary M. Birdseye, and their daughter, Irene Lucinda. To his brother Ezra Birdseye and wife of Penn Yan, Yates County, New York, he left the interest from five thousand dollars "for their comfortable maintenance so long as they live." The remainder of his estate after these provisions was to be divided equally between his wife and daughter in this original will. In a codicil to his will dated May 12, 1859, Birdseye left half of his deceased daughter's share to four of his wife's nieces and nephews, and half to Eben Chaffee, his sister Hannah's son. His brother-in-law, Rev. T. D. P. Stone, father of four of his legatees, was named executor of his estate.[18]

By the time of his arrival in East Tennessee in 1838, Ezekiel Birdseye had become an ardent abolitionist, as is evident throughout his extensive correspondence with Gerrit Smith between 1841 and 1846. From these letters, however, it is also clear that, like most other men of conscience who became converted to the abolitionist cause, the process was gradual and constantly evolving over a period of decades. In relating the incident concerning the angry slaveholders' plot to murder James G. Birney if he published an antislavery newspaper in Danville, Kentucky, Ezekiel Birdseye makes a revealing confession. "I thought it my duty to apprise him of his danger by letter," he writes, "but am mortified to recollect that it contained a censure on abolitionists for going ahead of public sentiment." By the 1840s, Birdseye would be convinced that abolitionists should publish their message as vigorously as possible at every opportunity, but in 1835 he was hesitant to offend southern sensibilities on the issue of slavery.[19]

Ezekiel Birdseye's mature views on slavery, once he had become a convinced abolitionist by the 1840s, were similar, if not identical, to those of the majority of his contemporaries in the antislavery crusade which was gaining increasing momentum throughout the North. First, he viewed human enslavement fundamentally as a moral issue; slavery was damaging both to slave and master and on that account alone was morally wrong. Second, he focused on the physical and psychological cruelties that he believed abounded in the South. These ranged from the extremes of burning alive in public executions slaves accused of crimes, or savagely beating them to death with no accountability before the law for such murder; to depriving a man, of whatever race, of just wages for work done, or depriving him of all opportunity for self-improvement.[20]

Birdseye also deplored the fact that slave marriages were not recognized by law, as well as the frequent separation of slave children from their mother at an early age, due to the capriciousness or financial insolvency of the master. He also was well aware of the licentiousness of southern slaveholders, who had ready sexual access to their female slaves. Both these problems were apparent in a slave auction in Greene County, Tennessee, which Birdseye described in 1842. James McMurtrey, owner of forty-five slaves, "died leaving his estate indebted so as to render a sale legally necessary." About fifteen of the slave children had a white father, presumably McMurtrey himself. One observer stated "that the resemblance is so striking to the other children of McMurtr[e]y as to leave no doubt of the fact in the mind of anyone who will observe them." He noted, "Here were parents and children bound together by all those ties which could be supposed to exist in that relation then to be separated forever." "Slavery in its best estate is a bitter cup," Birdseye concluded, "but who can describe a scene like this—of such unutterable woe."[21]

One major difference between Birdseye and many of his fellow abolitionists is that he nowhere appears to have any racial prejudice. If a single thread runs through the letters he wrote to Gerrit Smith between 1841 and 1846, it is the attempt to purchase and set free a slave named William, who, despite enormous suffering, exhibited qualities of character and intelligence which made him appear superior in any setting. Birdseye tried to purchase William, or "the Captain," as he was sometimes called, first from Nicholas W. Woodfin in Asheville, North Carolina, in 1841, and then, in 1845, from another owner, David Davis. "He is a smarter man than I am," observed Mr. Franklin, another former owner of William. Gerrit Smith offered the money to purchase William, in order to display his "strict integrity of character" and "natural talents" of the "first order" before a northern audience as an antidote to racism. Birdseye believed that William "will be an acquisition to the good cause" because "he has firmness talents and the evidences of barbarities of the section on his person which will do much to influence our Northern people." Evidently both Woodfin and Davis were warned by other slaveholders not to sell William, however, and the purchase never was effected. Woodfin had promised to give Birdseye an option on buying "the Captain," should he ever sell him, but later he disregarded this pledge.[22]

Birdseye's lack of racial prejudice is also apparent in his description of Sion Harris, a former slave and carpenter-farmer from Knox County, Tennessee. Harris, in 1830 at age nineteen, after obtaining his freedom, had gone to Liberia on the ship *Liberia*. Following many adventures, such as capturing a boa constrictor and surviving some harrowing attacks by hostile natives in his adopted country, he eventually became a member of the Liberian House of Representatives. Harris married Martha Erskine, the daughter of George Erskine, a former slave who had been freed and educated by Dr. Isaac Anderson at Maryville College. George Erskine had been ordained and sent as a Presbyterian missionary to superintend church and school work in Liberia in 1820. Harris returned to the United States in 1841 and addressed a camp meeting of the Presbyterian church in Maryville, Tennessee, which was presided over by Dr. Anderson, founder and president of Maryville College. Anderson was Birdseye's friend and also an ardent abolitionist. Birdseye thus described Sion Harris's address to over a thousand people in Maryville:

> On the next morning I attended the meeting. The interest to hear Harris was so great that he was again invited to address the meeting. He commenced and spoke probably an hour and a half with a well timed and appropriate address manifesting natural talents of a high order and showing that in the few years he had been free in Africa he had acquired much. With all the prejudice in the South against the African I was gratified to see an audience listening attentively to one, and acknowledging him to possess talents of a high order. After his address they inquired earnestly as to the influence on the natives and the extent and opening for missions.[23]

Perhaps the single characteristic of Ezekiel Birdseye which most differentiated him from other northern abolitionists, however, was his basic sympathy toward individual slaveholders. He believed that all men were essentially good, and that most slaveowners were capable of being converted peaceably through moral suasion. "Almost every day I have conversations with slaveholders on the subject of slavery," he wrote in 1842. "It has not procured me an unkind word," he concluded, "and when done in a spirit of kindness I have little fear it will." Birdseye argued that more extensive correspondence with northern abolitionists was needed to spread "light" throughout the South. He also urged repeatedly the necessity of northern churches taking a strong public stance against slavery. Like the temperance reformation, any movement which gained widespread popularity in the North must simultaneously affect public opinion in the South, he argued.[24]

The actual number of slaveholders who frankly confessed their own private doubts about the peculiar institution to Birdseye is amazing. Evidently his demeanor inspired confidence, even from relative strangers. One such was William Wadsworth of Carthage, Moore County, North Carolina, who had served in the legislature of that state and assured Birdseye that Romulus M. Saunders and Gov. John Motley Morehead, prominent politicians, also were opposed to slavery. Later Birdseye met Saunders in Knoxville and reported a lengthy conversation with him condemning slavery, although "these public men are afraid of injuring their popularity," he observed, and consequently "express themselves with caution." Ironically, the southern slaveholders most likely to take issue with Birdseye's antislavery views were clergymen. "In defending slavery," he commented, the southern clergy "have the most bitterness and least charity of all its defenders."[25]

It must be remembered, however, that the men Birdseye befriended usually were well-educated, wealthy businessmen or prominent politicians, attorneys, or judges who often were very interested in attracting northern investment to their respective states. In this sense, Birdseye was an unconscious elitist in his friendships and close associations, although he made frequent protestations of democratic egalitarianism. "I am not a lawyer," he wrote in 1841 in one such disclaimer, "but a very plain farmer." Nevertheless, he conducted very sophisticated legal and commercial transactions throughout his career. At the time of his death in 1861, this "very plain farmer" had an estate valued at $182,731.[26] It is also well to note that the majority of Birdseye's conversations with slaveholders took place, as he reported to Smith, in 1841 and 1842. These years saw a worsening economic depression throughout the South, and the loss of markets made many southern planters bitterly question every aspect of an economic system which threatened to impoverish them. Ten years later, during the 1850s, when the cotton market revived, their attitude toward slavery often would be quite different.

Nor was Ezekiel Birdseye without critics during these years. In April 1842 he noted that someone was attacking him in the *Knoxville Register* "as the colonizationist in the Mountains." He was confident that his opponents "will venture no open attack on me" but feared that they might employ an assassin. Earlier, in March of that year, the editor of the *Knoxville Post*, "a tolerably fair specimen of a Southern swaggerer," vented his spleen against northern abolitionists and thundered "forth some anathemas for my special benefit." In December 1841 he had reported that hostile postmasters had threatened to withhold delivery of his mail at Mossy Creek and New Market because they recognized Gerrit Smith's handwriting. "Individually they profess friendship for me as they do for my friend Caldwell," he noted, "while in the narrow circle of slaveholding they privately express opinions in terms familiar here that we are 'ugly customers.'"[27]

On at least one occasion, Ezekiel Birdseye's friendship with an elderly slaveholder led him to attempt to persuade a runaway slave, Chamberlain, to return to his master. Birdseye was aware of the moral ambiguity of this particular course of action but attempted to justify it on the grounds that Mr.

Fowler, his friend, was the kindest and most conscientiously humane and mild master he knew. After an altercation with his master's wife, Chamberlain, presumably under the influence of alcohol, ran off and suffered severe privation while "lying out" in the surrounding mountains. Birdseye, acting as an intermediary for Fowler, spoke to Chamberlain's mother and promised his own guarantees of kind treatment and no punishment if the slave would return promptly. At first Birdseye believed that Chamberlain had fled to the free states, but in September 1842 the poor slave in question returned to his owner after ten months' wandering about in the forest starving. Later, Birdseye questioned Simon, another slave owned by Fowler, about the suffering he had endured while living in the mountains to escape capture as his friend Chamberlain had done. The slave poignantly responded that his physical privations were "but a trifle" compared to the "idea of being sold and carried off by a slave trader."[28]

To Birdseye's credit, whenever an opportunity presented itself he talked directly with individual slaves in order to obtain more accurate impressions of slavery's effects on its victims. Confidential conversation with slaves was "one of the most difficult things in the slave states," he reported; for "the master is jealous" and inclined to "raise a popular tumult against the individual who attempts it." "Should the slave report the conversation and it should happen to be of an 'incendiary' character he would be in danger of his life in most of the South." Nevertheless, most slaves were well aware of Birdseye's abolitionist views, one slave informed him, and, because he was considered a friend of the slave, they were more inclined to speak frankly to him.[29]

In one of many instances of small acts of kindness, he paid for the enlargement of a keepsake gold ring for a young slave who had been a waiter in a Knoxville hotel, when the silversmith refused credit. On another occasion, he warned a free black barber not to accept the offer of liberal wages from a slaveowner seeking to induce him to come to Mississippi as his coachman. Too many such incidents of free blacks being lured back into slavery by such attractive offers were reported in the newspapers for Birdseye to be sanguine about this particular situation. At another time, Birdseye actually talked one angry slaveowner out of "one of those terrible scourgings so common with unrestrained despotism" five miles below Athens, Tennessee, by calmly reasoning with him about his offending slave. Characteristically, he remarked that this particular master, Mr. Rice, "appeared a little mortified that he had indulged such violent passions," charitably noting that "Mr. Rice in his usual intercourse with society has nothing of the appearance of the tyrant about him."[30]

Most of Birdseye's time after his arrival in East Tennessee in 1838 was spent at Newport, Cocke County, where he owned and operated a lumber mill. He had numerous other business ventures throughout this region, however, and traveled frequently. Blount, Greene, Jefferson, Knox, McMinn, and Monroe counties were most frequently mentioned in his correspondence, but he also visited Asheville, North Carolina, and Chattanooga in Hamilton County, Tennessee. Although he was nowhere explicit about his political allegiances, it is evident that he was a strong Whig, as was his brother, Victory Birdseye. Of course, he actively supported James G. Birney and the newly formed Liberty Party, as did Gerrit Smith. He criticized Andrew Jackson on account of his dueling and generally deplored the prevalence of dueling and the lamentable propensity to violence he found so evident among southerners:

> One of the most unhappy features in the character of the slaveholding states is their proneness to violence. The evil may be traced to the frequent examples of cruelty to the slaves and the want of parental government. Children grow up without restraint—[being] rather taught to indulge than govern their passions. As they become grown up frequent collisions occur of a serious nature, often fatal and seldom punished, if among the aristocracy. I am happy to be able to say that they occur less frequently in E[ast] Ten[nessee] than in most parts of the South, but are quite too frequent here. Nashville and the vicinity have been most afflicted with these occurrences of any part of our state and seem to occur there most among the aristocracy.[31]

Closely allied to Birdseye's abolitionism were his belief in evangelical religion and his enthusiasm for the temperance crusade. "The temperance reformation and religious revivals we hope are preparing them for other great changes and improvements in Christian morals," he noted in 1842. That so many Tennesseans could be induced for conscience's sake to give up alcoholic beverages was an illustration he used to counter southern claims that slavery was so deeply entrenched in society it would not be easily eradicated. Like so many other reformers of his generation, Birdseye repeatedly expressed a deep optimism about human nature and his faith in the perfectibility of man. He generally spoke very favorably of the clergy he encountered in East Tennessee; "most of them are humble pious self-denying men," he reported in 1841. The Presbyterians and Methodists particularly numbered among their members many antislavery advocates, men like Isaac Anderson, Spencer Henry, and the aged divine, Abel Pearson, whom Birdseye greatly admired. Pearson had written a book in which he predicted the near approach of the millennium and the downfall of slavery. "An enlightened clergy is one of the greatest blessings which can attend a free country," Birdseye concluded, while "an ignorant bigoted vicious clergy is among if not the greatest calamity."[32]

Not all clergy were enlightened, however. A few Presbyterian ministers, such as Dr. Thomas A. Anderson and Rev. Gideon S. White, were strongly proslavery, as was the sometime Methodist minister, William G. Brownlow. From 1840 until his removal to Knoxville in 1849, Brownlow was editor of the *Jonesboro Whig*, fighting with characteristically fierce vituperation against a rival political paper in the same town, the Democratic *Jonesboro Sentinel*, established in 1836 and edited for a time by Thomas A. Anderson. After espousing "the cause of slavery with some degree of vehemence," Birdseye noted with asperity, Anderson's "next error was editing an administration paper in the same village with Brownlow." Fortunately for the sensibilities of the religious community, Anderson had resigned as editor by 1840, when Brownlow was shot by his successor, Landon Carter Haynes, so Jonesboro was not forced to witness the melancholy spectacle of two ministers of the gospel dueling each other! Ironically, Brownlow, who in the 1840s was very active in the temperance movement and for a time helped to edit the *Sons of Temperance* in Knoxville, Birdseye had reported as "drinking too freely" in a political campaign in February 1840 and actually fighting a duel with one of his political opponents.[33]

Gideon Stebbins White (1803–1863), despite having been educated at Maryville College under Dr. Isaac Anderson, was outspoken in his defense of slavery. At the time Birdseye argued with him over slavery in 1841, he was serving two churches, Shunem Presbyterian Church at Strawberry Plains, Jefferson City, and the Washington Presbyterian Church in Knox County. What right did the people of one state have "to interfere with the institutions of another state," White angrily asked Birdseye. Cleverly, Birdseye inquired whether White supported missions to India, where widows routinely were burned on the funeral pyres of their husbands. White replied this was an entirely different matter. To be sure, Birdseye responded, "but not a greater sin." Indian widows voluntarily complied with a swift death; American slaves endured the greater protracted agony of being separated forever from their children and spouses. Reverend White was "a man of strong sectarian feelings," Birdseye concluded, expressing his view that White "has a mistaken view of his duty" and "exhibits feelings which should not enter the pulpit."[34]

Birdseye discovered that most Baptist ministers were proslavery, particularly in Georgia and South Carolina, where often they were "the most cruel of petty tyrants" to their own slaves. He criticized sermons delivered by many Baptists as "an unintelligible jargon which could enlighten no one and leaves no more favorable impression on the intelligent than that the poor man had mistaken his disinclination for some industrious employment for a special call from the Holy Spirit to preach the gospel." Often these Baptist clergy "deride learning, abhor missions ridicule Temperance reformation pour out anathemas on the abolitionists and defend slavery." In other letters, however, Birdseye characteristically found admirable antislavery Baptist ministers and praised their efforts. One such was the Reverend Joseph Manning of Cocke County. "A very useful man and much distinguished for his piety," Manning said that slavery was so "great an evil that he feared it would be the ruin of the country."[35]

Only two ministers in East Tennessee openly preached abolitionism from their pulpit, according to Birdseye's observations. In 1840, the Reverend William Mack, a graduate of Princeton Theological Seminary, was invited to become pastor of the Second Presbyterian Church in Knoxville. Mack warned the local presbytery quite frankly that he was "an *abolitionist*" of strong convictions and unlikely to change; he supposed this conviction would cause an immediate objection to him from some members of the congregation. To his surprise, however, "every member avowed his concurrence with Mr. Mack in regard to abolition," and he became their pastor "honestly avowing his opinions" from the pulpit until he left to serve another church in 1844. In a visit in May 1842 to Knoxville, Mack told Birdseye that he believed slavery in the South would end only by violence.[36]

Thomas S. Kendall, minister of the Seceder Church in Blount County, also fearlessly preached abolitionism from his pulpit. This heroic man, according to Birdseye, had been tarred and feathered some years earlier in South Carolina for similar heresy. In a public meeting extraordinary in a slave state, Kendall actually delivered an antislavery address to a large crowd in Louisville, Blount County, Tennessee, in 1842. When some proslavery men heard of the planned meeting, they threatened to mob Kendall if he attempted to speak. At this point, many Blount County residents armed themselves to defend Kendall, and, according to Birdseye, "what may appear very extraordinary was a number of slaveholders there with their rifles ready to defend the liberty of speech." No attack was made, but "had one been attempted it would have proved disastrous to the aggressors." Many members of this particular church later emigrated with their entire families to the free states of Illinois and Iowa to escape slavery.[37]

Ezekiel Birdseye also joined many northern abolitionists in condemning the removal of the Cherokees from East Tennessee and northern Georgia in the 1830s. In November 1841 he visited one of the internment camps at Charleston, McMinn County, Tennessee, where "the Cherokees were quartered before removing to the West." He bitterly condemned the "frail tenements" in which they had been sheltered here and the "dram shop" where they "were tempted to drunkenness." The unaccustomed idleness in which they were kept before final removal in 1838, Birdseye believed, contributed to their despondency "under the injustice with which they were robbed of their country," causing them to die "in great numbers." Earlier that year, at Maryville College, he renewed his acquaintance with William Potter, whom he had known as a missionary at Creek Path, Alabama, in the 1820s. Potter now was working for the American Board of Commissioners for Foreign Missions and fully shared Birdseye's convictions about temperance, abolitionism, and the mistreatment of the Cherokees by both the State of Georgia and the federal government.[38]

Most of the reform movements which Ezekiel Birdseye passionately espoused—temperance, abolitionism, pacifism, and Indian rights—were shared to a remarkable degree by the recipient of his letters from East Tennessee, Gerrit Smith. Smith, unlike other famous abolitionists such as William Lloyd Garrison, was moderate and remarkably tolerant of those who disagreed with him. Modern historians employ a two-camp schema to describe abolitionists, dividing the latter into "radical" Garrisonians and "conservative" Tappanites. Smith belongs in neither camp, because he enjoyed good relations with members of both groups. Consequently, later generations of Americans have failed to appreciate his importance. In his own lifetime, however, Smith's vast wealth and highly publicized philanthropy made his name analogous to that of John D. Rockefeller in the twentieth century. As a reformer, he disbursed much of his great fortune in backing various liberal movements of the day, from women's rights and land and educational reforms to support of James G. Birney for president in 1840 at the head of the newly-formed Liberty Party.[39]

Like Birdseye's, however, Smith's ideas evolved slowly over time. Born of a wealthy family in Utica, New York, he graduated from Hamilton College in 1818 with honors and eventually became one of the most successful financiers in the country, parlaying his inheritance into a vast fortune through land speculation in New York state. He suffered a temporary setback during the depression that followed the Panic of 1837, but by the mid-1840s again was managing to accumulate a vast fortune. An advocate of cultural voluntarism through activity on the local level, Smith's fortune allowed him to retire to Peterboro in central New York to devote his full attention to various reform movements. During the last ten years before his death in 1874, his annual income was eighty thousand dollars.[40]

Smith elaborated upon his "voluntary principle" to argue by 1840 that individuals who were free of cultural or institutional restraints automatically would act in their own best interests; in doing so, they would serve the best interests of society by building railroads, schools, churches, etc. Where such freedom prevailed, Smith argued further, there was an inner compulsion to behave morally. As a corollary to his concept of cultural voluntarism, Smith condemned aristocracy, believing that all men should have equal opportunity to develop their talents, without the restrictions of distinctions of rank or inherited wealth or privilege. In this sense, slavery represented to Smith the worst form of aristocratic privilege, since slaves were automatically denied "the inherent right of self-ownership."[41] So Smith's basic philosophy of cultural voluntarism led directly to a theoretical condemnation of chattel slavery, a condemnation that became more personal as he learned more about the worst abuses of that institution from correspondents such as Ezekiel Birdseye.

An early supporter of the American Colonization Society, Smith by the mid-1830s, again like Birdseye, began seriously to doubt whether this organization honestly addressed the deeper problems of American slavery. In 1835, Smith, at the urging of abolitionist friends Beriah Green and Alvan Stewart, enrolled in the New York Anti-Slavery Society, a first step toward active abolitionism. This path eventually would lead Smith, in 1859, to give moral and financial support to John Brown and thereby to become an accessory before the fact in the raid on Harper's Ferry, which solidified southern hostility toward all abolitionists.[42]

In 1841 and 1842, however, when he received a majority of Birdseye's letters, Gerrit Smith still was a moderate who deplored Garrison's extremism and who had considerable sympathy for southern slaveholders as individuals and faith that, through moral suasion, they might voluntarily give up their peculiar institution. Although in later years, particularly after the passage of the Fugitive Slave Act in 1851, Smith's sympathy for the plight of southern slaves would lead him toward extralegal means of freeing them, in the early 1840s he exercised his compassion by buying individual slaves in order to liberate them. In 1841, for example, he purchased an entire slave family—husband, wife, and five children—from a Mississippi owner, Mr. Worthington, whose address he had obtained from Ezekiel Birdseye. Birdseye's best friend in East Tennessee, Judge Jacob Peck, had a son living in Mississippi who was able to secure Worthington's exact address.[43]

At this point, Birdseye's precise relationship to Gerrit Smith becomes critically important in assessing the accuracy and veracity of his accounts of slavery in East Tennessee. Clearly, Birdseye acted as a business agent for Smith, as he did for another famous and wealthy abolitionist, Lewis Tappan. Most of Birdseye's letters were edited by Smith and published in either the *Emancipator*, which in 1834 became the American Anti-Slavery Society's official publication, or *Friend of Man*, a weekly antislavery paper published in Utica, New York, under the auspices of the New York Anti-Slavery Society. Both papers enjoyed Smith's financial assistance and frequently published articles by him, so Ezekiel Birdseye was conscious of writing what would be used as abolitionist propaganda by his employer and potential benefactor. Birdseye's only stipulation was that Smith should omit the names of his friends, so as to prevent any embarrassment or persecution that might be occasioned by their antislavery sentiments, should these newspapers happen to circulate in the South.[44]

Birdseye himself believed that he gave an accurate account of slavery in East Tennessee and of the reaction to slavery by both slaveowners and nonslaveowners in the community. In sending what he characterized as "some hasty sketches of the lights and shades of slavery," he wrote in June 1842, "I may not always select such incidents as would be the best but I have endeavoured to be accurate and impartial." The most important evidence corroborating the veracity of Birdseye's descriptions is the amazing amount of minute detail he includes and the number of witnesses he specifically names. Broad generalizations about slavery or slaveowners occur briefly and usually at the end of his letters. Almost all the important points he makes involve some story or specific example, naming exact locations and the particular people involved. Even hearsay evidence usually is presented in terms of the reliability or reputation of the person giving the narration. The details of the lives and careers of Birdseye's principal witnesses, men such as Isaac Anderson, Jacob Peck, Spencer Henry, and John Caldwell, all are corroborated by other sources. Birdseye often praised the qualities of mind and character of individual slaveholders; as he discerningly argued in 1842, "when only bad men held slaves they would not hold them long." The balanced picture he presented of slaveowners lends credibility to Birdseye's other testimony, although to a northern audience he at times must have seemed overly sympathetic to individual planter aristocrats.[45]

In the final analysis, however, the greatest value of Birdseye's letters lies in the hidden world of private opinions about slavery expressed to him by prominent southerners in confidential conversations. This distillation of public opinion, particularly the outrage expressed over murders of slaves or cruel treatment of them, is the nearest approach documentary evidence offers to the real mind of the community. Time and again, Ezekiel Birdseye emphasized the prevalence and importance in East Tennessee of "a restraining public sentiment which discountenances cruelty to the poor slave."[46] An interior road map of the moral landscape of this public sentiment, coupled with a geographical tour and careful description of the exterior of East Tennessee during the early 1840s, is precisely Birdseye's most important contribution to a better understanding of both slavery and abolition in one part of the Appalachian South.

3.
Entrepreneurship, Capitalism, Economic Progress, and Abolitionism

If Ezekiel Birdseye miraculously had survived into the last decade of the twentieth century, he would not be surprised in the least over the connection historians now draw between the rise of capitalism and the nearly simultaneous emergence of organized antislavery.[1] His own perspective, however, was at once narrower and more simplistic. Not only was slavery unprofitable in its own right, Birdseye—in common with many abolitionists of his generation—believed, but also it harmed slaveowners economically as well as morally. Its very presence blighted both entrepreneurial zeal and progressive capitalist expansion. Indeed, one of his major and most frequent arguments to slaveholders in East Tennessee was the inhibiting effect slavery had on commercial and industrial development throughout the region. As early as 1837, Birdseye, in a letter published in the *New York Emancipator and Republican,* critically compared Ohio's commercial progress with Kentucky's backwardness, concluding that, in Kentucky, "if slavery was immediately abolished there, the land would at once rise to more than the present market value of the slaves" and that "this increase would continue in a compound ratio by the improvements that would be made in railroads, turnpikes, canals, and other works, which would arise from an introduction of the arts and well directed industry."[2]

After his removal to Newport, Cocke County, East Tennessee, in 1838, Birdseye continued to see the land around him in terms of its *potential* development, through establishment of railroads, turnpikes, and canals, into a manufacturing and commercial district that would bring prosperity to all classes. Once the encumbrance of slavery was removed, the abundant natural resources of East Tennessee would attract the necessary capital from the North and abroad. Birdseye was concerned in particular with the plight of the poor whites, whom he believed slavery "grinds to the dust" more than any other group in the South. Neglected and "suffered to grow up without education or education as mechanics," most poor whites were "willing to work and would hail with joy any manufacturing or company that would employ them at a low price," he argued.[3]

The focus of the confluence between abolitionism and capitalism in East Tennessee lay in mining, mineralogy, and the constantly expanding search for new metals of commercial value. This connection already existed among certain capitalists in East Tennessee long before Birdseye's arrival there. In fact, one of these men, Elihu Embree, began publication of a weekly antislavery paper in March 1819 entitled the *Manumission Intelligencer.* This newspaper, published for the Tennessee Manumission Society at Jonesboro, county seat of Washington County in the northeastern corner of Tennessee, contained far too little antislavery information, however, and before the year was out, Embree gave up the effort as a financial failure because the *Manumission Intelligencer* had failed to attract a national audience.[4]

His next effort, the monthly *Emancipator,* was in contrast immediately successful, achieving a subscription list of two thousand in a very short time. Begun in April 1820 as a result of Embree's renewed zeal over the Missouri controversy, it concentrated entirely on the antislavery cause and reached interested readers throughout the United States. Embree entered the debate with a fierce, polemical spirit and solicited articles from other zealous advocates of antislavery in the North. His fiery rhetoric and outspoken militancy on behalf of abolitionism clearly echoes the radicalism of his most famous successor, William Lloyd Garrison, a decade later. That Elihu Embree is not remembered today is primarily due to his untimely death from a "bilious fever" on December 4, 1820, at the age of thirty-eight, just as the *Emancipator* was at the height of its fame.[5]

Embree's achievement as the founder of the first periodical in the United States devoted exclusively to antislavery, however, obscures his reputation as a prominent iron manufacturer and early industrialist in East Tennessee. Together with his brother Elijah, he owned and operated an extensive network of iron manufacturing plants, including furnaces, forges, and a nail factory in Washington and Sullivan counties. One of these operations at Bumpass Cove,

Washington County, bought by the Embrees in 1814, produced a wide variety of cast-iron products applauded by one contemporary, who noted that these items otherwise could be obtained only from Baltimore and Richmond. In 1811, a larger ironworks in Sullivan County had been purchased by the Embrees and given the name "Pactolus" from classical mythology. The account books of the Pactolus ironworks offer a minute description of Elihu's daily involvement in the furnace, forge, and nail factory, as well as related operations such as digging, hauling, and burning iron ore; cutting and burning wood for charcoal; mining of limestone; and the operation of mill dams and races for blowers for the furnace and the forge. Accordingly, the *Nashville Gazette* praised Elihu Embree in 1820 for introducing into the state "the most improved and best constructed machinery used in manufacturing nails and tacks."[6]

It is little wonder, then, that *Niles' Weekly Register* hailed Elihu Embree as "one of the most enterprising citizens of the state" in its notice of his death. Three years earlier, this same newspaper had published an 1816 petition from the Manumission Society of Tennessee asking all Christians to unite in their efforts to abolish slavery, signed and probably written by Embree. After his death in 1820, the State of Tennessee made a loan from public school funds to Elihu's brother, Elijah, in recognition of the economic benefits to the entire region brought by the Embrees' ironworks.[7] Ezekiel Birdseye never met Elihu Embree, but the two shared a common vision of a brighter future for East Tennessee combining abolitionism and the progressive exploitation of the region's mineral wealth through manufacturing and enlarged commerce.

A mutual acquaintance of both Birdseye and Elihu Embree was the likeminded abolitionist and entrepreneur, the Reverend Isaac Anderson, founder and first president of Maryville College. A prominent Presbyterian minister, Anderson brought black students into his home and at his own expense educated them for the ministry along with white students in his seminary. Two notable early examples were George M. Erskine and John Gloucester, both of whom were ordained by the Union Presbytery before 1810. Erskine, who later went to Liberia as a Presbyterian missionary, actually had obtained his freedom from the Blount County Court in 1815, at Dr. Anderson's request. Both Gloucester and Erskine were such powerful and effective orators that they greatly impressed white congregations wherever they preached; Dr. Anderson used these ministers as examples to combat the prevailing racism of his day. Birdseye noted this subtle message when Erskine's son-in-law, Sion Harris, another black Liberian missionary, preached in Dr. Anderson's church in Maryville in 1841.[8]

Dr. Anderson was an early member of the Manumission Society of Tennessee; on a petition seeking the abolition of slavery, sent by that organization to the Tennessee legislature in 1817, his name appears with Elihu Embree's. The pervasive stance on abolitionism at Anderson's seminary in Maryville is revealed in a letter by one of the students, published in the *Emancipator* in 1838. He averred that at least half of the students at Maryville were decided abolitionists who "take the liberty to uphold and defend our sentiments, whether it is agreeable or not to the selfishness of the slaveholder." After the Civil War, one prominent judge argued that Isaac Anderson had had more to do with fixing the stand "taken by East Tennessee for the Union and against slavery" than had any of the region's political leaders.[9]

Birdseye frequently stayed at the home of "my worthy friend" Dr. Anderson, conversing frankly with him about problems within the antislavery movement. Like Birdseye and Gerrit Smith, Anderson, an early supporter of the colonization of American slaves to Liberia, by 1841 no longer believed this experiment was the answer to freeing all slaves. Like Birdseye, too, Dr. Anderson was an ardent entrepreneur, investing heavily during the 1830s in a road to make minerals more accessible to North Carolina across the Great Smoky Mountains. In the 1840s, he invested in various mining ventures with Dr. Calvin Post, a physician-abolitionist who represented New York mineral interests. Dr. Post had married the sister of the wife of Dr. Anderson's only son; like Birdseye, Post sent abolitionist letters to northern newspapers while simultaneously exploring East Tennessee's mineral wealth. According to his first biographer, Dr. Anderson intended to use wealth gained from these minerals to promote missionaries and to assist the colonization effort in Liberia. Regardless of his motives, ample evidence of his various entrepreneurial ventures exists in the Blount County records.[10]

Both of Isaac Anderson's biographers, John J. Robinson and Samuel Tyndale Wilson, were less than completely candid about his active involvement in the antislavery movement, possibly because of the pejorative connotation the word *abolitionist* had throughout much of the nineteenth century. There is overwhelming evidence, however, that both Anderson and at least one other professor in his seminary, the Reverend John S. Craig, indeed were ardent abolitionists. Evidence also indicates that the Maryville seminary's reputation for sympathy toward antislavery had spread to the Lower South. Indeed, Birdseye reported a conversation in November 1841 with a minister returning from a conference of Presbyterian clergy in Cassville, Georgia, where a proposal to locate a new southern theological seminary at Maryville had been rejected by the delegation from South Carolina on the grounds that the Presbytery of Kingston there was decidedly antislavery.[11]

Birdseye found Dr. Anderson to be a kindred spirit in other reform issues also, particularly temperance and sympathy for the plight of the Indians. As early as 1824, three Cherokees were studying for the ministry in his seminary, where he also welcomed sons of the Presbyterian missionaries to the Creeks and Cherokees. Birdseye met one such missionary, William Potter, in Maryville in 1841. Anderson, also very supportive of the efforts of Gideon Blackburn and other noted missionaries, was as a consequence appointed by the Union Presbytery as an annual examiner of the Indian schools established and operated by those missionaries. In his abortive attempt to construct a road across the Great Smoky Mountains to North Carolina in the 1830s, Anderson employed many Cherokees as laborers and was revered for his scrupulous fairness and considerate treatment of them.[12]

No individual better exemplified the combined devotion to abolitionism, mineral exploration, and entrepreneurship, however, than did Birdseye's best friend in East Tennessee, Judge Jacob Peck. This energetic man was born in Virginia in 1779 but removed to Tennessee with his family at an early age. His father, Adam Peck (1753–1817), had been the first settler of Mossy Creek (now Jefferson City), in Jefferson County, and represented that county in Tennessee's constitutional convention in 1796. Subsequently he served in the first state house of representatives between 1796 and 1799. Jacob Peck, "a large, jovial man, of bright intellect, and quick at repartee," studied law and was licensed to practice in 1808. Rising rapidly in his profession, he was a state senator in 1821–23 and in 1822 was elected to the Tennessee Supreme Court, where he served as a justice until the courts were reorganized by Tennessee's constitutional convention of 1834.[13]

Something of an anomaly in East Tennessee society, which in the early nineteenth century was just emerging from its frontier status, Jacob Peck was an unusually gifted man who had an exceptional fondness for painting, poetry, and music and took great delight in the study of zoology and mineralogy. He was one of the founders of Emory and Henry College in 1836 and raised a large family of nine children, among them a medical doctor and a brigadier general in the Confederate army. A wealthy man with wide-ranging investments, Judge Peck already owned thousands of acres of land in Tennessee and North Carolina at the time of Birdseye's arrival in 1838. In 1839, Peck became Birdseye's partner in a sawmill in Cocke County which would be Birdseye's principal business in East Tennessee during the early 1840s.

He also actively assisted Birdseye in buying thousands of acres of unclaimed land in Tennessee. As a justice on the Tennessee Supreme Court, Peck "was noted for his positiveness and independence of spirit"; his readiness to dissent from the opinions of the other justices is evident in the volume of decisions he edited in 1822–24.[14]

Yet this able and articulate man, who seemed to share all Birdseye's convictions about slavery, appeared timid about revealing his true antislavery opinions publicly. In an 1841 letter to Gerrit Smith, Peck asked Smith to correspond with him through his friend Birdseye to avoid such exposure. "Not but that I have the moral courage, to advocate all I have said in any public place," Peck explained, but he feared his neighbors would become hostile if they discovered his true sentiments. Like an earlier abolitionist-entrepreneur, Elihu Embree, Judge Peck in fact owned slaves himself; but, also like Embree, he rationalized this ownership of human property on the grounds of the difficulty in emancipating slaves under Tennessee law, and his concern for their welfare if forced to remove from the state.[15] For these reasons, a modern critic might well question Judge Peck's real motives, wondering if his antislavery feeling was only an opportunistic ploy to cultivate Birdseye and to gain access to Gerrit Smith's well-known philanthropy in funding various abolitionist ventures.

The answer to this fundamental question of character lies in the numerous cases before the Tennessee Supreme Court, in which, over a period of time, Judge Peck invariably betrayed a deep sympathy for the plight of slaves and exhibited a clear and personal aversion to the institution of slavery itself. As early as 1821, Peck chaired a committee on slavery in the Tennessee legislature which unanimously recommended removing the current restrictions on emancipation and solicited further research into freeing "those yet unborn," in order to end an "evil, whose root is perhaps dangerously entwined with the liberty of the only free government." When he asserted in this report that emancipation was "consistent with the rights of freemen," who ought "to have, and exercise the power of yielding obedience to the dictates of conscience and humanity," Peck's language is particularly reminiscent of later abolitionist writing. Perhaps because of its appeal to antislavery sentiment in the North, Peck's committee report was published in *Niles' Weekly Register,* November 10, 1821, where it received national attention.[16]

In reviewing an 1825 case in which a slave convicted of murdering a woman and her daughter was sentenced to death by a special slave tribunal consisting of three justices of the peace and a jury of slaveowners in White

County, Judge Peck argued that the superior court had the right to review such tribunals on appeal, even though the writ of certiorari was not specifically conferred by statutory law:

> It would seem strange, that while that power exists in civil proceedings to the fullest possible extent, that any should deny it in criminal proceedings. Color, rank or situation can make no difference; even the slave has such rights as the statutes of the country have afforded him. The exercise of these rights rests with the courts according to the exigency. And say for argument sake, he cannot speak himself, the law has given to the master the right to speak for him. His plea, when presented, must be heard; and if he save his beast of the plough from being sacrificed by the sheriff under an unjust judgment, by suing forth the writ demanded in this case, is it less reasonable that his more valuable property, the life of his slave, should be jeopardized or taken away, because on a proper application made, in a case proper for revision, the remedy has been denied, where it should have been granted.[17]

In an 1835 case, which resembles the later famous *Dred Scott* decision, Judge Peck argued that legal niceties should not obviate "the justice of the case." An elderly man, Joshua Hadley, had conveyed his slaves to George S. Latimore with careful instructions to take them to the free state of Illinois in order to emancipate them. Latimore followed these instructions, but after emancipation in Illinois, Hadley's former slaves wished to return to Tennessee. The heirs of Hadley sued for recovery of these slaves, but Judge Peck ruled that "once free in Illinois, the return to Tennessee does not replace them in the condition of slaves." The justice of the case should not be denied because of some technicality in state law, Peck argued, especially in this case "where the matter to be settled is of more consequence to one of the parties than a mere right of property." He further stated that if Tennessee "designed to make such acts as this record presents nullities, then express enactments should be shown." "We cannot, for the sake of preserving what is termed our policy from violation, make the law," he concluded with asperity, "it is enough for us to administer such as are made to our hands."[18]

Yet, in an earlier case involving the legal process of emancipating slaves by will, Judge Peck actually declared an act of the Tennessee legislature unconstitutional. In the somewhat complicated 1834 case of *Fisher's Negroes v. Dabbs*, the legislature had provided in an act of 1829 that a case of emancipation of slaves by will could be completed in chancery court if the administrator of the will in question "shall fail or refuse" to petition the county court. An 1831 amendment to this act subsequently demanded that any such suit instituted before the district chancery court prior to the original 1829 act be "stricken from the docket." This 1831 amendment seemed to infuriate Judge Peck. "It is not the business of the legislature to keep the chancellor within his jurisdiction," he warned, "and the least meddling with it is an attempt to interfere with the administration of justice as the same has been committed to him." If the courts did not stand up "firmly and independently" before the legislature, "then there is an end of the administration of law, and a reign of terror at hand," he lamented.[19] Regardless of the legal complexity of the case or the circumlocution of Peck's judicial reasoning, however, his decisions invariably benefited the slave. By declaring the 1831 act unconstitutional, the slaves in this particular case were left free to pursue their emancipation in the chancery court.

Perhaps the most poignant case in which Judge Peck explicitly revealed his true sympathy for slaves was *William Fields v. State of Tennessee* (1829). Fields, a white man, was indicted in the circuit court of Maury County for killing a slave; the jury found him guilty not of murder, but rather of the lesser crime of manslaughter, for "feloniously slaying the Negro slave, Peter." Fields' lawyer questioned whether any punishment was legal, since manslaughter against a slave "does not in point of law exist." Judge Peck adamantly argued for the basic humanity of slaves and ridiculed the notion that in such circumstances the laws of Africa obtained. "How can it be urged," Peck asked, "that of necessity the horrors of slavery must not abate when introduced here, from the degraded conditions it was found in where it had its origins." Was cannibalism to be permitted, he jeered, because it was legal in those localities from which some slaves were transported? So "ludicrous as this may seem," Judge Peck continued, "it falls exactly within the train of that argument, which can only be supported by supposing the slave on a footing with the livestock on a farm." Rather than submit to such absurdity, Judge Peck appealed to the precepts of Christianity as a higher law, guaranteeing all slaves the right to remain and be regarded as human beings, at least in the sight of God and the Tennessee Supreme Court! He finally ruled that, since slaves were indeed *reasonable creatures* (i.e., human), no master had the right to take their lives arbitrarily. "Law, reason, Christianity and common humanity, all point out one way," he concluded, affirming the circuit court's decision to punish Fields for murdering the slave Peter.[20]

Like Birdseye's old friend on the South Carolina Supreme Court, John Belton O'Neall, Jacob Peck consistently ruled in favor of slaves, even when such a ruling conflicted with the rights of property. When, in an 1832 case, creditors demanded seizure of the slave Ephraim, loaned to William Walter, Jr., by his father, Peck argued that, while possession of a slave for five years did indeed confer ownership, nevertheless Ephraim had in the interim returned to the senior Walker, and his subsequent return to the son "was a new lending, and five years not having elapsed since such last loan, these creditors, even had they valid judgments, could not seize and sell this property." Likewise, in another 1832 case, Peck strongly disavowed the forcible and violent seizure of a female slave, regardless of the defendants' supposed legal title to her. Numerous other cases in which the rights of slaves were upheld found Peck concurring with the other justices, although he did not write the opinion of the court. A notable example is the 1827 case of *Abraham Vaughan v. Phebe, a Woman of Color*. Phebe claimed her freedom on the basis of being descended from an Indian ancestor; although hearsay evidence in the form of "common reputation" was her chief defense, a unanimous Supreme Court ruled in her favor.[21]

Anecdotal evidence indicates that Judge Peck's sympathy for slaves and free blacks was not unknown within the black community. Birdseye recounts an incident in Newport in 1841 in which an aged free black, "Free Isaac," personally appealed to Judge Peck to prevent an unscrupulous white neighbor, Mr. Courtney, from claiming part of his farm in a survey and subsequently fencing in the disputed area. "Judge Peck said if they would not agree to remove their fence and pay him all damages he would sue them at once," Birdseye reported in an eyewitness account of this meeting. Thereafter Judge Peck listened with great sympathy to Free Isaac's recitation of all his past difficulties in purchasing his wife's freedom. "Isaac will have his rights well protected," Birdseye concluded from this interview.[22]

Although Jacob Peck's deep sympathy for the plight of slaves is fully recorded in the reports of cases decided by Tennessee's supreme court, not until recently has documentation been discovered of his amazing interest in, and knowledge of, mineralogy and geology. His elaborate, detailed notebook, purchased by the McClung Historical Collection of the Knox County Public Library in 1994, reveals a sophisticated knowledge of nineteenth-century geology, as well as accounts of numerous field expeditions recording mineral outcroppings in Tennessee, Kentucky, Georgia, and western North Carolina. Peck wrote an extensive analysis of geological principles based upon the published works of Abraham Gottlob Werner (1750–1817), the father of German geology, and those of Sir Charles Lyell (1797–1875), widely regarded as the father of modern geology. Peck's analyses of these pioneering scientists' works reveal more than a superficial knowledge of their theories, however wrong or misguided parts of these works now may seem to a modern scholar. He was somewhat attracted, for example, to Werner's doctrine of the aqueous origins of rocks, later repudiated by Lyell's research. The proponents of these competing theories were called Neptunists and Vulcanists, respectively, terms which occur frequently in Peck's writings.[23]

The purpose of all the theoretical study of geology in Judge Peck's notebook, however, clearly was to enable him better to explore for minerals of commercial value. Careful maps of coal lands in Campbell County and various mineral deposits in Blount, Cocke, Greene, Sevier, and Washington counties emphasize the search for mining properties. Elaborate descriptions of the copper mines at Ducktown, Tennessee, and of a silver mine discovered in Greene County by John Hale were typical of the majority of Peck's entries, although occasionally his scientific curiosity got the better of him, as indicated, for example, in his description of "ancient mining at Jacob Kirkpatrick's upper end of Jefferson County." Extensive notes and a map of the "auriferous region in the Cherokee country" also reveal Peck's intimate knowledge of the Georgia gold rush during the 1830s. Considerable attention also was given to these Georgia gold mining areas in a scholarly article Peck published in the prestigious *American Journal of Science and Arts* in 1833, entitled "Geological and Mineralogical Account of the Mining Districts in the State of Georgia—Western Part of North Carolina and East Tennessee, With a Map."[24]

All Peck's descriptions of these various locations include careful and specific information about topography and mineral type and formation. Many surveys are included, including one done by unspecified engineers of "the whole descent of the French Broad from Newport to Knoxville." Lengthy and detailed descriptions also are given of geological surveys conducted by Peck himself. "In August 1832 I made a geological survey of Cumberland Mountain near Sparta," he writes at one point in his notebook, giving a detailed description with a map of the area. Another minutely recorded survey was made by Peck in the winter of 1834–35 of the salt formation of the Cumberland Mountain in Kentucky. Not infrequently, he sponsored or had others dig a shaft so as further to examine minerals at a promising locale.[25]

Specimens from all these varied sites were sent by Peck for scientific analysis to experts, usually in the North; indicative is an 1856 report from the "Analytical Laboratory & Office of Consulting Chemistry" in New York City, wherein is reported that the specimen in question contained "no tin but a compound of sulfur iron silica & alumina." Before 1850, however, most of this sort of scientific analysis was done in Nashville by Peck's good friend, Gerard Troost (1776–1850), Tennessee state geologist from 1831 until 1850 and professor of geology and mineralogy at the University of Nashville since 1828. Dr. Troost was one of the most capable scientists in the United States; a scholar of international renown, he played a major role in the evolution of American geology from the time of his arrival in the United States until his death in 1850. Educated in his native Holland, he received the degree of doctor of medicine from the University of Leyden and master of pharmacy degree from Amsterdam. He also had studied in Germany under Abraham Gottlob Werner, the pioneering geologist so frequently cited in Judge Peck's notebook. Many maps and surveys of Tennessee prepared by Dr. Troost were duly recorded in Peck's notebook, and at least one letter written in August 1840 to Peck asks him to give his "respects to Mr. Birdseye." Birdseye, in an 1841 letter to Gerrit Smith, indeed had identified Dr. Troost as a personal acquaintance and as "one of the most scientific Geologists in the country and a man of profound learning." Iron ore was the only metal of commercial value in the Cocke County lands of Peck and Birdseye, but before 1850 Dr. Troost also reported on numerous other specimens from a wide range of locales for Judge Peck. Troost's published reports as state geologist did much to attract the interest of northern and foreign capitalists to Tennessee's mineral resources, a goal long endorsed by both Peck and Birdseye.[26]

Finally, Judge Peck's notebook lists specific land grants by number belonging to him or his family or business associates. These lands, in the East Tennessee counties of Blount, Cocke, Greene, Jefferson, Sevier, and Washington, presumably had commercially valuable minerals. A summary of the total number of acres thus recorded reveals that Ezekiel Birdseye owned 7,985 acres, all in Cocke County. Birdseye and Peck together owned another 12,500 acres. Judge Peck and his immediate family owned 80,514 acres; maps were given for many but not all of these grants, indicating where each particular mineral was located. These totals in Judge Peck's notebook do not necessarily include all the land in either Tennessee or North Carolina owned by Peck or Birdseye, but other sources of pertinent information are not readily available. All the land deeds for Cocke County before the Civil War, for example, were destroyed in an 1876 courthouse fire; only an 1839 tax list survives, listing a total of 37,516 acres belonging to Ezekiel Birdseye in the first and sixth civil districts of that county. The sheer number of these acquired acres enumerated in Peck's notebook, however, indicates the serious commitment of both Judge Peck and Birdseye to the commercial exploitation of East Tennessee's mineral wealth.[27]

The culmination of this partnership between Judge Peck and Birdseye, perfectly illustrating their interest in combining abolitionism and the development of East Tennessee's mineral resources for commercial profit, was their scheme to develop a free labor colony on their lands, "wholly excluding slave labor." Such colonies were discussed widely by northern abolitionists in the 1840s and 1850s, although Gerrit Smith feared that such ventures could not succeed when confronted with the overwhelming pressures of slavery. Nevertheless, both Birdseye and Judge Peck believed that the greater efficiency of free laborers, using superior techniques and tools, finally, by sheer productivity, would convince neighboring slaveowners that slavery was unprofitable economically as well as morally. Both men wrote to Gerrit Smith in 1841 soliciting financial support for this project. Birdseye said that he and Judge Peck owned sixteen miles on the French Broad River which had been acquired specifically for a free labor colony. Judge Peck wrote Smith that in 1838 he had first introduced Birdseye to this project, "which may result in profit to himself and humanity to others." He offered the additional inducement that East Tennessee, aided by this moral example, in a very short time "may become a separate and free state."[28]

No greater mistake could be made by historians, however, than to view this proposed free labor colony in East Tennessee solely as a disinterested philanthropic undertaking. Clearly both Peck and Birdseye planned to make tremendous profits from the exploitation of mineral wealth and from subsidiary manufacturing within this colony. Birdseye is explicit in his correspondence to Gerrit Smith about the mineral resources, ideal sites for manufacturing towns, and abundant iron ore. The French Broad River "would make a fine place for a Rolling Mill or manufacturing towns," he noted at one point. The key piece of evidence submitted to Smith in an effort to persuade him to contribute to their free labor colony, moreover, was Dr. Troost's geological report enumerating commercially valuable minerals on the site of their proposed experiment.[29]

Why the colony never materialized, after all Birdseye's efforts, is difficult to determine; the most probable reason is the severe financial stress on his own business ventures in the continuing depression of the early 1840s. At one point, he optimistically indicated to Smith that "no class of citizens have been more anxious to have a free labor community in this country than slaveholders. They say: 'we want you to bring on 500 of your Northern good farmers and good mechanics.'" Evidently Smith, always skeptical about this particular sort of venture, was unwilling or unable at this time to make a financial contribution, although he did mention this proposal in 1841 in a letter to William Ellery Channing:

Amongst my Southern correspondents is Mr. Ezekiel Birdsey[e] of East Tennessee. Mr. B. is a man of truth and good common sense. He is very desirous of the establishment of a "free labor colony" upon the highlands of N Carolina or E. Tennessee. Could the measure be brought about, I should hope for good from it. But I apprehend that the measure will not be found easily practicable, whilst slavery is strong and rampant in those states; and should it be, there would be reason to fear, that the bold tone of freedom, which would characterize the beginnings of the Colony, would become faint & fainter still under the presence and influence of slavery.

By April 1842 Birdseye wrote Smith that someone was attacking him publicly in the *Knoxville Register* "as the colonizationist in the Mountains," so public opinion in East Tennessee was not unanimously in favor of the scheme, as he earlier had believed.[30]

The free labor colony idea also offers insight into Birdseye's opinion concerning the importance of manual labor in the South's moral and physical regeneration. Like many other abolitionists of his generation, Birdseye believed that physical labor played an important part in developing a wholesome American national character. He applauded efforts to introduce Fellenberg schools throughout the state: "I hope the public mind may continue directly to them so as to produce a good effect and render the idle dissipated sickly habits of the young men of the South unpopular and be followed by a system well calculated to develop the highest mental and physical qualities. It is for want of these habits and science that slavery exists."[31]

So the free labor colony, in Birdseye's view, would create an example of the habits of industry so lacking among degenerate and effete southern slaveholders. Together with the profitability of the entire enterprise, this powerful moral display would establish a compelling argument in the midst of slavery. In the moral economy of neither Judge Peck nor Ezekiel Birdseye was there any conflict whatsoever between public benevolence and private gain. Both men would identify completely with that felicitous phrase in an earlier East Tennessee abolitionist's obituary which singled out for particular praise Elihu Embree's enterprises, which, "though embarked in for individual benefit, were of a nature which tended much to the public good."[32]

In contrast to Judge Peck, Birdseye's other close friend and business associate in East Tennessee was a man who openly and unashamedly had advocated the cause of antislavery throughout the region since 1815. John Caldwell (1790–1869) wrote to Gerrit Smith in 1841 that he had presided over the organization of an antislavery society in Jefferson County in 1815; throughout the 1820s and 1830s, he continued to espouse abolitionism at every opportunity. A largely self-educated man, Caldwell was described by Oliver P. Temple as a "strong, brave, clear-headed Covenanter Presbyterian," who in 1861, on the eve of the Civil War, "was still true to his original convictions." This "remarkable man—robust, determined, conscientious," also was an ardent Unionist and Whig, as well as one of the state vice-presidents of the American Colonization Society when Henry Clay was its president. According to Ezekiel Birdseye, Caldwell had an enviable reputation throughout the South for his bold defense of antislavery, being fearless in his zeal despite the growing hostility of slaveowners. Like Birdseye, Caldwell also was active in the temperance movement, but the consistency and longevity of his antislavery stance, attested to by his name on numerous abolitionist petitions to the Tennessee state legislature, distinguish him from earlier Tennessee abolitionists who either moved out of the state or altered their positions on slavery during the 1850s.[33]

John Caldwell worked indefatigably to end slavery through smaller, practical means, when other abolitionists despaired of abolishing slavery in East Tennessee. Birdseye tells us, for example, that he was tireless in writing wills for his neighbors which provided for the emancipation of slaves at their death, although he had no formal legal training. Likewise, Caldwell ran a boarding school in his home for the sons of southern aristocrats, providing them with surreptitious but effective antislavery training by a Presbyterian minister, Mr. Haynes. In October 1841 Birdseye was invited by Caldwell to meet Sion Harris, the noted black missionary to Liberia and former slave, who was visiting Caldwell's brother at this time. Caldwell's grandson, Joshua W. Caldwell (1856–1909), a prominent Knoxville lawyer and author, tells us that his grandfather was particularly fond of writing to notable men such as the presidents of the United States, Henry Clay, and Gerrit Smith, usually in regard to Liberia and the colonization movement.[34]

The continuing economic depression of the 1840s prompted John Caldwell to write one such letter to Gerrit Smith in June 1841 seeking a loan of fifteen hundred dollars to forestall bankruptcy. Birdseye earlier had described his friend's predicament to Smith, extolling Caldwell's long and outspoken service in the antislavery cause and noting that local slaveholders in Jefferson County were conspiring to ruin him by "bringing his creditors to press him all at once." For five years before this time, Caldwell had taken herds of horses and mules to Florida for sale, but the bills of credit in which he was paid had so depreciated that in 1841 he found himself four thousand dollars in debt and his own Jefferson County farm threatened by creditors. Evidently Smith was unable to assist Caldwell at this point, and in an October 1841 letter, Birdseye indicated that Caldwell "had not met with the disasters which he anticipated." But in January 1842 John Caldwell finally was forced to sell his fine farm "on which there has never been slave labor," for the sum of four thousand dollars to William Brazelton, one of the group of "despotic slaveholders," according to Birdseye, who had been working actively to force him into bankruptcy because of his antislavery convictions.[35]

John Caldwell's chief fame, however, came not for his abolitionism but rather for his pioneering efforts to develop East Tennessee's mineral wealth. Although an amateur and self-taught geologist, Caldwell is credited with discovering many of the region's principal mineral deposits; both Dr. Gerard Troost and his successor as state geologist, James M. Safford, actively sought Caldwell's assistance in their own investigations. He was one of the founders, in 1849, of the copper region at Ducktown, Polk County, in the southeastern corner of Tennessee. Although at the time he owned "one twenty dollar bill," he was so impressed by the copper outcroppings there that he called a meeting of the citizens of the township and made a speech to them extolling the potential value of copper mining in the area's economy. To his claim that "civilization, intelligence, comfort and wealth" was to be derived from mining copper ore, one disgruntled citizen acidly replied that "a large portion of the inhabitants had come here to get away from civilization, and that if it followed them, they would run again." Despite such reservations, at the end of Caldwell's speech, he drew up a memorial to the state legislature "praying the passage of a law authorizing the commissioners to give a mining lease on this school section." Signed by a majority of those citizens attending the meeting, this memorial was taken by Caldwell himself to Nashville, where he secured its passage by his own inimitable style of lobbying.[36]

The unique intermingling of evangelical religion, philanthropy, and entrepreneurship typical of Ezekiel Birdseye and his friends is nowhere better exhibited than in John Caldwell's own account of how, after starting a Sabbath school for miners, he obtained funding from them to build a road to transport copper ore from Ducktown across the mountains to the nearest railroad at Dalton, Georgia:

> We were tantalized by one of the miners, who exclaimed, on a certain occasion: "Good God Almighty! does that old mud-sucker think he can worship Jesus and work a copper mine?" While this same miner was planning a way to pack copper ore out of the mountains on mules, I surveyed the Ocoee river, and determined to make a road eighteen miles through an impassable

desert. I had no means but a strong determination to surmount every obstacle. Going to a Methodist camp meeting, I obtained permission to make a road speech, in the recess of divine service. The speech over, we took up a collection, principally on credit and payable in trade. This, however, served the purpose, and on the 6th of October, 1851, the work was commenced. On the first day, three hands worked, on the second, two; and on the third, worked *alone*—public opinion, strong and powerful, being against the enterprise; on the fourth day hired a dozen Cherokees. Thus began one of the most important projects in the State—which was consummated in two years, at an expense of about $22,000. The Tennessee Company came early to help in the enterprise, but the Hiwassee held back till 14 miles of the road were passable for wagons. At the close of the first year, Robt. McCampbell was employed as the engineer of the road, after which I again turned my attention to mining.[37]

John Caldwell thus "preached" the benefits of mining copper and building a road to market it, in much the same fashion he exhorted his fellow citizens to embrace abolitionism, colonization, temperance, and evangelical Christianity of the Presbyterian variety. Yet these exhortations evidently worked remarkably well, and the Ocoee Road, completed in 1853, was critical to the success of the copper industry at Ducktown before the completion of the East Tennessee and Georgia Railroad from Dalton, Georgia, to Cleveland, Tennessee. At various stages, Caldwell was incorporator and major shareholder in at least three copper companies. The Tennessee Mine was opened by him in October 1851; by 1852, the Congdon interests of New York had taken over Caldwell's original Tennessee Mine and begun working it as the Tennessee Mining Company. In February 1852 Caldwell was one of the owners of another mine, the Ocoee Mining Company, which received incorporation from the state that same year. The Polk County Mine, opened in November 1852 by Caldwell, was located on deposits of copper ore so immense that the hill where it stood was named Copper Hill. This was the fourth mine opened at Ducktown, but in April 1854 Caldwell and his partners sold this mine to the Polk County Copper Company. Caldwell also was among the incorporators of the Ocoee Turnpike and Plank Road Company, organized in 1854 to maintain the road to Dalton, Georgia.[38]

Although John Caldwell was one of the principal actors in the formation and transfer of numerous mining companies at Ducktown during the 1850s, he did not fail to include his old friend, Ezekiel Birdseye, in the lucrative profits from copper mining. In an inventory of Birdseye's estate, made in 1862 following his death in Knoxville in June 1861, is listed an "interest in Caldwell Copper Mining Company in East Tennessee, being one quarter of the same according to original investment," valued at $75,000. It is ironic that an outspoken abolitionist and strong Unionist—John Caldwell—played the major role in developing the copper industry in Polk County, while a New England abolitionist made a contributing investment. These mines at Ducktown later were to furnish 90 percent of the copper mined in the Confederacy during the Civil War. After the Confederacy lost control of these Ducktown copper mines with Bragg's defeat at Chattanooga in November 1863, the Ordnance Bureau was reduced to salvaging badly needed copper from turpentine and apple brandy stills in North Carolina and sugar-boiling kettles in Louisiana.[39]

Caldwell and Birdseye also were associated in several other business ventures involving the commercial exploitation of valuable minerals. In July 1854 Birdseye and Caldwell bought three hundred acres of land in Claiborne County for fifteen hundred dollars. This land contained rich deposits of calamine, or silicate of zinc, which both men thought commercially valuable. James M. Safford visited this site in July 1855 and pronounced its zinc "the best we have seen in the State." He carefully noted the location "on Powell's River, between Tazewell and Jacksboro', about sixteen miles from the former place," and said that the owners, Caldwell and Birdseye, were making arrangements to test its value.[40]

How abolitionism and entrepreneurship in developing mineral wealth were combined in men like Ezekiel Birdseye and his friends is perhaps best explicated in a remarkable letter to the editor of the *Nashville Daily Press and Times* from John Caldwell, published February 12, 1868, a year before his death. Caldwell was writing to urge the Tennessee legislature to pass a bill loaning $100,000 to develop the iron ore at Embreeville Iron Works, Washington County—interestingly, at a site originally established by East Tennessee's first abolitionist-entrepreneur, Elihu Embree. Caldwell compared the wealth to be derived in Washington County with that realized from Polk County's copper industry and then presented an elaborate argument for the social utility of this development, an argument remarkably similar to one he had made earlier against slavery:

> In my boyhood I lived in a community that was self-sustaining, that produced all the fibrous material that was necessary to clothe the body (wool, cotton, flax, and hemp), and all the provisions necessary for the sustenance of man and beast. We tanned the leather and made our own shoes. We

made our own hats from the fur of the animals we hunted. We had a forge in the wilderness, and even manufactured our own iron, and from it we made agricultural implements, tools, etc. We lived in independence, and made progress in the world morally, mentally and materially. Our labor system, however, became corrupted and degenerated in the midst of our prosperity, and our commercial independence was lost. I long for a renovation of our system, when my State will adopt the principles and the policy of the community alluded to. The bill now before the Senate contemplates a revival of the policy referred to, in Washington County. These iron works are capable of giving support to over a thousand families, not only employment, but education and religious influence. They will not only form the basis for a self-sustaining community, but will create a new source of revenue to this state.[41]

The corruption and degeneration of the labor system to which Caldwell referred was, in the opinion of most of his abolitionist-entrepreneur business partners, caused by slavery. During the four decades before the Civil War, Caldwell repeatedly argued that ending slavery and developing East Tennessee's mineral resources were both necessary to recover the "self-sustaining community" of his childhood, in which citizens had full opportunity to advance, according to their ability and own labor. Ezekiel Birdseye and his friends always argued that slavery harmed poor whites more than any other group in the South, because slavery distorted the labor market by devaluating their honest labor and consequently caused them to lose their healthy independence and self-sufficiency. In a similar fashion, men like Caldwell, Birdseye, and Judge Peck believed that the regional economy was badly distorted when Tennesseans were forced to depend on foreign or northern sources of iron or other products produced at great expense in faraway factories. In this same letter, Caldwell explicitly condemned importing iron rails from England, or buying from Cincinnati iron casting for the front of Gov. William G. Brownlow's new printing office. "Is it possible that a community can live and thrive under such a system," he asked, noting the disproportionate cost of these iron goods manufactured at such a great distance from Tennessee.[42]

Sadly, this illuminating dream of an independent, self-sufficient community in East Tennessee, in which industrialization or the exploitation of the region's commercially valuable minerals would enable the common man to "make progress in the world morally, mentally, and materially," was destined not to become a reality. As historian Ronald D Eller has demonstrated so ably, extractive industries controlled by outside capital instead left large portions of the Appalachian region deeply impoverished, its landscape scarred, and its citizens often embittered and dependent on low wages and sporadic employment. Minerals such as coal, copper, and iron ore simply were removed from Appalachia, and the enormous profits derived therefrom benefited mostly remote capitalists in the North or Europe, who had made the initial investments.[43]

Actually, this process, by which foreign or outside investors took control of East Tennessee's mineral deposits, already was accelerating during the 1850s, long before the Civil War, in areas originally developed by Birdseye and his abolitionist-entrepreneur friends. Several companies in the Ducktown copper-producing area of southeastern Tennessee were purchased in 1858 by capitalists in New York, Charleston, and Savannah; the new company, the Union Consolidated Mining Company of Tennessee, capitalized at $2,200,000, was controlled by a home office in New York. The iron manufacturing company at Embreeville, in Washington County in upper East Tennessee, continued through various reorganizations to be controlled by local capitalists, but their lack of financial resources limited production so drastically that they were unable to provide even the rails for the East Tennessee and Virginia Railroad being built through their own neighborhood in the 1850s. The Embreeville Iron Works finally were sold in 1890 to a group of British capitalists.[44]

Ezekiel Birdseye himself evidently gave up on owning or developing manufacturing plants by the 1850s, and seems to have spent most of his time acquiring leases for mineral rights on behalf of various New York firms. In March 1854 he signed an agreement to sell three "leases of mines and mining rights" in East Tennessee to Stearnes and Sturges Mining Company of New York City for ten thousand dollars per lease. Two of these leases were "certain," or already in his possession; the third lease Birdseye was still negotiating to obtain. About this third lease, he claimed to be "possessed of the knowledge of the existence and locality" whose "particular description" he would convey later, once it was properly acquired. In order to "devote my entire time to these objects until accomplished excepting only what shall be necessary to enable me to protect other interests which I now have in said State," Birdseye was to receive a monthly salary of one hundred dollars from Stearnes and Sturges, so in effect he was acting as their agent. Evidently, however, he was not their exclusive agent; in May 1860 he sold several tracts of land containing minerals in Greene County to Augustine W. Daby of New York City for five thousand dollars. Birdseye also was actively seeking and obtaining leases for mineral rights on behalf of various other New York mining companies in Anderson, Claiborne, Jefferson, and Union counties during the 1850s. He served as a business agent for other ventures, too; in 1845 he was conducting business in Kentucky for his friend Lewis Tappan, another famous and wealthy northern abolitionist. In 1846, he casually mentioned in a letter to Gerrit Smith doing some additional business for Tappan in Virginia, suggesting that a complete catalog of all his business activities for northern companies throughout the South will be difficult to obtain.[45]

In any event, the constant threat of bankruptcy, about which he had complained so frequently to Gerrit Smith in the early 1840s, seems to have lessened by 1845, when he related his interest in obtaining a charter from the state legislature to manufacture iron. "I hope to escape bankruptcy and am more encouraged now," he wrote in November 1845. Throughout these years, Birdseye held title to large amounts of "wild" land in East Tennessee, which he constantly was attempting to sell to northern investors. He told Smith in 1845 that he had between fifty and sixty thousand acres, "generally new and unproductive," in Cocke and Greene counties. In 1846 he was still at Long Creek Mills in Cocke County, the saw and grist mill he and Judge Peck had purchased in 1839. At some point during the 1850s he finally sold this mill, which had furnished his principal source of income. After that, he no longer resided in Newport, Cocke County, from which the majority of his extant letters to Gerrit Smith in the 1840s were written.[46]

Birdseye appears to have been particularly prone to litigation. Evidently, many tracts of land he purchased at speculative prices had titles of dubious legality and eventually were challenged in court. One such tract of 1,717 acres in Marion County, Ohio, purchased in 1833, had such a disputed title and had been in chancery court in Ohio for eleven years, still remaining undecided in 1845. Indeed, he and Judge Peck were involved in a lengthy case over the validity of the title to the Cocke County mill; the matter dragged on in the Jefferson County Chancery Court at Dandridge. Typical of Birdseye's many lawsuits, in which Birdseye was usually the plaintiff, was one brought against Marcellus B. Parham in 1843 before the Knox County Circuit Court. Birdseye alleged Parham's failure to pay five hundred dollars due for "a large quantity of white pine lumber" from Birdseye's mill in Newport. Victory in these ubiquitous lawsuits was uncertain and often pyrrhic; in the Parham case, for example, judgment finally was returned in Birdseye's favor, but only in the amount of thirty dollars.[47]

At his death in June 1861, much of Birdseye's estate appears to have been composed of these somewhat questionable claims to land in various parts of the country. An inventory of his estate, prepared for his executor and brother-in-law, Rev. Timothy D. P. Stone of Amesbury, Massachusetts, made May 2, 1862, lists a total value of $182,731 for all his property. Schedule A, real estate, listed 204,345 "acres of wild lands in the States of North Carolina, Tennessee, Indiana, and New York," valued at 23 cents per acre, for a total value of $51,086. A "perpetual lease" of a clay bed in Cornwall, Connecticut, Birdseye's hometown, was valued at $10,000; another "lease of coal mines, perpetual, at Coal Creek, in Anderson County, East Tennessee," was valued at $25,000. Schedule B, enumerating Birdseye's personal estate, included "Notes of hand, stocks, and Company shares and sums due on Commission" at $21,645. Schedule B also listed a one-quarter interest in the Caldwell Copper Mining Company in East Tennessee, valued at $75,000, which has been previously discussed.[48]

By October 1861 Birdseye's executor, Rev. Timothy D. P. Stone, had lost no time in reporting to the Probate Court at Cornwall that the Birdseye estate was insolvent and could not pay mounting claims against it. By 1864, an obviously weary Stone was complaining to the Probate Court about the enormous expenditure of his own time and funds in efforts to settle this estate, a process that appeared to be dragging on interminably. Because of the war, Stone informed the court, he had been unable to go to Knoxville, where Birdseye had died, "and furthermore has reason to believe that the Confederate States Officers have destroyed or confiscated the personal effects of the deceased, so that funds cannot be secured by their sale." No evidence exists to indicate that Ezekiel Birdseye died from other than natural causes, but some mystery surrounds his sudden death in June 1861. No obituary can be found in either the Knoxville or Nashville papers, and the site of his burial in Knoxville cannot be discovered.[49]

If the Confederate authorities did not commit violence on Birdseye's person, the same cannot be said of his property in East Tennessee. During and immediately after the war, much of his land there was sold at auction for delinquent taxes, for ridiculously low prices in a precipitous manner before the executor of his estate could intervene. Typical of these transactions was a sale of five thousand acres in Greene County. On July 1, 1861, when Birdseye's corpse was scarcely cold, the tract was conveyed to George Jones, Sr., the father of Sheriff James Jones, who had initially brought the suit before the Greene County Court! The new owner paid $21.80, the exact amount of back taxes owed on this property. Birdseye's estate remained unsettled in the Probate Court of Cornwall as late as 1869; his executor, Reverend Stone, continued to ask for additional time. Sadly, for all Birdseye's entrepreneurial efforts, it is highly improbable that his heirs ever derived any substantive benefit from his final estate settlement. Perhaps there was indeed a grain of prophetic truth in Gerrit Smith's assertion that slavery had been a particular curse to Birdseye. "Were it abolished, the immediate and great rise in the value of your immense real estate would make you one of the wealthiest men in the country," he wrote to his friend in December 1845, "whilst as it is, slavery making most of your property unsaleable, you have to struggle to keep your head above water."[50]

In the final analysis, the link between abolitionism and entrepreneurial capitalism in the minds of Isaac Anderson, Ezekiel Birdseye, John Caldwell, Elihu Embree, and Judge Jacob Peck was based upon assumptions about the nature of the moral and political economy of slavery, indigenous to their time and place in nineteenth-century America, which some modern historians now dispute. All these men, for example, fervently believed and preached that slavery was, at bottom, unprofitable and actually harmful to the whole fabric of the economy, irrespective of its moral or political consequences. To southerners, slaveholders and nonslaveholders alike, who communicated with Birdseye during the depression of the 1840s, there did indeed seem to be a "curse on the land," the likeliest cause of which was human bondage. But in other times, particularly in the subsequent prosperous decade of the 1850s, when cotton prices again soared, slavery seemed quite profitable, strictly from a economic point of view. On the other hand, scholars from Ulrich B. Phillips to Peter Kolchin have pointed out that, although antebellum southern economic growth seems impressive, it was based on the production of a small number of staple crops, mainly cotton, and an argument can be made that slavery ultimately distorted and kept the southern economy backward, a proposition with which Ezekiel Birdseye would agree completely.[51]

Actually, the broad-based prosperity of the 1850s also bound East Tennessee's economy more closely to that of the Lower South, a process ironically accelerated by the completion of the railroad through this section. It is ironic because during the 1840s, Ezekiel Birdseye had hailed the coming railroads as messengers bringing light, civilization, and progressive ideas from the North. But, as historian W. Todd Groce has demonstrated, the East Tennessee and Virginia Railroad, in the decade of the 1850s, increasingly made East Tennessee's economy interdependent with that of the Lower South and Virginia. There was a boom in wheat raised for this market, a concomitant 21 percent increase in the region's total number of slaves between 1850 and 1860, and unprecedented economic prosperity, based on the sale of foodstuffs to the Lower South. Such prosperity and closer economic ties with the Lower South led inevitably to more proslavery feeling and eventually to an increase in the number of merchants and businessmen in the region who subsequently supported the Confederacy, Groce argues persuasively.[52]

Yet what finally is important to determine is what set of ideas Birdseye and his fellow abolitionist-entrepreneurs earlier held to be self-evident maxims concerning the ultimate good of both abolition and industrial development for East Tennessee's economy and society. This mental furniture determined their subsequent actions and, in every instance, remained largely unchanged and permanently linked or intertwined in their minds until their deaths. Their ideal future society always remained a self-sufficient, independent community whose citizens could prosper "morally, mentally, and materially," in John Caldwell's phrase, once the impediments of slavery were removed and the incentive created for industrialization through the proper exploitation of the region's abundant natural resources. If personal wealth should crown their individual efforts in pursuit of the larger public good, neither Ezekiel Birdseye nor his friends could conceive of any moral contradiction or possible metaphysical objection. In their minds, slavery always would be as damaging economically as it was morally; how self-evident this truth was they demonstrated by continuous references to the collective and individual maltreatment of slaves in their midst, the focus of the next chapter.

4.
The Legal Status and Actual Treatment of Slaves

"If you knew the interest which your letters produce in the columns of the F[riend] of Man and in other papers that copy them," Gerrit Smith enthusiastically wrote to Ezekiel Birdseye in December 1840, "you would feel well repaid for your labor, and write me more frequently." No small part of this widespread interest was due to the intensity and honesty with which Birdseye detailed the lives and tribulations of individual slaves in his letters. "Mr. B[irdseye] is a man of truth and good common sense," Smith wrote William Ellery Channing in 1841, but, in fact, Birdseye possessed an almost novelistic ability to represent simultaneously the vast horrors of the institution of slavery together with the common humanity of particular slaves about whom he wrote.

Yet it is precisely this problem of determining the actual effect of slavery upon the lives of its victims which places Ezekiel Birdseye's letters, so widely circulated in northern abolitionist newspapers, at the center of a current historiographical debate. Like twentieth-century scholars, readers of abolitionist newspapers during the nineteenth century wondered both about the veracity of such reporters, usually of northern origin but living in the South; and about how widespread, or representative, throughout the region were the abuses of slavery which they so graphically depicted.[1]

One historian, James L. Huston, argues persuasively that scholars during the last two decades have virtually severed the connection between the experiential reality of southern slavery and the motivation and behavior of nineteenth-century abolitionists. Too narrow a focus on the social and economic context of abolitionism in the North, Huston maintains, has downplayed the shock experienced by northerners who saw slavery's most inhumane features—whippings, family separations, mutilations, and coffles of bewildered captives bound in chains for the auction block. Yet this experience is a crucial factor in explaining why so many Americans, southerners as well as northerners, became passionate advocates in the crusade against slavery.[2]

In most respects, Ezekiel Birdseye fits the collective profile of abolitionists which has emerged within the last twenty years. He was born after slavery had been abolished in the North and grew up amid the economic revolution wrought by transportation improvements and incipient industrialization. Throughout his life, while full of anxiety over rapid social and economic changes surrounding him, he struggled to become wealthy. He, like other abolitionists, routinely condemned the backward state of the southern economy, the lack of discipline in southerners, the instability of family life in the South, and the ubiquitous sexual abuse of female slaves. And, like other abolitionists of his generation, he saw the solution to the problems of the South in legitimizing free labor and the free market, contesting the power and arrogance of the planter elite, and educating southerners in self-discipline, piety, frugality, and the dignity of manual labor.[3]

But the single most important accomplishment throughout Birdseye's life was his eyewitness account, on a daily basis, of the horrors of slavery and the reactions of its victims. Southern proslavery defenders often accused northern abolitionists of attacking slavery in the abstract and exaggerating only its worst features, with little knowledge of, or perspective on, the day-to-day operation of the peculiar institution, which, slaveowners insisted, was benign and paternalistic in the vast majority of cases, *most* of the time. Ezekiel Birdseye knew better; since 1818, from the age of twenty-one, he had lived most of his adult life in many parts of the South. Furthermore, he had lived in a wide variety of slave states for protracted periods of time—South Carolina, Alabama, Georgia, Kentucky, and Tennessee—in addition to traveling on business frequently throughout the other southern states.[4]

Three characteristics of Ezekiel Birdseye's interaction with southerners emerge from a careful reading of his correspondence, tending to corroborate the veracity of his observations of the impact of slavery upon its victims. First, Birdseye was highly aware of, and constantly measured, public opinion, which he referred to as "public sentiment." In 1841, he was "mortified to recollect" that he once wrote James G. Birney a letter which "contained a censure of

Abolitionists for going ahead of public sentiment." Otherwise he noted widespread divergence on this issue throughout the South, but found "a restraining public sentiment" in East Tennessee which operated to the slave's benefit.

Second, Birdseye was an affable, friendly, nonbelligerent "gentleman" to whom southerners of many classes found it easy to talk. To a degree remarkable for an outsider, he seems to have penetrated the folk mind and gained access to much more specific and detailed information about abuses of slaves than he would have had time or opportunity to observe personally. People confided openly to Birdseye, and evidently privacy was no more prized in East Tennessee than in his native New England; his neighbors seemed to know everyone's business and relished gossiping to him about the community's darkest secrets.[5]

Third, Ezekiel Birdseye formed warm friendships with many slaveowners and did not condemn them as individuals. He readily admitted that many slaveholders were kindly masters, but pointed out the obliquity of slavery under even the most favorable circumstances. Many southern slaveholders privately confided their own doubts or fears about the institution, and Birdseye listened sympathetically to the woes of both slave and master. "When only bad men held slaves," he observed in October 1842, "they would not hold them long." He noted in this same letter that he had "conversations with slaveholders on the subject of slavery" almost daily. He gave these slaveholding friends antislavery tracts and papers to read, noting that it "has not procured me an unkind word and when done in a spirit of kindness I have little fear that it will."[6]

In some instances, in fact, Birdseye's friendship with individual slaveholders made him appear too sympathetic toward the master—almost at the expense of his own antislavery principles. No better example of Birdseye's empathy for such slaveholding friends exists than his response to the request of one Cocke County master, Mr. Fowler, who urged him to see his runaway's slave's mother in order to persuade the slave to return. Chamberlain's master, in Birdseye's opinion a "very worthy man," was "one of the most kind" masters, "conscientious humane and mild," who promised no punishment and continued kind treatment if his slave would return promptly. Birdseye did in fact convey these assurances to Chamberlain's elderly mother, who was owned by another slaveholder fifteen miles above Knoxville. Some months later, he also agreed to talk to Mr. Foster's other slave, Simon, and offer the same assurances of kind treatment for Chamberlain, if he would return. Simon presumably had some sort of contact with his runaway friend, who appeared to be "lying out" in the surrounding mountains. Although Birdseye surmised that Chamberlain long since had fled to the free states, as his elderly mother suggested, in fact the slave finally returned in September 1842, after enduring nine months of "hunger, cold and wet" while wandering about in the forests and mountains. Chamberlain had run away out of fear that he was about to be sold and carried off by a slave dealer. Birdseye believed, in this instance, that remaining with a kind master was better than suffering alone in the wilds without food or shelter. Mr. Fowler, in contrast, clearly was taking advantage of his friendship with Birdseye and utilizing his friend's well-known reputation as a "friend of the slaves."[7]

This episode with Chamberlain also illustrates the larger problem of historical interpretation of particular events involving slavery, because, characteristically, Birdseye in the final analysis saw Chamberlain's plight as yet another damning indictment of slavery under even the best of circumstances. Even those slaves with kind masters, he observed, lived in constant fear of being sold, should their master die or become insolvent, since slaves were tangible, attachable property liable to be seized like any other real or personal property under the state's bankruptcy laws.

Historian Stanley M. Elkins in 1959 pointed out the difficulty of determining the actual treatment of slaves from traditional sources. Scholars like Ulrich B. Phillips, who saw slavery as having a mild or beneficent effect upon its victims, drew their conclusions from essentially the same manuscript sources as did historians like Kenneth Stampp, who condemned the treatment of slaves as harsh, brutal, and dehumanizing. Although this ongoing historiographical battle appears in the 1990s to be swinging again toward the latter emphasis, the problems involved in determining historical reality from Birdseye's letters continue to present an interpretative minefield which should be approached with great caution.[8]

That conflicting historical interpretations can be derived utilizing essentially the same evidence is well illustrated with regard to the condition or experience of free blacks in Tennessee before the Civil War. Free blacks living in slave states were always a problematic counterpoint of the whole slavery issue, perceived as a threat by slaveholders and as unfree victims by abolitionists. A 1941 study of free blacks in Tennessee by James Merton England concluded that most of these people were basically happy and lived lives of relative peace and security, unmarred by the vicissitudes which abolitionists erroneously had attributed to their often marginal existence. Using essentially the same source materials, Roger R. Van Dyke in 1972 substantially challenged these conclusions. Even the adaptive strategies free blacks employed to "get by," self-effacement and "Uncle Tom" behavior, Van Dyke argued, were "inherently demeaning" and inevitably resulted in psychological damage. Always the free Negro's legal, social, and economic status was defined in accord with racist assumptions enforced at the community level by social norms below the reach of formal law. Most lived in abject poverty, being socially, economically, and politically marginalized by ubiquitous white suspicions and by a pernicious racism, the inevitable corollary of slavery, which constantly bombarded them on many different psychological levels.[9]

Other dimensions further complicate any definitive portrayal of slaves and slavery within the state. Attitudes toward blacks changed within the South following the 1831 Nat Turner revolt, and the mounting abolitionist attacks from without during the 1840s and 1850s inevitably led to harsher laws and more stringent regulation of slaves. Merton L. Dillon ably demonstrates that, with each passing decade after the American Revolution, slaveholders' fears of black subversion and insurrection grew, and this fear, in turn, increasingly dominated both their anger toward abolitionists and their reactive and often punitive treatment of the slaves. In this sense, if Ezekiel Birdseye's letters predicting the imminent demise of slavery in the South and widely circulated in northern newspapers were read by any southerners, he became in their minds part of a threat that began with the revolt of slaves in 1791 in Saint-Domingue and continued in an unbroken line from Denmark Vesey to Nat Turner.[10]

So in Tennessee there never was any exact concomitance between state laws regulating slave behavior and the fluctuating wishes of the body politic; by the time the legislature passed a new law on the subject, yet another crisis already had eroded public confidence. Nor were the laws regularly or uniformly enforced throughout Tennessee's ninety-six pre–Civil War counties or at the myriad levels of local magistrates. The evolving laws on the emancipation of an individual slave by an owner illustrate the complex and irregular nature of Tennessee jurisprudence in this regard. Although, according to English common law, the decision to emancipate one's own slaves was an absolute right of the master, a 1777 North Carolina statute restricted this right by establishing the precedent that the state also had a substantive interest in emancipation. When the North Carolina statutes were adopted by the new state of Tennessee in 1796, the state's formal assent consequently was required in such proceedings. North Carolina had feared the presumably dire consequences of having too many free blacks within the community, as a result of individual emancipation, and demanded meritorious service on the part of the prospective freedman as a condition of its consent to his freedom.[11]

Tennessee modified its inherited North Carolina manumission requirement in a more liberal statute enacted in 1801, ending the meritorious service stipulation and vesting complete power to free slaves in the county courts. The meritorious service requirement often had prevented entire families from being liberated together, since presumably only an individual could achieve such merit. Furthermore, the legislature was growing weary of considering so many individual petitions for nonmeritorious emancipation. This hope of ending petitions to the legislature asking freedom for individual slaves proved vain, however; until the Civil War, such petitions continued to come to Nashville and often were acted upon by the legislature. The only stipulations imposed by this liberal 1801 statute were that the county court be of the opinion that an individual slave's emancipation was consistent with the interest and policy of the state, and that the owner give a bond for an amount determined by the county court to reimburse the county if the slave became "chargeable," or indigent, requiring public assistance.[12]

Since most slaves were emancipated by will, an 1829 law prevented recalcitrant executors from keeping slaves in bondage, by providing that slaves in such circumstances could file a bill in chancery court for their freedom through a "next of friend." A subsequent 1831 amendment to this act removed jurisdiction of these cases instituted before the 1829 statute from the chancery courts. The 1831 amendment, however, was ruled unconstitutional by the Tennessee Supreme Court. Justice Jacob Peck, Birdseye's close friend and business partner, had in this instance sharply admonished the legislature not presumptuously to interfere with the prerogatives and authority of the judiciary.[13]

A major shift in Tennessee's comparatively liberal policy toward emancipation occurred in 1831, as a direct result of hysteria caused by the Nat Turner revolt in Virginia, however. This new 1831 statute forbade future emancipation, except on condition that such slaves were removed from the state immediately. The emancipator, in addition, had to enter into bond for an amount equal to the value of the slave being emancipated, to guarantee removal. In 1834, the Tennessee Supreme Court upheld this drastic expulsion provision and ordered that all slaves emancipated in the future be deported to Africa. This decision probably was influenced by an 1833 state law providing payment of ten dollars to the Tennessee Colonization Society for every free black transported from the state to Liberia. Some modification of this harsh expulsion provision was provided by an 1833 law exempting slaves who had contracted for their freedom prior to the 1831 act.[14]

In the confusion following the expulsion provision of 1831, as even token enforcement proved virtually impossible, the state legislature began to comprehend the complexity of ensuring any sort of uniformity in emancipating slaves. An 1842 act, implicitly admitting this failure, reenacted the liberal 1801 policy giving the county courts power to grant emancipation and the right of freedmen to remain in the state, provided they were of good character and gave a bond of five hundred dollars to guarantee not becoming chargeable to the county. If the freedman failed to meet these conditions, however, he subsequently had to leave the state. In 1849, the state again dramatically reversed its policy, returning to the harsh 1831 requirement of expulsion from the state as a nonnegotiable requirement for emancipation.[15]

Throughout all these abrupt reversals in state policy toward emancipating individual slaves, the key thing to remember is that, in actual practice, many masters continued to free their slaves despite prevailing state law. County courts, circuit courts, chancery courts, the Tennessee Supreme Court, and even the Tennessee legislature itself, in granting petitions to free individual slaves, continued to make decisions involving individual freedmen which were in direct violation of state law regarding expulsion of all freedmen. In actual practice, a growing class of "nominal" slaves, neither bond nor free, emerged; these quasi-free slaves were granted freedom from their masters, but the state had not consented to their freedom officially, and they continued to reside within its borders. An 1852 law tried to provide for these nominal slaves by instructing county courts to appoint trustees to hire them out and apply the proceeds to their support. Trustees were to have "all the rights, powers, and privileges, and be subjected to all the responsibilities of the master of the said slave," so these nominal slaves were returned to a condition of virtual slavery.[16]

In 1854, the Tennessee legislature repealed this 1852 act and passed its final policy concerning manumission before the Civil War. According to this new law, all emancipated slaves henceforth were to be transported to the western coast of Africa. If freedmen lacked money for such a trip, they were to be hired out by the clerk of the county court until their accumulated wages sufficed to pay for the voyage to Africa. Exempted from transportation were former slaves "who from age or disease are unable to go with safety." In a final irony, the legislature in 1860 actually passed a law allowing nominal slaves voluntarily to reenter a state of servitude as an alternative to transportation![17]

By 1858, the last year before the Civil War when Tennessee's laws were codified, an elaborate body of laws regulated slave behavior. No slave could carry a gun, sword, or club, or any other weapon, without written permission from his master; penalty for such conduct was "twenty lashes on his or her bare back," required to be performed by the constable "without further order or warrant." Likewise, no slave could leave her or his owner's plantation without a written certificate of permission. Three or more slaves conspiring to rebel or make insurrection constituted a felony punishable by death. "Any Negro, mulatto or Indian, bond or free," who was found guilty of giving false testimony received a mandatory "thirty-nine lashes, well laid on his or her bare back." A slave caught selling the master's possessions likewise received thirty-nine lashes; the same penalty obtained if a slave happened to be caught with a forged pass. Although slaves could not give evidence against a white person, their testimony against any free black was permitted.[18]

By an 1819 statute, murder, arson, burglary, rape, and robbery, if committed by a slave, became capital offenses punishable by death. In 1833, any assault on a white woman "with intent to commit a rape," was to be punished by hanging. By 1858, capital crimes committed by slaves had been expanded to include assault on a white person with intent to commit murder; being an accessory to the murder of a white person; preparing any sort of "poison, potion, or medicine whatever" intended to kill any person; having sexual intercourse with a free white female under twelve years of age; *merely* consulting among three or more slaves to "advise or conspire to rebel, or make insurrection," or "conspire to murder any person"; and finally, the "ringleader or chief instigator of any plot to rebel, or to murder any white person" lawfully could be killed, evidently on sight, if he was lying out and refused to surrender.[19]

Runaway slaves were jailed; if unclaimed by their owner, they were to be sold by the sheriff at auction. Within two years of such an auction, however, the original owner could redeem his slave by paying all court costs. Slaves could not traffic in "spirituous liquors" or "go about the country under the pretext of practicing medicine, or healing the sick." This latter prohibition evidently inspired a petition to the legislature in 1831 from citizens of the counties of Bedford, Giles, Hardeman, Lincoln, Maury, and Williamson to allow a Negro doctor, Jack, to continue practicing medicine. Interestingly, another case involving a slave physician, also named Jack, was heard by the Tennessee Supreme Court in 1844. Although evidence clearly showed that the slave Jack was "an obedient, exemplary slave, a most successful practitioner of medicine" who "had performed many cures of a most extraordinary character," the court nevertheless upheld his conviction for violating the prohibition against slaves' practicing medicine. Justice Green delivered the opinion of the court, noting that "a slave under pretence of practising medicine might convey intelligence from one plantation to another of a contemplated insurrectionary movement, and thus enable the slaves to act in concert to a considerable extent, and perpetrate the most shocking massacres."[20]

In 1835, the circuit courts were given exclusive jurisdiction "of all offenses committed by slaves, which are by law punishable by death." Previous to this act, special slave courts composed of justices of the peace and slaveholders in the district adjudicated cases involving slave crimes without benefit of jury. These slave courts clearly were more concerned with punishment and control of slaves than with justice, although they did cloak their activities in some procedural formality. Interestingly, a petition to the legislature in 1829 from the citizens of Greene County protested an 1825 act prohibiting nonslaveholders from acting as jurors in the trials of slaves. Such "discriminating regulations," the Greene County petitioners feared, "will ultimately destroy the spirit of our free institutions and build an aristocracy upon the ruins of public liberty." Although all slave courts eventually were abolished by the legislature in 1854, between 1835 and that date these tribunals still exercised wide jurisdiction over slaves. Finally, in the 1858 code, more elaborate directions were given for slave patrols, and greater discretion was entrusted to magistrates dealing with "riots, routs, unlawful assemblies, trespasses, seditious speeches by a slave or slaves, or any insulting or provoking language used by a slave to any white person."[21]

These statutes regulating slave behavior have been analyzed and interpreted by many students of Tennessee history, with conflicting and often contradictory results. Perhaps the critical questions to be asked are: How uniformly were such laws enforced? And what were the consequences of such regulations for the day-to-day life of the typical Tennessee slave?

Historian Chase C. Mooney argued in 1957, as Ulrich B. Phillips had done earlier, that most slaves within the state lived happy, carefree lives, because it so obviously was in the best interests of masters to protect their slave property. As evidence that most laws regulating slave conduct were not stringently enforced, Mooney cites an 1858 decision by Justice Robert J. McKinney of the Tennessee Supreme Court. In this case, *Jones v. Allen*, involving the slave Isaac's attendance at a cornhusking in the neighborhood without written permission from his master, Justice McKinney observed that it was widely accepted in Tennessee that slaves "are allowed by universal sufferance, at night, on Sundays, holidays, and other occasions, to go abroad, to attend church, to visit . . . and to exercise other innocent enjoyments, without its ever entering the mind of any good citizen, to demand *written authority* of them." Despite the statute, then, it was not always necessary for a slave to have written permission to attend a social gathering, Mooney surmised from this incident, which he judged representative of a general laxity in the enforcement of the slave code in Tennessee. It was, however, a moot point for the slave Isaac, who, without any provocation, had been mortally stabbed by an uninvited drunken white man on this occasion![22]

If the irony of Isaac's violent death—evidently considered only a minor corollary to the universal laxness in enforcing the requirement for slaves to have written permission to travel away from their masters' plantations—escaped Mooney, the incident nevertheless illustrates how vulnerable slaves were to violence from masters and strangers alike. In a thoughtful study of the treatment of slaves and free blacks in Tennessee's state and local courts, historian Arthur F. Howington found only three instances in which whites brought to trial for the murder of slaves were convicted. Two of these white defendants were convicted in the 1820s of a lesser degree of homicide than murder, and both were branded by the letter "M" as their only punishment. The third white defendant, convicted in 1849 of murder in the second degree for brutally shooting a black man through the back of the head without any provocation, evidently was sentenced to ten years in the penitentiary, only because public opinion was so outraged over this incident. Most whites accused of felonious assault upon slaves received no punishment at all, or only petty fines ranging from five to fifty dollars, which often were suspended. Howington cites one particularly gruesome crime of "inhuman butchery" perpetrated on a female slave in 1855 in Williamson County by Ellen Bolton, her mistress. Mrs. Bolton beat her slave with a shovel, hanged her and scalded her entire body with boiling water, but was released on nominal bail and never appeared for trial. Howington's conclusions echo Birdseye's assertion that a white man never received punishment in the South for murdering his own slave.[23]

Court cases or instances such as that of Mrs. Bolton have seemed to many historians only a rare phenomenon, the exception rather than the rule in the general treatment of slaves. It is difficult, of course, to reconstruct the daily life of average slaves in Tennessee from the impersonal language of formal statutes or from admittedly extraordinary cases tried before the supreme court. Clearly the vast majority of punishments meted out for minor slave offenses were adjudicated at the local level by justices of the peace, and such punishment was executed by the local constable. Whipping by the lash on the bare back of the slave seems to have been the most common form of such punishment for minor offenses. One of the most chilling, and heretofore overlooked, indications that such beatings indeed were commonly performed on recalcitrant slaves is to be found in an 1859 Tennessee constable's guide, which offers the following instruction:

> All criminal offences committed by slaves, except those for which the penalty is death, are triable before a justice of the peace, and are punished by

the infliction of stripes; so, too, are several offences when committed by free persons of color.

In these cases the punishment is inflicted by the constable. In discharging this disagreeable duty, he should on the one hand remember, that the object of punishment is not revenge for the past, and on the other that the infliction is visited on the culprit as a warning to all "like offenders." He should administer the prescribed punishment without anger, and without comment,—with as little publicity as practicable, yet without any attempt to conceal his purpose, and with no pandering to a mawkish sentimentality.[24]

Historian Arthur F. Howington offers persuasive evidence that, with the glaring exception of violence against slaves, Tennessee law and courts accepted the humanity of slaves, even while giving primacy to their property aspect. Such admitted humanity conferred certain human rights that generally were respected throughout the state's court system. "A slave is not in the condition of a horse or an ox," Justice Nathan Green wrote in a famous 1846 case confirming this basic recognition of the slave's humanity:

> He is made after the image of the Creator. He has mental capacities, and an immortal principle in his nature, that constitute him equal to his owner, but for the accidental position in which fortune has placed him . . . the laws . . . cannot extinguish his high born nature, nor deprive him of many rights which are inherent in man . . . he can make a contract for his freedom, which our laws recognize, and he can take a bequest of his freedom, and by the same will he can take personal or real estate.[25]

In an earlier case, *Bob, a Slave, v. The State,* Howington sees the Tennessee Supreme Court moving from a "crime control model" of justice to a due process model, by broadening the trial rights and procedural guarantees of slave defendants well beyond those required by statute, eventually to include the same judicial protection accorded all free defendants. Jacob Peck, Birdseye's friend, was instrumental in this particular case, but throughout the 1840s and 1850s, most of the Supreme Court justices continued to interpret laws governing criminal trials as applicable to slaves unless expressly prohibited by the legislature. Out of thirty-three cases involving slave defendants which were appealed to the Tennessee Supreme Court, Howington discovered that twenty-three of these cases were decided in favor of the slave defendant. Furthermore, in these cases the Tennessee Supreme Court was quite willing to reverse trial court convictions of slaves based on procedural irregularities, unconvincing evidence used against the defendants, or technicalities in the substantive law. Some scholars have argued that such outcomes were due more to the value of these slaves as property than to judicial recognition of their human rights. Others see these results as rhetorical flourishes designed to refute abolitionist criticism. Howington vehemently rejects these hypotheses, however. In the final analysis, he argues, Tennessee's judicial policymakers genuinely and conscientiously were determined to protect the human rights of slave defendants.[26]

Howington discovered that the slave's right to a fair trial generally was respected in the lower circuit and criminal courts of Tennessee, too. After 1835, state law required that all slaves accused of capital crimes be tried in the same courts as free men. Court-appointed attorneys for slaves in such instances usually were of high caliber, and slave defendants were allowed to challenge as many prospective jurors as a free white person in similar circumstances. Howington did find rather pronounced regional differences among Tennessee's three grand divisions in the final outcomes of trials involving slaves accused of capital crimes: 82 percent of such slave defendants were acquitted in East Tennessee; 59 percent were acquitted in Middle Tennessee; and only 49 percent of slave defendants were acquitted in West Tennessee. Howington speculated that these discrepancies were due to the much smaller total slave population in East Tennessee. The outcome lends credence to, but does not definitely corroborate, Ezekiel Birdseye's oft-repeated claim that slaves were treated better in this section than anywhere else in the South.[27]

Previous interpretations of how slavery affected its victims in Tennessee have relied disproportionately upon these notable cases before the Tennessee Supreme Court, largely because so little other documentation of slave life is available. Although Tennessee's record at this level is indeed luminous in comparison to that of most other state courts in the South, the question of how representative such cases were remains unanswered. Helen Tunnicliff Catterall pointed out that, although the Tennessee Supreme Court had no problem defining specific rights and protections for nominal or quasi-slaves, other southern courts scornfully rejected as impossible the logic of any such distinction. Yet there is no clear evidence of how these nominal slaves were treated, or of how such rights as they were permitted by the supreme court were honored by innumerable local magistrates at the civil district level or by common consensus and usage within Tennessee's myriad rural communities.[28]

At this point, Ezekiel Birdseye's observations do offer insight into the daily lives of slaves in East Tennessee. Although he told Gerrit Smith that he "endeavoured to be accurate and impartial," one must nevertheless continually bear in mind Birdseye's predisposition as an abolitionist to see only the dark side of slavery. In analyzing his reports on abuses of slaves, however, it is important to note that most narratives and critical details came from other southerners who betrayed a moral disapprobation of such cruelties equal to or greater than Birdseye's own compunction. More than the actual details of abuses themselves, then, these reactions of other southerners to cruelties in their midst form the most valuable part of Birdseye's letters. Like a good novelist, he allowed the reactions and attitudes of friends and neighbors who told him about various atrocities to give his narratives both a rich texture and illuminating subplots.[29]

Good examples of this technique are to be found in his many reports of the most commonplace violence against slaves throughout the South: beatings or whippings as punishments, deserved or not. In the second week of November 1841 Birdseye encountered in passing a slave tied to a tree, preparatory to being beaten, some five miles below Athens. Although he had been introduced only once to the master, Mr. Rice, Birdseye determined to "call and see if I could not dissuade him from such barbarity." Carefully, Birdseye inquired if Rice's servant ever had given him trouble previously and then suggested taking milder measures to redress his grievances. Mr. Rice, appearing mortified at the extremity to which his anger had led him, readily agreed. Birdseye characterized Rice as a man of ardent but tender feelings who "in his usual intercourse with society had nothing of the appearance of the tyrant about him." His conclusion was simply that the institution of slavery itself routinely and almost inadvertently brought out barbarous cruelty in the characters of otherwise ordinary and decent men.[30]

In June 1842 Birdseye's landlady in Newport, Mrs. Spencer Henry, wife of the Methodist minister there, reported overhearing a terrible beating of a female slave by R. W. Pulliam, a prominent local merchant. Some two hundred stripes were administered to the poor woman, cutting her back to pieces and covering Pulliam with blood. Her screams were heard throughout the village. Mrs. Henry, "whose piety seems to be beyond all doubt," lamented this "deplorable evil" and wondered why no one in the neighborhood had intervened. Pulliam only recently had joined the church, but this action made Mrs. Henry doubt his conversion. She noted that too often churches attempted to cover up or ignore such actions on the part of their members. Other church members were consequently so offended that they declared that, if men like Pulliam were not expelled for such cruelty, they themselves would withdraw from the congregation. Mrs. Henry's fears were prescient, because two years later, in 1844, the Methodist church indeed would split over the issue of slavery.[31]

Some masters, deeming it necessary to keep their slaves constantly "cowed," routinely whipped them without any apparent cause, as Birdseye witnessed on more than one occasion. In March 1841 he unwillingly witnessed Calloway Hodges whipping six of his slaves on the Sabbath morning, just before breakfast, for no obvious reason. His amazement on this occasion was reserved for the other members of Hodges' family, who appeared completely undisturbed and nonchalant during the successive beatings just outside the door. Birdseye earlier had conversed with Hodges about slavery. Although Hodges had been "friendly to me individually," he noted, "he said harsh things about abolitionists." Perhaps these beatings were intended to convey some point to Birdseye, who also noted that Hodges' slaves were clothed in rags and stood barefoot in the cold March rain.[32]

On occasion, a master became passionately angry at the slave of another owner. In November 1841 Adam Meek "dangerously wounded" the slave of Mr. McBee because of an earlier fight between this slave and slaves owned by Meek. The most disturbing aspect of this narrative was Meek's predatory persecution of the hapless slave, whom he hunted down, almost gleefully, like a wild animal. When the slave attempted to defend himself with a club against Meek's savagely attacking bulldog, Meek and his associates threw sharp-edged stones at him until an artery in his neck was severed. Afterward, an infuriated McBee took personal vengeance by attacking and beating Meek with his cane. Birdseye's good friend John Caldwell told him the details of the Meek-McBee affair, noting that the slave who had been mauled so badly by Meek's bulldog was still alive but was expected never to recover fully.[33]

According to Birdseye, public opinion in East Tennessee could be incited against slaveowners who too frequently or too savagely beat their slaves. One such planter, William Moore, removed from South Carolina to Jefferson County, Tennessee, where he adopted such a "despotic system of discipline" against his slaves that it brought a response from the community. "The neighborhood was so shocked with his barbarity," Birdseye recorded in 1841, "that several planters waited on Moore and told him that it must be discontinued." Moore consequently "paid some attention to the remonstrance," Birdseye noted, "but is sufficiently barbarous yet." Later this planter spoke of the neighborhood as being too free for his taste and indicated a desire to move to Texas. Not infrequently, Birdseye's East Tennessee neighbors reported terrible beatings of slaves in other parts of the South. One such man, a wagoner from Jefferson County named Mansfield, reported an incident he witnessed while passing through Georgia, in which a slave had been whipped "to a jelly." "Cases of these enormous cruelties are so constantly reaching us from South Carolina," Birdseye noted, "that they excite little attention." Yet his East Tennessee neighbors, for the most part, did observe and comment on such cruelties witnessed in the Lower South.[34]

Such savage beatings frequently were the cause of slaves' running away from their masters. The slave William, or "the Captain," as he was called, at one point reportedly received five hundred lashes and, as a consequence of innumerable whippings, was "covered with ridges from his head to his feet." Birdseye's unsuccessful efforts to purchase the Captain for Gerrit Smith run like a leitmotif through all his correspondence. Smith believed that this slave's moral superiority, combined with his scarred body, would make him a splendid example to convince northern audiences of the barbarity of slavery. "My heart yearns toward him," Smith wrote Birdseye in December of 1840, "I want to comfort him—and I want to see him usefully employed at the North." Initially Birdseye failed to purchase him from Nicholas W. Woodfin in Asheville, North Carolina, because the price asked, $800, was too high. Subsequently, however, Woodfin sold him to another slaveholder, Mr. Davis, for $550, ignoring his promise to notify Birdseye should he ever be for sale. Arrangements to purchase the Captain from Mr. Davis collapsed in 1846, but Birdseye learned from Davis's wife that this slave had tried yet again to escape to the free states but had been apprehended and jailed in Kentucky.[35]

Runaways were frequent, although conditions while living in the wild always were harrowing. One slave, Simon, told Birdseye a particularly moving narrative of his own sufferings while running away during the winter. Simon admitted suffering much during this ordeal but said that such hardships "were but a trifle [compared] to the idea of being sold and carried off by a slave dealer." Yet being sold at public auction, most slaves' worst fear, resulted more often from the insolvency or death of a master than from an individual slave's misbehavior. Birdseye personally witnessed one such auction in Cocke County in June 1841, when a Mr. Jones, reputedly a kind master, died suddenly and in debt. His slaves were sold to owners living at great distances all over the South. Husbands and wives, mothers and children, all were separated, never to see each other again. "However mild slaves may be treated," Birdseye observed on this occasion, "they live in dread of these occurrences which separate them forever."[36]

The inevitable corollaries of the slave traffic—unscrupulous professional slave dealers, professional slavecatchers, nightly patrollers regulating the movement of slaves and looking for runaways—also were evident throughout East Tennessee, Birdseye was forced to admit. Coffles of slaves going further south or to Texas frequently were seen. He also noted one instance in Chattanooga in which an elderly blind slave, "Old William," had been abandoned to starve by his master. Fortunately, however, the citizens of that city rallied to his assistance after learning his story. Birdseye also reported as "another evil of considerable magnitude prevailing in the South," the practice of kidnapping free blacks in order to sell them into slavery. In one such instance, he warned a young black barber in Philadelphia not to be lured to Mississippi by the promise of liberal wages.[37]

Birdseye occasionally alluded to miscegenation; on one occasion he pointedly argued that "slavery in principle is not confined to color at the South." Many slaves were "as white as I am, where the offspring has been for generations from a white father," he continued, until "all trace of African blood has disappeared." Such slaves nevertheless were "bought and sold like cattle and the females often at a much higher price for being white." In 1842, he reported that, at the death of James McMurtrey in neighboring Greene County, some forty-five slaves were auctioned off to pay his debts. One of Birdseye's neighbors reported that fifteen of these slaves were the children of McMurtrey himself. The "resemblance is so striking to the other children of McMurtrey as to leave no doubt of the fact in the mind of anyone who will observe them," Birdseye's informant maintained:

> Here were parents and children bound together by all those ties which could be supposed to exist in that relation then to be separated forever. Mr. R says it was the most distressing sight he ever saw. All those poor slaves were in tears. The women embraced their husbands in the anguish of their hearts. The husband in quiet grief sustained his weeping wife. The child frantic with screams clung to the bosom of its mother. I did not attend the sale. It is sufficiently distressing to me to hear of it from one who did. Slavery in its best estate is a bitter cup but who can describe a scene like this—of such unutterable woe.[38]

In the final analysis, the fatal defect in Tennessee law, which makes mockeries of any other substantive or procedural guarantees to slaves, was the fact that masters could kill their slaves with impunity, while, on the other hand, slaves convicted of killing their masters in self-defense almost invariably were hanged. According to Birdseye's testimony, instances of slaves killing their masters were not uncommon in East Tennessee. When he reported an incident in which a woman, Mrs. McMahan, and her daughter were murdered by their slave near Athens in February 1842, he noted that this was the fifth such incident within the last three years. In April of the same year, he reported that a slave owned by John Thomas in Cocke County had killed a man by the name of Benson, dangerously wounded Thomas and his wife, and burned all his buildings. At this slave's trial, it was revealed that he was a well-known maniac, sold to Thomas knowingly as such "for a trifle." Previously he had murdered another slave in Blount County, washed his hands and face in the victim's blood, and then stuck the head on a pole. Later, Birdseye learned from a reputable farmer in Blount County that this slave's sister, after being sold to a slave dealer, had run away and hanged herself; "from that time he was crazed."[39]

In a moving letter published in 1843 in the *Christian Freeman*, Birdseye told about attending the trial of a young slave who had killed his master in self-defense. The slave Hannibal had been so frequently and cruelly scourged by his master that he intended to commit suicide. While he was covering a coal pit, his master assaulted him with a heavy club, and Hannibal accidentally killed him with his shovel. The slave's lawyer pointed out that the Tennessee Supreme Court had ruled that a slave had the right to resist, if his master attacked him with a dangerous weapon. It seemed plain to everyone attending this trial, Birdseye reported, that Hannibal was indeed guilty of only second degree murder, or manslaughter; nevertheless, the jury found him guilty of murder in the first degree. The following day, the judge, "one of the most amiable men living, who has freed his own slaves, and whose opinion of slavery corresponds with ours," reluctantly and with great emotion passed on Hannibal the sentence of death by hanging. Although "more than half the audience wept" at Hannibal's nobility and dignity in the face of death, the verdict was inexorable, according to Birdseye, who recalled having heard of eight or ten similar cases during the preceding five years in East Tennessee.[40]

Arthur F. Howington confirms the great reluctance of the Tennessee Supreme Court to countenance a slave's resistance to physical violence, no matter how excessively imposed, by his master. No clear standard ever was developed spelling out the proper limits of abuse which would permit slaves finally to claim self-defense as justification for such resistance. Sadly, the court always considered the sanctity of the slave's person subordinate to his duty to submit to punishment from his master; the permissible scope or boundaries of such punishment never were defined. In an 1842 case, *Jacob v. The State*, the supreme court upheld Jacob's conviction for murdering his master "because the law cannot recognize the violence of the master as a legitimate cause of provocation." In a similar 1850 case, the court upheld the conviction of Moses, a slave convicted of murdering his master, John Lauderdale, although Moses' attorneys argued that the slave was "alarmed at the character of the preparation for his punishment and under the fear and apprehension of death, or great bodily harm." Both the *Moses* and the *Jacob* cases clearly indicate that the Tennessee Supreme Court left virtually unchallenged the authority of masters over their chattel, even if such authority was maintained by physical violence against the slave that was excessive and possibly would result in death. Any resistance on the slave's part which resulted in the master's death, on the other hand, inevitably led to the offending slave's execution.[41]

Although Tennessee law provided that anyone who murdered a slave would be tried "as if such person so killed, had been a free man," there were three notable exceptions to this rule which rendered it, in practice, virtually meaningless. The law did not apply to a slave declared an "outlaw" by the legislature, to any slave resisting his lawful owner, or to any slave "dying under moderate correction." Although the Tennessee Supreme Court did uphold convictions of whites for murdering their slaves, problems of evidence and the inadmissibility of the testimony of slaves against a white man in reality meant that the vast majority of slave homicides never were reported or never went to any tribunal whatsoever.[42]

Birdseye reported one such instance in September 1842 in adjoining Greene County. A despotic slaveholder, Daniel Allen, emasculated his slave for returning later than usual in the morning after visiting his wife, who lived some miles distant. This slave's body turned up in a fish trap in the Nolichucky River; his mutilation was apparent to any witness. Birdseye's informant, Mr. J. Huff, also related that this same slaveholder had killed one of his slaves with a pitchfork the previous summer. Everyone in the community knew about these murders, but no action was taken against Allen. Although "no man doubts" the correctness of these reports, Birdseye concluded, "there is no legal proof as a slave cannot testify against a white man and none but slaves saw him commit the murders." The protection thus afforded by the law to slaves assaulted by a cruel or unstable master seemed to Birdseye nonexistent.[43]

Throughout all his letters to Gerrit Smith, Birdseye time and again reiterated his conviction that in East Tennessee slavery was milder or more humane in its effect on blacks than anywhere else in the South. The nadir of slavery's brutality for him, the absolute standard of horror by which he judged all other experiences, was the practice of burning slaves alive in South Carolina. The iniquity of this practice, which he had personally witnessed in his youth in South Carolina, was multiplied by the fact that such burnings always were undertaken as the result of mob action, outside the normal process of law.

Such an act could not occur in East Tennessee, Birdseye frequently argued, where a restraining public sentiment disapproved cruelty toward slaves.[44]

Yet, in reality, such lynchings were not uncommon in East Tennessee. In 1853, the daughters of one of Cocke County's most prominent citizens, Rev. Samuel Lotspeich, a Methodist minister, together with the husband of one daughter, Elisha Moore, a wealthy planter, were brutally murdered by their slave Tom on a farm in Jefferson County near the French Broad River, just opposite Cocke County. After these particularly brutal murders were discovered, bands of armed men scoured the country in every direction. On the Sunday after the murder of the Moore family, Tom was captured in the middle of the Nolichucky River, after being shot in one leg. He subsequently was tortured by having various parts of his body successively placed in a vise and smashed. All the bones in his hands and fingers were thus crushed before he confessed to the murders and to raping the unmarried sister of Mrs. Moore. He offered no reason for killing them other than his passion for Miss Lotspeich.[45]

Subsequently the hapless slave was taken without trial to a pen built around a small persimmon tree. A floor of unseasoned logs was placed at the base of this pen, but the pen itself was filled with the most combustible wood—the richest pine which could be found. Tom was handcuffed and chained to the persimmon tree, his arms extending above his shoulders and head. He appeared completely unrepentant, nonchalantly showing his wardens how to bind him properly to the persimmon tree, then laughing in the faces of the nearest bystanders. But after the flame, which burned slowly at first, leaped into a sheet of fire encircling his body, Tom cried, "God help me," before dying in agony. Six thousand people and nearly a thousand slaves gathered to watch this spectacle—a crowd similar to the large throngs Birdseye earlier had described as attending slave-burnings in South Carolina.[46]

We know of this incident only because of the private recollection of one individual living in Cocke County at the time; it appears in no public or court record, or any newspaper. Such occurrences usually were remembered in great detail and transmitted through oral tradition within the community, but their number or frequency is extremely difficult to determine from traditional manuscript sources. Birdseye's last extant letter to Gerrit Smith was written in 1846 from Newport, county seat of Cocke, but no record remains indicating when he left. The burning alive of the slave Tom in this county occurred in 1853; although the record is silent, Birdseye, even if he already had left the vicinity, likely heard about the incident from old friends in either Jefferson or Cocke County. One can only speculate whether this event changed his mind about the comparative mildness of slavery in East Tennessee, or whether he would have viewed it as only a momentary aberration. Although "we have slavery in a mitigated form in E[ast] Ten[nessee]," Birdseye had written presciently in 1842, "it has horrors enough here."[47]

Cases like that of the slave being burned alive in Cocke County and ample evidence, direct and indirect, in Birdseye's own testimony point toward much harsher treatment of slaves in East Tennessee than historians have previously assumed. Birdseye's contribution to this debate lies in uncovering so many instances of homicides involving slaves—whether the master was victim or perpetrator—which remain hidden, like a subterranean stream, below formal county court minutes or circuit and criminal court records. The oral tradition within the folk community concerning such violence nevertheless documents a historical reality which cannot be ignored; the agony suffered by slave victims of mob action or brutally cruel masters is no less real for not having achieved formal expression in extant written documents. So, too, is the reputation of abolitionists like Ezekiel Birdseye inextricably chained in a historiographical coffle to any assessment of slavery's effect on its victims. If that effect was benevolent or mild, abolitionists appear irrational fanatics continuously fueling unnecessary dissension within the social fabric of antebellum America. If, on the other hand, slavery indeed was an institution vicious in all its ramifications, men like Ezekiel Birdseye appear heroic crusaders, possessed of a rare vision beyond their time or place.

Epilogue

Historical records often baffle us by their sudden omissions and long silences, and Ezekiel Birdseye's letters to Gerrit Smith, which end abruptly in March 1846, are illustrative of this unfortunate occurrence. It would be especially valuable to have Birdseye's comments on East Tennessee during the 1850s, for example, as prosperity returned, bringing with it closer economic ties to the slaveholding Lower South. The destruction of Cocke County's records by fire in 1876 leaves unanswered, too, the questions of when Birdseye sold his lumber mill in Newport, and when, if ever, he sold his large holdings of "wild" lands in that county. Similarly, did Birdseye cease corresponding with his old friend, Gerrit Smith, in 1846, or did Smith simply destroy Birdseye's subsequent letters to him thereafter, as having little further significance in the antislavery cause?

One also wonders if Birdseye maintained his friendships with that colorful cast of Tennessee entrepreneurs—Judge Jacob Peck, John Caldwell, the Reverend Spencer Henry—or with a host of minor characters mentioned earlier in his letters to Smith. Evidence from surviving deeds for other parts of the section indicates that Birdseye's own prosperity was partially restored, as he continued to act as an agent purchasing mineral leases for various New York companies in East Tennessee during the 1850s. On a personal level, certainly he was saddened in 1858 by the sudden and unexpected death of his only daughter, Irene Lucinda, a schoolteacher who died just before she was to have been married.

Intriguing also is the unanswered question of how Ezekiel Birdseye reacted to the impending crisis of the Union, the outbreak of the Civil War, and East Tennessee's frantic but ultimately unsuccessful efforts to secede from the state rather than leave the federal Union in 1861. A tantalizing clue lies in a very brief letter he wrote to Andrew Johnson on February 20, 1861, informing him that his course of action was meeting widespread approval throughout East Tennessee, and that his reputation as a statesman was growing in the North. Birdseye further hoped that Johnson's "efforts to reconcile these difficulties may be successful." The letter is addressed from Knoxville, where Birdseye still was residing at the time of his sudden and unexpected death in June 1861. Since his personal effects were destroyed after his death by the Confederate authorities, we have no record of what his feelings or thoughts were regarding the East Tennessee Convention's momentous secession meetings in Knoxville and Greeneville during the last month of his life. Was he now reminded of those exhilarating times twenty years earlier, in 1841 and 1842, when he had been in the middle of East Tennessee's earlier effort to form a separate state?

Although he was fated never to see the promised land of an American nation entirely free from slavery, Birdseye's correspondence clearly shows that, throughout much of his life, he lived and worked for that elusive goal, and he seems never once to have doubted, even for a moment, its ultimate realization. Given his great humanity and basic rationality, he surely must have dreaded the prospect of a long and bloody civil war—and all the more if, by some prophetic premonition, he had foreseen that his beloved "state" of Frankland would suffer far more destruction because of her divided loyalties than virtually any other section of the country. Like his Biblical namesake, the prophet Ezekiel, he had served too long as an unappreciated and largely unheeded watchman for freedom. But because his total rejection of bigotry and racism seems strangely modern in both tone and discourse, Ezekiel Birdseye's following letters often transcend their historical context of time or place and still speak to us compellingly and very directly today.

Notes

Chapter 1. Political Abolitionism and Separatism

1. *Emancipator,* Apr. 30, 1820; EB/GS, Mar. 22 and Nov. 4, 1841; EB/GS, Feb. 7 and Oct. 17, 1842.
2. John Allison, *Dropped Stitches in Tennessee History* (Nashville: Marshall and Bruce Co., 1897), 80; Oliver P. Temple, *East Tennessee and the Civil War* (Cincinnati, Ohio: Robert Clarke Co., 1899), 84; Chase C. Mooney, *Slavery in Tennessee* (Bloomington: Indiana Univ. Press, 1957), 8; Joshua W. Caldwell, *Studies in the Constitutional History of Tennessee* (Cincinnati, Ohio: Robert Clarke Co., 1907), 148. One historian argued that the constitutional convention of 1796 "intentionally and deliberately enfranchised" the free black. Caleb P. Patterson, *The Negro in Tennessee, 1790–1865: A Study in Southern Politics* (Austin: Univ. of Texas Press, 1922), 166.
3. *Knoxville Gazette,* Jan. 23, 1797; Robert H. White, "Sketch of the Author," in Robert H. White, ed., *The Emancipator (Complete), Published by Elihu Embree, Jonesborough, Tennessee, 1820: A Reprint of* The Emancipator, *to Which Are Added a Biographical Sketch of Elihu Embree, Author and Publisher of* The Emancipator, *and Two Hitherto Unpublished Anti-Slavery Memorials Bearing the Signature of Elihu Embree* (Nashville: B. H. Murphy, 1932), v; Caldwell, *Studies in*

Constitutional History, 215; *Emancipator,* Apr. 30, 1820; Stephen B. Weeks, *Southern Quakers and Slavery: A Study in Institutional History* (Baltimore, Md.: Johns Hopkins Univ. Press, 1896), 235. For correspondence between the Tennessee Manumission Society and the Manumission and Colonizing Society of North Carolina, see H. M. Wagstaff, ed., *Minutes of the North Carolina Manumission Society, 1816–1834* (Chapel Hill: Univ. of North Carolina Press, 1934), 211–13. The letter from the Tennessee Manumission Society was dated Mossy Creek, Jefferson County, Nov. 12, 1817, and signed by the corresponding committee of John Underhill, Barachia Macy, and William Brazelton.

4. Asa Earl Martin, "The Anti-Slavery Societies of Tennessee," *Tennessee Historical Magazine* 1 (Dec. 1915): 264–65; *History of Tennessee, Containing Historical and Biographical Sketches of Thirty East Tennessee Counties* (Chicago and Nashville: Goodspeed Publishing Co., 1887; reprinted Greenville, S.C.: Southern Historical Press, 1991), 881–82; Temple, *East Tennessee,* 85–87; White, "Sketch of the Author," ix. According to signatures on the second 1817 memorial, James Jones was president and Elihu Embree was clerk.

5. Asa Earl Martin, "Anti-Slavery Societies of Tennessee," 264–66; Asa Earl Martin, "Pioneer Anti-Slavery Press," *Mississippi Valley Historical Review* 2 (Mar. 1916): 511–13; Merton L. Dillon, *Benjamin Lundy and the Struggle for Negro Freedom* (Urbana: Univ. of Illinois Press, 1966), 16–17; Weeks, *Southern Quakers,* 235–38; Charles Osborn, *Journal of that Faithful Servant of Christ, Charles Osborn, Containing an Account of Many of His Travels and Labors in the Work of the Ministry, and His Trials and Exercises in the Service of the Lord, and in Defense of the Truth, as It Is in Jesus* (Cincinnati, Ohio: Achilles Pugh, 1854), 1–147; Ruth Ann Ketring, *Charles Osborn in the Anti-Slavery Movement* (Columbus: Ohio State Archaeological and Historical Society, 1937), 11–71; *DAB,* 14:66–67.

6. *DAB,* 5:332–33; A. T. Rankin, *Truth Vindicated and Slander Repelled* (Ironton, Ohio: Privately printed, 1883), 1–17; Asa Earl Martin, "Anti-Slavery Societies of Tennessee," 264; Dwight Lowell Dumond, *Antislavery: The Crusade for Freedom in America* (Ann Arbor: Univ. of Michigan Press, 1961), 91, 134–35, 348; John R. McKivigan, *The War Against Proslavery Religion: Abolitionism and the Northern Churches, 1830–1865* (Ithaca, N.Y.: Cornell Univ. Press, 1984), 31; Paul R. Grimm, "The Rev. John Rankin, Early Abolitionist," *Ohio State*

Archaeological and Historical Quarterly 46 (1937): 215–59. Rankin once said that in his boyhood "a majority of the people of East Tennessee were Abolitionists." Temple, *East Tennessee,* 90. Among Samuel Doak's other students at Washington College were Gideon Blackburn, James Gallagher, Samuel Houston, Jesse Lockhart, and Samuel Kelsey Nelson. It was probably due to Doak's teachings that many years later Houston, as governor of Texas, took a strong pro-Union stance and vetoed the Texas ordinance of secession. William Birney, *James G. Birney and His Times* (New York: D. Appleton and Co., 1890), 73–76.

7. Temple, *East Tennessee,* 90–91; *DAB,* 13:414–15; Dumond, *Antislavery,* 91, 199, 233–36. Merton Dillon said that David Nelson and his son, David Deaderick Nelson, "formed what surely must have been one of the most outspoken and eloquent teams of abolitionists to be found in the West." Merton L. Dillon, "The Antislavery Movement in Illinois, 1809–1844" (Ph.D. diss., Univ. of Michigan, 1951), 287–88. Other abolitionist Presbyterian emigrants to the West from East Tennessee were Gideon W. Blackburn and James Gallagher, who emigrated from Hawkins County, Tenn., to Cincinnati in 1830. Gordon E. Finnie, "The Antislavery Movement in the South, 1787–1836: Its Rise and Decline and Its Contribution to Abolitionism in the West" (Ph.D. diss., Duke Univ., 1962), 473–79.

8. Asa Earl Martin, "Anti-Slavery Societies of Tennessee," 266–68; *DAB,* 11:506–7 and 6:124; Dillon, *Benjamin Lundy,* 34–54. As recently as 1989, Herbert Aptheker endorsed the tradition of a "direct line" of Tennessee abolitionists, from Osborn and Embree to Lundy and Garrison. Herbert Aptheker, *Abolitionism: A Revolutionary Movement* (Boston: Twayne, 1989), 2–3. Another major theme in Stanley Harrold's book is that northern abolitionist reform culture continued to value antislavery activity in the South throughout the 1840s and 1850s, a contention certainly supported by the Birdseye correspondence with Gerrit Smith. Stanley Harrold, *The Abolitionists and the South, 1831–1861* (Lexington: Univ. Press of Kentucky, 1995), 10–20, 149–70.

9. Merton L. Dillon, "Three Southern Antislavery Editors: The Myth of the Southern Antislavery Movement," *East Tennessee Historical Society's Publications* 42 (1970): 54–55; Asa Earl Martin, "Pioneer Anti-Slavery Press," 520–26; Finnie, "Antislavery Movement in the South," 330–31. Lundy's eulogy for James Jones in the April 1830 issue of *Genius of Universal Emancipation* was effusive: "A great man

has fallen, one of the brightest stars in the galaxy of American Philanthropists has set, has set to rise no more. James Jones, president of the Manumission Society of Tennessee—the steady, ardent and persevering friend of universal emancipation, is numbered with the dead. . . . No language can impress upon the mind an adequate idea of his many virtues. Suffice it to say that few men living can fill the station that he held, with equal honor and usefulness. Long shall the poor oppressed African mourn his irreparable loss."

10. *Genius of Universal Emancipation,* Oct. 13, 1827; Asa Earl Martin, "Anti-Slavery Societies of Tennessee," 272–77; Asa Earl Martin, "Anti-Slavery Activities of the Methodist Episcopal Church in Tennessee," *Tennessee Historical Magazine* 2 (June 1916): 98–109; John Berry McFerrin, *History of Methodism in Tennessee* (Nashville: Southern Methodist Publishing House, 1871), 2:494–95; James Allen Ledford, "Methodism in Tennessee, 1783–1866" (M.A. thesis, Univ. of Tennessee, 1941), 47–66; Lewis McCarroll Purifoy, "The Methodist Episcopal Church, South, and Slavery, 1844–1865" (Ph.D. diss., Univ. of North Carolina, Chapel Hill, 1965), 1–65; Donald G. Mathews, *Slavery and Methodism: A Chapter in American Morality, 1780–1845* (Princeton, N.J.: Princeton Univ. Press, 1965), 46–48; James W. Patton, "The Progress of Emancipation in Tennessee, 1796–1860," *Journal of Negro History* 17 (1932): 85–88.

11. For these conclusions I have examined all petitions submitted to the Tennessee legislature between 1799 and 1859 on microfilm. *Petitions to the Tennessee General Assembly,* Rolls 1–20, Tennessee State Library and Archives, Nashville. These petitions are cited as Petitions, with appropriate year.

12. I could locate only one antislavery petition in 1841 not seeking emancipation of a particular slave, with no date and no county, using the identical language of a printed petition widely circulated in the 1820s:

> Your humble petitioners hereunto subscribed, feeling solicitous to promote the rights of man as exhibited in the Constitution of the United States of America, and declaration of rights upon which it was established, are induced to petition your honorable body to take into consideration the deplorable situation of the people of colour, held in slavery in our highly favored and highly professing country; and in your wisdom, devise some plan and pass it into a

law for their relief; such as allowing masters who are convinced of the impropriety of holding slaves, to emancipate them on terms that will not involve themselves or their estates for their maintenance, provided the court should be of opinion that the slaves so offered for emancipation, are, in all probability, capable of maintaining themselves.

And further, we would suggest to you the justice, the good policy etc., of your honorable body, passing a law, declaring agreeable to the purport of the above declaration of rights, and the laws of nature, that all men are and ought to be free, that all the descendants of slaves, born after the passage of said law, shall be free at some age, which your honorable body, doing as you be done by, may fix upon; meanwhile, enjoining on those who may have the raising of such, to teach them some useful occupation, and learn them, if practicable, to read the scriptures, that they may be qualified to become members of civil society; and also, that your honorable body will prohibit, by law, the inhuman practice of separating husbands and wives, within the limits of this state; & your petitioners, as in duty bound, shall ever pray. (Petitions, 1841)

13. Petitions, 1837.
14. Arguing against compulsory colonization in Africa, Foute said that most freedmen would "in due time leave if their condition is as miserable and degraded as alleged." *National Banner and Nashville Whig*, Nov. 21, 1833. Jacob Fauble Foute (1796–1861) represented Blount, McMinn, and Monroe counties in the 20th Tennessee General Assembly (1833–35). He served as clerk of the Blount County Court in 1817–36, after having practiced law in that county. In 1850, he was practicing law in Hinds County, Miss., where he died on July 7, 1861. *BDTGA*, 1:260–61; Inez E. Burns, *History of Blount County, Tennessee, from War Trail to Landing Strip, 1795–1955* (Nashville: Tennessee Historical Commission, 1957), 39, 135, 139, 210, 223; *History of Tennessee, Containing Historical and Biographical Sketches*, 833.
15. Patton, "Progress of Emancipation," 98–101; *Niles' Weekly Register*, 45:182; *Tennessee Acts*, 1833, ch. 64, sec. 1; Mooney, *Slavery in Tennessee*, 73–77; Patterson, *Negro in Tennessee*, 93–98. In 1850, the Tennessee Colonization Society was incorporated; it could sue and be sued, and was allowed to receive gifts of money, goods, and real estate,

provided the total value of such gifts did not exceed $10,000 in any one year. *Tennessee Acts,* 1850, ch. 130, secs. 5 and 8.

16. *African Repository and Colonial Journal* 9 (Dec. 1833): 319–20; Finnie, "Antislavery Movement in the South," 234–35; Lester C. Lamon, *Blacks in Tennessee, 1791–1970* (Knoxville: Univ. of Tennessee Press, 1981), 12–13; Asa Earl Martin, "Anti-Slavery Societies of Tennessee," 270; EB/GS, Oct. 11, 1841; Tom W. Shick, *Emigrants to Liberia, 1820–1843: An Alphabetical Listing* (Newark, Del.: Liberian Studies Association in America, 1971), 43; Bell I. Wiley, ed., *Slaves No More: Letters from Liberia, 1833–1869* (Lexington: Univ. Press of Kentucky, 1980), 215–36.

17. Petitions, 1834; Chase C. Mooney, "The Question of Slavery and the Free Negro in the Tennessee Constitutional Convention of 1834," *Journal of Southern History* 12 (Nov. 1946): 487–89; Patterson, *Negro in Tennessee,* 189–95.

18. *Journal of the Constitutional Convention of 1834* (Nashville: W. H. Hunt, 1834), 125–30; Petitions, 1834. John A. McKinney began practicing law in 1807 in Rogersville, was appointed U.S. district attorney by John Quincy Adams, and died in 1845. "His great success was due to his thorough knowledge of the law, his untiring perseverance and his incorruptible integrity." *History of Tennessee, Containing Historical and Biographical Sketches,* 876.

19. *Journal of the Constitutional Convention of 1834,* 87–93.

20. Ibid., 98–104; *Nashville Republican and State Gazette,* June 28, 1834. Stephenson's protest was signed by John McGaughey of Greene County, Richard Bradshaw of Jefferson County, and James Gillespy of Blount County, all from strongholds of antislavery sentiment in East Tennessee. Mooney, "Question of Slavery," 498. Matthew Stephenson (1777–1838) was a Whig representative in the Tennessee General Assembly (1809–15 and 1831–35). He was one of the first merchants in Washington County, where he also served as clerk of the County Court (1822–24). *BDTGA,* 1:697–98. John McGaughey (1792–1874) served in the Tennessee house of representatives in 1827–33 and senate in 1835–37, representing Greene and Hawkins counties. One of the original directors of the East Tennessee, Virginia, and Georgia Railroad and active in its construction, he was a Unionist during the Civil War. *BDTGA,* 1:477; Oliver P. Temple, *Notable Men of Tennessee, from 1833 to 1875: Their Times and Their Contemporaries* (New York: Cosmopolitan Press, 1912), 52. James

Houston Gillespy (1799–1881) served in the Tennessee house of representatives in 1827–33, representing Blount County. He practiced medicine, was a commissioner promoting the Hiwassee Railroad, and held an interest in the East Tennessee, Virginia, and Georgia Railroad. *BDTGA*, 1:284–85.

21. Mooney, "Question of Slavery," 499–502; *Journal of the Constitutional Convention of 1834*, 125–31, 222–28. Gray Garrett (1800–1848) served in the U.S. Senate in 1827–29, representing Campbell, Claiborne, Grainger, and Jefferson counties. *BDTGA*, 1:277–78.
22. *Journal of the Constitutional Convention of 1834*, 71; Mooney, "Question of Slavery," 502–3. One of the greatest surprises of this final vote is that John A. McKinney, author of the report on slavery, voted against adoption of this provision.
23. Petitions, 1834.
24. Ibid.
25. Ibid.
26. EB/GS, Oct. 17, 1842; Temple, *East Tennessee*, 113; Joshua W. Caldwell, *Sketches of the Bench and Bar of Tennessee* (Knoxville: Ogden Brothers and Co., 1898), 155–59.
27. Amos Dresser, *The Narrative of Amos Dresser, with Stone's Letters from Natchez, an Obituary Notice of the Writer, and Two Letters From Tallahassee, Relating to the Treatment of Slaves* (New York: American Anti-Slavery Society, 1836), 1–15; EB/GS, June 25, 1841; EB/GS, Mar. 14, 1842; Carleton Mabee, *Black Freedom: The Nonviolent Abolitionists from 1830 through the Civil War* (London: Macmillan, 1970), 31–33, 35, 37, 152–57.
28. EB/GS, Jan. 25, 1841; EB/GS, Dec. 14, 1841; EB/GS, Apr. 16, 1842; EB/GS, June 18, 1842; EB/GS, Sept. 1, 1842. William Chesley Roadman (1784–1849) represented Carter and Washington counties in the Tennessee senate in 1815–17. He later removed to Cocke County, where he was a prominent merchant and postmaster. *BDTGA*, 1:621; Ruth Webb O'Dell, *Over the Misty Blue Hills: The Story of Cocke County, Tennessee* (Newport, Tenn.: Privately printed, 1951), 131–34. Roadman consistently voted against slavery in the 1834 constitutional convention and also against restricting the vote to white men. Temple, *East Tennessee*, 113, 119.
29. EB/GS, Oct. 11, 1841; EB/GS, Jan. 25, 1841; EB/GS, Nov. 4, 1841. Prof. L. F. Clark was appointed in 1839 as "Professor of Chemistry, Natural Philosophy and Natural History" at East Tennessee Univer-

sity. Stanley J. Folmsbee, "Blount College and East Tennessee College, 1749–1840: The First Predecessors of the University of Tennessee," *East Tennessee Historical Society's Publications* 17 (1945): 50.

30. Stanley J. Folmsbee, *Sectionalism and Internal Improvements in Tennessee, 1796–1845* (Knoxville: East Tennessee Historical Society, 1939), 112–215.
31. Ibid., 225–28; EB/GS, Nov. 27, 1841; EB/GS, Dec. 14, 1841. Elijah Embree, brother of the famous abolitionist editor, Elihu, was chairman of the December convention in Knoxville. The *Knoxville Post* argued that the Cumberland Mountains divided East Tennessee "as far asunder" from the remainder of the state as Maine from Georgia, and demanded that the state capital should be located in the eastern part of the state. *Knoxville Post,* Dec. 1, 1841.
32. Folmsbee, *Sectionalism,* 229; Henry Lee Swint, "Ezekiel Birdseye and the Free State of Frankland," *Tennessee Historical Quarterly* 3 (Sept. 1944): 226–36; Tennessee General Assembly, *Senate Journal,* 1841–42, pp. 288, 495; *House Journal,* 1842, pp. 662–63. Typical of the petitions is one from Cocke County requesting an "Independent Bank" in East Tennessee to fund common schools and "Internal Improvements": "From this, it will be readily perceived that the Eastern and Western sections of the State have derived, as yet, but little benefit from the appropriations of the Act above referred to, compared to those which have been obtained by the Middle Division of the State; . . . yet it will be apparent to all that it would be grossly unjust to withhold from the Eastern and Western sections the several amounts due to them in proportion to what has *already been received* by the Middle Section of the State." They also pointed out that, "in proportion to her population and commerce, East Tennessee has less Banking facilities than any other section of the State," and what banking capital "she has is controlled by the direction principally of Directors residing in the Middle section of the State, and who, from this circumstance, are wholly unacquainted with our trade, and are necessarily ignorant of the most advantageous manner in which Banking capital should be used in East Tennessee." Identical petitions were sent from Jefferson, Washington, and Knox counties. Petitions, 1843.
33. EB/GS, Nov. 4, 1841; EB/GS, Nov. 27, 1841; Folmsbee, *Sectionalism,* 216–67. During the 1840s there was genuine statewide two-party

competition in Tennessee between the Whigs and Democrats. See Paul H. Bergeron, *Antebellum Politics in Tennessee* (Lexington: Univ. Press of Kentucky, 1982), 64–102. In his letter of Nov. 4, 1841, Birdseye extensively discussed the state of completion on the Hiwassee Railroad, noting that it was graded from Knoxville to Murray County, Ga., and that the company had erected an iron manufacturing plant in Calhoun, Tenn., to make its rails.

34. W. Todd Groce, "Mountain Rebels: East Tennessee Confederates and the Civil War" (Ph.D. diss., Univ. of Tennessee, Knoxville, 1992), 1–26; Temple, *East Tennessee*, 87–88; Merton E. Coulter, *William G. Brownlow: Fighting Parson of the Southern Highlands* (Chapel Hill: Univ. of North Carolina Press, 1937), 89–109, 136–37, 152, 214–15. For an interesting examination of the bitter religious conflict between Methodist Brownlow and Presbyterian Frederick Augustus Ross, even though both were strong defenders of slavery, see Forrest Conklin and John W. Wittig, "Religious Warfare in the Southern Highlands: Brownlow versus Ross," *Journal of East Tennessee History* 63 (1991): 33–50.

35. Petitions, 1834. The handwriting of the 1834 antislavery petition which Brownlow signed seems very similar to Brownlow's own writing, but the age of the document and broad stroke of the pen used on this memorial from Jefferson County make any conclusive determination difficult. Brownlow at the Holston Conference of 1833 was assigned to the Dandridge Circuit, so he was living in Jefferson County at the time this antislavery petition was written. Richard N. Price, *Holston Methodism from Its Origin to the Present Time* (Nashville: Methodist Publishing House, 1908), 3:278.

36. EB/GS, June 21, 1841; EB/GS, July 10, 1841. Frederick Augustus Ross, "The Autobiography of Frederick Augustus Ross, D.D., in Letters to a Lady of Knoxville, Tennessee, Mrs. Juliet Park White," written in Huntsville, Ala., 1862–63, pp. 97–143; typescript in McClung Historical Collection, Knox County Library, Knoxville, Tenn. Frank Netherland, *A History of the Ross Silk Factory and Other Events of Rotherwood, Tennessee* (Rogersville, Tenn.: East Tennessee Printing Co., 1988), 1–14; Charles C. Ross, ed., *Story of Rotherwood, from the Autobiography of Rev. Frederick A. Ross, D.D.* (Knoxville: Bean, Warters, 1923), 1–35.

37. EB/GS, July 27, 1841; White, "Sketch of the Author," viii; Frederick Augustus Ross, *Slavery Ordained of God* (Philadelphia: J. B.

Lippincott, 1857); Frederick Augustus Ross, *Position of the Southern Church in Relation to Slavery: As Illustrated in a Letter of Dr. F. A. Ross to Rev. Albert Barnes* (New York: J. A. Gray, printer, 1857).

38. Temple, *East Tennessee*, 147–365; Temple, *Notable Men*, 51–55. The best modern studies of East Tennessee and the Civil War are Charles F. Bryan, "The Civil War in East Tennessee: A Social, Political, and Economic Study" (Ph.D. diss., Univ. of Tennessee, Knoxville, 1978), and Groce, "Mountain Rebels." See also John C. Inscoe, "Mountain Unionism, Secession, and Regional Self-Image: The Contrasting Cases of Western North Carolina and East Tennessee," in *Looking South: Chapters in the Story of an American Region*, ed. Winfred B. Moore, Jr., and Joseph F. Tripp, 115–29 (Westport, Conn.: Greenwood, 1989).
39. Groce, "Mountain Rebels," 27–52; Verton M. Queener, "East Tennessee Sentiment and the Secession Movement, November 1860–June 1861," *East Tennessee Historical Society's Publications* 20 (1948): 59–83; Mary Emily Robertson Campbell, *The Attitudes of Tennesseans Toward the Union, 1847–1861* (New York: Vantage Press, 1961), 136–212; Ezra J. Warner, *Generals in Gray: Lives of the Confederate Commanders* (Baton Rouge: Louisiana State Univ. Press, 1959), 231.
40. Temple, *East Tennessee*, 245–74; David Warren Bowen, *Andrew Johnson and the Negro* (Knoxville: Univ. of Tennessee Press, 1989), 45–79. For an examination of the prevailing anti-aristocratic, republican ideology prevalent in East Tennessee and the Upper South in general during the antebellum period, see Daniel W. Crofts, *Reluctant Confederates: Upper South Unionists in the Secession Crisis* (Chapel Hill: Univ. of North Carolina Press, 1989), 158–59. My figures on the referendum of June 8, 1861, are taken from Campbell, *Attitudes of Tennesseans*, 291–92.
41. Caldwell, *Sketches of the Bench and Bar*, 152–59; W. A. Henderson, *Life and Character of Judge McKinney: A Paper Read before the Bar Association of Tennessee, Thursday, July 3rd, 1884* (Nashville: Privately printed, 1884), 4–11. For cases before the Tennessee Supreme Court showing Justice Reese's attitude toward slavery, see *Elias et al. v. Smith et al.*, 25 Tenn. 18–21 (1845); *McCullough v. Fanny Moore, Etc.*, 17 Tenn. 233–34 (1836); *Lewis and Others v. Daniel, Administrator*, 23 Tenn. 209 (1849); *Elijah, a Slave, v. The State*, 20 Tenn. 100–101 (1839); and *Henderson v. Vaulx and Wife*, 18 Tenn. 22–30 (1836). For

similar cases showing Justice McKinney's attitude, see *Lewis v. Simonton*, 27 Tenn. 150 (1847); *The Case of F. Gray*, 28 Tenn. 347–49 (1848); *Sam v. The State*, 31 Tenn. 63–64 (1851); *Ann v. The State*, 30 Tenn. 113–14 (1850); *Jim, a Slave, v. The State*, 23 Tenn. 279–82 (1843); and *W. E. Jones v. John J. Allen*, 38 Tenn. 353–60 (1858).
42. Caldwell, *Sketches of the Bench and Bar*, 139–46; Arthur F. Howington, *What Sayeth the Law: The Treatment of Slaves and Free Blacks in the State and Local Courts of Tennessee* (New York: Garland, 1986), 3–21, 74–81, 167–82, 214, 271.
43. George W. Featherstonhaugh, *Excursion Through the Slave States, from Washington on the Potomac to the Frontier of Mexico; with Sketches of Popular Manners and Geological Notices* (London: John Murray, 1844), 1:163; Frederick Law Olmsted, *A Journey Through the Back Country in the Winter of 1853–54* (New York: Mason Brothers, 1860), 221–90, 293.
44. Olmsted, *Journey Through the Back Country*, 291–330; John C. Inscoe, "Olmsted in Appalachia: A Connecticut Yankee Encounters Slavery and Racism in the Southern Highlands," *Slavery and Abolition* 9 (Sept. 1988): 171–82.
45. Inscoe, "Mountain Unionism, Secession, and Regional Self-Image," 115–29.
46. EB/GS, Mar. 22, 1841.
47. Bryan, "Civil War in East Tennessee," 6–16; Folmsbee, *Sectionalism*, 264–67.
48. Bryan, "Civil War in East Tennessee," 17–19. The percentage of slaves in the total population of East Tennessee varies, depending upon which counties are included. Campbell, *Attitudes of Tennesseans*, 11–33.

Chapter 2. Ezekiel Birdseye

1. Samuel Orcutt, *A History of the Old Town of Stratford and the City of Bridgeport, Connecticut* (New Haven, Conn.: Tuttle, Morehouse and Taylor, 1886), 2:1149. The final *e* occasionally was omitted in earlier references to the Birdseye name.
2. George F. H. Birdseye, comp., and Lucien H. Birdseye, ed., "Outline of the Birdseye Family in America," 1951, typescript in the Connecticut State Library, Hartford, Conn., pp. 26–27.

3. Cornwall Vital Records, 2:65, in Barbour Collection of Connecticut Vital Records Prior to 1850, in the Connecticut Historical Society, Hartford; Orcutt, *History of the Old Town*, 2:1150–51.
4. Ezekiel Birdseye, letter in *New York Emancipator and Republican*, Feb. 23, 1837.
5. Mary Merwin Stone, Birdseye's second wife, whom he married on Feb. 5, 1834, was listed in the 1850 census as living in Cornwall in the home of her parents, the Reverend Timothy and Mary Stone, 7th U.S. Census, 1850 Population Schedule, Litchfield County, Conn.; Cornwall Vital Records, 3:37, in Barbour Collection; George F. H. Birdseye and Lucien H. Birdseye, "Outline of the Birdseye Family," 62. "I hope to be able to leave this spring, and see my wife and daughter," Birdseye wrote in a letter of Feb. 15, 1843, printed in *Christian Freeman*, Apr. 14, 1843.
6. In Newport, Cocke County, Tenn., Birdseye resided in the public house kept by the wife of his good friend, Rev. Spencer Henry. EB/GS, Oct. 11, 1841. Examples of Birdseye's residence during the 1850s being listed as Cornwall, Litchfield County, Conn., are Greene County Deeds, 31:1; and Anderson County Deeds, Book S, 437. All Tennessee county record citations are from the microfilmed collection in the Tennessee State Library and Archives, Nashville, unless otherwise noted.
7. George F. H. Birdseye and Lucien H. Birdseye, "Outline of the Birdseye Family," 61; Will and Inventory of Estate of Ebenezer Birdseye, Court of Probate for the District of Litchfield, Conn., 14:111–12; Cornwall Deeds, 12:6; 12:64; 13:428; MS 72754, Birdseye, Ebenezer (1752–1829), Account Store Book, Cornwall, 1789–1828, in Connecticut Historical Society Library, Hartford.
8. Edward C. Starr, *A History of Cornwall, Connecticut: A Typical New England Town* (New Haven, Conn.: Tuttle, Morehouse and Taylor, 1926), 400.
9. Theodore S. Gold, comp., *Historical Records of the Town of Cornwall, Litchfield County, Connecticut*, 2d ed. (Hartford: Hartford Press, 1904), 277; *BDAC*, 595; George F. H. Birdseye and Lucien H. Birdseye, "Outline of the Birdseye Family," 63–64; O'Dell, *Over the Misty Blue Hills*, 184.
10. Ezekiel Birdseye, letter in *New York Emancipator and Republican*, Feb. 23, 1837.
11. Emily Bellinger Reynolds and Joan Reynolds Faunt, *Biographical Directory of the Senate of South Carolina, 1776–1964* (Columbia: South

Carolina Archives Dept., 1964), 244; N. Louise Bailey, Mary L. Morgan, and Carolyn R. Taylor, *Biographical Directory of the South Carolina Senate, 1776–1985* (Columbia: Univ. of South Carolina Press, 1986), 2:792–93; EB/GS, July 2, 1842; EB/GS, Oct. 17, 1842.

12. *Cyclopedia of Eminent and Representative Men of the Carolinas of the Nineteenth Century* (Madison, Wis.: Brant and Fuller, 1892), 1:219–20; EB/GS, July 2, 1842; Bailey, Morgan, and Taylor, *Biographical Directory of the South Carolina Senate*, 2:793.

13. Stephen Meats and Edwin T. Arnold, eds., *The Writings of Benjamin F. Perry: Essays, Public Letters and Speeches* (Spartanburg, S.C.: Reprint Co. for the Southern Studies Program, Univ. of South Carolina, 1980), 3:127–32; John Belton O'Neall, *Biographical Sketches of the Bench and Bar of South Carolina* (Charleston, S.C.: S. G. Courtenay, 1859), 1:xiii–xxv; EB/GS, June 25, 1841.

14. Rosser H. Taylor, *Ante-Bellum South Carolina: A Social and Cultural History* (Chapel Hill: Univ. of North Carolina Press, 1942), 170; Lacy K. Ford., Jr., *Origins of Southern Radicalism: The South Carolina Upcountry, 1800–1860* (New York: Oxford Univ. Press, 1988), 149, 199, 225, 235; *DAB*, 14:42–43; John Belton O'Neall, *The Negro Law of South Carolina* (Columbia, S.C.: J. G. Bowman, 1848), 1.37–44, 2.35–57; A. E. Keir Nash, "Negro Rights, Unionism, and the Greatness of the South Carolina Court of Appeals: The Extraordinary Chief Justice John Belton O'Neall," *South Carolina Law Review* 21 (1969): 141–90; Alan Watson, *Slave Law in the Americas* (Athens: Univ. of Georgia Press, 1989), 150–52.

15. Will and Inventory of Estate of Lucinda Pierce Birdseye, Court of Probate for the District of Litchfield, Conn., 14:112; Cornwall Vital Records, 2:65, in Barbour Collection; Jean Waldrop Smith, comp., *Limestone County, Alabama, Orphan's Court Minutes, 1822–1830* (Athens, Ala.: Privately printed, 1950), 99, 114, 212, 162; Ezekiel Birdseye, letter of Feb. 15, 1843, in *Christian Freeman*, Apr. 14, 1843. Lucinda Birdseye was buried in the old Athens City Cemetery. Faye A. Axford, ed., *Limestone County, Alabama, Cemeteries: Athens City and Additions* (Athens, Ala.: Limestone County Historical Society, 1979), 3:196. Her tombstone listed her name, date of death as "May, 27, 1828," and the inscription "wife of Ezekiel" and born in "Cornwall, Connecticut."

16. EB/GS, June 21, 1841; EB/GS, Mar. 14, 1842; Ezekiel Birdseye, letter in *New York Emancipator and Republican*, Feb. 23, 1837; Betty Fladeland, *James Gillespie Birney: Slaveholder to Abolitionist* (Ithaca,

N.Y.: Cornell Univ. Press, 1955), 90–124; Inventory of Ezekiel Birdseye's Estate, Court of Probate, Cornwall, Conn., Nov. 8, 1862, 2:210.

17. Cornwall Vital Records, 3:37, in Barbour Collection; George F. H. Birdseye and Lucien H. Birdseye, "Outline of the Birdseye Family," 62.

18. Knox County, Tenn., Administrative Settlements, 15:7–12, 15:33, Knox County Archives, Knoxville, Tenn. Birdseye's will and codicil were recorded in Knox County, where he died in June 1861. His estate later was probated in Cornwall, Conn., Court of Probate, vol. 2, pp. 121, 123, 126, 127, 128, 142, 210, 212, 220, 223, 224, 251, 303, 351.

19. Indications that 1838 was the date of Birdseye's arrival in East Tennessee are interspersed throughout his correspondence. One such is his statement in November 1841 that he "brought 300 Saxon sheep with me three years ago anticipating a ready sale but I found to change the habits of people more especially southern people was a difficult matter." EB/GS, Nov. 4, 1841; EB/GS, June 21, 1841. By 1845, Birdseye was arguing that "it is often asserted in the Northern states that the condition of the slave is made worse by the influence of the abolitionists. Such assertions are incorrect. The abolition excitement has had a beneficial influence on the condition of the slave." EB/GS, June 18, 1845.

20. EB/GS, Jan. 25, 1841; EB/GS, June 21, 1841; EB/GS, Oct. 11, 1841; EB/GS, Nov. 4, 1841; EB/GS, May 21, 1842. See also Lawrence J. Friedman, *Gregarious Saints: Self and Community in American Abolitionism, 1830–1870* (Cambridge, England: Cambridge Univ. Press, 1982); Merton L. Dillon, *The Abolitionists: The Growth of a Dissenting Minority* (DeKalb: Northern Illinois Univ. Press, 1974); Mabee, *Black Freedom*; Louis Filler, *The Crusade Against Slavery, 1830–1860* (New York: Harper, 1960); Lewis Perry and Michael Fellman, eds., *Antislavery Reconsidered: New Perspectives on the Abolitionists* (Baton Rouge: Louisiana State Univ. Press, 1979).

21. EB/GS, Oct. 17, 1842. This incidence of miscegenation recalls Mary Boykin Chesnut's famous comment in 1861: "Like the patriarchs of old, our men live all in one house with their wives and their concubines; and the mulattoes one sees in every family partly resemble the white children." C. Vann Woodward, ed., *Mary Chesnut's Civil War* (New Haven, Conn.: Yale Univ. Press, 1981), 29–31.

22. EB/GS, Jan. 25, 1841; EB/GS, Mar. 22, 1841; EB/GS, Apr. 16,

1841; EB/GS, July 2, 1842; EB/GS, June 18, 1845; EB/GS, Nov. 28, 1845; EB/GS, Dec. 29, 1845; EB/GS, Jan. 20, 1846. Nicholas W. Woodfin, prominent Asheville lawyer and legislator, was the second largest slaveholder in western North Carolina in 1860. He did make financial sacrifices upon occasion, however, to respect black family ties. A strong Whig who would later support the Confederacy, Woodfin generally was a permissive, kindly master who had a sense of moral responsibility toward his slaves. John C. Inscoe, *Mountain Masters, Slavery, and the Sectional Crisis in Western North Carolina* (Knoxville: Univ. of Tennessee Press, 1989), 65, 91, 104, 144.

23. EB/GS, Oct. 11, 1841. Dr. Anderson had one other black theological student who was ordained to the ministry in Maryville by the Union Presbytery before 1810. Following Dr. Anderson's tradition, Maryville College admitted blacks after the Civil War until they were barred by a state law in 1901. *Maryville Record,* July 8, 1904; Burns, *Blount County,* 39, 59, 161; Shick, *Emigrants to Liberia,* 43; Wiley, *Slaves No More,* 215–36, 240, 309.

24. EB/GS, July 10, 1841; EB/GS, June 18, 1842; EB/GS, Oct. 17, 1842. See also McKivigan, *War Against Proslavery Religion,* 18–92.

25. EB/GS, Mar. 22, 1841; EB/GS, June 21, 1841; EB/GS, June 25, 1841. According to his biographer, Morehead did not believe in slavery and earlier had voted for allowing free Negroes to vote and for the education of Negroes. He owned slaves but had presented Quaker memorials against slavery to the state legislature. He nevertheless believed that, while slavery was a "curse to the American people," it was so established by law and custom that nothing could alter its existence. Burton Alva Konkle, *John Motley Morehead and the Development of North Carolina, 1796–1866* (Philadelphia: William J. Campbell, 1922), 194–95. The best and most thorough study of the antislavery movement in North Carolina concludes that abolitionism never captured a substantial following among any group in that state other than the Quakers, and that whatever feeble effort they were able to mount was substantially moribund prior to the rise of northern abolitionism. John Michael Shay, "The Antislavery Movement in North Carolina" (Ph.D. diss., Princeton Univ., 1971), 501–14.

26. EB/GS, July 27, 1841; Inventory of Ezekiel Birdseye's Estate, Court of Probate, Cornwall, Conn., Nov. 8, 1862, 2:210.

27. EB/GS, Apr. 16, 1842; EB/GS, Mar. 14, 1842; EB/GS, Dec. 14, 1841.

28. EB/GS, June 18, 1842; EB/GS, Sept. 1, 1842; EB/GS, Sept. 24, 1842; EB/GS, Oct. 17, 1842.
29. EB/GS, Sept. 1, 1842. Tennessee law prescribed "confinement in the penitentiary at hard labor for a period of not less than five nor more than ten years" for inciting a slave to "insubordination, insurrection, or rebellion" by any writing or by "words or gestures, with malicious intent." Return J. Meigs and William F. Cooper, eds., *The Code of Tennessee, Enacted by the General Assembly of 1857–58* (Nashville: E. G. Eastman and Co., State Publishers, 1858), 517–18.
30. EB/GS, June 25, 1841; EB/GS, Sept. 2, 1841, EB/GS, Feb. 7, 1842.
31. EB/GS, June 25, 1841. The best scholarly examination of southern honor, violence, and dueling is Bertram Wyatt-Brown, *Southern Honor: Ethics and Behavior in the Old South* (New York: Oxford Univ. Press, 1982).
32. EB/GS, Mar. 22, 1841; EB/GS, June 21, 1841; EB/GS, Aug. 7, 1841; EB/GS, May 21, 1842; EB/GS, June 18, 1842, EB/GS, Oct. 17, 1842. Abel Pearson (1779–1856), a student of Dr. Isaac Anderson at Maryville College, in 1815 petitioned the Blount County Court for the emancipation of George Erskine, a black later educated by Dr. Anderson and sent to Liberia as a missionary. Pearson moved to Hamilton County, Tenn., where he organized and served as the first minister of the Soddy Presbyterian Church in 1828. Burns, *Blount County*, 39; Zella Armstrong, *The History of Hamilton County and Chattanooga, Tennessee* (Chattanooga: Lookout Publishing Co., 1931), vol. 1, pp. 114, 199, 242, 244, 266, 318; Abel Pearson, *An Analysis of the Principles of the Divine Government* (Athens, Tenn.: William P. Reid, 1833). Birdseye's description of the close links in East Tennessee among temperance, abolitionism, and evangelical religion supports the analysis of James Brewer Stewart, "Evangelicalism and the Radical Strain in Southern Antislavery Thought During the 1820s," *Journal of Southern History* 39 (Aug. 1973): 379–96.
33. EB/GS, Mar. 22, 1841; EB/GS, June 21, 1841; EB/GS, Dec. 14, 1841; *History of Tennessee, Containing Historical and Biographical Sketches*, 899; Coulter, *William G. Brownlow*, 38–40, 120. Recent scholarship on Parson Brownlow's temperance activities contains no indication that he himself occasionally drank "too freely." See Forest Conklin, "Parson Brownlow Joins the Sons of Temperance, Part I," *Tennessee Historical Quarterly* 39 (Summer, 1980): 178–94; Forest

Conklin, "Parson Brownlow—Temperance Advocate, Part II," *Tennessee Historical Quarterly* 39 (Fall 1980): 292–309.
34. EB/GS, Dec. 14, 1841; Mary U. Rothrock, ed., *The French Broad–Holston Country: A History of Knox County, Tennessee* (Knoxville: East Tennessee Historical Society, 1946), 500–501; Mayme Parrott Wood, *Hitch Hiking Along the Holston River, 1792–1962* (Gatlinburg, Tenn.: Brazos Printing Co., 1964), 63–64.
35. EB/GS, Sept. 2, 1841; EB/GS, Aug. 7, 1841. Joseph Manning (1806–1883) was a leader in organizing the East Tennessee Association of Baptists. He preached in primarily East Tennessee Baptist churches for 50 years, serving in Cocke County for 21 years. James J. Burnett, *Sketches of Tennessee's Pioneer Baptist Preachers* (Nashville: Marshall and Bruce, 1919), 345–49.
36. EB/GS, Oct. 11, 1841; EB/GS, May 21, 1842; W. Russell Briscoe and Katherine Boies Buehler, *Her Walls Before Thee Stand: History of the Second Presbyterian Church, 1818–1968* (Knoxville, Tenn.: Privately printed, 1968), 15.
37. EB/GS, Mar. 14, 1842; Burns, *Blount County*, 59, 105; Asa Earl Martin, "Anti-Slavery Societies of Tennessee," 278, 280.
38. EB/GS, Feb. 7, 1842; EB/GS, Oct. 11, 1841; EB/GS, Dec. 14, 1841. William Potter (1796–1891), a native of Lisbon, Conn., served as missionary and established a school at Creek Path, Ala. (present-day Guntersville), that operated from 1821 to 1837. Robert Sparks Walker, *Torchlights to the Cherokees: The Brainerd Mission* (New York: Macmillan, 1931), 46; William G. McLoughlin, *Cherokees and Missionaries, 1789–1839* (New Haven, Conn.: Yale Univ. Press, 1984), 196, 209, 235, 256, 301, 306, 309. Conflict between evangelicals and abolitionists in the American Board of Commissioners for Foreign Missions is carefully analyzed in Robert T. Lewit, "Indian Missions and Antislavery Sentiment: A Conflict of Evangelical and Humanitarian Ideals," *Mississippi Valley Historical Review* 50 (June 1963): 39–55.
39. Lawrence J. Friedman, "The Gerrit Smith Circle: Abolitionism in the Burned Over District," *Civil War History* 26 (Mar. 1980): 18–38; Ralph Volney Harlow, *Gerrit Smith: Philanthropist and Reformer* (New York: Henry Holt, 1939), 237–85; Octavius Brooks Frothingham, *Gerrit Smith: A Biography* (New York: G. P. Putnam's Sons, 1878), 44–266.

40. Gerald Sorin, *The New York Abolitionists: A Case Study of Political Radicalism* (Westport, Conn.: Greenwood, 1971), 26–38; Lawrence J. Friedman, *Gregarious Saints*, 29–126; Harlow, *Gerrit Smith*, 22–45; *DAB*, 17:270–71; Lewis Perry, *Radical Abolitionism: Anarchy and the Government of God in Antislavery Thought* (Ithaca, N.Y.: Cornell Univ. Press, 1973), 62–63, 106, 179–81.
41. Lawrence J. Friedman, *Gregarious Saints*, 105. Merton Dillon argues that Gerrit Smith, in an 1842 speech to a Liberty Party convention, made a critical shift "away from the policies of pacifism and disengagement" of the American Anti-Slavery Society, a shift that "stands as a milestone in the process that would lead to the destruction of slavery." Merton L. Dillon, *Slavery Attacked: Southern Slaves and Their Allies, 1619–1865* (Baton Rouge: Louisiana State Univ. Press, 1990), 208.
42. Sorin, *New York Abolitionists*, 31–37; Alice Hatcher Henderson, "The History of the New York State Anti-Slavery Society" (Ph.D. diss., Univ. of Michigan, 1963), 100–383; Harlow, *Gerrit Smith*, 391–422; Frothingham, *Gerrit Smith: A Biography*, 230–47; Dillon, *The Abolitionists*, 230–32.
43. Harlow, *Gerrit Smith*, 270; EB/GS, Jan. 25, 1841; EB/GS, Mar. 22, 1841; EB/GS, Nov. 27, 1841. Even in the late 1850s, Gerrit Smith still was endorsing compensation of slaveholders who emancipated their slaves. Lawrence J. Friedman, *Gregarious Saints*, 124.
44. EB/GS, Nov. 28, 1845; EB/GS, Jan. 20, 1846. The best study of Lewis Tappan is Bertram Wyatt-Brown, *Lewis Tappan and the Evangelical War Against Slavery* (Cleveland, Ohio: Press of Case Western Univ., 1969). For Lewis Tappan's correspondence with Ezekiel Birdseye, see Papers of Lewis Tappan, Container 6, Reel 3, Letterbook Mar. 10, 1846–Nov. 4, 1847, pp. 69–92, Library of Congress, Washington, D.C. Publication of Ezekiel Birdseye's letters in abolitionist newspapers is difficult to verify because of the incomplete collection available for both *Emancipator* and *Friend of Man*. The following examples have been located: EB/GS, Oct. 11, 1841, was published in *Friend of Man*, Nov, 9, 1841; EB/GS, Nov. 27, 1841, in *Friend of Man*, Jan. 11, 1842; EB/GS, Mar. 14, 1842, in *Emancipator*, Apr. 28, 1842; EB/GS, June 18, 1845, in *Utica (N.Y.) Liberty Press*, July 19, 1845; and EB/GS, Mar. 2, 1846, in *Emancipator*, May 13, 1846. Internal evidence exists in the Birdseye correspondence that many more letters were published than are present in the Smith

Collection. E.g., in EB/GS, Mar. 22, 1841, Birdseye mentions two errors in the printed copy of his letter in *Friend of Man*, Jan. 19, 1841. Four letters from Gerrit Smith to Ezekiel Birdseye are in the Smith Papers.
45. EB/GS, June 18, 1842; EB/GS, Oct. 17, 1842.
46. EB/GS, Nov. 4, 1841.

Chapter 3. Entrepreneurship, Capitalism, Economic Progress, and Abolitionism

1. Thomas Bender, ed., *The Antislavery Debate: Capitalism and Abolitionism as a Problem in Historical Interpretation* (Berkeley: Univ. of California Press, 1992); David Brion Davis, *The Problem of Slavery in Western Culture* (Ithaca, N.Y.: Cornell Univ. Press, 1966); David Brion Davis, *The Problem of Slavery in the Age of Revolution, 1770–1823* (Ithaca, N.Y.: Cornell Univ. Press, 1975); Eugene D. Genovese, *The Political Economy of Slavery* (New York: Pantheon, 1965); Eric Foner, *Politics and Ideology in the Age of the Civil War* (New York: Oxford Univ. Press, 1980); and Eric Williams, *Capitalism and Slavery* (Chapel Hill: Univ. of North Carolina Press, 1944).
2. Ezekiel Birdseye, letter in *New York Emancipator and Republican*, Feb. 23, 1837.
3. EB/GS, July 27, 1841; EB/GS, Jan. 25, 1841. A common theme among abolitionists was that slavery denigrated labor in the South by identifying work with servility, and this denigration had particularly pernicious effects on poor whites. Robert William Fogel, *Without Consent or Contract: The Rise and Fall of American Slavery* (New York: W. W. Norton, 1989), 328. For the application of this theme to East Tennessee, see Thomas William Humes, *The Loyal Mountaineers of Tennessee* (Knoxville: Ogden Brothers and Co., 1888), 30–31.
4. Dillon, *Benjamin Lundy*, 33, 43–44. Although initially a slaveholder himself, Elihu Embree freed most of his slaves after conversion to abolitionism in 1812 and kept several others only because he wished to keep the family of slaves together. He successfully explained these circumstances in *Emancipator*, Aug. 31, 1820. Other scholars have noted that in 1808 Embree paid Alfred M. Carter $1,000 for a skilled Negro worker whom he probably used in his iron works. Robert T. Nave, "A History of the Iron Industry in Carter County to 1860" (M.A. thesis, East Tennessee State Univ., 1953), 73; Frank Merrit,

Early History of Carter County, 1760–1861 (Knoxville: East Tennessee Historical Society, 1950), 153. "I repent I ever owned one," Embree said in regard to his connection to slavery. "And indeed the crime is of such a hue, that the time may yet come, that a man who has, in a single instance, gone astray thus far, may never be able in his life time to regain public confidence; and should this change of public sentiment take place in my day, and render me disqualified to act in the promotion of this glorious cause, I hope to acquiesce in, and be resigned to suffer the just judgment, and be more humble under a sense of my past misconduct." Quoted in Patterson, *Negro in Tennessee,* 184–85.

5. Asa Earl Martin, "Anti-Slavery Societies of Tennessee," 261–81; Asa Earl Martin, "Pioneer Anti-Slavery Press," 509–28; Dillon, "Three Southern Antislavery Editors," 47–56; Elijah Embree Hoss, "Elihu Embree, Abolitionist," *American Historical Magazine* 2 (1897): 113–38; White, "Sketch of the Author," v–xi. See also Finnie, "Antislavery Movement in the South," 208–57.

6. Paul M. Fink, "The Bumpass Cove Mines and Embreeville," *East Tennessee Historical Society's Publications* 16 (1944): 48–64; Raymond F. Hunt, Jr., "The Pactolus Ironworks," *Tennessee Historical Quarterly* 25 (Summer 1966): 176–96; L. R. Ahern, Jr., and R. F. Hunt, Jr., "The Boatyard Store, 1814–1825," *Tennessee Historical Quarterly* 14 (Sept. 1955): 271; Samuel Cole Williams, ed., "Journal of Events (1825–1873) of David Anderson Deaderick," pt. 2, *East Tennessee Historical Society's Publications* 9 (1937): 93–110; Pactolus Iron Works Account Book, 1811–15, in Southern Historical Collection, Wilson Library, Univ. of North Carolina at Chapel Hill. Sullivan County Deeds, Book 2, pp. 371, 506; Book 3, pp. 185, 187; Book 4, p. 699; Book 6, p. 403; Book 7, pp. 124, 315; Book 8, p. 63; Book 10, pp. 41, 43, 45, 285, 286. See also Washington County Deeds, Books 9–15, *passim,* for Elihu Embree's numerous transactions. The editor of the *Nashville Gazette* knew Embree personally and in his obituary noted that Embree's iron works, "though embarked in for individual benefit, were of a nature which tended much to the public good." Quoted in Philip M. Hamer, ed., *Tennessee: A History, 1673–1932* (New York: American Historical Society, 1933), 1:459–60.

7. *Niles' Weekly Register,* Feb. 3, 1821, 9:384; *Niles' Weekly Register,* July 4, 1818, 14:321; *Tennessee Acts,* 1821, ch. 161.

8. Burns, *Blount County,* 39, 59, 161; Samuel Tyndale Wilson, *A Century of Maryville College, 1819–1919, A Story of Altruism* (Maryville, Tenn.:

Maryville College, 1919), 30; Samuel Tyndale Wilson, *Isaac Anderson*, 38; Shick, *Emigrants to Liberia*, 43; Wiley, *Slaves No More*, 215–36, 240, 309; EB/GS, Oct. 11, 1841. The most complete information I have found on the later careers of George M. Erskine and John Gloucester is in Rankin, *Truth Vindicated*, 5–6.

9. White, "Sketch of the Author," x; *Emancipator*, Mar. 8 and 16, 1838; Asa Earl Martin, "Anti-Slavery Societies of Tennessee," 278; Will A. McTeer, *A History of New Providence Presbyterian Church, Maryville, Tennessee, 1786–1921* (Maryville, Tenn.: New Providence Church, 1921), 43–44. The letter from a student at the Maryville Theological Seminary, dated Feb. 27, 1838, to the editor of the *Emancipator* also was partially quoted in *The New England Anti-Slavery Almanac for 1841* (Boston: J. A. Collins, 1841), 30.

10. EB/GS, Oct. 11, 1841; EB/GS, Dec. 14, 1841; Burns, *Blount County*, 41, 187; *Tennessee Acts*, 1833, ch. 34; *Tennessee Acts*, 1851–52, ch. 261; Blount County Deeds, 1840–60, *passim*; John Preston Arthur, *Western North Carolina: A History from 1730 to 1913* (Raleigh, N.C.: Edwards and Broughton, 1914), 241; Durwood Dunn, *Cades Cove: The Life and Death of a Southern Appalachian Community, 1818–1937* (Knoxville: Univ. of Tennessee Press, 1988), 80, 84–88, 111, 125, 140, 168, 217n, 278n, 284n; John J. Robinson, *Memoir of Rev. Isaac Anderson, D.D.* (Knoxville, Tenn.: J. A. Rayl, 1860), 153–56.

11. Robinson says that Anderson "in his benevolence was no respecter of persons. The African, the Indian, the foreigner from whatever land, was to him as a brother"; Robinson, *Memoir of Anderson*, 146. Samuel Tyndale Wilson, *Isaac Anderson*, 71–72; EB/GS, Nov. 27, 1841; EB/GS, Dec. 14, 1841. See also Lester C. Lamon, "Ignoring the Color Line: Maryville College, 1868–1901," in *The Adaptable South: Essays in Honor of George Brown Tindall*, ed. Elizabeth Jacoway, Dan T. Carter, Lester C. Lamon, and Robert C. McMath, Jr., 64–68 (Baton Rouge: Louisiana State Univ. Press, 1991).

12. Robinson, *Memoir of Anderson*, 153–54; Samuel Tyndale Wilson, *Isaac Anderson*, 63–71, 88, 118; EB/GS, Oct. 11, 1841.

13. *History of Tennessee, Containing Historical and Biographical Sketches*, 858; John W. Green, *Lives of the Judges of the Supreme Court of Tennessee, 1796–1947* (Knoxville: Archer and Smith, 1947), 80–81; *BDTGA*, 1:577–78; Caldwell, *Sketches of the Bench and Bar*, 62–63; George Braden Roberts, *Genealogy of Joseph Peck and Some Related Families* (Washington, D.C.: Privately printed, 1955), 24.

14. O'Dell, *Over the Misty Blue Hills*, 128–29; Caldwell, *Sketches of the*

Bench and Bar, 63; Hari von Beck, *Chronicles of the Peck Family* (Jefferson City, Tenn.: Privately printed, 1956), 1–13. Judge Peck's reports are in *Reports of Cases Argued and Adjudged in the Supreme Court of Errors and Appeals of the State of Tennessee, Commencing September Term, 1822, and Ending with May Term, 1824, by Jacob Peck, One of the Judges* (N.p: n.d.). During the 19th century, cases from the Tennessee Supreme Court were cited by the editor of that particular volume; e.g., *Gordon v. Farquhar*, Peck 155, June 1823. Hereafter, cases will be cited using the name of the case, volume in *Tennessee Reports*, page nos., and year.

15. Jacob Peck to Gerrit Smith, Nov. 30, 1841, Smith Papers; EB/GS, Nov. 27, 1841; EB/GS, Dec. 14, 1841.
16. *Niles' Weekly Register*, Nov. 10, 1821, 21:173–74; Temple, *East Tennessee*, 110–11.
17. *Bob, a Slave v. The State*, 10 Tenn. 155–72 (1826). For an extensive analysis of this particular case, see Howington, *What Sayeth the Law*, 142–43, 148, 158–63. This was not the first instance in which a slave court decision was appealed; Judge Peck wrote in this decision that he knew of "two instances, where the circuit court has controlled the convictions of slaves by such tribunal." See also Andrew Fede, "Toward a Solution of the Slave Law Dilemma: A Critique of Tushnet's *The American Law of Slavery*," *Law and History Review* 2 (Fall 1984): 301–20.
18. *Blackmore and Hadley v. Negro Phill*, 15 Tenn. 297–307 (1835). According to Tennessee law at the time, slaves could not be liberated without the assent of the legislature or the county court of the county where the owner resided. An act passed in December 1831 made it unlawful for any court or owner to emancipate a slave except on express condition that such slave "shall be immediately removed from this state." The owner was to give bond for the fulfillment of this requirement equal to the value of the slave. *Tennessee Acts*, ch. 102, sec. 2.
19. *Fisher's Negroes v. Dabbs and Others*, 14 Tenn. 78–111 (1834). Judge Peck argued at great length in this case about the need for courts jealously to guard jurisdictions entrusted to them:

> Courts to whom a jurisdiction is given by express terms are always jealous of encroachment upon that jurisdiction, and this for an

obvious reason. The care of certain rights is committed; the courts should see these rights are preserved. It belongs to them; and the mind of the judge, of necessity, must be directed to the objects of its care. Hence the writ of prohibition which is used in those cases where a jurisdiction is assumed which cannot be rightfully exercised; as, where a military tribunal was proceeding, having no jurisdiction of the person charged. So, too, in the cases in our own state, where military tribunals imposed fines, not having jurisdiction of the person (Durham's case), and in the still more noted case of the Indian Tassels, in Georgia. These all illustrate the necessity of the court having jurisdiction taking care that no encroachment shall be made upon that jurisdiction which is obviously clothed with the right; and this jealousy is just as important in questions of property or freedom as in the case affecting life.

20. *William Fields v. State of Tennessee,* 9 Tenn. 141–50 (1829). See also Howington, *What Sayeth the Law,* 85–86.
21. *Walker and Others, v. Wynne and Others* 11 Tenn. 62–73 (1832); *Black, Bates, and Parmington v. The State,* 11 Tenn. 588–89 (1832); *Abraham Vaughan v. Phebe, a Woman of Color,* 8 Tenn. 389–404 (1827). In this last case, Judge Crabb delivered the unanimous opinion of the court, concluding that "it is difficult to suppose a case where common reputation would concede to a man the right to freedom if his right were a groundless one." Freedom was "something substantial," he argued, which placed a man, "even if he be black," in "many respects on an equality with the richest and the greatest and the best in the land."
22. EB/GS, Aug. 7, 1841.
23. Peck's Notes, McClung Historical Collection, Knox County Public Library, Knoxville, Tenn. Unfortunately, the pages in this valuable manuscript are not numbered. For an appraisal of Abraham Gottlob Werner and Sir Charles Lyell in the development of 19th-century geological science, see Mott T. Greene, *Geology in the Nineteenth Century: Changing Views of a Changing World* (Ithaca, N.Y.: Cornell Univ. Press, 1982), 24–144.
24. Peck's Notes; Jacob Peck, "Geological and Mineralogical Account of the Mining Districts in the State of Georgia—Western Part of North Carolina and East Tennessee, with a Map," *American Journal of Science*

and Arts 23 (1833): 1–10. One recent historian of the Georgia gold rush says that Jacob Peck's 1833 article in the *American Journal of Science and Arts* is the closest thing to contemporary documentation about the origins of the Georgia gold rush. David Williams, *The Georgia Gold Rush: Twenty-Niners, Cherokees, and Gold Fever* (Columbia, S.C.: Univ. of South Carolina Press, 1993), 22.

25. Peck's Notes.
26. Ibid.; L. C. Glenn, "Gerard Troost," *American Geologist* 35 (Feb. 1905): 72–94; *DAB*, 18:647–48; Henry Grady Rooker, "A Sketch of the Life and Work of Dr. Gerard Troost," *Tennessee Historical Magazine,* 2d ser., 3 (1935 for 1933): 3–19; James X. Corgan, "Early American Geological Surveys and Gerard Troost's Field Assistants, 1831–1836," in *The Geological Sciences in the Antebellum South,* ed. James X. Corgan, 39–72 (Tuscaloosa: Univ. of Alabama Press, 1982); EB/GS, Aug. 7, 1841. Dr. Troost presented 10 reports on the geology of Tennessee to the state legislature between 1832 and 1850; all of these reports are extant except the last, presented in 1850. Troost had studied in Paris as the pupil of the famous French mineralogist and crystallographer, Abbé René Just Hauy (1743–1822). Troost was a member of many learned societies in Europe and the U.S.; a bibliography of his writings contains articles on geology, natural history, chemistry, ethnology, mineralogy, and crystallography; Glenn, "Gerard Troost," 90–94. For his academic career at the Univ. of Nashville, 1828–50, see Henry Lee Swint, "Higher Education in the Tennessee-Kentucky Region a Century Ago," *Tennessee Historical Quarterly* 2 (July 1943): 133–36.
27. Peck's Notes; Pollyanna Creekmore, comp., "Early East Tennessee Taxpayers: XIII. Cocke County, 1839," *East Tennessee Historical Society's Publications* 37 (1965): 126, 138.
28. Jacob Peck to Gerrit Smith, Nov. 30, 1841, Smith Papers; EB/GS, Jan. 25, 1841; EB/GS, Mar. 22, 1841; EB/GS, June 21, 1841; EB/GS, July 10, 1841; EB/GS, Aug. 7, 1841; EB/GS, Nov. 27, 1841; EB/GS, Dec. 14, 1841.
29. EB/GS, Jan. 25, 1841.

> The first locality of iron ore that I examined was near Long Creek, on the property of Mr. E. Birdseye. On his premises are found several deposites, which are remote the one from the other, but not so far but that the ore from them may with convenience be

employed at one furnace. These ores are not of the same quality. The quality of iron which each contains will be mentioned in another part of this report. I will here only state there seems to be no doubt but that there is great abundance of ore. It is situated in gently rolling country, which is mostly all under cultivation, possessing an excellent soil, which is not always the case in mining countries. Indeed there is found here everything requisite for the establishment of iron works, plenty of ore, abundance of timber of the best kind for coal, ample quarries of good limestone, and I believe Long Creek will afford a copious supply of water to drive any machinery needed for such an establishment; at least it afforded a sufficient quantity when I was there in September of this year, a year remarkable for the long continued drought, which has drained most of our streams; but even if this creek should fail, these deposites are only about two miles from the French Broad, which never gives out. (Gerard Troost, *Fifth Geological Report to the 23rd General Assembly of Tennessee, Made November, 1839* [Nashville: J. Geo. Harris, Public Printer, 1840], 23)

30. EB/GS, Aug. 7, 1841. "They will venture no open attack on me," Birdseye wrote in regard to the article in the *Knoxville Register*, "but may try to employ some assassin." EB/GS, Apr. 16, 1842. Gerrit Smith to William Ellery Channing, Sept. 6, 1841, letterbook copy, Smith Papers. For an excellent analysis of these antislavery colonies in the Upper South, see Harrold, *Abolitionists and the South*, 107–26.
31. EB/GS, Aug. 7, 1841. Fellenberg schools in the U.S. were patterned after Philip Fellenberg's school, Hofuyl, near Berne, Switzerland, a 200-acre farm where young men and women from all classes engaged in physical labor along with academic training to demonstrate that all labor was useful and honorable. For the best discussion of the connection between abolitionism and the manual labor movement, see Paul Goodman, "The Manual Labor Movement and the Origins of Abolitionism," *Journal of the Early Republic* 13 (Fall 1993): 355–88.
32. *Nashville Gazette*, Dec. 23, 1820. Judge Peck expressed an identical sentiment when he boasted to Gerrit Smith of having introduced Ezekiel Birdseye "into a business which may result in profit to himself and humanity to others." Jacob Peck to Gerrit Smith, Nov. 30, 1841, Smith Papers.
33. Temple, *East Tennessee*, 87–88; *History of Tennessee, Containing*

Historical and Biographical Sketches, 862, 882, 1163–64; EB/GS, July 10, 1841; John Caldwell to Gerrit Smith, June 14, 1841, Smith Papers.

34. EB/GS, June 21, 1841; EB/GS, July 10, 1841; EB/GS, Oct. 11, 1841; Joshua W. Caldwell, *A Memorial Volume Containing His Biography, Writings and Addresses: Prepared and Edited by a Committee of the Irving Club of Knoxville, Tennessee* (Nashville: Brandon Printing Co., 1909), 7–8, 55–56.

35. EB/GS, July 10, 1841; EB/GS, July 27, 1841; EB/GS, Oct. 11, 1841; EB/GS, Nov. 27, 1841; Jefferson County Deeds, Book W, 570–71; John Caldwell to Gerrit Smith, June 14, 1841, and Aug. 28, 1842, Smith Papers.

36. Mayme Parrott Wood, *Drifting Down Holston River Way, 1756–1966* (Maryville, Tenn.: Privately printed, 1966), 41. According to Wood, John Caldwell held no office except that of pension agent at Knoxville under Andrew Johnson. James Merrill Safford, *A Geological Reconnaissance of the State of Tennessee; Being the Author's First Biennial Report, Presented to the 31st General Assembly of Tennessee, December, 1855* (Nashville: G. C. Torbett and Co., State Printers, 1856), 61. Safford stated in a later book that, "in July 1858, John Caldwell, Esq., of Jefferson County, was kind enough to accompany me through this group of coves. His knowledge of the country, and the researches he himself has made in this region, enabled him to render valuable assistance." James M. Safford, *Geology of Tennessee* (Nashville: S. C. Mercer, 1869), 52.

37. John Caldwell to Dr. R. O. Currey and C. A. Proctor, Ducktown, 1855, quoted in Richard Owen Currey, *A Sketch of the Geology of Tennessee: Embracing a Description of Its Minerals and Ores, Their Variety and Quality, Modes of Assaying and Value; with a Description of Its Soils and Productiveness, and Palaeontology* (Knoxville: Kinsloe and Rice, 1857), 75–76. This letter first appeared in print in somewhat abbreviated form in Safford, *Geological Reconnaissance,* 61–62.

38. R. E. Barclay, *Ducktown Back in Raht's Time* (Chapel Hill: Univ. of North Carolina Press, 1946), 46–134. Judge Jacob Peck commented extensively on the productivity of the Ducktown copper mines before and after the Civil War. Peck's Notes, *passim.*

39. Inventory of Ezekiel Birdseye's Estate, Court of Probate, Cornwall, Conn., Nov. 8, 1862, 2:210–11; Clement Eaton, *A History of the*

Southern Confederacy (New York: Macmillan, 1954), 136; Frank E. Vandiver, *Ploughshares into Swords: Josiah Gorgas and the Confederate Ordinance* (Austin: Univ. of Texas Press, 1952), 201–2. During the war, Confederate authorities confiscated the Ducktown mines, which were owned largely by northern capitalists. Interest in these mines was returned to the rightful owners after the war, but there is no indication that a separate "Caldwell Copper Mining Company" survived. Barclay, *Ducktown,* 87–101.

40. Claiborne County Deeds, Book W, 391–93; Safford, *Geological Reconnaissance,* 72.
41. *Nashville Daily Press and Times,* Feb. 12, 1868.
42. Ibid., EB/GS, Jan. 25, 1841; EB/GS, July 27, 1841; EB/GS, Aug. 7, 1841; EB/GS, Oct. 11, 1841.
43. Ronald D Eller, *Miners, Millhands, and Mountaineers: Industrialization of the Appalachian South, 1880–1930* (Knoxville: Univ. of Tennessee Press, 1982), 39–242. See also Gordon B. McKinney, *Southern Mountain Republicans, 1865–1900: Politics and the Appalachian Community* (Chapel Hill: Univ. of North Carolina Press, 1978), 30–141; and Henry D. Shapiro, *Appalachia on Our Mind: The Southern Mountains and Mountaineers in the American Consciousness, 1870–1920* (Chapel Hill: Univ. of North Carolina Press, 1978), 157–84.
44. Barclay, *Ducktown,* 78–80; Fink, "The Bumpass Cove Mines and Embreeville," 48–64. Successful completion of railroad construction in East Tennessee was delayed until the 1850s because of financial problems resulting from the depression following the Panic of 1837 and bitter intrastate sectional rivalry. As a delegate from Cocke County, Ezekiel Birdseye attended a convention in Knoxville on Dec. 13–14, 1841, to attempt to resolve differences among competing interests opposed to completing a railroad through East Tennessee—specifically, the Hiwassee Railroad from Knoxville to the Georgia state line. Failure of the legislature to act upon this convention's recommendations, due to consistent opposition from Middle Tennessee, led directly to the development of a vigorous movement for separate statehood for East Tennessee, a movement enthusiastically supported by Birdseye. Folmsbee, *Sectionalism,* 222–32; EB/GS, Dec. 14, 1841. Another major regional industry, the East Tennessee Iron Manufacturing Co. in Chattanooga, was purchased in 1858 by Thomas Webster and R. D. Mann, both English immigrants. Al-

though slave labor probably was used in this industry, the majority of Chattanooga's skilled industrial work force was foreign immigrant labor, trained either in Europe or the American Northeast before coming to Tennessee. R. Bruce Council, Nicholas Honerkamp, and M. Elizabeth Will, *Industry and Technology in Antebellum Tennessee: The Archaeology of Bluff Furnace* (Knoxville: Univ. of Tennessee Press, 1992), 69, 75.

45. Anderson County Deeds, Book S, 437–38; Claiborne County Deeds, Book W, 389–92 and 415–17; Greene County Deeds, 31:1–13; Jefferson County Deeds, 4:59–62, 3:1–13, 3:75–80; EB/GS, Nov. 28, 1845; EB/GS, Jan. 20, 1846. For Lewis Tappan's correspondence to Ezekiel Birdseye, see Papers of Lewis Tappan, Container 6, Reel 3, Letterbook Mar. 10, 1846–Nov. 4, 1847, pp. 69–70, 76, 85–89, Library of Congress, Washington, D.C. For Lewis Tappan's efforts to acquire mercantile agents in the South, see Wyatt-Brown, *Lewis Tappan*, 226–47.

46. EB/GS, Sept. 24, 1842; EB/GS, Nov. 28, 1845; EB/GS, Jan. 20, 1846. The only existing public records of land owned by Ezekiel Birdseye in Cocke County, other than an 1839 tax list, concern two tracts, one for 3,000 acres acquired Sept. 29, 1841, the other for 5,000 acres acquired Sept. 1, 1840. State of Tennessee, Surveyor's Office, Cocke County Land Entries, pp. 444–45, Tennessee State Library and Archives, Nashville.

47. EB/GS, Nov. 28, 1845; Jefferson County Chancery Court Minutes, Book I, pp. 155–61, 321, 389–90, 508–9; First Circuit Court of Knox County, Execution Docket Books, vol. D, Aug. 1842–June 1847, pp. 215–16; Knox County Circuit Court Case Files, 1844, No. 3217/2184, Box 5–1, Knox County Archives, Knoxville, Tenn.

48. Inventory of Ezekiel Birdseye's Estate, Court of Probate, Cornwall, Conn., Nov. 8, 1862, 2:210–11. Birdseye's will and codicil were also recorded in Knox County, Tenn., the place of his death in June 1861. Knox County Administrative Settlements, 15:7–12, 15:33, Knox County Archives, Knoxville, Tenn.

49. Court of Probate, Cornwall, Conn., vol. 2, pp. 128, 141, 210–16, 220–24, 251, 303, 351. Knox County Court Minutes, Book 23, pp. 205, 238.

50. Greene County Deeds, 33:492–93; Goldene Fillers Burgner, comp., *Greene County, Tennessee: Wills, 1783–1890* (Easley, S.C.: Southern Historical Press, 1981), 65; Gerrit Smith to Ezekiel Birdseye, Dec. 13, 1845, letterbook copy, Smith Papers.

51. Peter Kolchin, *American Slavery, 1619–1877* (New York: Hill and Wang, 1993), 174–79. For the scholarly debate over the profitability of slavery, see Alfred H. Conrad and John R. Meyer, *The Economics of Slavery and Other Studies in Econometric History* (Chicago: Aldine, 1964); Robert William Fogel and Stanley L. Engerman, *Time on the Cross: The Economics of American Negro Slavery* (Boston: Little, Brown, 1974); Fogel, *Without Consent or Contract*; Harold D. Woodman, "The Profitability of Slavery: A Historical Perennial," *Journal of Southern History* 29 (Aug. 1963): 303–25; Herbert G. Gutman, *Slavery and the Numbers Game: A Critique of* Time on the Cross (Urbana: Univ. of Illinois Press, 1975); Paul A. David et al., *Reckoning with Slavery: A Critical Study in the Quantitative History of American Negro Slavery* (New York: Oxford Univ. Press, 1976); Peter Kolchin, "More *Time on the Cross?* An Evaluation of Robert William Fogel's *Without Consent or Contract*," *Journal of Southern History* 58 (Aug. 1992): 491–502; Gavin Wright, *The Political Economy of the Cotton South: Households, Markets and Wealth in the Nineteenth Century* (New York: Norton, 1978); Fred Bateman and Thomas Weiss, *A Deplorable Scarcity: The Failure of Industrialization in the Slave Economy* (Chapel Hill: Univ. of North Carolina Press, 1981); Laurence Shore, *Southern Capitalists: The Ideological Leadership of an Elite, 1832–1885* (Chapel Hill: Univ. of North Carolina Press, 1986); and Barbara Jeanne Fields, *Slavery and Freedom on the Middle Ground: Maryland during the Nineteenth Century* (New Haven, Conn.: Yale Univ. Press, 1985).
52. Groce, "Mountain Rebels," 1–26. Another historian points out that, in southwestern Virginia, the coming of the railroad provided more avenues for slave labor and actually was one of the reasons slaves were increasing in number in this section during the late 1850s. The Virginia and Tennessee Railroad, completed in 1856, linked East Tennessee to Virginia. Kenneth W. Noe, *Southwest Virginia's Railroad: Modernization and the Sectional Crisis* (Urbana: Univ. of Illinois Press, 1994), 67–84.

Chapter 4. The Legal Status and Actual Treatment of Slaves

1. Gerrit Smith to Ezekiel Birdseye, Dec. 21, 1840, letterbook copy, Smith Papers; Gerrit Smith to William Ellery Channing, Sept. 6, 1841, letterbook copy, Smith Papers. William Ellery Channing (1780–1842) was a well-known religious leader whose first-hand

observations of slavery while serving as a tutor to a family in Richmond, Va., led him to oppose slavery as detrimental to slave and master alike. Channing nevertheless had a firm respect for the integrity of slaveholders, unlike other abolitionists. His books, *Slavery* (1835) and *The Abolitionist* (1836), constituted effective propaganda for Birdseye to distribute in the South, since Channing did not attack slaveholders directly. *DAB,* 4:4–7. Birdseye argued that "Dr. Channing is a very candid writer and so mild that I should think his writings could offend no one" when, in 1841, a proslavery clergyman, Thomas A. Anderson, objected to his distributing one of Channing's books; EB/GS, June 21, 1841. For examples of Birdseye's letters published in northern newspapers, see the following: *The Emancipator,* Feb. 23, 1837, and Nov. 15, 1838; *Friend of Man,* Nov. 9, 1841, and Jan. 11, 1842; *Emancipator and Free American,* Apr. 21 and 28, 1842; Nov. 10, 1842; and May 4, 1843; *Liberty Press,* July 19, 1845; *Emancipator and Weekly Chronicle,* May 13, 1846.
2. James L. Huston, "The Experiential Basis of the Northern Antislavery Impulse," *Journal of Southern History* 56 (Nov. 1990): 609–40.
3. Ibid., 616–20; Thomas L. Haskell, "Capitalism and the Origins of the Humanitarian Sensibility," pts. 1 and 2, in Bender, *Antislavery Debate,* 107–60; Davis, *Problem of Slavery in the Age of Revolution,* 251–467; EB/GS, Jan. 25, 1841; EB/GS, June 21, 1841; EB/GS, July 27, 1841; EB/GS, Aug. 7, 1841; EB/GS, Oct. 11, 1841; EB/GS, Nov. 4, 1841; EB/GS, Nov. 27, 1841.
4. Ezekiel Birdseye letter, Feb. 15, 1843, in *Christian Freeman,* Apr. 14, 1843; EB/GS, June 21, 1841; EB/GS, June 18, 1845.
5. EB/GS, June 21, 1841; EB/GS, Mar. 22, 1841; EB/GS, Nov. 4, 1841.
6. EB/GS, Oct. 17, 1842.
7. Simon told Birdseye that "it was understood by the colored people that I was opposed to slavery." EB/GS, Apr. 16, 1842; EB/GS, June 18, 1842; EB/GS, Sept. 1, 1842; EB/GS, Sept. 24, 1842; EB/GS, Oct. 17, 1842.
8. Stanley M. Elkins, *Slavery: A Problem in American Institutional Life* (Chicago: Univ. of Chicago Press, 1959), 1–26; Ulrich Bonnell Phillips, *American Negro Slavery: A Survey of the Supply, Employment and Control of Negro Labor as Determined by the Plantation Regime* (New York: D. Appleton, 1918); Kenneth M. Stampp, *The Peculiar Institution: Slavery in the Ante-Bellum South* (New York: Knopf, 1956);

John W. Blassingame, *The Slave Community: Plantation Life in the Antebellum South* (New York: Oxford Univ. Press, 1972); Eugene D. Genovese, *Roll, Jordan, Roll: The World the Slaves Made* (New York: Pantheon, 1974); Herbert G. Gutman, *The Black Family in Slavery and Freedom, 1750–1925* (New York: Pantheon, 1976), Lawrence W. Levine, *Black Culture and Black Consciousness: Afro-American Folk Thought from Slavery to Freedom* (New York: Oxford Univ. Press, 1977); and Orlando Patterson, *Slavery and Social Death: A Comparative Study* (Cambridge, Mass.: Harvard Univ. Press, 1982).

9. James Merton England, "The Free Negro in Ante-Bellum Tennessee" (Ph.D. diss., Vanderbilt Univ., 1941), 215–350; Roger R. Van Dyke, "The Free Negro in Tennessee" (Ph.D. diss., Florida State Univ., 1972), ii–vii, 156–72. England further elaborated on the theme that abolitionist propaganda distorted the basically carefree existence of free blacks in J. Merton England, "The Free Negro in Ante-Bellum Tennessee," *Journal of Southern History* 9 (Feb. 1943): 37–58.

10. Dillon, *Slavery Attacked*, 4–242.

11. *North Carolina Acts*, 1777, ch. 6, sec. 2. According to the North Carolina Cession Act of 1790, these North Carolina statutes would remain in effect in the ceded territory until the new legislature in Tennessee, once duly established, should change them. Patterson, *Negro in Tennessee*, 22.

12. *Tennessee Acts*, 1801, ch. 27, sec. 1. According to sec. 3 of this act, the motives for emancipating a particular slave were to be set forth in the petition; nine or a majority of the justices had to be present for the county court to receive such a petition; two-thirds of the justices present had to concur for emancipation to be allowed. See also Charles C. Trabue, "The Voluntary Emancipation of Slaves in Tennessee as Reflected in the State's Legislation and Judicial Decisions," *Tennessee Historical Magazine* 4 (Mar. 1918): 50–68.

13. *Tennessee Acts*, 1829, ch. 29, sec. 1; *Tennessee Acts*, 1831, ch. 101; *Fisher's Negroes v. Dabbs and Others*, 14 Tenn. 78–111 (1834).

14. *Tennessee Acts*, 1831, ch. 102, sec. 2; 1833, ch. 64, sec. 1; 1833, ch. 81, secs. 1 and 2. Commenting on this much harsher policy of 1831, Chief Justice A. O. P. Nicholson in 1871 remarked that "this policy was based upon the belief that the peace of the State would be endangered by an increase of the number of free colored persons." *C. R. Jameson, Administrator, v. James McCoy*, 52 Tenn. 107–23 (1871).

15. *Tennessee Acts*, 1842, ch. 191, secs. 1 and 2; 1849, ch. 107. Enormous

pressure was placed on the legislature to repeal the 1842 law; typical is one petition from Wilson County, signed by 40 residents: "Your petitioners are fully persuaded of the wisdom and humanity of the 1831 act, ch. 102, which provided that no slave could be emancipated but upon the condition of removal. The practical effect of that law was most salutary in preventing the increase of a base born free population in the State—a population which can do little or no good for itself, that is injurious to the Free White population and ruinous to the slaves of the country. Since passage of the 1842 act, as your petitioners are informed, crowds of slaves have not only been emancipated, but the privilege of remaining has been granted with little consideration of the character of the applicants, so that the state is now more than ever likely to have a large Free Negro population with all its attendant evils." Petitions, 1843.

16. *Tennessee Acts,* 1852, ch. 300, secs. 2, 3, 4. Tacit recognition by the state of the existence of a nominal slave class is indicated in an 1839 law forbidding slaves to live as if they were free persons of color. *Tennessee Acts,* 1839, ch. 47, sec. 1. The Tennessee Supreme Court in 1834 admitted that this nominal class of blacks existed: "The idea that a will emancipating slaves, or deed of manumission, is void in this state is ill founded; it is binding on the representatives of the devisor in the one case, and the grantor in the other, and communicates a right to the slave; but it is an imperfect right until the state, the community of which such emancipated person is to become a member, assents to the contract between the master and the slave." *Fisher's Negroes v. Dabbs and Others,* 14 Tenn. 83 (1834).

17. *Tennessee Acts,* 1854, ch. 50, sec. 1; 1860, ch. 128, sec. 1. See also Patterson, *Negro in Tennessee,* 159. One scholar estimated that the number of nominal slaves was equal to those whose freedom had been formally recognized by law. England, "Free Negro in Ante-Bellum Tennessee," 46. Tennessee also prohibited free blacks from moving into the state; *Tennessee Acts,* 1831, ch. 102, sec. 1. This 1831 prohibition against free blacks immigrating into Tennessee was upheld in an 1838 decision of the Tennessee Supreme Court: *The State v. Claiborne,* 19 Tenn. 337–40 (1838). See also Lawrence M. Friedman, *A History of American Law* (New York: Simon and Schuster, 1973), 194.

18. R. L. Caruthers and A. O. P. Nicholson, *A Compilation of the Statutes of Tennessee, of a General and Permanent Nature, from the Commencement of the Government to the Present Time. With References to Judicial*

Decisions, in Notes, to Which Is Appended a New Collection of Forms (Nashville: Steam Press of James Smith, 1836), 673–86.

19. Meigs and Cooper, *Code of Tennessee, 1858*, 362, 500–528, 880.
20. Ibid.; *Tennessee Acts*, 1831, ch. 103, sec. 3; Petitions, 1831; *Macon v. The State*, 23 Tenn. 411–13 (1844).
21. Meigs and Cooper, *Code of Tennessee, 1858*, 500–507, 510–11, 881; Howington, *What Sayeth the Law*, 116–53; Petitions, 1829. In 1860, the legislature made it a capital offense for slaves to "endanger the safe running" of railroad locomotives or cars. *Tennessee Acts*, 1860, ch. 118.
22. Mooney, *Slavery in Tennessee*, 92–93; *W. E. Jones v. John J. Allen*, 38 Tenn. 353–60 (1858). Mooney's belief that masters, out of rational self-interest, routinely protected their slave property ignores the laws punishing citizens for abusing and cruelly mistreating, or neglecting, their farm livestock—also valuable property. Meigs and Cooper, *Code of Tennessee, 1858*, 352.
23. Howington, *What Sayeth the Law*, 93–94. Williamson County Circuit Court Minutes, Nov. 1855, 304–5; and July 1856, 378. *Nashville Republican Banner*, Sept. 21, 1855, and Dec. 21, 1859; *Nashville Daily Gazette*, Sept. 22, 1855.
24. W. C. Kain, *The Constable's Guide: Being a Practical Treatise on the Powers, Duties and Liabilities of Constables in the State of Tennessee, Both in Criminal and Civil Proceedings. With Approved Forms, Adapted to Every Service and Duty Required. To Which Is Added, an Appendix, Containing the Laws of Tennessee Respecting Partnerships, Assignments, Wills, Etc., with a Variety of Reliable Business Forms* (Knoxville, Tenn.: Jesse A. Rayl, 1859), 77.
25. *Ford v. Ford*, 26 Tenn. 75 (1846); Howington, *What Sayeth the Law*, 247–54.
26. *Bob, a Slave, v. The State*, 10 Tenn. 155–72 (1826); Howington, *What Sayeth the Law*, 154–85. Justice William B. Reese stated, in an 1839 case that disallowed prohibiting a master from testifying on behalf of his slave, who was accused of killing a white man: "The relation of master and slave is, indeed, different; but in a case like this the law, upon high grounds of public policy, pretermits, for a moment, that relation, takes the slave out of the hands of his master, forgets his claims and rights of property, treats the slave as a rational and intelligent human being, responsible to moral, social, and municipal duties and obligations, and gives him the benefit of all the forms of trial which jealousy of power and love of liberty have induced the freeman

to throw around himself for his own protection. If, then, the master know any fact tending to save the life of the slave, shall society, who have taken from him the slave for the purpose of trial, say to him, not that you are master and we will weigh your credit, but you are master and shall not speak at all? On the grounds of public policy, of common humanity, of absolute necessity, the master must be held to be competent as a witness for or against the slave." *Elijah, a Slave, v. The State,* 20 Tenn. 78–80 (1839).

27. Howington, *What Sayeth the Law,* 186–216. See also Edward L. Ayers, *Vengeance and Justice: Crime and Punishment in the Nineteenth-Century American South* (New York: Oxford Univ. Press, 1984), 133–36; Mark Tushnet, "Approaches to the Study of the Law of Slavery," *Civil War History* 25 (Dec. 1979): 329–38; Andrew Fede, "Legitimized Violent Slave Abuse in the American South, 1619–1865: A Case Study of Law and Social Change in Six Southern States," *American Journal of Legal History* 29 (Apr. 1985): 93–150; Fede, "Toward a Solution of the Slave Law Dilemma," 301–20; Daniel J. Flanigan, "Criminal Procedure in Slave Trials in the Antebellum South," *Journal of Southern History* 40 (Nov. 1974): 537–64; Mark V. Tushnet, *The American Law of Slavery, 1810–1860: Considerations of Humanity and Interest* (Princeton, N.J.: Princeton Univ. Press, 1981).

28. Helen Tunnicliff Catterall, ed., *Judicial Cases Concerning American Slavery and the Negro,* vol. 2: *Cases from the Courts of North Carolina, South Carolina, and Tennessee* (Washington, D.C.: Carnegie Institution of Washington, 1929), 479–31. See also David J. Bodenhamer and James W. Ely, Jr., eds., *Ambivalent Legacy: A Legal History of the South* (Jackson: Univ. of Mississippi Press, 1984), 123–70.

29. "At a leisure moment I drop you an occasional line in giving you some hasty sketches of the lights and shades of slavery. I may not always select such incidents as would be the best but I have endeavoured to be accurate and impartial." EB/GS, June 18, 1842.

30. EB/GS, Feb. 7, 1842.

31. EB/GS, June 18, 1842. See also Mathews, *Slavery and Methodism,* 30–290; C. C. Goen, *Broken Churches, Broken Nation: Denominational Schisms and the Coming of the Civil War* (Macon, Ga.: Mercer Univ. Press, 1985), 1–63.

32. EB/GS, Mar. 22, 1841.

33. EB/GS, Feb. 7, 1842. Meek's attack on McBee's slave was specifically prohibited by state law: "No person shall wantonly, and without

sufficient cause, beat or abuse the slave of another person. Any such offender may be indicted in the Circuit or Criminal Court where the offence was committed; and, on conviction, shall be punished in the same manner as for a similar offence committed on the body of any white person." Meigs and Cooper, *Code of Tennessee, 1858,* 515.

34. EB/GS, Mar. 22, 1841. This particular despotic master, Col. William Moore, had moved to Ray County, Mo., by 1854. *History of Tennessee, Containing Historical and Biographical Sketches,* 1169.
35. EB/GS, Jan. 25, 1841; EB/GS, Mar. 22, 1841; EB/GS, Apr. 16, 1841; EB/GS, June 21, 1841; EB/GS, July 2, 1842; EB/GS, June 18, 1845; EB/GS, Nov. 28, 1845; EB/GS, Dec. 9, 1845; EB/GS, Jan. 20, 1846; EB/GS, Mar. 2, 1846; Gerrit Smith to Ezekiel Birdseye, Dec. 21, 1840, letterbook copy, Smith Papers.
36. EB/GS, June 21, 1841; EB/GS, Sept. 1, 1842; EB/GS, Oct. 17, 1842. The Tennessee Supreme Court allowed courts of equity to have jurisdiction of disputed title to slave property, which provided the owner with the means to compel the actual return of a specific slave. Slaves were "property in intellectual and moral and social qualities, in skill, fidelity, and in gratitude"; the "mutual feelings of dependence, affection, and humanity" between master and slave could "not be compensated in money." *Womack v. Smith and Tinsley,* 30 Tenn. 329 (1850); *Henderson v. Vaulx and Wife,* 18 Tenn. 28 (1836); *Whitmore v. Parks and Jackson,* 22 Tenn. 85 (1842). Justice John Catron echoed Birdseye's horror at slave auctions in an 1833 case: "Nothing can be much more abhorrent to these poor people, or to the feelings of every benevolent individual, than to see a large family of slaves sold at sheriff's sale; the infant children, father and mother, to different bidders." *Loftin v. Espy and Others,* 12 Tenn. 75 (1833).
37. EB/GS, June 25, 1841; EB/GS, Nov. 4, 1841; EB/GS, Feb. 7, 1842; EB/GS, May 21, 1842.
38. EB/GS, Mar. 14, 1842; EB/GS, Oct. 17, 1842. In an 1835 case, the Tennessee Supreme Court declared that the physical appearance of a woman whose freedom was in dispute constituted sufficient evidence that she was not a slave. If the woman in question "was of fair complexion, with straight hair, high, thin nose, with all the other indications of European descent," and had established "that she had lived two years in the neighborhood without any person having the least suspicion that she had any African blood," Justice Nathan Green wrote, she must be considered free unless more compelling evidence

to the contrary was presented. *Miller v. Denman,* 16 Tenn. 156–59 (1835).

39. EB/GS, Feb. 7, 1842; EB/GS, Apr. 16, 1842; EB/GS, May 21, 1842.
40. Ezekiel Birdseye, letter of Feb. 15, 1843, in *Christian Freeman,* Apr. 14, 1843.
41. Howington, *What Sayeth the Law,* 71–97, 186–216; *Jacob v. The State,* 22 Tenn. 481–509 (1842); *Moses, a Slave, v. The State,* 30 Tenn. 160–67 (1850). Justice Nathan Green, in a separate opinion in the *Jacob* case, offered the following *obiter dictum*: "I think proper to announce distinctly, as my opinion, that there may exist cases in which the killing of a master by his slave would be manslaughter. What circumstances of torture, short of endangering life or limb, would so reduce a homicide, it is not easy to indicate. Every such case must rest upon its own peculiar facts. The rights and duties of the parties must form the *criteria* by which an enlightened court and jury should act. But the present case is destitute of a single mitigating circumstance, and is most clearly one of murder."
42. Meigs and Cooper, *Code of Tennessee, 1858,* 512–15. Historian Bertram Wyatt-Brown points out how, within the southern system of honor, few masters suffered legal complications from murdering their slaves, and excessive beatings of slaves were motivated more by fear of appearing weak or not in command. He also points out the danger of treating appeals cases as typical instead of exceptional, a point which Birdseye's observations of cases of slave abuses or murders that were never tried seem to corroborate. Wyatt-Brown, *Southern Honor,* 373–76.
43. EB/GS, Sept. 24, 1842. The Tennessee Supreme Court upheld the conviction of Gabriel Worley in 1850 for castrating his slave Josiah. Justice A. W. O. Totten delivered the opinion of the court: "We utterly repudiate the idea of any such power and dominion of the master over the slave, as would authorize him thus to maim his slave for the purpose of his moral reform. Such doctrine would violate the moral sense and humanity of the present age." *Worley v. The State,* 30 Tenn. 110–22 (1850).
44. Ezekiel Birdseye, letter in *New York Emancipator and Republican,* Feb. 23, 1837; EB/GS, Jan. 25, 1841; EB/GS, Mar. 22, 1841; EB/GS, Nov. 4, 1841.
45. Anna Roe Mims, comp., *Tennessee Records of Cocke County: Scrap Book*

of W. J. McSween (Nashville: Works Progress Administration, 1936), 28–29.
46. Ibid., 29–30.
47. EB/GS, Feb. 7, 1842. Other Tennesseans believed that slavery was milder in its effect on blacks in Tennessee than in other southern states. One justice of the supreme court, William B. Reese, of Jefferson County, the brother of Dr. Joseph B. M. Reese, an antislavery friend of Birdseye's, made the following comments in regard to slaves being transported from Tennessee to Mississippi:

> We have a mild penal code, as regards slaves as well as others; they might be taken where this would be otherwise. We have a much greater portion of free than of slave population and the slave, without severity, is kept in a due and safe subordination; they might be taken where the proportion is the other way, and where weakness on one side and rashness on the other might lead to insurrection and consequent destruction of the slave. Here there is a liberal philanthropy and protective public sentiment to the slave; there it might be otherwise. Here the annual profit of the slave's labor bears no very large proportion to his own value, and of course interest is on the side of humanity, and he may not be over-worked; there the annual profit may be one-third of his entire value, and the temptation would be to overwork him. Here the moderate annual profit of the slave's labor makes an increase of the stock an object, and mothers and children are tenderly treated; there a different state of things may produce a different feeling and a different course. Here we have a temperate, healthful climate; there the climate may be less favorable to life. *(Henderson v. Vaulx and Wife,* 18 Tenn. 29 [1836])

Part II
Ezekiel Birdseye's Letters

1. To the *New York Emancipator and Republican*,[1] February 23, 1837

THE INFLUENCE OF SLAVERY ON THE PROSPERITY OF THE SOUTH

On this subject I give the testimony of Ezekiel Birdseye, Esq., who spent six years in South Carolina, four years in Alabama, a part of two in Georgia, and much time in other slaveholding states. Mr. Birdseye is a gentleman of uncommon powers of observation, and everything he relates may be relied on as strictly true.

He says, "Kentucky was settled before Ohio, and I believe is equally fertile and equally rich in mineral productions, and every way as well adapted to sustain a dense population.

There is now in Cincinnati, in possession of Dr. Drake,[2] a newspaper printed at Lexington, between 40 and 50 years ago, which states that 'a road had been cut out from Lexington, to the mouth of Licking River (opposite to where Cincinnati is now situated), that there was there a good situation for a town, which the proprietors were about to lay out.' From this Cincinnati took its rise, and now contains about 30,000 inhabitants. McAdamized roads lead from it in every direction. Of these, there are five. The country, as in almost every part of Ohio, is flourishing. Land for farming purposes, from 2 to 5 miles from Cincinnati, readily brings from $65 to $300 per acre; while land of equally good quality, opposite in Kentucky, the same distance from the city, is sold for from $10 to $20 per acre. Lands generally command better prices in Ohio, though the disparity is not always equally great.

Above Cincinnati, near the upper part of Kentucky, there are iron works in the vicinity of the river, worked by slave labor, while on the opposite side of the Ohio, there are iron works possessing no more than equal natural advantages. Those in Ohio are flourishing and more than usually prosperous; while those in Kentucky make comparatively but slow progress and produce but limited profits.

In Ohio, there are about 450 miles of canal made by the state, and considerable by private companies. The state has also much stock in roads, and is making improvements in the rivers by slack water navigation. The state has ordered surveys for rail-roads, and probably will render great aid to this useful improvement. A number are in progress and about 50 charters granted; most of which will probably be made, traversing the state in every direction. To carry on her public works, Ohio has advanced about fifteen millions of dollars by loan, and so high is her credit, that the Ohio state stocks fluctuate less in London, than the stocks of England herself.

In Kentucky, few improvements of this kind have been made; the amount by the state is very small. In conversing with a gentleman from England, who was a correspondent of capitalists both in London and Paris, he stated as his opinion that Kentucky could not obtain a loan there on the credit of the state for any considerable amount. He had travelled much in Kentucky, and was probably well prepared to give an opinion. Kentucky has but few good roads, one canal, Louisville and Portland, two miles long, one rail road of 32 miles, from Lexington to Frankfort. None of these were made or owned by the state. The state has made some small appropriations to improve the navigation of her rivers, and to a McAdamized road from Lexington to the Ohio, opposite Cincinnati.

It is my opinion, and I have been much in Kentucky, that if slavery was immediately abolished there, the land would at once rise to more than the present market value of the slaves—that slavery is an incumbrance which, if removed, property would appreciate to a greater amount than the incumbrance, and that this increase would continue in a compound ratio by the improvements that would be made in railroads, turnpikes, canals, and other works, which would arise from an introduction of the arts and well directed industry."[3]

Influence of Slavery on the Morals of the South

I give again the testimony of Mr. Birdseye:

"I went," he says, "to South Carolina in 1818, and for a while resided in Union District, Unionville, or as commonly called, Union Court House, containing about 30 dwelling houses. The district is a cotton growing one, the labor, as is usual in that state, is mostly done by slaves. The sons of the planters in a very large proportion spend their time in idleness or fashionable sports.— They collect in the villages, and become licentious to a degree which I have never known in the towns and villages of the free states. Dr. Divitt, one of the 4 or 5 physicians at Union, told me that his practice in the disease, which God has sent as a judgment on licentiousness, was worth $600 annually. I am inclined to think that his practice in this branch was not greater than that of the other physicians. ($2,400 for one district!) The idle habits of the young men with their means, and opportunity for indulgence, cut off thousands in the morning of life, or leave them with a broken constitution.—From long habits of ease, they become unfitted for active labor, and when the parent dies, they soon exhaust their patrimony, and live drones in society, unfitted to be useful members of it or the heads of families.

"I am of opinion that the females in the slaveholding states, are more virtuous than the males. Greater care is taken in their education, and known departures from virtue are followed with loss of character. Dissipated men, who have apparently but little regard for their own reputation, appear anxious that that of their wives, sisters and daughters should stand fair. The education of the females is too often of the showy, rather than the useful, kind. Where there are slaves it is not common for the daughters to labor in the kitchen, or to become acquainted with the drudgery of the family.[4] A greater proportion of them do not marry than in the free states. They view domestic duties as the appropriate employment of slaves. Whenever reduced by misfortune to a state of dependence, they too often lose that virtuous pride, which those who can rely on their own industry maintain. It is said that among the unfortunate females in the cities in the slave states, and on their borders, a large proportion are those who have been trained in fashionable idleness, or are from the ruined families of the slave states. I am inclined to believe, from all the information I have, that this is true."

Burning Alive

"A man by the name of Waters," says Mr. Birdseye, "was killed by his slaves, in Newberry District. Three of them were tried before the court, and ordered to be burnt. I was but a few miles distant at the time, and conversed with those who saw the execution. The slaves were tied to a stake, and pitch pine wood piled around them, to which the fire was communicated. Thousands were collected to witness this barbarous transaction. Other executions of this kind took place in various parts of the state, during my residence in it, from 1818 to 1824. About three or four years ago, a young negro was burnt in Abbeville District for an attempt at rape."

The Slaves without Protection

Mr. Birdseye says: "During my residence at the South, I knew of no instance, where a white man was executed for killing a negro; while in no instance did I know a white man escape the gallows for stealing a slave, except one, where the criminal broke jail."

He relates the following facts: "A Baptist clergyman in Laurens District, S.C., whipped his slave to death, whom he *suspected* of having stolen about $60. The slave was in the prime of life, and was purchased a few weeks before for $800 of a slave trader from Virginia or Maryland. The trader had given him at parting a silver dollar, which he had passed. This led his master to suspect that he had stolen his money, and to whip him to make him confess it. The coroner, Wm. Irby,[5] at whose house I was then boarding, told me, that on reviewing the dead body, he found it beat to a jelly, from head to foot. The master's wife discovered the money a day or two after the death of the slave. She had herself removed it from where it was placed, not knowing what it was, as it was tied up in a thick envelope. I happened to be present when the trial of this man took place at Laurens Court House. His daughter testified that her father untied the slave, when he appeared to be failing, and gave him cold water to drink, of which he took freely. His counsel plead that his death might have been caused by drinking cold water in a state of excitement. The Judge charged the jury that it would be their duty to find the defendant guilty, if they believed the death was caused by the whipping; but if they were of opinion that *drinking cold water* caused the death, they would find him not guilty! The jury found him—NOT GUILTY.

"While I lived in Limestone County, Ala., in 1826–27, a tavern keeper of the village of Moresville discovered a negro carrying away a piece of old carpet. It was during the Christmas holidays, when the slaves are allowed to visit their friends. The negro stated that one of the servants of the tavern owed him some twelve and one-half or twenty-five cents, and that he had taken the carpet in payment. This the servant denied. The inn keeper took the negro to a field near by, and whipped him cruelly. He then struck him with a stake, and punched him in the face and mouth, knocking out some of his teeth. After this, he took him back to the house and committed him to the care of his son, who had just then come home with another young man. This was at evening. They whipped him by turns with heavy cowskins, and made the *dogs shake him.* A Mr. Phillips, who lodged at the house, heard the cruelty during the night. On getting up, he found the negro in the bar-room, terribly mangled with the whip, and his flesh so torn by the dogs, that the cords were bare. He remarked to the landlord, that he was dangerously hurt, and needed care. The landlord replied, that he deserved more. Mr. Phillips went to a neighboring magistrate who took the slave home with him, where he soon died. The father and son were both tried, and acquitted!! A suit was brought, however, for damages in behalf of the owner of the slave, a young lady by the name of

Agnes Jones.[6] I was on the jury when these facts were stated on oath. Two men testified, one that he would have given $1000 for him, the other $900 or $950. The jury found the latter sum.

"At Union Court House, S.C., a tavern keeper by the name of Samuel Davis, procured the conviction and execution of his own slave, for stealing a cake of gingerbread from a grog shop. The slave raised the latch of the back door and took the cake, doing no other injury. The shop keeper, whose name was Charles Gordon, was willing to forgive him, but his master procured his conviction and execution by hanging, because he had one arm, and an order on the State Treasury by the Court that tried him, which also assessed his value, brought him more money than he could have obtained for the slave in the market."

NOTES

1. *Emancipator*, a weekly antislavery newspaper, was published in New York, N.Y., between 1833 and 1841, and then in Boston, Mass., from 1841 to 1850. Also called *Emancipator and Free American* and *Emancipator and Republican*, it was edited in 1833 by Charles Denison, in 1834 and 1835 by William Goodell, and in 1835–41 by Joshua Leavitt. In 1834, the *Emancipator* became the official publication of the American Anti-Slavery Society. Under Joshua Leavitt's editorship, the paper became the leading organ for the expression of political abolitionism in its support of the Liberty Party. Gerrit Smith was a major contributor to this paper, in terms of both financial support and letters to the editor. Gerald Sorin, *The New York Abolitionists: A Case of Study of Political Radicalism* (Westport, Conn.: Greenwood, 1971), 21, 59, 69; Ralph Volney Harlow, *Gerrit Smith: Philanthropist and Reformer* (New York: Henry Holt, 1939), 119–20, 161, 179, 215, 262, 269–70; Alice Hatcher Henderson, "The History of the New York State Anti-Slavery Society" (Ph.D. diss., Univ. of Michigan, 1963), 31–45, 81–92.
2. Dr. Daniel Drake (1785–1852), Cincinnati's most famous physician and booster, published numerous books promoting the city. The most widely known account, *Natural and Statistical View, or Picture of Cincinnati and the Miami Country*, was first published in 1815 and contains precisely the information Birdseye cites. *DAB*, 5:426–27; Richard C. Wade, *The Urban Frontier: Pioneer Life in Early Pittsburgh, Cincinnati, Lexington, Louisville, and St. Louis* (Chicago: Univ. of Chicago Press, 1959), 155–57; Emmet Field Horine, *Daniel Drake, 1785–1852: Pioneer*

Physician of the Midwest (Philadelphia: Univ. of Pennsylvania Press, 1961).

3. Although Birdseye here uses many statistics drawn from Dr. Drake's publications, it should be pointed out that Drake himself was not at all in sympathy with the abolitionists. Drake's solution to the growing sectional tensions over slavery was to completely exclude all free blacks from the free states and to end emancipation of any slave in the South. He believed that emancipated former slaves living in the North fueled abolitionist extremism and that the actual living conditions of slaves in the South were improving steadily. All Drake's arguments, of course, would be the antithesis of Birdseye's beliefs. Daniel Drake, *Dr. Daniel Drake's Letters on Slavery to Dr. John C. Warren, of Boston, Reprinted from the National Intelligencer, Washington, April 3, 5 and 7, 1851* (New York: Schuman's, 1940), 8–47.

4. In reality, managing a large household placed innumerable burdens and responsibilities, including many menial chores, upon the southern plantation mistress after marriage. Catherine Clinton, *The Plantation Mistress: Woman's World in the Old South* (New York: Pantheon, 1982), 16–35.

5. William Irby (1797–1860), a physician and large planter, was educated at South Carolina College and attended the Medical Department of the University of Pennsylvania, 1818–19. He served in both the South Carolina house of representatives (1840–46) and the state senate (1846–52). He was coroner of Laurens District in 1822–26. Emily Bellinger Reynolds and Joan Reynolds Faunt, *Biographical Directory of the Senate of South Carolina, 1776–1964* (Columbia, S.C.: South Carolina Archives Dept., 1964), 244.

6. Agnes Jones is listed as a minor over 14, requiring a guardian to be appointed for her estate on Dec. 16, 1826. Jean Waldrop Smith, comp., *Limestone County, Alabama, Orphan's Court Minutes, 1822–30* (Athens, Ala.: Privately printed, 1950), 82, 114.

2. To Gerrit Smith, January 25, 1841

Newport[,] Cocke Co[unty,] Ten[nessee,]
Jan[uary] 25th, 1841

My Dear Sir

After about three weeks absence I found your highly interesting letter at Newport last week. I was much affected with your liberality to enable me to procure the liberation of the poor slave sold by Franklin to Woodfin. I had much wished that I had the means to liberate him but poverty has come on us like an armed man. I find it impossible to collect but a small part due me. Distress prevails throughout the state and I believe the whole South.

Immediately on receiving your letter I wrote The Rev[erend] D R McAnally[1] of the Methodist Church at Asheville and stated my object. A day or two after The Rev[erend] Robert H Lea[2] of the same church joined with me in another letter to him. I am in the daily expectation of his answer. I stated that my object was to purchase him to give him his freedom and requested him to ascertain what Woodfin would take for him and should I not be mistaken in supposing that motives of humanity would influence him he might suggest it to him. As Woodfin[3] is an attorney he may be at a distant court. If so I shall learn at what time I can meet with him and see him personally. The man I learn is with him and comfortably provided for and receives kind treatment.

Mr. Lea informs me that Woodfin's father was a philanthropist who labored earnestly for the poor slaves that his brother a clergyman in the Methodist Church was also one but was killed suddenly, his horse took fright and ran with his carriage by which he was instantly killed.[4]

From these circumstances I hope to find that the principles cherished by the father and brother will be found in the one who owns the slave. Should he refuse to take $450, I will try to meet the difference if not too great. Whatever the cost of the purchase may be I will pay one half as soon as my means will permit or at the first convenient time with interest.

Aaron Clarke[5] an intelligent honest laboring man who is in my employ has labored with this slave. He says that he is a man of very superior natural talents between 25 or 30 years old strong active and one of the best laborers he ever worked with. He told Mr. Clarke that for more than ten years he had been making repeated efforts to get to the free states and gave him such a detail of his sufferings as it would appear impossible for any man to live through.

He says he is healthy and strong with one of those firm constitutions that can endure incredible hardships. When taken in Buncombe County he was in company with another runaway slave lying out in the mountains. In running near one of his pursuers he threw a stone which so much injured him that they took him. The other escaped. All who know him speak of him as strictly honest. No report of any other crime has ever reached me.

The pamphlet—Your letter to Mr Clay and the Emancipator of the 17 Dec[ember] reached me safely. For both please accept my thanks. I will give them a circulation where I hope they will do much good. The letter to Mr Clay I handed to my worthy friend Lea who read it through and expressed himself so highly pleased with it that he should esteem it a priviledge to have a correspondence with the author. He is a pious clergyman who has labored much for the colored people. He had a Saboth school of upwards of 40 most of them slaves in Jefferson County whom he taught with encouraging prospects untill threatened with a prosecution. He was compelled to abandon his school. Should you find it convenient to correspond with him you may obtain much valuable information, much that I could not give. His Post Office will be in Morgan County[,] Ten[nessee]. If you could send him some Antislavery publications directed to him Morgan County they would be sent to the county seat—where they would find him. I hope that great good may be done by keeping up an active correspondence with the South. An opinion is gaining ground at the South that slavery cannot continue long.

The whole South has been in some degree influenced by the Abolitionists. Barbarous punishments are less frequent. Burning slaves alive was a barbarity that prevailed in South Carolina untill about 1830. The last instance that I heard of in that state was in Abbeville District a young Negro man said to be about twenty years old. He was sentenced/tried by a court composed of two magistrates and five freeholders and executed near the part of the District if I am correctly informed where were the plantations of John C Calhoun and George McDuffie. W[illia]m C Roadman[6] the intel[l]igent Postmaster of Newport in this county was present at the execution. He told me that there was a very large collection of people and as near as he could judge 3000 blacks— That before the fire was kindled a sermon was preached by I think the Rev[erend] Mr Capers that he saw the poor young man who was about to suffer distinctly. That he appeared composed—so much so, that he thought he did not believe that they really intended to burn him. When the dreadful sentence was about to be executed, they piled pitch pine faggots around him and applied the fire. His screams were loud and piercing. No language could describe his agony. The plain dealing of the Abolitionists has put a stop to this mode of execution, I trust forever. The slave market was when I was in

Charleston in the most public part of the city. When the Abolitionists were handling them as they thought rather roughly they removed it to a more private place. These are among the important signs of the times. Where there is shame there is a hope of something better.

In the late fall a planter the owner of some 50 or 60 slaves from Edgefield district which joins Abbeville on the east spent a night at the house where I am now writing. Speaking of the Abolitionists[,] he said they made horrid pictures and exhibited them publicly of slaves chained together and of others flogging them in the most cruel manner. I asked him if their pictures exceeded the reality. He said they did. I told him I thought not, that I had met slaves everywhere chained, that while the trade continued it was an every day occurrence in the South that in Laurens district one was whipped to death by a Baptist clergyman and more recently one burned to death in Abbeville two districts immediately adjoining the one in which he lived. He admitted the fact and that there was much cruelty on the plantations. Frequent instances of this kind have occurred which are important [in] so far as they show that slaveholders are not wholly insensible to shame and that the pictorial representations and severe criticisms of the Abolitionists are doing much good.

Some two or three weeks since I spent a night at my friend John Caldwells[7] in Jefferson County. I met there with a Mr Patterson the President of the Manumission society of that part of Jefferson county. I inquired about the present situation of the society—its numbers, etc. He stated that the society had over 600 members—that he had a list of their names which he should be happy to show me. The society had not opened their meetings owing to the oppressive laws of the state. Mr Patterson has sold his farm and purchased in Indiana[, being] unwilling to remain longer in a state where freedom was denied him.

This excellent man gave me a pressing invitation to visit at his house which I hope to be able to do before he leaves the state. I inquired of him if during this time of trial he had kept up an active correspondence at the North. He said not but little had been done by any of the society. It is too true that these good men become much discouraged by the mobs of the North and the oppressive laws of the South—I think too much so. I believe these societies might be openly held without any danger of prosecution and that by corresponding with the North they would soon learn that there was much cause for rejoicing. Mr Caldwell thinks that the antislavery influence is about to arise with redoubled vigor at the South. One of the most effectual means will be by extensive and active correspondence. Should my Northern friends be willing to undertake the labor I think I can do something to induce a very extensive correspondence with this part of the South.

In my acquaintance with the South I have been induced to believe that the improved communications between the North and South would contribute greatly to the overthrow of slavery. The South are in want of manufactures, tools, and implements of any kind. Agriculture is in a low state. The poor are neglected [and] suffered to grow up without education or education as mechanics[,] yet most are willing to work and would hail with joy any manufacturing or company that would employ them at a low price.

There is a turnpike in a state of forwardness from Cincinnati to Lexington K[entuck]y, from there to Cumberland Gap from which a long pike road will soon be completed to S[outh] C[arolina] by this place. Steam now extends to Raleigh N[orth] C[arolina;] from thence a turnpike will probably be made to Asheville by this place to Knoxville which will make the communication from this to the East or West easy and direct. Judge Peck and myself own very large tracts of land in this Co[unty,] the adjoining counties[,] and North Carolina on which we are anxious to establish improvements wholly excluding slave labor. These lands are healthy [and] have great natural resources Iron ore water power timber lime & rich mountain pasture grounds. We own French Broad for about 16 miles. The river would make a fine place for a Rolling Mill or manufacturing towns. Paint Creek Brush Creek long Creek on this side Wolf Creek and Big Creek on the south side of F[rench] B[road] would all be sufficient for furnaces and abound in iron ore and good timber. Should our friends at the North think our opinions worthy of consideration I shall be happy to correspond with them on the subject. This is the most thoroughly antislavery part of the South. A press might soon be established here and much done to redeem the South which needs a practical example of the advantages of Free labor. We have the analysis of iron ores. I took the liberty to for[war]d you Dr Troost's Geological Report[8] where you will find our lands spoken of. You may assure any capitalists of the North or Europe that if they are disposed to associate with us we will put in our lands at nominal prices and invite an examination of them. I am not acquainted with Mr Worthington but will inquire of my Miss[issippi] friends. You may do well to trace him from his last residence and probably would find the P[ost] Masters ready to give you information if you have no other acquaintances. In this way I found it generally easy to find the residence of any men much known.

In another letter I will give you some names with whom you or your friends might find it convenient to correspond or send antislavery documents and papers. I will add a few only. Rev[erend] Josiah Rhoton[9] Tazewell, Claiborne Co[unty,] E[ast] Ten[nessee] Dr J M Reese[10] Mossy Creek Mr Kirkpatrick[11]

Post Master Bent Creek Jefferson Co[unty] Thomas Lane same office. These men will circulate any papers you send them one being a P[ost] Master few will be lost or destroyed. I will try to furnish the means of paying for such papers as I order for the South. Judge W[illia]m B Reese[12] of the Supreme Court is an antislavery man [in] Knoxville Ten[nessee]. Seth J. W. Lucky[13] Esq[quire] Att[orne]y at Law Jonesboro E[ast] Ten[nessee] an intelligent and pious man his influence is extensive.

Yours sincerely,
Ezekiel Birdseye

WRITTEN ACROSS PAGE 1:
I hope to see my Brother before he takes his seat in Congress and shall labor to convince him that cringing to the South is not the way to gain their respect or discharge his duty to the North. Rev[erend] Robert H Lea Montgomery Morgan Co[unty] E[ast] Ten[nessee]

NOTES

1. David Rice McAnally (1810–1895), was born in Grainger County, Tenn., licensed to preach in 1828, and admitted the following year to the Holston Conference, which included Asheville, N.C., at the time Birdseye met him. In 1840, the Holston Conference disapproved of McAnally's editorship of the *Highland Messenger,* a political newspaper published in Asheville. McAnally subsequently was the author of numerous biographies of prominent Methodist ministers. In 1851, he transferred to the St. Louis Conference in Missouri, where he edited the *St. Louis Christian Advocate* and was a very successful and popular preacher who "did more to build up Methodism in Missouri and adjacent states than any other one man." He was arrested and imprisoned in 1861 for being a southern sympathizer, and his paper was suppressed thereafter. Richard N. Price, *Holston Methodism from Its Origin to the Present Time,* 5 vols. (Nashville: Methodist Publishing House, 1903–13), 3:385–86, 4:109–12.
2. Robert H. Lea evidently was a local preacher in the Holston Conference, since no record remains of his ministry. He was listed in an 1839 tax list of Cocke County as owning one slave. Pollyanna Creekmore, comp., "Early East Tennessee Taxpayers: XIII. Cocke County, 1839," *East Tennessee Historical Society's Publications 37* (1965): 129.
3. Nicholas W. Woodfin (1810–1875), prominent Buncombe County

lawyer and state representative in 1844–52, was western North Carolina's second largest slaveholder in 1860. He was an entrepreneur, like Birdseye, active in promoting a railroad for his section. Evidently he was something of a humanitarian, opposed to selling slaves when it would separate family members and exhibiting permissiveness, kindness, and a sense of moral duty toward his own slaves. Like Birdseye, also, he was a strong Whig; initially a Unionist, he became one of the section's leading secessionists. John C. Inscoe, *Mountain Masters, Slavery, and the Sectional Crisis in Western North Carolina* (Knoxville: Univ. of Tennessee Press, 1989), 65, 79, 91, 104, 144, 200, 251.

4. The brother was Archibald Woodfin (1808–1836), who was admitted on trial to the Holston Conference in 1829. He was thrown from a sulkey at Taylorsville, Tenn., and subsequently died from injuries sustained in this accident. His horse was frightened by a man in a red shirt. Price, *Holston Methodism,* 3:237; Getha Gina Bell, *The Bells in U.S.A. and Allied Families, 1650–1977* (Buford, Ga.: Privately printed, 1977), 654.

5. Aaron R. Clark is listed in an 1839 Cocke County tax list, next to Birdseye in the 6th Civil District. Creekmore, comp., "Early East Tennessee Taxpayers," 138.

6. William Chesley Roadman (1784–1849) represented Carter and Washington counties in the Tennessee senate in 1815–17. Later he became a prominent merchant in Cocke County and served as postmaster of Newport in 1819–47. A representative to the 1834 constitutional convention, he consistently voted against proslavery provisions. BDTGA, 1:621; D. R. Frazier, comp., *Tennessee Post Offices and Postmaster Appointments,* 1789–1984 (Dover, Tenn.: Privately printed, 1984), 237; Oliver P. Temple, *East Tennessee and the Civil War* (Cincinnati, Ohio: Robert Clarke Co., 1899), 113.

7. John Caldwell (1790–1869), one of Birdseye's closest friends in East Tennessee, had been an early abolitionist and remained faithful to the cause throughout the Civil War. He was also one of the pioneer entrepreneurs in developing East Tennessee's mineral resources, notably the copper industry at Ducktown in southeastern Tennessee. He was early active in the American Colonization Society; like Birdseye, he was a Whig, a temperance advocate, and a strong Unionist. Temple, *East Tennessee,* 87–88; *History of Tennessee, Containing Historical and Biographical Sketches of Thirty East Tennessee Counties* (Chicago and Nashville: Goodspeed Publishing Co., 1887; reprinted Greenville, S.C.:

Southern Historical Press, 1991), 882, 1164; Mayme Parrott Wood, *Drifting Down Holston River Way, 1756–1966* (Maryville, Tenn.: Privately printed, 1966), 41.

8. Gerard Troost, *Fifth Geological Report to the Twenty-third General Assembly of Tennessee, Made November, 1839* (Nashville: J. Geo. Harris, Public Printer, 1840), 23.
9. Josiah Rhoton (1803–1860) joined the Tennessee Conference of the Methodist Church in 1822 and located in the Holston Conference in 1827. Thereafter he studied medicine and was a successful practitioner until his death. As a local preacher he was active and useful, maintaining an unblemished reputation, and he simultaneously attained a leading position in the medical profession. Price, *Holston Methodism,* 3:170–73.
10. Dr. Joseph B. M. Reese (1792–1848), brother of Judge William B. Reese, was a well-known physician in Jefferson County. *History of Tennessee, Containing Historical and Biographical Sketches,* 1162, 1193.
11. William M. Kirkpatrick was postmaster at Bent Creek, Jefferson County, from 1838 until this post office was discontinued on June 11, 1841. Frazier, *Tennessee Post Offices,* 466.
12. William B. Reese (1793–1859), born in Jefferson County and educated at Blount College and Greeneville College, was admitted to the bar in 1817. He served on the Tennessee Supreme Court (1835–47), where he was considered one of the most scholarly of supreme court justices. He ran for the U.S. Senate in 1847 but was defeated by John Bell. He thereafter served as president of East Tennessee University and actively promoted the movement to secure railroads for East Tennessee during the 1850s. His father, James Reese, also a lawyer, was a prominent supporter of the state of Franklin in the late eighteenth century. Joshua W. Caldwell, *Sketches of the Bench and Bar of Tennessee* (Knoxville: Ogden Brothers and Co., 1898), 152–54; Samuel Cole Williams, *History of the Lost State of Franklin* (Johnson City, Tenn.: Watauga Press, 1924), 318.
13. Seth J. W. Lucky was admitted to the bar in 1830 at Jonesboro and quickly became one of the leading attorneys. Between 1836 and 1841, he was clerk and master of the chancery court in Washington County; from 1836 until 1854, he was judge of the first judicial circuit. From 1854 until his death in 1869, he was chancellor. A man of unquestioned integrity and high attainments, his judicial decisions rarely were reversed. Active in promoting the East Tennessee and Virginia Railroad, he was an abolitionist who, before 1830, emancipated his own slaves.

History of Tennessee, Containing Historical and Biographical Sketches, 897; Paul M. Fink, *Jonesborough: The First Century of Tennessee's First Town, 1776–1876* (Johnson City, Tenn.: Overmountain Press, 1972), 77; Temple, East Tennessee, 107.

3. To Gerrit Smith, March 22, 1841

NEWPORT COCKE COUNTY E[AST] T[ENNESSEE]
MARCH 22, 1841

My Dear Sir

A few days since I met with Doctor Isham T Peck of Vicksburg Mississippi son of Hon[orable] Jacob Peck[1] of New Market E[ast] Ten[nessee]. Doctor Peck says he is acquainted with the Mr. Worthington[2] whose residence you wish to ascertain. He states that his Post Office is Princeton Washington County Miss[issippi] which is about 100 miles above Vicksburg near the river. He says he came there from K[entuck]y [and] is confident he is the same man for whom you inquire.

In the printed copy of my letter in the Friend of Man[3] Jan[uary] 19[,] I discover two errors which if I said escaped my attention. I should have said North Carolina instead of Mississippi as the state referred to by Mr McAnally. In speaking of this county as opposed to slavery I meant to have said "A very large proportion who own slaves are. While but few are despotic slaveholders." Colored persons even if free are not permitted to own slaves at the South.

I have just heard that the slave in Bunscombe [*sic*] County who was sold by Franklin[4] to Woodfin was well a few days since [and] still with Woodfin.

I have rec[eive]d no letter from Mr. McAnally in answer to mine but shall hear this week by one of my friends who has gone up from this neighborhood to Bunscombe County who will see McAnally and Woodfin if at home. It is 54 miles from my mills to Asheville. My engagements have been such that I could not leave to go up there. I hope to be able to go as soon as the first week in next month and I hope be able to effect the purchase of that poor slave whose sufferings if laid before our good people of the North I think might do much to enlighten them on the subject.

The public sentiment here revolts at such barbarities but it should be recollected that we are in a district where there are but few slaves and one more enlightened on the subject than most others at the South. Cases of equal cruelty are constantly taking place in South Carolina, Georgia, Ala[bama] & Mi[ssissippi]. In fact in all the cotton growing parts of the country where they are put under overseers. A waggoner with whom I am acquainted from Jefferson County by the name of Mansfield passed here some three or 4 days since on his return from Augusta G[eorgi]a stated that on his way he staid at the house of John Smith on this side of the Saludee River at Nealy Ferry. Smith had an overseer who stripped a negro man tied his hands together drew them over his knees—ran a stick thro[ough] above his arms then with one of those heavy slave drivers whips struck him three times. The whip cut entirely through the skin which being strained spread open. He then took a lighter whip and whipped him to a jelly to use his own words from his head to his feet. All this was for a report which the overseer had heard that the negro said that the overseer should not whip him a second time—which the negro declared then and the next day to be entirely untrue. Cases of these enormous cruelties are so constantly reaching us from South Carolina that they excite little attention.

There is a planter at the Great Bend of Nolichucky River Jefferson County by the name of William Moore[5] from S[outh] C[arolina] who has about 40 slaves who adopted this despotic system of discipline. He first tried a Tennessee overseer with whom I am somewhat acquainted, but who resigned his office very soon as he could not be as cruel as his employer required. Moore then hired one from S[outh] C[arolina]. The neighborhood was so shocked with his barbarity that several planters waited on Moore and told him that it must be discontinued. Moore paid some attention to the remonstrance but is sufficiently barbarous yet. He complains of the country as being too free for him. Report says he has purchased lands in Texas.

Some two weeks last Saturday while on my way to Knoxville I was compelled to stop at the house of Calloway Hodges[6] 5 miles below New Market in a severe rain. He is one of the despots of the county, tho[ugh] keeping a public house. I had never stopped with him. I had several times conversed with him on the subject of slavery. I met with no harsh treatment. His professions were friendly to me individually, tho[ugh] he said hard things of the abolitionists. I should think he had about 20 slaves, clothed in rags—some of them barefoot, in this cold March rain. On Sabbath morning, while breakfast was preparing, a slave came to the door and spoke to him. He took a leather covered whip with a lash about 12 in[ches] long, called here a waggoners whip. With this he stepped into his yard and whipped some 5 or 6 of his slaves. Every blow could be counted. I should suppose they were as severe as a strong man could make them and probably averaged about 20 to each slave. He returned, laid by the whip. The family continued their engagements as usual[,] no more excited than if he had been to the door to speak to his slaves. What their offences were was unknown to me. There is always enough with such despots, even should there be no other they say it is best to keep them "cowed."

There is uneasiness in Kentucky this state and North Carolina and in all of them a majority of the legal voters opposed to slavery. Marshals letters[7] published in the Louisville Journal have probably reached you. I have seen but one—that in the paper of Feb[ruary] 3. The Kentucky travellers tell me that the antislavery influence there is on the gain. It is in this state. Many good men are discussing it openly. There are some who call themselves abolitionists. Of the number is my excellent friend, James A. Deaderick,[8] Esq[uire,] cashier of the R[ail] Road Bank in Knoxville. He has freed his slaves—and he assured me that he thought it no dishonor to be known as an abolitionist. A family of slaves have lately been made free in Greenville, that were owned by the clerk of the court. I think they were about 15. About the same number owned in Jefferson by a Mr. Knight[9] will probably be taken to Indiana and made free. Mr. K[night] is offering his place for sale for that purpose. My good friend Judge Peck says in a few years all will be made free. When I saw him last week I loaned him your reply to Mr. Clay. He assured me it was his intention to write you. This unimportant as it may appear is worthy of some regard as it will do much to show that the most intelligent men at the South have much respect for the abolitionists.

Last week William Wadsworth[10] Esq[uire] of Carthage, Moore County North Carolina stopped here on his return from Texas where he had been for some months selling the estate of a son who died there. He spent a night with us on his way out. I found him an interesting man thoroughly opposed to slavery. He assured me he had long exerted himself to overthrow it in North Carolina. He has been seven years a member of the legislature and assured me that he knew the opinion of most of the leading men of that state on the subject. He states that there is now a majority in the state opposed to it. He was much gratified when I assured him that our antislavery people of the North would be glad to correspond with him. I gave him your address. You will probably receive a letter from him soon. If the tax is too great on your time some of our friends will I hope find it convenient. If I am not mistaken a door is now opened which if rightly improved will give us access to the whole antislavery influence in N[orth] C[arolina]. All that is wanting there to make it effectual is to make it active and energetic.

I think the resolution of the abolitionists to act politically at the North excellent. Assure our proslavery friends that we will remember them at the polls they will soon become sparing of their abuse. If generally adopted at the North it will find its way across Mason & Dixon line & then the days of slavery are numbered.

A large proportion of the Presbyterian and Methodist clergymen that I am acquainted with at the South are opposed to slavery. Most of them are humble pious self-denying men. I am sorry to say that we have some proslavery clergymen in this state. Among the most conspicuous is an editor of a political paper published at Jonesboro E[ast] T[ennessee]. His name is William G. Brownlowe.[11] But few papers leave his office without some denounciations of the abolitionists.

A year last Feb[ruary] he made one of a delegation from Washington County to the Knoxville Whig Convention. With some I may say many good traits of character, he is excitable and indiscreet. On his way at Greensville he procured a red flannel *petticoat* [and] carried it himself on a pole some 20 feet long as an expression of contempt for a slander on Gen[eral] Harrison. Such a strange exhibition drew squads of both parties out to see what was passing. When he saw Locofocos[12] he called to them with a familiar sang-froid "look here you rascals" as the roads were bad they had some 20 or 30 miles to ride on the sabath yet Mr Brownlowe carried his flag to the door of his hotel in Knoxville in the afternoon. In the excitement on Monday evening he drank too freely. His severe personal remarks soon bro[ugh]t him into a quarrel with one of the adverse party. It was said that in this his adversary was the aggressor. Brownlowe sent to Baltimore by Gen[eral] W[illia]m Brazzleton for a select pistol. Soon after receiving it he met his adversary in the street for a personal encounter. But his foe got the first shot and wounded him severely in the thigh. This man gives a detailed account of these transactions with the exception [of his] drinking too freely at Knoxville and that he yet preaches—in his paper. I have heard that he would not be permitted to remain in the Methodist Church without reformation but as yet I have not heard of his expulsion. His is here a very unusual case. But the proslavery clergy of the South as at the North sometimes act apparently in the absence of religious influences.

My hasty letter has so much that is personal that it would be probably imprudent to publish it. Should anything be selected I request that it should be such as could not easily be traced back. Judge Peck and myself are anxious to get up a free labor community or settlement where slave labor will be entirely excluded. There are great natural resources here for such a location. I am anxious to have an active correspondence between the antislavery portion of the North and South. Steady patient efforts with the blessing will eventually succeed.

Sincerely your friend
E Birdseye

WRITTEN ACROSS PAGE 1:
P.S. My friend has returned from Asheville McAnally was from home. Woodfin was gone to return on the 12th April when I shall endeavour to see him.

WRITTEN ACROSS PAGE 2:
*Valentine Sevier[13]

Notes

1. Judge Jacob Peck (1779–1869) served on the Tennessee Supreme Court from 1822 until 1834. He was a man of unusual culture, interested in music, painting, mineralogy, and zoology. His interest in geology led him to invest widely in lands containing mineral ores. He was Birdseye's best friend in East Tennessee, and a sympathetic abolitionist whose humanity towards slaves was revealed in many of his decisions as judge. He served as Birdseye's lawyer, advisor, and partner in various land speculations, and left behind a fascinating journal of his geologic investigations. Caldwell, *Sketches of the Bench and Bar*, 62–63; Peck's Notes, McClung Historical Collection, Knox County Public Library, Knoxville, Tenn.; BDTGA, 1:577–78.
2. In 1841, Gerrit Smith bought a slave family—man, wife, and five children—from Mr. Worthington of Mississippi. In an earlier letter to Birdseye, Smith said that his wife, when young, inconsiderately had given a slave girl to her brother, James Fitzhugh of Maryland, who afterward sold her to Mr. Worthington. Seeking to free this slave girl and her family, Smith inquired if Birdseye knew Worthington's address in Mississippi. Harlow, *Gerrit Smith*, 270; Gerrit Smith to Ezekiel Birdseye, Dec. 21, 1840, letterbook copy, Smith Papers.
3. *Friend of Man*, one of the official newspapers of the New York Anti-Slavery Society, was sponsored in part by Gerrit Smith and edited by William Goodell from 1836 to 1842. It was therefore a logical source for publication of many of Birdseye's letters to Smith. Sorin, *New York Abolitionists*, 60.
4. This person may well have been Isaac Franklin, Sr., a well-known slave trader and stagecoach driver who lived in Cocke County, Tenn., but operated from New Orleans to Alexandria, Va. Ruth Webb O'Dell, *Over the Misty Blue Hills: The Story of Cocke County, Tennessee* (Newport, Tenn.: Privately printed, 1951), 263. See also Wendell Holmes Stephenson, *Isaac Franklin: Slave Trader and Planter of the Old South* (Baton Rouge: Louisiana State Univ. Press, 1938).

5. Col. William Moore was a planter from South Carolina who moved to Jefferson County, Tenn., after 1834. He was living in Ray County, Mo., by 1854, so he did indeed leave East Tennessee as Birdseye suggested. *History of Tennessee, Containing Historical and Biographical Sketches*, 1169.
6. Calloway Hodge later was cited by the *Knoxville Daily Register*, June 5, 1861, for kind treatment shown to soldiers injured on a train derailed near Strawberry Plains, Tenn. Mayme Parrott Wood, *Hitch Hiking along the Holston River, 1792–1962* (Gatlinburg, Tenn.: Brazos Printing Co., 1964), 111.
7. Thomas F. Marshall (1801–1864), nephew of John Marshall, was a Kentucky lawyer and state representative (1832–36, 1839–39, 1854), elected as representative to the 27th U.S. Congress (1841–43). In the *Louisville Journal*, he wrote comparing the population of Virginia and Kentucky, attributing the latter's success to the absence of slavery: "There is but one explanation of the facts I have shown. The clog that has stayed the march of her [Virginia's] people, the incubus that has weighed down her enterprise, strangled her commerce, kept sealed her exhaustless fountains of mineral wealth, and paralyzed her arts, manufactures, and improvements, is Negro slavery." This view of the economic blight imposed by slavery was identical to Birdseye's. Dwight Lowell Dumond, *Antislavery: The Crusade for Freedom in America* (Ann Arbor: Univ. of Michigan Press, 1961), 288; BDAC, 1340. In later years, Marshall was denounced by Henry Clay as an "apostate Whig" and became a proslavery leader. J. Winston Coleman, Jr., *Slavery Times in Kentucky* (Chapel Hill: Univ. of North Carolina Press, 1940), 309–13.
8. I believe Birdseye has mistakenly given the wrong name here to David Anderson Deaderick (1797–1873), who in 1839 was appointed cashier of the Southwest Railroad Branch Bank at Knoxville. Mary U. Rothrock, ed., *The French Broad–Holston Country: A History of Knox County, Tennessee* (Knoxville: East Tennessee Historical Society, 1946), 409–10.
9. Tristam Day Knight (1798–1857), a native of Maine, did indeed write to Gerrit Smith in 1845, asking him for a loan to discharge all his debts in order to emancipate his slaves. He said he had immigrated to Tennessee in 1820, married the daughter of a slaveholder there, and subsequently pledged not to leave the state while his father-in-law lived. His wife inherited the slaves from her father; when Knight's cotton manufacturing failed after the Panic of 1837, he was forced to give a deed of trust for the slaves for $5,000. Smith replied to Knight very sympathetically but informed him that his own estate was in such jeopardy that he could not assist him. Gen. T. D. Knight to Gerrit Smith, Apr. 17, 1845;

Gerrit Smith to Gen. T. D. Knight, May 5, 1845, letterbook copy, Smith Papers.

10. William Wadsworth (1788–1851), representing Moore County, served three terms in the North Carolina House of Commons (1826–27, 1827–28, and 1828–29). John L. Cheney, Jr., *North Carolina Government, 1585–1979: A Narrative and Statistical History* (Raleigh: North Carolina Department of the Secretary of State, 1981), 288, 290, 291; Anthony E. Parker, comp., *A Guide to Moore County Cemeteries* (Carthage, N.C.: Moore County Historical Association, 1975).

11. William Gannaway Brownlow (1805–1877), sometime Methodist minister and the irascible and vituperative editor of the *Knoxville Whig,* became a leader of the Unionist movement in 1861 in East Tennessee and later served as Reconstruction governor of the state. During the 1840s and 1850s, however, he was one of the region's staunchest defenders of slavery. E. Merton Coulter, *William G. Brownlow: Fighting Parson of the Southern Highlands* (Chapel Hill: Univ. of North Carolina Press, 1939), 110–293.

12. Locofocos were the radical wing of the Democratic Party, Jacksonians who favored states' rights and particularly championed the common man. The name, derived from a common type of friction match, first was used in politics when a group of New York Jacksonians used these matches to light candles when their opponents tried to break up their meeting by turning off the gaslights. Locofocos argued against granting any subsidies or favors to private business and advocated a policy of total *laissez faire* in the economy. Robert V. Remini, *Andrew Jackson* (New York: Twayne, 1966), 180.

13. Valentine Sevier (1780–1854), prominent merchant, later lawyer, represented Greene County in the Tennessee house of representatives (1821–23). A Whig, he served as Greene County Court Clerk in 1802–10, circuit court clerk in 1810–54, and mayor of Greeneville in 1818. A Presbyterian, he was a trustee of Greeneville College and a director of the Hiwassee Railroad in 1836. Earlier he had set all his slaves free and was an abolitionist, so it is logical that Birdseye knew him and wrote his name as a possible correspondent for Gerrit Smith. *BDTGA,* 1:661–62; Temple, *East Tennessee,* 107.

4. To Gerrit Smith, April 16, 1841

ASHEVILLE BUNCOMBE COUNTY NORTH CAROLINA
APRIL 16TH, 1841

My Dear Sir

I have today had an interview with N. W. Woodfin Esq[uire] in order to learn whether he would sell the man he bought of Franklin. Mr. McAnally has spoken to him on the subject before and informed him that the object was to give him his freedom.

Mr. W[oodfin] says that he found this man in jail here that he became interested in his case and bought him intending never to sell him, but to make him a good home where he should live as well as he did; that he has become much attached to him.

He says he does not know a better laborer or a more honest man. He is confident that he would not be willing to leave him unless it was to obtain his freedom. I think he has but one other man. He notes that they are so trustworthy that he is gone two or three months at a time. On returning he finds everything in good order and faithfully done, so much so that he is in the habit of making him a present or payment in money for extra labor.[1]

He says as he is now situated he should have to purchase another of his father in law for which he should have to pay $800. That as the object is a benevolent one he will take that for this man if it would be his wish to go. If he should be unwilling to go he would decline selling him. He asked if I had a personal knowledge of the character of the man who wished to buy him. I assured him that his character was well known to me that a good home and kind treatment could be relied on. He replied that from what he had heard of me he was satisfied with the assurance. I am gratified with the kind attentions I had from the Rev[erend] D R McAnally. He expressed much anxiety to accommodate and further my views tho[ugh] he said it was but a week since he had the opportunity meeting with Mr. W[oodfin] and making the inquiry. Mr. W[oodfin] remarked incidentally that if he should find that he could replace him for less it would make a difference in the price of this man.

Mr. Woodfin paid specie $600 and in addition paid his jail fees. I do not know what they amounted to.

It is too true that with the character he gives him that he would readily bring 800 dollars in specie if offered for sale. There is no danger that he will be [sold] for any other purpose than to obtain his freedom. Mr. W[oodfin] assures me that no sum would induce him to set a price on him.² Mr. W[oodfin] requested me not to speak to him on the subject untill our arrangement was finally conducted as it might make him dissatisfied or uneasy. I assured him that I would not that the Reverend McAnally was the only person in the county to whom I had spoken and to him confidentially.

Woodfin is a young man apparently not over 33 mild interesting readily acknowledges his aversion to slavery and deeply deploring the slave trade. Mr. McAnally is an interesting man and briefly remarked "that is our misfortune in the South that a few people do the thinking for all the rest."

It is gratifying to me as it must be to you to learn that this man who has been subjected to much barbarity is now comparatively comfortable but whether we can purchase him at the price asked is a question for his friends to consider. The sum is large. I had hoped it would be less. Prices have given way in the cotton growing districts beyond what they have in the others and are declining.

Mr. Woodfin observed that should my friend want a confidential servant industrious honest and affectionate he could not find a better. This agrees with the character my tenant Mr. Clarke gives him. Personally I have no acquaintance with him.

There is another view of the case which is important. That is, what would be the effect in our community if this man should lay his case personally before them. His character for truth is undoubted. Mr. W[oodfin] says he is one of the most candid men he knows that he has in no case found him to deviate from the strictest veracity. He has seen much of slavery and experienced it in all its horrors as his lacerated body will abundantly testify. Of this nothing should be said which would if known here prevent his going North—or if influential slaveholders should learn that our purpose was to lay his case before our community they might and probably would interfere. Mr. Woodfin will go out on his circuit and be much from home. A letter addressed to him may reach him soon and would be promptly attended to. He is strictly honorable. It would be safe to remit to him and address me at Newport Ten[nessee]. I shall readily contribute a share should it be thought expedient to buy him but that would have to be on near one y[ea]rs time. If you should think it inexpedient to buy him at the price we shall derive consolation in knowing that he is so far comfortable.

We are mourning the death of Gen[eral] Harrison.³ I formed a personal acquaintance with him soon after he returned from S[outh] America tho[ugh] I regretted his subservency to slavery. I believe even on that ground we had gained something. He was an amiable generous man. His sympathies for the poor or unfortunate were easily excited. His generosity even led him into faults.

As he is taken from us by a mysterious Providence I hope he will obtain forgiveness for every error at the Bar of a merciful God.

With this I send you a paper published here and one of the temperance papers. This is a pleasant town has a brick court house two churches one a New Brick Presbyterian the other a good Methodist. It is a mountaineous district. The town is high and healthy. Situated in a grazing country or one naturally so there is green fields which add beauty to the town. There is much improvement in morals and much that does honor to the Old North state.

This is one of the most hopeful states of all the South. I see nothing like personal violence and what must be gratifying to all of our friends they speak with much hostility against slavery. I write in great haste. I shall be happy to hear from you my dear Sir.

With great respect
I am Y[ou]rs
E. Birdseye

Notes

1. This comparative liberality toward slaves, and willingness by some masters to allow their slaves greater autonomy, was not atypical of western North Carolina slaveowners, according to Inscoe, *Mountain Masters*, 87–114.
2. Woodfin actually did sell this slave within one year for $550, to another slaveowner. EB/GS, July 2, 1842.
3. William Henry Harrison (1773–1841), 9th U.S. president, contracted pneumonia and died in office on Apr. 4, 1841. In 1829 he had served as minister to Colombia. *DAB*, 8:348–52.

5. To Gerrit Smith, June 21, 1841

Newport Cocke County
June 21st, 1841

My Dear Sir

Yours of the 29th April came safely to hand. The Friend of Man accompanied it—a very acceptable present.

I am clearly of the opinion that you have taken the best course with regard to the purchase of the freedom of the slave in Asheville. He has a kind master and is where he has moral and religious influences around him. The greatest induc[e]ment to his purchase would appear to be to further the interests of the good cause. I have been so long from the North that I am not well prepared to say how much such influences may be needed at the present day. I hope less than they were a few years since. The sum is large, probably the same amount expended in some other way might do more good. Mr. Woodfin will not sell him as a slave for any sum as he well assured me. He is much attached to him. So strong is the mutual friendship that he thought it doubtful whether he would leave him; he said he would for no other purpose but to gain his freedom. Prices of slaves have not declined in the mountain districts as they have in the cotton growing. I am confident that prices must come down further in all. Should the cause of abolition need the aid of this man better terms would probably be listened to in a year. In a few years[,] if I am not mistaken in the sighns of the times, Woodfin will give him his freedom and find his greatest happiness in doing justice without payment. The slave I find communicated more to Mr Clarke my tenant that I was aware of. It was understood to be confidential. The poor fellow had such a dread of getting back into the hands of the barbarians from whom he had escaped that he disclosed nothing where he tho[ugh]t he could be betrayed. At the time he labored with Clarke he was bailed out of jail. His history was briefly this. He was sold to a slave dealer in V[irgini]a taken on to the west and traded from one savage to another. Finding life a burden he attempted to escape was several times recaptured and whipped. He stated to Clarke that they had whipped him as many as 500 lashes at one time so that he is covered with ridges from his head to his feet. His last escape was from Apalachicola Bay. He soon fell in company with one who had probably escaped from Arkansaw. Their plan was to follow the mountains to the free states. They were so much harassed that they made slow progress. One winter they lived in a cave in the mountains and subsisted mainly on dry corn which they parched by their fire. At other times they were followed by dogs and narrowly escaped being caught. One night after a fatiguing days walk they crawled into a pen where there was a quantity of corn husks. Very soon after they lay down they were surrounded by a company of men and dogs. They broke thro[ugh] and were followed by the dogs. They called to the dogs as if to set them on something ahead. This succeeded. The dogs ran past doing them no harm. They were often supplied with provisions by other slaves. Sometimes they suffered with hunger. They saw plenty of game but could not take it for want of a gun. They were on the Great Smoky M[oun]t[ain] in

Cocke County and found themselves pursued by dogs and men. They ran untill they came to the Big Pigeon River. The ice was running in the river at the time. They plunged in and swam across. The dogs and the more savage men could not stand so cold a bath, and gave up the pursuit. The night was cold, they were hungry, without fires, wet, their clothes froze on them. The poor fellow stated to Clarke that in all of his sufferings, that night was the most severe, and one that brought him the nearest to death. They wandered about the mountain a few days longer and seeing a hunter at a distance by the name of Davis they went to him and voluntarily surrendered themselves. All who have seen this man describe him as a man of the first order of natural talents—of strict integrity of character. When I met Franklin inquiring for him He said "He is a smarter man than I am." Mr Woodfin said that his veracity was so strict that he would always tell the truth if against himself. There are thousands whose cases would be a parallel to his. In Mississippi they are hunted with blood hounds. If a slave attempts to run the pursuers shoot him down. This fertile state is suffering as if under the curse of Heaven. Dr. Peck tells me that as many as one fifth of the plantations are abandoned and it seems to be generally understood that the state is without character at home or credit abroad.

There are a great many instances where the slaves are kindly treated comfortably clothed and well fed, but with such the antislavery part of our people have little cause to apprehend difficulty. They do not denounce the abolitionists or speak unkindly of them. Many of them are zealous advocates for emancipation. Such slaves have not intellectual culture. On the death of a kind master, should he have neglected to provide for them by will, or die indebted, they must be sold publicly to the highest bidder. A case of this kind happened last winter in Cocke County. Mr. Jones a kind man to his slaves died sud[d]enly and in debt. He had some 9 or 10 slaves. Riding into Newport I overtook them near the town walking in a muddy road of a rainy morning. Two women had their children in their arms (infants) their husbands had some older ones. It was raining. They were tired with a walk of 8 miles in deep mud. Within half a mile of the place where they were to be sold to whom they knew not and to be separated perhaps for the last time. There appeared to be fortitude with a related melanchollia. They were sold in the Court House.

I went in for a few minutes; there appeared to be not more than twenty or thirty biders. Most of them from a distance. The first offered was a boy about 14 years old. He was sold on a credit of one year for $715. The next boy about the same age $720—the next a woman with infant child I think a fraction over $900. Her husband was sold to a man from North Carolina. It was said the purchaser assured him that he should be permitted to come into Tennessee and visit with his wife once a year. Possibly the promise may be regarded. The women were allowed to retain their infants, with that they appeared to think the claims of humanity satisfied. The others were scattered to places remote from each other. I have been since to the house of Mrs Jones. She appears to be a pious woman. She said it was distressing to her to have her colored family scattered so but she had no power to prevent it. However mild slaves may be treated, they live in dread of these occurrences which separate them forever.

A year ago there was much discussion in the South, the most in V[irgini]a, about the demand made on Governor Seward for the surrender of the "Fugitives from Justice."[1] There appeared to be some surprise that the Governor did not yield at once, the elections were pending and times unpropitious. It was said the correspondence was to be resumed and no doubt was entertained of success. The old expedients of raving and disunion with bullying was supposed would not fail to bring N[ew] York to terms. I had much anxiety for the issue and greatly to the honor of your executive he maintained his ground with dignity and firmness. For once this insolence of the South has been rebuked and compelled to yield. No circumstance that I recollect has raised the North more.

The South appear to feel as though their power was not so potent as they had supposed; and that the North may in future be less disposed to yield to their unreasonable demands. The repeal of your nine months law—the decision of the Supreme Court of Ohio and many other things indicate a favorable change of public sentiment in the North.

There are favorable signs even here. The letters of Mr Gurney to Henry Clay[2] are read attentively by slave holders. I have heard no one of them express an unfavorable opinion. For the present state of the South it is a most excellent work—so kind that none could take offence at it—the reasoning so clear and forcible as to be unanswerable. I hope it will have a general circulation at the South. I should think that in the present quiet state of the public mind it would be read in all parts of the South, and without any special effort to destroy it.

It was observed by some southern writer a year or two ago that the abolitionists were more dangerous to their institutions than was generally imagined. Tho[ugh] few in number they were industrious and persevering—I hope they may continue to deserve that character.

John Caldwell of whom I have frequently spoken showed me a will drawn for a widow a few days since in which she emancipated her six slaves at her death. Mr Caldwell has been in the habit of writing a great many wills for the last twenty years. He states that a great change has taken place within the last two years in emancipating slaves, and that this disposition to emancipate is on the increase. Judge Peck has expressed the same opinion and others also whose situation enabled them to obtain extensive information.

Mr C[aldwell] has one of the pamphlets (your letter to Mr Clay). The other I gave to John Doane[3] Esq[uire] near New Market. This man has been one of the most faithful laborers in the antislavery cause in E[ast] Ten[nessee]. He has writ[t]en much and always carries the influence with him. He laments the corrupting influence in the Church and says the Church must be freed from it.

I am happy to hear that my friend Birney[4] is married. No one of his friends can more sincerely rejoice in his happiness. My acquaintance began with him in Ala[bama]. He was then in the first rank of his profession at the Bar. The highest honors of the state were within his reach, if he would have accepted them. I next knew him while in K[entuck]y. While I was in the stage in the company with slaveholders between Maysville & Lexington they spoke of his paper intended to be published at Danville and said he should never survive the second number if he did the first. I thought it my duty to apprise him of his danger by letter—but am mortified to recollect that it contained a censure on Abolitionists for going ahead of public sentiment. I soon became convinced that Mr Birney was right and have only regretted that I could not do more for a cause in which so much is involved. I hope most sincerely that he may yet be the President of the United States. He has talents of the first order firmness and independence with all the qualifications necessary for the chief magistrate of a great nation—political changes are often as great. In the fall of 1828 I was in Nashville, a man who would there have spoken openly and decidedly against Andrew Jackson would have done it at the risque of his life. Now very few there do him reverence. His name has become a byword throughout the state.

Should the country become and continue calm on other subjects I think we may hope for a great change on that. When politicians learn that they must be orthodox on this point to insure the votes of abolitionists they will soon be correct in their views. I hope the antislavery freemen of the North will look on this as an indispensable qualification. When the people are right the candidates for their favor will find little difficulty in becoming so.

The Temperance reformation was most triumphant in Ten[nessee]. So much so that I do not recollect being aquainted with a respectable public house above Knoxville where wines or liquors are sold. There are two Hotels in Knoxville that attempted to keep it. The keeper of one of them was fined last spring court $100. I believe both were fined. The friends of the cause have made no special effort of late. In the most exciting political contest last year it suffered some I think. The Whigs I believe furnished only hard cider and but little of that. Sometimes it was a label only on the head of an empty cask. The public sentiment will sustain the present law which prohibits the sale of a less quantity than one quart and that not to be drunk in the house where sold (if I recollect correctly). Public sentiment makes it unfashionable and dishonorable. The friends of the cause speak of making special efforts very soon.

Rev[erend] F. A. Ross[5] Kingsport E[ast] Ten[nessee] anticipates great good to the cause of emancipation from the silk culture. His heart is much in the cause. He gave all his own slaves their freedom and has gone into the business extensively. He thinks it will make a profitable employment for the poor and raise them from the extreme depression and ignorance under which a great part of them labor. The culture of multicaulis is extending to almost every house. I should suppose one third of the families were growing some silk by way of experiment. Mr R[oss] proposes to buy the cocoons and make a ready market for them. If it should bring them but a very moderate compensation it will be a great blessing to them. The white poor are depressed in all the South, too often unlettered and exposed to all the nameless ills attendant on ignorance and vice.

Judge Peck and myself still hope to get up a small settlement of free laborers on our land debarring slavery forever. We have some interesting correspondents at Boston. Willard Badger David Gould our eastern people are very fearful of the South. There is a spirit of freedom in all the mountain region from P[ennsylvani]a to our districts. This region is healthy a large proportion of it fertile abounding in mineral wealth equal I should suppose to the mountains in P[ennsylvani]a.

Some 4 weeks since I met with Dr. Tho[ma]s A. Anderson[6] who lives near. The Doctor had been opposed to me in the political campaign last summer. He was understood to be proslavery but had always treated me with politeness. Such was the excitement of the time that political opponents seldom were very warm personal friends. The D[octo]r was until recently a Presbyterian clergyman. I believe his conduct was not very censurable untill he espoused the cause of slavery with some degree of vehemence. His next error was editing an administration paper in the same village with Brownlow, Jonesboro. It was difficult to determine which was the most violent as an editor. The doctor gave up his clerical character with all claims to his profession as a Christian. In every instance when I have found a Southern clergyman defending slavery there has been no signs of spiritual life. Some have given up their hopes [while] others seem to retain them as an incumbrance, which like Virgil's white horses do not pay the rearing. In defending slavery they have the most bitterness and the least charity of all its defenders.

The D[octo]r invited me to spend the night at his house and wished to have me become acquainted with the Rev[erend] Abel Pearson,[7] an aged divine for whom I had entertained a very high respect. I accepted his invitation and became much pleased with Dr Pierson. The D[octo]r bro[ugh]t his late papers. When I happened to lay down Dr. Channings[8] pamphlet on Emancipation the D[octo]r took the alarm said he wondered why our Eastern friends would not let us alone. He said some had the audacity to send abolition pamphlets to him. He had promptly sent them back and written them to send him no more. I replied Dr Channing is a very candid writer and so mild that I should think his writings could offend no one. It was all offensive. The very attempt to agitate the question would dissolve the Union. The South had too much value in slaves besides a representation of 25 members in Congress ever to allow the question to be discussed. D[octo]r you will admit that the North have a right to discuss this question. No they have no such right. The very attempt is unconstitutional and will lead to war and bloodshed. Could the South hope for any success by appealing to the fears of the North. The great law of love would lead us to discuss all questions connected with the well being of our fellow man. The D[octo]r left the room excited. I did not see him that evening again. Dr Pierson had a volume near him which he had written on the Prophesies, Piersons Analysis[9] in which he predicted the near approach of the millinium and the downfall of slavery. He read from his book explained his views in a very clear manner. He said slavery must soon terminate by the voluntary act of the Masters or by force. He inclined to think by the voluntary act of owners. Some of the Southern clergymen and politicians represent the South as being united all as one man ready to *do battle* for slavery at its bidding. Nothing can be further from the truth. Take the whole slaveholding South. They have less than a majority of the legal voters. It is only by withholding light and acting in concert as a privileged order that they maintain the ascendency. This is the reason why they are alarmed when an abolition paper or pamphlet finds its way among them. Slavery could not bear free discussion one year in the South. If by any means the non-slaveholding part of the community act in concert it must soon die. If the time comes and come it must when the subject is fairly taken up for discussion there are men of ardent feelings who will go to the work as though they were contending for life. I have heard expressions of commendation of your course not unfrequently. Something like a year since I happened in company with Mr Caldwell and a venerable old clergyman Rev[erend] Mr McCammel[10] of Dandridge. Mr. Caldwell read your letter to President Smucker.[11] Good old Mr McCammel said "Oh! that Gerritt Smith I love him as I would an only son."

Present my cordial good wishes to Mr Birney and Lady and accept the assurances of my sincere friendship.

Ezekiel Birdseye

Notes

1. Late in 1839, three black seamen, New York citizens, made an unsuccessful effort to help a slave escape from Virginia. Subsequently Virginia demanded that New York surrender these seamen, but Gov. William H. Seward refused, on the grounds that he did not consider human beings—slaves—as property. Seward's stand was popular among abolitionists in the North but caused a storm of protest from the South. Glyndon G. Van Deusen, *William Henry Seward* (New York: Oxford Univ. Press, 1967), 65–66.
2. Joseph John Gurney, *A Winter in the West Indies, Described in Familiar Letters to Henry Clay, of Kentucky* (London: John Murray, 1840). Describing improvements in the British West Indies after emancipation, Gurney argued that all aspects of the lives of both blacks and whites had dramatically improved, especially the value of land. Gurney's arguments were very similar to Birdseye's about the economic liabilities occasioned by slavery.
3. John Doan's name appears on many petitions from Jefferson County to the state legislature seeking the abolition of slavery. Petitions, 1821–34, *passim.*
4. James Gillespie Birney (1792–1857), southern antislavery leader, practiced law in Alabama in 1818–32, freed his own slaves, and did indeed plan an abolitionist newspaper in Danville, Ky.; but overwhelming opposition caused him to move to Ohio, where he began publishing the *Philanthropist* in 1836. Although initially a supporter of the American Colonization Society, by 1834 he had lost faith in gradual emancipation and colonization. In 1835 he founded the Kentucky Anti-Slavery Society; in 1840 and 1844, he was the presidential candidate for the Liberty Party, supported in part by his good friend Gerrit Smith. Betty Fladeland, *James Gillespie Birney: Slaveholder to Abolitionist* (Ithaca, N.Y.: Cornell Univ. Press, 1955), 25–251.
5. Frederick Augustus Ross (1796–1883), prominent wealthy Presbyterian minister, earlier had freed all his slaves. Unfortunately he lost his entire

fortune in the silk industry and became a leading proslavery advocate in the 1850s. In 1857 he published a book, *Slavery Ordained of God*, in which he claimed divine sanction for the peculiar institution. Charles C. Ross, ed., *Story of Rotherwood, from the Autobiography of Rev. Frederick A. Ross, D.D.* (Knoxville, Tenn.: Bean, Warters, 1923), 1–35; Frank Netherland, *A History of the Ross Silk Factory and Other Events of Rotherwood, Tennessee* (Rogersville, Tenn.: East Tennessee Printing Co., 1988); Frederick Augustus Ross, *Slavery Ordained of God* (Philadelphia: J. B. Lippincott, 1857).

6. Dr. Thomas A. Anderson, "a writer of great spriteliness," edited the Democratic *Tennessee Sentinel* for several years, until succeeded by Landon C. Haynes. Fink, *Jonesborough*, 143; *History of Tennessee, Containing Historical and Biographical Sketches*, 899. Parson Brownlow characteristically and vituperatively attacked Anderson, who was the son of former U.S. Sen. Joseph Anderson and brother of the current senator, Alexander Outlaw Anderson, as "the *profane swearer, apostate Presbyterian Preacher, and drunken blackguard* who now edits the *Jonesborough Sentinel*." Steve Humphrey, *"That D——d Brownlow,"* . . . (Boone, N.C.: Appalachian Consortium Press, 1978), 30–35.

7. Abel Pearson (1779–1856), a Presbyterian minister educated by Dr. Isaac Anderson at Maryville College, in 1815 petitioned the Blount County Court for the emancipation of George Erskine, a black later educated by Dr. Anderson and sent to Liberia as a missionary. Pearson subsequently moved to Hamilton County, Tenn., where in 1828 he organized the Soddy Presbyterian Church and served as its first minister. Inez E. Burns, *History of Blount County, Tennessee, from War Trail to Landing Strip, 1795–1955* (Nashville: Tennessee Historical Commission, 1957), 39; Zella Armstrong, *The History of Hamilton County and Chattanooga, Tennessee* (Chattanooga: Lookout Publishing Co., 1931), 1:114, 1:199, 1:242, 1:244, 1:266, 1:318.

8. William Ellery Channing (1780–1842) was a well-known religious leader whose first-hand observations of slavery while serving as a tutor to a family in Richmond, Virginia, had led him to oppose slavery as detrimental to slave and master alike. Unlike other abolitionists, Channing nevertheless had a firm respect for the integrity of slaveholders, so Birdseye was indeed correct in terming him "mild." Channing's books, *Slavery* (1835), and *The Abolitionist* (1836), therefore constituted very effective propaganda for people like Birdseye, who were trying to use moral persuasion to convert southern slaveholders. *DAB*, 4:4–7.

9. Abel Pearson, *An Analysis of the Principles of the Divine Government* (Athens, Tenn.: William P. Reid, 1833).
10. Rev. John McCampbell (1871–1859) was trained by his cousin, Dr. Isaac Anderson, and began preaching at Shunem Presbyterian Church, Strawberry Plains, Tenn., in 1805; he was ordained by Union Presbytery in 1807. His close association with Isaac Anderson probably accounts in part for his abolitionist sentiments. Wood, *Hitch Hiking*, 63; Samuel Tyndale Wilson, *Isaac Anderson, Founder and First President of Maryville College: A Memorial Sketch* (Maryville, Tenn.: Privately printed, 1932), 35, 80, 94, 136, 147.
11. In 1838 Gerrit Smith wrote to President Schmucker of the theological seminary in Gettysburg, Pa., explaining his reasons for becoming an anti-colonizationist: "If the Colonization Society had not come out against the doctrine of immediate emancipation, and inferentially against the doctrine of the sinfulness of slavery, I should, in all probability, have continued a member of it down to the present time." Basically, he continued, colonization as an absolute requirement for emancipation was racist. Octavius Brooks Frothingham, *Gerrit Smith: A Biography* (New York: G. P. Putnam's Sons, 1878), 169–70.

6. To Gerrit Smith, June 25, 1841

NEWPORT E[AST] TEN[NESSEE]
JUNE 25TH, 1841

My Dear Sir

I found on Monday the *"Signal of Liberty"*[1] published at Ann Arbor Mi[chigan] which you had the goodness to for[war]d. It is gratify[ing] to me to receive this among the many evidences of the spirit of liberty in the Northern states. I would hope that this spirit is progressive in all the free states. The reformation there will act directly on the South. The Temperance reformation did. All influences which extensively affect the North operate almost simultaneously on the South. While these evidences are reaching me of a favorable change in the North I find them silently making progress here.

The late census with the s[t]atistical information spread before the public has made an impression. The far greater increase of the North in wealth and population is soon to leave them (of the South) in a hopeless minority unless prevented by a timely change of policy. I hope it may have a good effect on the North by showing them that they are not necessarily subservient to the South.

In a late letter I made some observations on the influences of free principles in North Carolina. Mr Wadsworth of whom I spoke told me that he had conversed with Romulus M Saunders[2] and Governor Morehead[3]—that both were opposed to slavery. Both you will recollect were rival candidates for Gov[ernor] last year. A year [ago] last winter I stopped for the night at the Hotel in Knoxville. A gentleman was introduced to my room whom I learned to be Mr Saunders of N[orth] C[arolina]. I had some knowledge of his public character. This was the first personal acquaintance. I found him communicative agreeable and polite. He conversed freely on the proslavery excitements of the South. He said they had one at Raleigh. Some vague reports obtained circulation of an intended insurrection. He found the court house filled with slaves undergoing examination and was requested to attend. He found no cause for the excitement and expressed his opinion that the slaves were innocent. The public were excited and requested him to give the prisoners a *talk*. He addressed the slaves and endeavoured to impress their minds with the necessity of a quiet peaceable demeanor, that they should carefully abstain from every thing which should lead to suspicions of bad intentions which would only tend to expose them to harsh treatment and endanger their lives. With this they were dismissed. All went off quietly. At this time a young man from the North was boarding in his family teaching. He had expressed himself openly on the subject of slavery and was apprehensive of personal violence. He consulted Mr S[aunders] as to what would be expedient. Mr. S[aunders] told him to talk with him unreservedly on the subject but advised him to be guarded in his expressions to others. Finding that there was excitement arising which might endanger the young man he advised him to leave. He went to the North safely. Mr S[aunders] in the course of our conversation inquired why it was that no more of our people emigrated to their state while its natural advantages were so great and so much cheaper than at the Northwestern states. I replied that it was their dread of slavery and coming in contact with slaveholding institutions. He said he had supposed that to be the reason. These public men are afraid of injuring their popularity; and express themselves with caution. Mr. S[aunders] if I recollect correctly once presented a petition from the Friends in N[orth] C[arolina] for the abolition of slavery in the District of Columbia. I am disposed to believe that a profitable correspondence might be carried on with him if he was assured that it should be confidential. I wish I could give grounds to hope of S[outh] Carolina. It is out of my power. There are individuals there of great moral worth but they would fear being even suspected of heresy on this subject. The great body of the community there of both Church and State appear to unite in its support. The slaveholders are aristocratic, fond of show and living up to their means. The poor are ignorant and depressed. When I was in that state it was supposed that there was an average of 200 women at their courts in the interior of the state mixing with the crowd with an effrontery which too plainly indicated to what class they belonged. Whether these evils have increased or diminished the last few years I am not informed. If there is a redeeming spirit in all that state I should suppose it to be John B Oneal[4] one of the Judges of the Appellate Court. He is a pious man well acquainted throughout the state. I believe would answer any respectful inquiry which might be addressed to him at Newbury C[ourt] H[ouse] S[outh] C[arolina]. It is but a few days since two men said to be from this state (S[outh] C[arolina]) passed through Jefferson County having three runaway slaves. They were chained together around the neck—their arms fastened to each other with irons around their wrists. I did not see them. They passed the neighborhood where I was at the time. The cruelty was generally spoken of in terms of severe reprobation.

One of the most unhappy features in the character of the slaveholding states is their proneness to violence. The evil may be traced to the frequent examples of cruelty to the slaves and the want of parental government. Children grow up without restraint—rather taught to indulge than govern their passions. As they become grown up frequent collisions occur of a serious nature, often fatal and seldom punished, if among the aristocracy. I am happy to be able to say that they occur less frequently in E[ast] Ten[nessee] than in most parts of the South, but are quite too frequent here. Nashville and the vicinity have been most afflicted with these occurrences of any part of our state and seem to occur there most among the aristocracy.

In Jan[uar]y last some angry words passed between a Mr J G Harris[5] I think of New Hampshire and a Mr Foster a son of the late Senator. The dispute was political—Mr Newman[6] sh[eri]ff of Jefferson Co[unty] was at the Hotel where Harris boarded. Standing near Foster when Harris came in to supper— Mr N. told me, Foster said (if he understood him) "Gentlemen I wish to make a denunciation" immediately raised his pistole and fired at Harris—wounded him very dangerously with two balls—Harris has recovered. Foster was recently tried and as is customary acquitted. Some few weeks since[,] his father Ephraim H Foster[7] met with a lawyer by the name of Brown who had the day before refused to speak to his son who shot Harris. Brown spoke politely to the father E. H. F[oster], who expressed his surprise that he should condescend to speak to him when he had the day before refused to speak to his son. An angry conversation soon led Foster to strike him with his cane. Brown stabbed him with his knife giving him a very dangerous wound at the same time breaking the blade of his knife. He is recovering tho[ugh] his escape is a narrow one. With Mr F[oster] I have some personal acquaintance. He appears to be an amiable man in his general intercourse in society. He might have been the candidate for Governor with almost a certainty of being elected. The evil is greater when good men or men in elevated stations in society engage in such contests. Before these[,] sev[er]al personal encounters had proved fatal—one by a brother of James K Polk the present governor.

Ever since the disgraceful violence on Amos Dresser[8] at Nashville[,] that city and vicinity have been distinguished for violence and assassinations. Generally they originate in some trifling matter—often ending in the death of one of the parties.

The same remarks would apply to Vicksburg only in a greater degree. Since the assassination of a number of persons in the summer of 1835 they have been killing off each other. In the mean time the town has been on the decline attended with almost universal bankruptcy.

Another evil of considerable magnitude prevailing in the South which has not wholly escaped the attention of the North is the exclusion of free colored persons from the free states or selling them into slavery under various pretences. A few weeks ago I saw a Nashville paper in the possession of one of my friends in which was an advertisement of a runaway in jail who said his name was William (or something so) who says he is free. These advertisements have been frequent at the South for some years. A year or two since I sent some to my friend J H Lewis P[ost] M[aster] Terryville Con[necticut]. I would have sent you this but it contained matter which the owner wished to keep. I suppose the antislavery society must be in possession of a sufficient number of them. I think they have most frequently appeared in the Mississippi papers. When a runaway slave is apprehended a minute description of his person appears in the advertisement. The name of the owner to whom he says he belongs—in addition a letter of message is sent to him. When a free colored man is apprehended and lodged in jail the advertisement appears to be intentionally blind. Nothing appears in them to indicate the place where the man is from[,] who his friends are, or any notice to them unless some philanthropic man near makes special inquiry. Then if the unfortunate man happens to be in the hands of kidnappers any person interfering would have notice that he was doing it at his peril.

I have been led to suspect that a system of kidnapping was carried on by those who often appear at the North in the character of gentlemen. When last in Phil[adelphia] a young colored man a barber asked my advice about attending a man to Mississippi as a waiter with the promise of liberal wages employment as a coachman & I told him the design was undoubtedly to make him a slave not to go there. I have supposed that these credulous men were induced to go there under liberal promises—probably dismissed after a while and then thrown into jail and sold as runaway slaves. From the character and frequency of these advertisements, I am led to the opinion that the subject is one requiring investigation as well as the laws in the Southern states in relation to free colored persons from the free states—that the free states should refuse to give up any person claimed as a slave coming from states where the rights of free colored persons are invaded or taken from them by unconstitutional laws.

If free colored persons have no rights in the slave states slavery should have none in the free states. The sooner the South are made to understand that, the better. If the North deals with them firmly and decidedly, they will be respected accordingly. If they tamely yield their rights they will meet with insolence and insult.

With great respect I am

Sincerely yours
Ezekiel Birdseye

Notes

1. Guy Beckley and Theodore Foster, leaders of the antislavery movement in Michigan, edited the *Signal of Liberty* from 1841 to 1846. James G. Birney was living at Bay City, Mich., during this period and was enthusiastically supported by the *Signal of Liberty,* which was the official organ of the Michigan Anti-Slavery Society. Guy Beckley was a prominent Methodist clergyman who left New York City when the Methodist churches there were closed to him because of his antislavery advocacy. After lecturing on behalf of the antislavery movement in Vermont and New Hampshire, in 1839 he moved to Ann Arbor, Mich., where he became pastor of the First Methodist Church. Dumond, *Antislavery,* 187, 303, 405.
2. Romulus Mitchell Saunders (1791–1867), lawyer, legislator, congressman, and diplomat, became judge of the superior court in 1835 in North Carolina and rode the circuit until 1840, when he accepted the Democratic nomination for governor. He was defeated by the Whig candidate, John Motley Morehead. He served in the U.S. House of Representatives in 1821–27 and 1841–45. Defeated in his bid for the U.S. Senate in 1852, he was elected instead to a judgeship on the superior court, which he held until the end of the Civil War. William F. Powell, ed., *Dictio-*

nary of North Carolina Biography (Chapel Hill: Univ. of North Carolina Press, 1994), 5:285–86.
3. John Motley Morehead (1796–1866), lawyer, Whig governor of North Carolina, and promoter of internal improvements and the railroad, did not believe in slavery but, according to his biographer, generally acquiesced in the institution as it existed. Earlier, as a North Carolina state representative from Guilford County (1826–28), he had presented Quaker petitions against slavery when requested by his constituency. In February 1861 he served as a delegate of the abortive "Peace Conference" held in Washington, D.C., to stave off a civil war. Thereafter, however, he joined the Confederacy and served as one of the state's delegates to the Confederate Provisional Congress in 1861–62. Powell, *Dictionary of North Carolina Biography*, 4:321–22; Burton Alva Konkle, *John Motley Morehead and the Development of North Carolina, 1796–1866* (Philadelphia: William J. Campbell, 1922), 194–95.
4. John Belton O'Neall (1793–1863) was a distinguished South Carolina jurist who in 1859 was appointed chief justice of the South Carolina Supreme Court. In his writings he had expressed disapproval of some laws regulating slavery and advocated reforms such as allowing owners the regulated right to manumit slaves and leave bequests to them. Of Quaker ancestry, O'Neall was a leader of the temperance movement, president of the Greenville and Columbia Railroad, and a leader of the Upcountry Unionist faction; he vigorously opposed nullification and secession. *DAB*, 14:42–43; Lacy K. Ford, Jr., *Origins of Southern Radicalism: The South Carolina Upcountry, 1800–1860* (New York: Oxford Univ. Press, 1988), 149, 199, 225, 235; A. E. Keir Nash, "Negro Rights, Unionism, and Greatness of the South Carolina Court of Appeals: The Extraordinary Chief Justice John Belton O'Neall," *South Carolina Law Review* 21 (1969): 141–90; Alan Watson, *Slave Law in the Americas* (Athens: Univ. of Georgia Press, 1989), 150–52.
5. Jeremiah George Harris, a Massachusetts Democrat, became the editor of the *Nashville Union* in February 1839. Paul H. Bergeron, *Antebellum Politics in Tennessee* (Lexington: Univ. Press of Kentucky, 1982), 43.
6. Benjamin F. Newman was sheriff of Jefferson County between 1840 and 1846. *History of Tennessee, Containing Historical and Biographical Sketches*, 863.
7. Ephraim Hubbard Foster (1794–1854), one of the founders of the Whig party in Tennessee, served in the General Assembly in 1827–31 and 1835–37; he was speaker of the house in the 18th and 21st assem-

blies. He was an unsuccessful candidate for governor in 1845 on the Whig ticket, so Birdseye was prescient in suggesting this possibility in 1841. *BDTGA*, 1:257–58.
8. Amos Dresser was a student at Lane Theological Seminary who, selling Bibles in Nashville in the summer of 1835, was arrested and charged with distributing subversive antislavery materials. He was sentenced by a vigilante committee composed of some of Nashville's most prominent citizens and received twenty lashes on his bare back, after which he hastily fled the city. His case quickly became a *cause célèbre* among abolitionists, and this incident became the subject of a leading antislavery tract. Amos Dresser, *The Narrative of Amos Dresser, with Stone's Letters from Natchez, an Obituary Notice of the Writer, and Two Letters from Tallahassee, Relating to the Treatment of Slaves* (New York: American Anti-Slavery Society, 1836).

7. To Gerrit Smith, July 10, 1841

Mossy Creek[1] E[ast] Ten[nessee]
July 10th, 1841

My Dear Sir

I am now at the house of my friend John Caldwell Esq[uire] of whom I have often spoken in my correspondence with you whose moral courage in every good cause does him great honor. An antislavery man he has been for years one of the most conspicuous always ready to meet the arguments of slaveholders in public and private never fearing to do his duty. His influence has done much in Tennessee but is not confined to this part of the state or to this state. It extends to the whole South, east of the Mississippi. He cultivates the best farm I know in E[ast] Ten[nessee], on which there has never been slave labor. In the Temperance cause he has been equally conspicuous so that while we can boast of the most free community in E[ast] Ten[nessee] of the whole South, we can at the same time boast of the most temperate and industrious.

Mr. C[aldwell] has for some years purchased horses and driven to Florida, which has been generally profitable. Of late owing to the deranged state of the currency there and the general depression he finds it impossible to realize in current funds the avails of his sales. He has in notes on good men in Florida $3202 (dollars) in specie funds drawing 8 percent interest payable the first of Jan[uary] next. In the situation of the money market and the Banks of Florida this was probably the best arrangement that could have been made. Mr C[aldwell] is a good judge of securities and has probably good security for the payment or has dealt with planters of such responsibility and character for punctuality as will make these debts good when due.

He finds on his return that no accommodations are to be had at the Banks in E[ast] Ten[nessee]. They are not discounting to any one at this time. Loans cannot be effected here on any credit. In view of the difficulties which surround Mr. Caldwell he had concluded to offer his farm for sale at a great loss, on advising with me I have thought it best that this should not be done at present. Mr C[aldwell] has 450 acres of as good land as can be found in East Tennessee all fair and tillable. The geology is transition blue limestone; in fertility it would compare with the best lands in Cumberland Valley P[ennsylvani]a. It is rated for taxation by the commissioners at 17 dollars per acre. It adjoins the farm of Judge Peck who would concur with me in opinion as to quality and value.

There are two hundred acres in cultivation none of which has been exhausted by bad farming but kept in a fertile good condition by manuring and good management. It is so healthy that a Northern family might occupy it without risque.

Mr Caldwell would be so great a loss to our community that I have suggested to him that it was possible that by giving a mortgage or deed of trust on his farm that he might procure a loan or some assistance in the free states. The title is *undisputed* and *undoubted,* wholly unincumbered. Untill he could collect his debts in Florida and avail himself of debts due him or becoming due soon here, he would be accommodated by borrowing $4000 (Four thousand dollars) on from 18 months to two years time. In Florida he would buy exchange on New York and remit to meet the debt and interest at seven percent and would send on the mortgage or deed of trust (either) which might be preferred, and a certificate of record and a certificate of the clerk of the court that the property was wholly unincumbered. All the necessary papers would be prepared by Judge Peck who would state his opinion as to the value of the property and that the security was given in conformity to the laws of Tennessee. The property has three good dwelling houses two good barns has good water convenient to the houses—with other out houses and such fixtures as may be expected on the best farm. From my acquaintance with Mr Caldwell his integrity industry energy and economy I should think a loan made him on the security he would give to be as safe as any security could make it and as sure to be honorably discharged as from any man in the whole circle of my acquaintance.

In the very depressed state of property here I should estimate Mr Caldwells land to be worth in cash fifteen dollars per acre. It is true that this is higher than good farms sell for at this time with us but his is in a better state of cultivation has better buildings better fences and every way better improvements, the soil acknowledged to be the best laid out, the best arranged farm in E[ast] Tenn[essee] as well as the best improved. From a knowledge of every part of it and the improvements on it I am clearly of opinion that the improvements alone have cost the fifteen dollars per acre. His dwelling house of brick must have cost over $2000 and have been managed with economy at that.

Should you either have funds—or what is more probable have a knowledge of those who have and who would wish to make a safe investment and where it would confer a favor on merit, the opportunity would be a good one. If there should be no one who can find it convenient to accommodate my friend Caldwell I make the communication with less diffidence as I know his great moral worth will entitle any request on his behalf to a favorable consideration. If my name or rec[ommendation] of mine would add any thing to the security he would offer I would tender both cheerfully.

Mr. Caldwell would be willing to make his bonds payable anywhere in your state most convenient to the lender if agreeable in N[ew] Y[ork] City—4 months drafts on N[ew] Y[ork] sell to the banks at this time at 6 percent premium less the interest—drafts at sight or short sight are worth 8 percent at prem[ium]. Authority to draw at not over 4 months would be an available loan to Mr C[aldwell]. In either case the securities as above described would be forwarded duly authenticated and at his charge.

I have supposed that in the state of N[ew] Y[ork,] the money market was easier. It is with us at its worst or possibly the worst is past and that some signs of a better state of things exist.

Mr Caldwell has eight young men boarding in his family from Florida attending school of The Rev[erend] Mr Haynes a man zealous in the good cause. While it affords a fair pecuniary profit, it gives both the opportunity of inculcating *principles* of freedom where they may do good. Could our good Abolitionists of the North come here and witness the zeal of these men it would do much to strengthen and encourage them in the glorious work they have undertaken. I left Knoxville last evening. While there I spent some time with Judge Peck who is attending the Supreme Court. He says evidences of a healthy change of public sentiment are continually multiplying—that in a very few years he anticipates a change to free labor, or entire freedom, in all the states North of the South line of this state. We are sanguine in our project of establishing a free labor community on our lands—by perseverance we have in a measure released ourselves of pecuniary pressure.

I hear of Gurneys letters to Mr Clay. I have not heard a word of disapprobation in this state tho[ugh] I have often met with them in the hands of slaveholders. I saw an Alabama paper in Knoxville which sounded the old fashioned alarm to slaveholders but I should think it would do but little to suppress their circulation. That they will have an extensive circulation I hope and believe. At the same time it will be a salutary one. It is one of the favorable signs of the times, that they meet with consideration, and that too from slave holders. There is need everywhere of continued efforts. They should be kept up at the North. Universal abolition at the North will be followed by universal abolition at the South, or they would be nearly simultaneous. The public sentiment cannot be much influenced at the North without producing a corresponding influence at the South. I hope our Abolitionists will carry their influence everywhere with them and especially to the Polls. That will soon produce such correct sentiments in candidates for office as will surprise abolitionists themselves.

Generally we have a fruitful season. Wheat has proved an average crop, corn bids fair to be a full average. Oats, which now make a large part of the crop, are good. Hay is but little grown in E[ast] Ten[nessee], but increasing. Silk is gaining favor with our people. I saw at Knoxville cocoons bro[ugh]t in by a great many persons not a few of them the poor, and sold to the merchants for $3.50 per bu[shel]. I heard some remark that they could make one dollar per day at that. This bids fair to do something to raise our poor from the extreme depression to which they had fallen in all the South. Mr Ross of Kingsport E[ast] Ten[nessee] thinks this will have a favorable influence in the antislavery cause.

With my best wishes I am my dear Sir

Yours
E Birdseye

Note

1. Mossy Creek today is Jefferson City, Tenn.

8. To Gerrit Smith, July 27, 1841

NEWPORT COCKE COUNTY
JULY 27, 1841

Yours of the 8th inst[ant] is just re[ceive]d as I am in town and having leisure reply without delay.

In my last I wrote you in part respecting my friend Caldwell. It may not be improper in further explanation to say that he apprehends a united effort of some few slaveholders to break him down or to compel him to sell his plantation. Appearances make it probable that this is too true. Mr C[aldwell] has the respect and affection of the community. No open attack on him where the object was undisguised would be risqued. It would draw down the indignation of the community. It is only at a time like this that they can hope to succeed by discrediting him and bringing his creditors to press him all at once.

There are in Jefferson County about a dozen despotic slaveholders or slaveholders from principle. Among the number are the Hodges of one I spoke in a previous letter, Gen[eral] Brazleton[1] of New Market[,] Geo[rge] Brenner[2] of Mossy Creek and John Roper[3] of Dandridge. After my letter of the last date I found that all these men were using their influence to discredit him. Brazleton purchased a note on him of some $35 and sold it endorsing it without recourse. All I have named were said to be busy in using expressions or in conversations to produce a want of confidence. But as yet I have heard of no one suing him. His character has been so high as a prompt honest man[,] his industry and good judgment in managing his business [such] that his credit has been at the very best. With the united efforts of these men I doubt whether they can induce those to press him who are not compelled by their own circumstances to do so. Mr. C[aldwell] began with very small means. By diligence and good management he grew steadily into good circumstances and educated a large family well. Within a short time he has given three of his children that married a goodly portion to begin with. He also purchased his brothers farm adjoining his. All of which would not have produced a pressure had it been for very unusual circumstances. He sold horses in Florida on a credit. On collecting the money last winter he found the local currency there to be at some 40 or 50 percent discount. He deemed it prudent to loan his money to planters who were owing the Bank payable with interest in funds on a par with specie next winter, and to sell his horses or a part of his droves on a credit untill then. This he expects to receive next Jan[uary] in Bill on N[ew] Y[ork] drawn on cotton or in some way to be safe and available. This is the best reliable source and from his acquaintance and good judgment of securities I think this may be relied on. He has Bills receivable by Jan[uary] in Jefferson that am[oun]t to $900 that I am acquainted with and may be relied on. This and his Florida debt would meet his liabilities. In addition he has as large crops as I have known on his plantation, I think more than of any previous year. All this added to his real estate would seem to make his responsibility undoubted, but no loans are now made at the Banks or no new loans. I know of no private fund holders in East Ten[nessee] except a few who hold small am[oun]ts of specie who would not consider any application for a loan. Under these circumstances I should think three thousand dollars secured by real estate would relieve him as the remaining one thousand could be continued by those who could wait and who would be willing to do so. He would apply all he could next winter to reduce the debt and might perhaps liquidate it but in two years he might pay the whole. Should it be impossible to make any negotiations for him those expressions of sympathy encouragement and kind feelings which I hope he may receive will do much to sustain him.[4] Could you be here and see how many are made insolvent by the mad policy of slave holding legislation you would see additional reasons for dreading this baleful institution which does not stop with bringing distress on the poor slaves but grinds to the dust the poor whites.

To[o] much has been said about the demand of the Gov[ernor] of V[irgini]a on the executive of N[ew] Y[ork] and so important have been the results that I have thought it might be well to suggest a doubt I have had whether there was any obligation on the part of the free states to surrender slaves escaping from the District of Columbia. In the case of Bullock vs his slave—before the Supreme Court of Conn[ecticut][5] I [am] told that the opinion of the court was that slavery had no rights in the state of Conn[ecticut] beyond the clause in the constitution "That a person escaping from a state & should be delivered up to the party." The question which I would suggest is are the free states bound to surrender a slave escaping from the District of Columbia. It is not a state and does the constitution give them any authority to reclaim runaway slaves. An incident which you will recollect is the case of Lieutenant Randolph who assaulted President Jackson by taking him by the nose in a steamboat on the Potomac near the line of V[irgini]a.[6] A lawyer by the name of Stuart told me that Randolph crossed immediately into V[irgini]a and [went] on to Richmond and was demanded of the Gov[ernor] of V[irgini]a as a fugitive from Justice. His excellency consulted Judge Marshall who happened to be in Richmond. Judge Marshall was of opinion that the Constitution gave him no authority to make the demand as the District was not a state and that the Gov[ernor] was under no obligation to comply with the demand—that the compliance with the demand was refused accordingly—If I have the facts correctly—can there be any more authority to demand a fugitive slave. It may be something important that V[irgini]a has been the first to establish this precedent. I suppose that this might have escaped the friends of the slave. They may perhaps give it consideration and take counsel. I am not a lawyer but a very plain farmer. All the indications continue favorable. I gave your Friend of Man a circulation and all you have sent me. The letters of John G Gurney have a patient consideration in all parts of E[ast] Ten[nessee, and] so far as I am informed in all the South. Of late I sent you the Agriculturalist[7] of Nashville. It touches occasionally on slavery and its ruinous agriculture. I shall send you some other numbers as they will go to show the low state of agriculture in the South and the suggestions of the better men who would raise free labor and make it honorable as one of the means of discontinuing slavery. I think there will be something that you can use to advantage. I shall send you occasionally a temperance paper and perhaps one of any other as a specimen &. Of late I sent you one of the Rev[erend] Mr. Brownlowes papers should you have no use for it perhaps some of the Proslavery clergymen of the North should there be any might thank you for the loan of it. That part of my letter which speaks of Mr Caldwells affairs he would not like to have published. I will write you soon. Again there is nothing of very unusual importance. There are always some incidents that may do good if laid before our Northern people. Should there be a copy of Mr Adams[8] plea before the Supreme Court it would be a very acceptable present if convenient or anything that is sent I will try to use to do good.

Sincerely your friend
E Birdseye

Notes

1. Gen. William Brazelton (1792–1877), wealthy Jefferson County farmer and merchant, from 1839 to 1847 was major-general of the East Tennessee Militia. He owned a farm of 1,000 acres, one of the finest farms in East Tennessee, and was superintendent of the East Tennessee and Virginia Railroad, as well as a member of the Agricultural Bureau at

Nashville. *History of Tennessee, Containing Historical and Biographical Sketches,* 1162.

2. George Branner (1796–1847), wealthy Jefferson County merchant, served in the Tennessee house of representatives in 1833–35. He was a Jefferson County trustee (1825–34) and justice of the peace. *BDTGA,* 1:72.

3. John Roper was a tavern keeper in 1830 in Dandridge; by 1854, he had become president of the Bank of Dandridge. *History of Tennessee, Containing Historical and Biographical Sketches,* 859.

4. John Caldwell wrote to Gerrit Smith on June 14, 1841, apparently at Birdseye's urging, asking him for a loan. Evidently Smith was not able to accommodate him, because in January 1842 Caldwell was finally forced to sell his fine farm, "on which there has never been slave labor," to Gen. William Brazelton, one of the group of "despotic slaveholders" seeking to destroy his credit. John Caldwell to Gerrit Smith, June 14, 1841, Smith Papers; Jefferson County Deeds, Book W, 570–71.

5. In this 1837 case before the Supreme Court of Connecticut, to which Birdseye refers, Nancy Jackson, a slave born in Georgia in 1813, was taken to Connecticut by her master, James S. Bulloch, in June 1835 and remained there with Bulloch's family until June 1837. Bulloch returned to Georgia twice for an extended period of time between 1835 and 1837. In 1837, he wanted to take Nancy Jackson back to Georgia as his slave, but she filed a writ of habeas corpus claiming her freedom after two years residence in the free state of Connecticut. The justice who wrote the opinion of the court, granting Nancy Jackson her freedom, concluded that "it is a source of gratification both to my learned brother who concurs with me, and to myself, to know, that if our views on this subject are erroneous, their effect will not be unjustly to deprive a fellow-being of her liberty." *Nancy Jackson v. Bulloch,* 12 Conn. 38–69 (1837).

6. On May 6, 1833, on board a steamboat for Fredericksburg, Va., a former naval lieutenant, Robert B. Randolph, who had been dismissed from the service for attempted theft, slammed his fist into President Andrew Jackson's face while the latter was seated at a table reading a newspaper. Remini, *Andrew Jackson,* 170.

7. *Agriculturalist, and Journal of the State and County Societies* was published in Nashville between 1840 and 1845. Sam G. Riley, comp., *Index to Southern Periodicals* (Westport, Conn.: Greenwood, 1986), 31.

8. John Quincy Adams, although not thoroughly an abolitionist, led the protest in Congress against refusing to hear antislavery petitions from various parts of the country. Adams was acting on constitutional principles, seeking mainly to protect the right to petition. Adams (1767–1848) had been the 6th president of the U.S. In 1841, he appeared before the Supreme Court and successfully defended the African mutineers of the slave ship *Amistad*, which is probably the case to which Birdseye refers. In June 1839 the *Amistad* left Havana bearing some 50 Negro slaves, who subsequently rebelled and seized the ship. When the *Amistad* reached Long Island, it was taken into New London, Conn., where the rebels were charged with piracy and committed to prison for trial. John Quincy Adams was brought in for the final defense of the prisoners, who ultimately were freed. Louis Filler, *The Crusade Against Slavery, 1830–1860* (New York: Harper, 1960), 98–107, 167–69.

9. To Gerrit Smith, August 7, 1841

Newport
Aug[ust] 7th 1841

My Dear Sir

Here with I send you the Agriculturalist published at Nashville Ten[nessee] in April. You will learn something of the state of slaveholding agriculture from this and other numbers and from a source entitled to the fullest confidence. I am personally acquainted with two of the four editors Dr John Shelby[1] and Dr Gerard Troost. Dr Troost[2] is one of the most scientific Geologists in the country and a man of profound learning. The editors are all men of respectable talents and disposed to introduce valuable improvements into Tennessee. From occasional remarks in this work I infer that they are fully convinced of the ruinous policy of employing slave labor. You will notice the remark of Mr. Zolicoffer[3] that "one scientific laborer would produce as much as five of these ignorant slaves." This is true and this prompt avowal of it in a *popular* address—its publication and circulation throughout the South will do much to convince the planters of the South that they labor to great disadvantage in employing slave labor.

All these arguments which go to prove to them that their policy is bad does much to prepare them for a change. The efforts to introduce Fellenbergs schools[4] are popular throughout the state. I hope the public mind may continue directed to them so as to produce a good effect and render the idle dissipated sickly habits of the young men of the South unpopular and be followed by a system well calculated to develop the highest mental and physical qualities. It is for the want of these habits and science that slavery exists. Anything that has an influence to enlighten, to lead them to inquire and discuss their true interests, is important and will aid in the great reformation which soon awaits Ten[nessee] and K[entuck]y, I hope more and more eventually the whole South.

No class of citizens have been more anxious to have a free labor community in this country than the slaveholders. They say: "We want you to bring on 500 of your Northern good farmers and good mechanics." This experiment I trust is about to be tried on a small scale. If found to operate well it will extend to much of the mountain region of the South. The climate will be healthy for Northern people superior to all that are predisposed to pulmonary habits. If I am not mistaken mountains are the most favorable for the developement of both physical and intellectual strength. Our people here are independent in discussing all subjects nowhere surpassed in the South. The clergy are inquiring good men, with some exceptions. This is no unimportant consideration. An enlightened clergy is one of the greatest blessings which can attend a free country. An ignorant bigoted vicious clergy is among if not the greatest calamity that can happen to an unfortunate community.

I am sorry to say that a part of the Baptist clergy in S[outh] C[arolina] and Georgia are of this latter class. The manner that they become ministers is often a little curious. Not unfrequently at a public assembly a rustic arrives and announces the fact that he has had a special call to preach. How the Spirit has communicated this important fact they do not always tell. Some have attributed it to a mysterious dream others to a strong impression which came forcibly to their mind that they must leave all and preach the gospel which he attempts to do by an unintelligible jargon which could enlighten no one and leaves no more favorable impression on the intelligent than that the poor man had mistaken his disinclination for some industrious employment for a special call from the Holy Spirit to preach the gospel. These men deride learning abhore missions ridicule the Temperance reformation pour out anathemas on the abolitionists and defend slavery. Often if they become the owners of slaves these poor creatures are the most cruel of petty tyrants. If the man happens to be a young man or a widower his sacred office gives him an introduction to ladies of fortune. The more slaves she has the more attractive her choice.

This evil prevails much in the South most in S[outh] C[arolina] Geo[rgia] & Ala[bama] and where a rich clergy are found, reformations will be found the most hopeless. The Baptist church in this state, in view of these evils which distracts it, divided and greatly to the benefit of the enlightened part, among whom there are examples of piety that shine brightly on all around.

After having had a visit from one of these divines from Georgia you will not be surprised to learn that such men defended the imprisonment of Dr Butler & Worcester[5] of the Cherokee nation in the G[eorgi]a penitentiary. To their influence in exciting the public mind against these men may be attributed the outrages on them.

On the 5th ultimo I rhode out with Mr. J. Chunn to his plantation on the west bank of Pigeon River three miles from Newport at his request. Mr. C[hunn] is a reformed inebriate, I hope in other respects a reformed man, the son of a wealthy man of Asheville N[orth] C[arolina]. His habits had been such as is very common with the young men of the South, intemperate, gambling, with other nameless habits that his wife an amiable woman had left him. Last spring his buildings were burned on a plantation at the confluence of the Nolichucky and French Broad rivers which he also owned[,] supposed to have been by persons whose acquaintance he would not be willing to acknowledge. He was a young man of natural and acquired talents of a high order. Want of employment wealth and evil communications had led him to the brink of ruin.

He has an inquiring mind reasons well and with frankness. We rode to the house a small cabin on the plantation called the Quarters. He introduced me to his overseer whose name was Edmunds & lady also from Buncombe County both persons more intelligent and refined than is often met with in such situations. Mrs. E[dmunds] said she saw no friends had no society—and found it a lonesome life. Both Mr. E[dmunds] & lady were evidently dissatisfied with their business. I heard his report to Mr. C[hunn] who had not been there for some time. He stated that he had got on with the plantation as well as he could have expected, that he was and had been at all times up with his work that the hands had performed their labor well that he had found it necessary to punish but one and that a boy slightly. They had been diligent orderly and obedient. He remarked that his hands did not deserve the bad character that the overseer had given them the year before "who was so constantly cutting and slashing that he kept some of them all the while lying out." He had seen no necessity for it. The hands were at the house their hoes hanging on the fence. In the situation of the crop they were not using them. They use the heavy plantation hoe with long heavy handles. These are used by male and female hands. I inquired of Mr. C[hunn] whether he would find it better to use the light Northern hoe with light handles which in my opinion would be more durable and not weigh more than one third as much. He said he had no doubt it would be better but they had been in the habit of using that kind of hoe. We rode into the corn field which was alluvial and very rich land. There was one hundred and twenty five acres. They were plowing it the last time and expected to finish that week. The corn appeared to have been mainly cultivated with the plow. Between the rowes it was tolerably clean but weedy about the hill or stalk. The roots of the corn were bare for want of sufficient earth about them. There was generally but one stalk in the hill full 4 feet distant. The corn of a large Southern or gourd seed. Compared with other crops it looked well and might be expected to produce from 35 to 40 bushels to the acre. The plow is here called a shovel plow consisting of a triangular piece of iron some 10 inches long by a breadth or lip of about 8 in[ches] a little turned at the point fastened to a stud by a single bolt which was at an angle of about 45 deg[rees] with the beam. They plow but a light furrow and running to a point at bottom leave the ground badly tilled. In proportion to the quantity of earth they move they must be of heavy draft. The season has been favorable for corn if a long dry spell of weather happens during the cropping season the corn never suffers owing to the shallow plowing. I inquired of Mr. Edmunds what would be the comparative expense of cultivating the plantation if he were to hire free laborers such young men as were in want of employment and who would make efficient hands—compared with the expense of cultivating it with slave labor. He said the free labor would be less than one half and if the families would come and live on the plantation they could be paid mainly in the produce of the farm. I inquired if it would not be more agreeable to him to cultivate the plantation with free than slave labor. He said decidedly so—if to that was added good northern plows heavy farm horses and thorough tillage with perhaps a change to the Dutton corn. I should suppose one hundred bushels to the acre might be grown. Mr Chunn said he had no doubt the plantation could be cultivated for less than half the expense with free labor but we have got into the habit of cultivating our lands with slave labor and are slow to change our habits when bad.

There was in this plantation a field of oats a heavy crop and falling down. No meadow but excellent land for meadow in all about 200 a[cres] alluvial about 400 a good upland not cleared. He was anxious to sell the plantation at $6000. He also offers the plantation at mouth of Nolichucky between 11 & 1200 a[cres] for sale at $6300, on one two and three years credit. That is a very handsome piece of land lying on the north side of French Broad below the mouth of N[olichucky] River bounded on both and sloping gently to them land well calculated for meadow or any other crop and being at the confluence of the two rivers has been thought to be one of the most desirable situations on either for a town but such is the extreme depression at the South that they have but little courage for building up towns & villages.

My remarks of this plantation or two may fatigue you but they may give you some idea of Southern agriculture. The same remarks would apply to a large share of the plantations only that Mr Edmunds manages better than is common. I don't know of an overseer that has done as well being new at the business. He has not become brutalized. It may be something important in the signs of the times that slaveholders are willing to reason on the subject of slave labor and to admit that compared to free labor it is unprofitable.

When in a room with Judge Peck at Newport last week a free colored man came in apparently over 60. He states to the judge that he would like to have him bring a suit against his neighbor. The person is Mr. Courtney. Free Isaac as he is called said that some years ago Mr Courtney took out a grant for a tract of land and run it so as to take in his bottom (alluvial) land. He said he told Mr. Courtney he would sue him if he took out a grant covering any part of his land. Mr Courtney said the court would laugh at them both that it saved some trouble to run a straight line which never could injure him as he had an older grant which made him an undoubted title. But said Isaac Master Courtneys boys claimed the land and had fenced in a part of it. Judge Peck said if they would not agree to remove their fence and pay him all damages he would sue them at once. Isaac has his grant and states his case like a man of business. He would have his claims as patiently considered as any man in the county. I had heard him spoken of as a good farmer but had little knowledge of him before. Judge Peck inquired of him how he became free. "I bought myself sir." Have you a good farm. I have a good farm Sir in a good state of cultivation and intended to live very well if others would not attempt to take my land from me in my old age. But thank God I have money enough to pay my lawyer. I have told them if they would have my land they must get it at court for the old man has worked it a good while and has the oldest title for it. Your title is good Isaac. Is your wife free. Yes Sir, I bought her freedom and had much trouble in getting her. How so Isaac. Why Sir she was owned by a young man not 21. I was to give him $300 for her which he was satisfied to take. I was going into Kentucky to be gone some time and went to pay him. A man by the name of Porter, a neighbor told me I would be unsafe to do so, that the young man would not be of age for three weeks and if I paid him the money when he became of age he might refuse to comply with his contract and make me pay the money all over again.

Mr. Porter said I had better go on my journey that if the young man wanted the money before I came back he would pay it to him for me. I thought I could depend on Esq[uire] Porter[6] and went on well contented, master and when I came back I found Esq[uire] Porter had bought my wife of her young master for $300 he supposed he was selling her for me. Esq[quire] P[orter] then sold her to a negro trader for $400. I had to go all the way to Nachee and to New Orleans to find her. Then I had to pay $900 to get her. Yes old master, I had a world of trouble for trusting Mr. Porter. I had to sell my farm worth $2000 to raise the money—and at a great sacrifice too. Well Isaac she ought to have been a good wife. She has done her part well sir. I have no cause to complain. Isaac will have his rights well protected. This Mr. Courtney I have heard before left his negroes free by his will and a plantation for their care untill they should go to a free state. His heirs are said to have taken the land from them and treated them harshly. There are I think 15 of them. He owed a debt of some $6000. They I believe cannot go untill that is paid. My informant said that $2500 remained in debts and that would be paid out of the estate without endangering the freedom of the negroes.

I met with a part of Mr. Rayner's[7] speech last week on a torn piece of the globe. I have not seen it in any paper of this or N[orth] C[arolina]. Mr. R[ayner] is mistaken in some of his statements[;] if he is not aware of how[,] the time is soon coming when he will be. I am astonished that men making pretensions to character should make such reckless statements. If their object is to deceive the North or to intimidate them I should suppose they could succeed with but few.

Judge Peck remarked that he had been much occupied with professional engagements with some indisposition, that he should write you soon. I have feared the influence of his son Dr. I. T. Peck who married a wealthy lady near Vicksburg some months since. Judge Peck and myself were conversing with him about our intention of settling our lands with free persons only. He replied that K[entuck]y and Tenn[essee] ought to be free states. I flatter myself that it will not be long before I can return to the North. Judge Peck says he is interested to accompany me.

Sincerely yours
Ezekiel Birdseye

Notes

1. Dr. John Shelby (1785–1859), physician, wealthy capitalist, and Whig politician, served in the Tennessee senate in 1815–17. He was treasurer of the Tennessee Medical Society (1838–43), was elected to life membership in the state society (1857), and served as president of the Tennessee medical convention (1847). *BDTGA*, 1:667–68.
2. Gerard Troost (1776–1850) earned degrees in medicine and pharmacy from the universities of Leyden and Amsterdam; in 1828 he became professor of geology and mineralogy at the University of Nashville. From 1831 to 1850, he was state geologist of Tennessee.

A member of many learned societies in both Europe and America, Troost was a scientist with an international reputation, fully deserving the praise Birdseye gives him. He was acquainted with both Birdseye and Judge Jacob Peck, and corresponded with them frequently about mineral samples from various locations in East Tennessee. *DAB*, 18:647–48; L. C. Glenn, "Gerard Troost," *American Geologist* 35 (Feb. 1905): 72–94.

3. Felix Kirk Zollicoffer (1812–1862) was a prominent Whig who, in addition to editing the *Southern Agriculturalist*, in 1841 became editor of the *Nashville Republican Banner*, the state organ of the Whig Party. He represented Davidson County in the Tennessee senate (1849–51). His chief claim to fame, however, was as brigadier general in the Confederate army, assigned in 1861 to East Tennessee to check the strong Unionist sentiment there. *BDTGA*, 1:832–33.

4. Fellenberg schools in the U.S. were patterned after Philip Fellenberg's school, Hofuyl, near Berne, Switzerland, a 200-acre farm where young men and women from all classes engaged in physical labor along with academic training, to demonstrate that all labor was useful and honorable. For the best discussion of the connection between abolitionism and the manual labor movement, see Paul Goodman, "The Manual Labor Movement and the Origins of Abolitionism," *Journal of the Early Republic* 13 (Fall 1993): 355–88.

5. After the Georgia legislature passed a law making it illegal for white persons to reside in the Cherokee territory without a license from the state and without taking an oath of allegiance to Georgia, two missionaries, Samuel A. Worcester and Elizur Butler, were thrown into prison for refusing to comply. The Union Presbytery of East Tennessee, under the leadership of Isaac Anderson, issued a public protest. The case eventually was appealed to the Supreme Court, which in 1832 decided, in *Worcester v. Georgia*, that the Georgia law in question was a violation of the Constitution, which had given to Congress the right to regulate intercourse with the Indians. William G. McLoughlin, *Cherokees and Missionaries, 1789–1839* (New Haven, Conn.: Yale Univ. Press, 1984), 239–99.

6. George M. Porter was clerk of the Cocke County Court in 1828–36. *History of Tennessee, Containing Historical and Biographical Sketches*, 867.

7. Kenneth Rayner (1810–1884) was a wealthy North Carolina planter and lawyer who served in the North Carolina house of commons and senate between 1836 and 1857. He was a member of Congress in 1839–45. Generally a conservative, he idolized John C. Calhoun and was a strong

states-rights man who ultimately favored secession, for which he voted with enthusiasm in 1861, as a member of North Carolina's secession convention. In 1863, disaffected with the Davis administration, he secretly joined the peace movement in North Carolina led by William J. Holden. He was a man of fiery and impulsive character and often appeared somewhat unstable. *DAB,* 15:416–17.

10. To Gerrit Smith, September 2, 1841

NEWPORT E[AST] TENNESSEE
SEPT[EMBER] 2, 1841

Dear Sir

In a late letter speaking of the culture of corn in E[ast] Ten[nessee] I inadvertently made an error in saying that the field I spoke of had generally one stalk in the hill. I should have said two which is the custom among planters of the south to plant two grains to the hill. This state is now the first in the culture of corn probably at the greatest product[ion] that it will reach. It is an exhausting crop. Where the lands lie uneven or as termed here rolling the continued culture of corn impoverishes the soil. Much of it is lost by washing rains, but with the great product[ion] of corn but little is exported beyond the state. It is used to make bread, and is fed to all kinds of stock in the ear. In winter it is thrown to cattle in the ear on the ground, much of it wasted when eaten. It is a wasteful mode of feeding stock. The culture of this and tobacco has been a great cause of the sterility of the older Southern states.

It may be proper to say in explanation of my remarks on the state of society in S[outh] Carolina that it is a custom for great crowds to attend their courts—their courts being a kind of fair where many attend to transact business unconnected with lawsuits. Mixed in these crowds are a great many females. Some are no doubt compelled to attend as witnesses. Many probably attend from innocent but idle curiosity—manifesting a want of well directed industry—a want of education and in many a want of good morals. I could refer to many who were well acquainted with the state of society in S[outh] C[arolina] at that time whose opinions would concur with mine.

Last week I was in the village of Newport. A colored woman was there taking her leave of her friends. She had been sold to a man living near Nashville. She was owned by a man by the name of Holland. Another woman was sold to the same individual by a Mr. Haynes. Both these men are known to me. They are in debt and parted with their slaves with reluctance but unable as they supposed to avoid it. They had the reputation of being kind masters, but misfortunes in business overtook them so that they were under the necessity of giving up their property. It is such calamities that operate with cruelty on the poor slaves at an hour when unexpected to themselves (except anticipated from the embarrassed situation of their master) they are notified that they are sold and are to leave their husbands wives or children to meet with them no more. About a year since I was riding through Jefferson County when I overtook a colored man apparently about 45. He said he was unacquainted with the road and asked permission to ride with me. We rode some miles in company. I found him to be a man of easy address [and] intelligent—a man who understood how to express himself correctly with dignity and grace. I inquired if he was free. He said that he belonged to Esq[uire] Rogers who lived near French Broad (I was acquainted with his master a very worthy man). I replied you have a kind master. He said "very kind, master has always been kind to me." I inquired if he had a wife and children. He said he had a wife and seven children. I said you have no fear have you that your master could be induced to sell you or any of your family? He said "not unless he was compelled to— master is in debt. I have sometimes had fears that he would not be able to get through but he says he will sell everything else first. He has often told me if he could sell his plantation for enough to pay his debts he would go with us to a free state where we could not be taken for debt." "Have the slavedealers ever applied to him to buy you?" "Yes Sir, they have tried Master every way. One came from Georgia some time since begged Master to set a price on me. The Master told him he might go and talk with me about it, so he came into the field where I was plowing and told me if I would go with him He would give me a suit of fine clothes make me his coachman and give me fifteen dollars in money. I knew slave dealers would promise anything. I was sorry the poor man would think I would part with my wife and children for such trifles. But I thought I would not offend the man, so I told him I would think of it. He then went to master and told him I had agreed to go with him. When I came to the house Master asked me how that was if I had agreed to go with him. I told him the man was mistaken; I was not willing to go with him. He then offered Master $800 in cash if he would let him tie me and take me off. Master told him no—nothing would induce him to do that."

I had much other conversation with this man in which he manifested strong affection for his wife and children kind feelings toward and confidence in his master. Esq[uire] Rogers is so much embarrassed that he is now supposed to be insolvent. In a little time in all human probability this poor man who so much dreads a separation from his wife and children will be compelled to see them sold one after another to the highest bidder and go where he may never meet with them again.

Last fall I was in Knoxville. On entering the shop of Samuel Bell,[1] a silver smith, I met with Daniel a young colored man who had been a waiter at the hotel. He was apparently about 25 years of age well formed and handsome features—a young man of ardent feelings who had manifested so much happiness on meeting with me and doing little acts of kindness that I felt interested in his welfare. Daniel was trying on a gold ring which Mr Draper the smith had enlarged for him. He placed it on his finger and after viewing it [with] scrutiny he said Master "how much do you charge me for putting in the piece." "One dollar" was the reply. "Could you not take less master?" "No" was the reply. "If you do not pay that you must leave it." "Then I shall have to leave it Master for I have but half a dollar." He pulled it off and laid it down upon the counter and stepped toward the door looking back to the ring. He stepped again to it and tried it on [and] with great anxiety said again "Master could you not take a half a dollar it is all the money I have." Mr. D[raper] said "No you must pay a dollar or leave it." "Then I must leave it Master." You can call and take it some other time was the reply. "No Master I shall never call again. It was a present from a lady Sir. She wished me to wear it but I must leave it Sir." I had thought it was a boyish fancy to have something fine untill then. It was a present from one on whom he had placed his affections—the matter was soon arranged. Daniel left with his ring. In a day or two he went with a drove of horses to Florida. When in Knoxville last I met the man with whom he went, at the hotel. I inquired of one of his fellow servants if Daniel had come back. He said no he has not come back sir. I suppose his late master to be insolvent. The profuse expenditure of public funds in Florida has made something of a market for slaves and horses. The cruelty does not stop with the Indians. The money enables them to purchase slaves and break those ties which bind them to all they value on earth.

In my intercourse with society here, and frequently with travellers from Mississippi to the Carolinas, I should think that there was a silent influence operating favorably. Very often I meet with individuals of avowed and decided free principles. A few days since one lodger at this house from Morganton N[orth] C[arolina] said he was fully convinced we were right that the free states were more happy more virtuous and more prosperous than the slave states. Yet he said he was not sanguine in any immediate change. He said although the South might be convinced, such was the force of custom that a change could only be brought about after a long time. He said the abolitionists had been represented as the enemies of the South. He gave no credit to that. He believed their motives pure and originated in no unkind feelings to the South. Similar opinions and expressions are not infrequent. Recently a gentleman from Iredell County N[orth] C[arolina] stopped here. He had been to Mississippi and Louisiana. He said there were shocking cruelties in the treatment of slaves there. I told him I understood that instances of cruelty were not frequent in Iredell County. He said they were not—that there was a restraining public sentiment which was increasing, while in Mississippi and Louisiana there appeared to be no restraining influences. He lives at the C[ourt] H[ouse] village. I do not now recollect his name. A conviction that slave labor is less profitable [and] that the free states are more prosperous more happy and more virtuous than the slave holding is becoming very general. Occasionally I meet with such opinions in paragraphs in papers otherwise objectionable. With this I sent you another number of the Agriculturalist where you will see a paragraph of this kind marked with my pencil. On the Island of St. Domingo if the writer had said Broomsedge in place of log wood with a few other alterations it would have answered very well for S[outh] Carolina.

Last Sabath I rhode a few miles with the Rev[erend] Mr. Manning[2] of the Baptist Church, on his return from preaching. He is a very useful man and much distinguished for piety. Our conversation turned on the subject of slavery. He said it was as great an evil that he feared it would be the ruin of the country. I inquired if he thought it would cause a dissolution of the Union. No was his reply. Not particularly so. He said there was so much wickedness connected with it that he feared that our country would be visited with great jud[ge]ments. He lives near Newport, said he regretted that he had not an opportunity of reading more on the subject.

Sincerely your friend,
E. Birdseye

Notes

1. Samuel Bell (1798–1882), silversmith and jeweler, came to Knoxville in 1819 from Pennsylvania. He was elected mayor of Knoxville in 1840–42 and again in 1844–46. He left Tennessee for San Antonio, Tex., in 1852. Rothrock, *French Broad–Holston Country*, 378–79.
2. Joseph Manning (1806–1883) was a prominent Baptist minister who served churches mainly in Cocke and Jefferson counties for a period of 50 years. He was one of the leaders of the East Tennessee Association of Baptists, and Birdseye's high opinion of him seems to have been universally shared by his contemporaries. James J. Burnett, *Sketches of*

Tennessee's Pioneer Baptist Preachers (Nashville: Marshall and Bruce Co., 1919), 345–49.

11. To Gerrit Smith, October 11, 1841

SWEET WATER P[OST] O[FFICE] MONROE CO[UNTY]
E[AST] TEN[NESSEE] OCT[OBER] 11TH, 1841

Dear Sir,

I am now in this county, about 100 miles from Newport on business which will require my stay some weeks. Below this possibly I may go into the near counties of Georgia.

As my sojourn has been new I have had some opportunity to learn something in relation to slavery. Mixing considerably with society I have had more opportunity to learn the current of public sentiment than I expected. Some few incidents have occurred which may interest you which I will notice.

On my way to Newport 8 miles I met the mail stage with a colored woman. Following the stage was her owner. I learned in town that she had been sold that morning to a man from Yancey Co[unty] N[orth] C[arolina] by one of the merchants, Mr. Pulliam.[1] No cause was assigned for selling her beyond the pecuniary inducement. No pressure on the part of her owner compelled him to make the sale. He had bid a part of the purchase money and voluntarily offered a credit on the remainder. With the feelings of the poor woman when parting with her family and friends he appeared no more affected than his horse. The effect appeared to have been different on others. Mrs. Henry the lady of a Methodist clergyman who keeps a public house said it was distressing, that her screams were heard through the village and made her regret that she was compelled to be a witness to such cruelty. These feelings were entertained by others, but, with most they appeared to be transient. Business required my stay untill the following day, when intimations were given to the man who had made the sale that he had credited a man who was supposed to be insolvent or doubtful. Alarmed for fear of the loss of his debt he took some of his acquaintenances with him followed the stage and demanded a return of the slave. The man claimed her as his property. He was told that it was a case where the law had but little to do, that if he did not consent to return her and take his money they should compel him by superior force. Yielding to such an argument, which if not altogether clear to him, was short and explicit, he gave her up. Next morning she returned in the stage and appeared quite overjoyed to meet her friends from whom she supposed she was separated forever. At Mossy Creek I re[ceive]d your letter and called on my friend Caldwell. He had not met with the disasters which he anticipated. I hope will not, all that he would seem to require is time, his farm is the best cultivated that I have seen in the county, I suppose equals any in E[ast] Ten[nessee]. He has over 100 acres in corn with a good proportion of other crops, his corn I should suppose could not be sold for more than 18 or 20 cents for cash. I doubt it could be sold at even 15¢. Horses hogs cattle have been difficult of late. The news is from all parts of the cotton growing region that the planters will be able to buy but little and will want that little on credit. The depression has been long continuing and appears unabated. It is ruinous to many, oppressing to most but may end in doing much good. It is weaning them from a dependence on the cotton grower and leading them to begin to rely on their own manufacturers. This is now taking place in most parts of Tennessee. They say that the North is prosperous while the South is ruined; and often ascribe it to the right cause, *slavery*. The culture of cotton is being abandoned in this state. Farming and improving their breeds of cattle horses and sheep now engage their attention. They inquire much about manufacturing and appear disposed to profit by a more close acquaintance with the North, and not unfrequently declare their intention of abandoning slavery and all its works. Mr. Caldwell invited me to his brothers where Sion Harris[2] was to spend the evening. He was a black who has been 12 years in Liberia. It rained excessively so that we were disapointed in finding him there.

The day following I met with one of my Quaker friends who had heard of the mob at Cincinnati. A member of their church or rather two preachers were in Cincinnati and had just gone from his house for Blount County.

Much was said in this neighborhood (near New Market) about the mob. Invariably it was condemned and I have not up to this time heard a man speak of it in any other terms than of decided disapprobation. About two miles above Knoxville I met with the Rev[erend] Mr. Mack[3] of Rochester. He was walking out on foot. I had heard him preach and being strongly prepossessed in his favor I introduced myself to him. A year last May my worthy friend Rev[erend] L. F. Clarke[4] a professor in the University who died in Aug[ust] a year since related an occurrence which interested me much in Mr. Mack. He was invited to become the pastor of the Presbyterian church in Knoxville. He told them that there would probably be an objection to him which would prevent his settlement with them, that was that he was an *abolitionist* that he was conscientiously so and could give them no reason to expect a change of sentiment. The committee ap[p]rised him that they concurred with him but would consult the church. They did so. When every member avowed his concurrence with Mr. Mack in regard to abolition he became their pastor honestly avowing his opinions and continues in that relation yet faithful in his duty and successful in his labors.

Mr. Clarke was one of the most ardent abolitionists with whom I have become acquainted and one of the most heavenly minded men with whom I have had the happiness to associate. His labors among the colored population of Knoxville were successful and placed him so high in their affections that they yet speak of him with warm affections and lament his death.

Some five miles below Knoxville I met with Sion Harris. He called in the evening at a house where I had stopped for the night. He had been when young acquainted with the hand cuff. There was much interest manifested and many inquiries made about Africa; and particularly if he intended to return. He replied certainly nothing could induce me to stay here. We have a free country there. We are governed by our own laws and are now prosperous and getting on very well. He came in part to induce his brother and connections to join him on his return. Next morning I met him at Wright Ferry three miles below at the house of his brother a free man. He said there had been some men there looking after a runaway slave—that they had torn up the floor ransacked the house and treated them with much harshness, but did not find him there. After crossing the Ferry I saw them at the house of Dr. Wright.[5] They had caught their slave. There were two of them. It would seem difficult for men in human form to have a more savage and ferocious aspect. They had huge whiskers, sullen swarthy countenances whose whole appearance seemed to denote a morbid appetite for cruelty.

At Maryville I called out in the evening to see my worthy friend Dr. Anderson[6] President of the collidge. In his many inquiries he asked if I had had any later letters from my friend Smith. I had had one not long since. He said he felt interested in hearing from him. In the morning I got acquainted with the Rev[erend] Mr. Taylor of Lee County V[irgini]a—a pious young clergyman, who had been educated at the collidge at Maryville. Mr. Taylor had great success in the temperance cause, it is said was successful in his ministry. I also met with Mr. Potter[7] and lady[,] late of the Cherokee mission now an agent for the Am[erican] B[oard] of Missions. I had known them at Creek Path[8] Cherokee and feeling much interest in them was glad to renew my acquaintenance. While I stopped in the village there was a protracted camp meeting of the Presbyterian Church. Dr. Anderson before the close of the meeting announced the arrival of Harris from Africa—that he would then address the meeting. I should think that there were over 1000 persons present.

All gave good attention. He made a very good address—stated the present state of the colony gave a circumstantial account of an attack on Hedding[9] and out station by the natives, their schools the present state of religion their efforts to instruct the natives etc. Dr. A[nderson] gave me an invitation to spend the evening at his house. He remarked that as a means of terminating slavery he viewed the colony of no importance but as a means of extending the gospel into Africa he thought it of very great importance, and hoped measures would be taken to correct their errors and aid furnished to carry missions into all parts of Africa. On the Sabath 2nd day of the meeting Dr. Anderson administered the sacrament. He invited all who were in good standing of their own or other evangelical churches to partake with them—but if there were any who were in the practice of making or vending distilled liquors they were not invited to commune with them. The efforts to reform the church in this respect I should think had been crowned with success. I do not know an instance in E[ast] Ten[nessee] where a member of the Presbyterian Church is engaged in the practice of making or vending the poison. In the evening while Mr. Potter was ad[d]ressing the audience and again urging the importance of missions to the heathen, he was disturbed by a gang of patrollers dragging a poor fellow immediately by the meeting. They had caught him at the neighboring house without a *pass* and were dragging him on to the village where they tied him to a post and gave him twenty lashes with great severity. What could have induced this act of cruelty I was wholly at a loss to determine. The law requiring a pass is allmost obsolete in this part of Ten[nessee] to those who go out of an evening to see a friend living near them. I thought it not improbable that the attentions shown Harris might have offended them. The transaction caused some excitement. On my way from the camp ground one of the citizens gave myself and a friend with me a pressing invitation to spend the night at his house. We excused ourselves on the ground that we had a room at the public house, while he was much thronged with company. He said he would excuse us if we would call and spend the remainder of the evening. As much earnestness appeared to characterize the request we complied with it. The occurrence of the evening gave rise to the subject of slavery. The conversation appeared to be unreserved. The company of ten or 12 persons were present. Our friend whose name I regret that I cannot at this time recollect inquired what was the situation and prospects of the antislavery cause in the free states. I stated to him that from all the information I had I was confident that it was progressive—that the public sentiment was becoming more favorably disposed toward it—that those who were more especially engaged in the cause were not disposed to relax in their efforts. He next inquired whether the letters of Gurney addressed to Henry Clay were real or fictitious, to which I replied that of their reality their could not be a doubt. The author was well known to be a man entitled to confidence—that these letters were addressed to Mr. Clay by his permission. He said he had no doubt of the fact, but the slave holders strenuously denied their reality[,] declaring them all fiction, got up for a catch penny. I assured him that Mr. Clay would no doubt confirm their authenticity if inquiry should be made of him. He said they would have a vast influence in the South that slavery was fast approaching its final struggle—that its time was short. Much as I had heard and witnessed I was hardly expecting such sentiments so publickly expressed even there. On the next morning I attended the meeting. The interest to hear Harris was so great that he was again invited to address the meeting. He commenced and spoke probably an hour and a half with a well timed and appropriate address manifesting natural talents of a high order and showing that in the few years he had been free in Africa he had acquired much. With all the prejudice in the south against the African I was gratified to see an audience listening attentively to one, and acknowledging him to possess talents of a high order. After his address they inquired earnestly as to the influence on the natives and the extent and opening for missions. I should suppose that there were but few slaveholders in the congregation.

In the evening or afternoon of Monday I called on a friend ten miles on this side of Maryville. When within half a mile of his house I inquired for him. When the man of whom I had requested information called me by name and introduced himself as Robert Bogle.[10] He said he had heard of me and must request me to return and spend the night with him. I had no doubt of his good intentions, but did not hesitate when he assured me he had a good assortment of antislavery papers, among them the Emancipator the American & Foreign Antislavery Reporter.[11] I found him an intelligent man well informed on the subject. We conversed till 10. He then gave me his papers with a candle and a room with a good fire, where I found much that was new to me. Mr. Bogle said that a man came there from Pittsburg and influenced them to form an association. They found sixteen subscribers for the Antislavery Reporter, and could have had more but for the difficulty of making payment. Each loaned his papers and living in various parts of the county, each could use much influence. They had a day appointed for a meeting for publickly discussing slavery at one of the county churches. They apprehend no disturbance and in all human probability they will have the county thoroughly abolitionized in a very short time. I have supposed that these discussions could not long be suppressed. They will be apt to extend to the northern abolitionist. They will be important as showing the great necessity of correct public sentiment at the north on slavery. The south is full of antislavery. When the north is strong and decided it will burst like a flame in the south the worst yet. He could give you some facts and a letter from the south might strengthen your hand a little. I will write you soon again, My Dear Sir. Should my letters hastily written and necessarily in haste do anything to advance the good cause I shall rejoice.

Sincerely yours
E. Birdseye

Notes

1. Robert W. Pulliam was one of the early merchants of Cocke County, a partner in the firm of Rankin and Pulliam. O'Dell, *Over the Misty Blue Hills*, 201.
2. Sion Harris went to Liberia on the ship *Liberia* in 1830, at the age of 19. He was a carpenter-farmer from Knox County, Tenn. Records do not indicate whether he was a former slave, but Birdseye seems to imply that he once had been enslaved. Tom W. Shick, *Emigrants to Liberia, 1820–1843: An Alphabetical Listing* (Newark, Del.: Liberian Studies Association in America, 1971), 43.
3. Rev. William Mack, a graduate of Princeton Theological Seminary, was appointed pastor in 1840 at the age of 33 by Second Presbyterian Church, Knoxville. He served in this capacity for three years, until 1844. W. Russell Briscoe and Katherine Boies Buehler, *Her Walls Before Thee Stand: History of the Second Presbyterian Church, Knoxville, 1818–1968* (Knoxville, Tenn.: Privately printed, 1968), 15.
4. In addition to his teaching responsibilities at East Tennessee University (now the University of Tennessee, Knoxville), Prof. L. F. Clark in 1840 published the *Tennessee Farmer* in Knoxville. Rothrock, *French Broad–Holston Country*, 77.
5. Dr. Isaac Wright operated Wright's Ferry near the mouth of Little River as early as 1810. Burns, *History of Blount County*, 234.
6. Rev. Isaac Anderson (1780–1857) was a prominent Presbyterian minister, the founder and president of Maryville College, Maryville, Tenn. He shared many of Birdseye's views on slavery, abolition, temperance, and the treatment of the Cherokee Indians. Samuel Tyndale Wilson, *Isaac Anderson*, 35–137.
7. William Potter (1796–1891), born in Lisbon, Conn., in 1821 arrived at the Creek Path Mission in Alabama, where he established a school for the Indians and labored faithfully until 1837. He removed to the

mission at Dwight, Ark., in 1839. Robert Sparks Walker, *Torchlights to the Cherokees: The Brainerd Mission* (New York: Macmillan, 1931), 46.

8. Creek Path Mission is present-day Guntersville, Ala. It was founded in 1820 by the American Board of Commissioners for Foreign Missions and continued until 1837. Ibid., 69.

9. The attack on Heddington, Liberia, and many other adventures which Sion Harris probably shared with his East Tennessee audience are vividly described in his letters in Bell I. Wiley, ed., *Slaves No More: Letters from Liberia, 1833–1869* (Lexington: Univ. Press of Kentucky, 1980), 215–23.

10. Robert Bogle at an early date operated a large tanyard and mill near the large spring at Spring View, Blount County, Tenn. Burns, *History of Blount County,* 241.

11. In 1840, the American Anti-Slavery Society split into two factions, one led by William Lloyd Garrison and the other led primarily by Lewis Tappan. Tappan organized, controlled, and financed a new organization, the American and Foreign Anti-Slavery Society, whose official organ was the *American and Foreign Anti-Slavery Reporter.* Dumond, *Antislavery,* 286–87.

12. To Gerrit Smith, November 4, 1841

ATHENS TENNESSEE
NOV[EMBER] 4TH 1841

Dear Sir

I am now at this town which is the principal town and seat of justice for McMinn County. The town is pleasantly situated on a fine creek running through it which affords good water power. The buildings are principally of brick built a good many of them in an elegant style. There are three churches all of brick one Presbyterian one Methodist and one Cumberland Presbyterian. There is a Court House Academy two branch banks three public houses. The inhabitants about 1000. I think it the most pleasant town in E[ast] Tenn[essee]. The county is comparatively new but of excellent land much like that of Jefferson Co[unty] less worn and better cultivated. Both appear to be a continuation of the Cumberland Valley[,] differing but little from the Valley in P[ennsylvani]a except in a greater abundance of mineral wealth. This county has lead copper and iron ores, the last in greater abundance than I ever saw elsewhere but in all the Counties of E[ast] Ten[nessee] there is enough. The Hiwassee R[ail] Road[1] now graded from Knoxville to Murray County Georgia 98 m[iles] runs by the town. The small part about 15 miles between the state line and New Echota is partially graded. The grade except a few miles, something near 20 is done from there to Madison Morgan County Geo[rgia] from thence lines run to Augusta and from opposite Augusta to Charleston. The R[ail] R[oad] Co[mpany] are now erecting iron works to make their rails on the south Bank of the Hiwassee in a small village called Calhoun near their road. I regard these channels of commerce or thoroughfares as important as light through them will find access to the community. These R[ail] Road Companies are embarrassed and doing but little. The Community appears to be seriously embarrassed and rather growing worse. When cotton became the staple article of the South[,] East Tennessee grew it and furnished provisions and stock for districts more exclusively cotton growing. The culture is now abandoned here and in all of E[ast] Ten[nessee;] it is growing less throughout the state. Stock growing is continued; hogs are fattened and driven to S[outh] C[arolina] and Geo[rgia] but the business is miserably unproductive. Those who drive stock horses hogs mules and cattle return with the report that the sales are effected with difficulty at loosing prices and this annually growing worse. The farmers usually sell their stock for the scrip issued by the Rail Road Companies, now so depreciated that that issued here is exchanged for Bank notes current at the Banks of the state at a discount of 23 per cent, the Banks themselves suspended and at a discount of 10 per cent per specie funds.

   In this dreadful state of the Country bankruptcy appears inevitable to the debtor portion of the inhabitants. The suffering poor are much to be pitied. It is difficult for them to obtain employment where the payment for their labor can be made to purchase rainment for themselves or families. Winter is now coming on they have neither shoes nor flannel for their children. Our poorest families at the North would appear to be quite comfortable in comparison with the poor here. Fortunately for them provisions are plenty and cheap so that most that have not adequate rainment are comfortably fed. The more intel[l]igent are making some efforts to recover from this unpleasant situation. They try to improve in farming to improve their stock particularly that much neglected and despised animal the sheep but they have a difficulty which to many is discouraging. The mountains of Spain are not better than those of E[ast] Ten[nessee] for this most useful animal. But since cotton engrossed their attention the flocks declined untill but a few coarse misformed animals could be found. Aware of the necessity of an improvement in this kind of stock I brought 300 Saxon sheep with me three years ago anticipating a ready sale but I found to change the habits of people more especially southern people was a difficult matter. The pressure has made it necessary for them. They are now buying my Saxons readily tho[ugh] at low prices and procuring fine cords to work the wool. There is here an agricultural society. Could slavery be abolished I should hope that in a few years it would become a highly agricultural community and a manufacturing one. I became a member of this agricultural society and entered my sheep for a premium and had a silver cup awarded me but being a member of the water drinking society I could dispense with the cup without inconvenience; and requested them to apply the amount to extend the usefulness of the society. Dr. Joseph B M Reese the President of the Jefferson County agricultural society gave a letter to his friends here and stated that he had purchased Saxon sheep of him more than two years since that the stock was a great improvement in both the full breed and as a cross in the common stock. His Lady had made jeans of the wool and an article of plain cloth where she used silk for the warp of her own make. He came down with his good Lady and exhibited the articles of her manufacture. They obtained a premium. He spent some days in the county and visited the principal farmers and used a very effective influence to induce them to improve their stock of sheep. I have I believe before spoken of him. He is a brother of one of the judges of the Supreme Court a planter of considerable wealth and the owner of some slaves I would think 15 or 20. He is an advocate for emancipation. Rev[erend] R. H. Lea told me he had heard him address the public on the subject before the bloodhounds of the South forced them into silence. You would perhaps give him little credit for candor when he continued a slaveholder. His reasons would be that his slaves were connected by marriage with those around him[,] that he could not free them here without adding them to the persecuted class of free negroes, that he had not confidence in colonization; to send them into the Northwest would also expose them to persecution. Under all the circumstances he may judge it best to let them remain under his guardianship untill the law would permit him to free them and have them near him. Request is frequent from all parts of E[ast] Ten[nessee] to me to bring out some good farmers and manufacturers. Much influence might be gained to our cause if a beginning could be made where agriculture and manufacturers could be introduced in the most improved forms. I have found the embarrassments of the last three years too oppressive to wish to bring others into difficulty. Any plan for improving the lands or manufacturing should be well considered before it is undertaken. The public sentiment would be favorable but pecuniary aid here would be doubtful. Any establishments however small should have the means to go on of their own.

The Gov[ernor] Mr. Jones[2] has recommended agriculture to the favorable attention of the Legislature, particularly wool growing and manufacturing. The change from cotton growing or a dependence on cotton growers would seem to lead them to view the institutions of the free states with more favor and in the same degree to wean them from Slavery. I would hardly expect to hear slavery spoken of with more disapprobation in the State of Connecticut than I do here.

When I wrote you last I was at Sweetwater Creek. I spent a night with Mr. Johnstone[3] the Post Master. In the morning a man called on him and informed him that a slave that had run away was caught the day before and lodged in jail in Madison[ville] Monroe Co[unty]. Mr Johnstone told me that his father Samuel Johnstone Sr had been annoyed by the pursuers. He said his Father openly avowed himself an Abolitionist and that that exposed him to such annoyances. He was himself opposed to slavery but thought it imprudent for a man to avow himself an abolitionist. His father was a man of talents had been an author of a pamphlet of about 100 pages of which he gave me a copy which he published some years since in opposition to *Free Masonry*. I believe that society is entirely dis[s]olved in E[ast] Ten[nessee]. I had passed the house of Mr Johnstone near Madison.[4] He was absent but at the time I knew nothing of his history.

I spent a night with Col[onel] John Bradford[5] two miles South of this town. He is a member of the Bar a man of talents and energy. His Lady is one of the best informed that I have become acquainted with in E[ast] Ten[nessee]. They had six interesting children. Mr B[radford] is a man of wealth one of the directors in the Bank, pleasantly situated but intends selling his property and removing to Iowa. He said he did it for the benefit of his children. He remarked that no man could calculate the injury to a family in being brought up in a slave holding state. He thought slavery one of the most enormous evils that could befall a country, but said to turn them all loose here he thought would produce disorder and not operate well. He has slaves. I inquired if he would take them with him. He said yes that they would not leave him. I should think they would not. He is kind to them. I called yesterday on a Mr. Sullins[6] 2 miles S[outh] W[est} of this town. He had the best cultivated farm I have seen but no slaves. He said he was conscientiously opposed to owning slaves. He appeared gratified to learn that I was also opposed to slavery. I found him so very interesting that I spent an hour or two at his house. He said a man from V[irgini]a spent a night with him a short time before who remarked that slaves were treated with too much kindness in E[ast] Ten[nessee] that he had often seen them in conversation with a white man with their hats not off that in V[irgini]a no slave would dare converse with a white man without his hat off. It is true there is a difference between the treatment of slaves here and in V[irgini]a. They are there aristocratic fond of their prejudices and ready to remind the traveller from the North that he is in the old dominion and that some homage is expected. Here we meet with nothing of that kind. Feelings are manifested and a wish expressed for more intimate acquaintance with the North. There is a restraining public sentiment which discountenances cruelty to the poor slave.

I met last week a small drove of poor slaves some 15 or 16 going on to Ala[bama]. It was the first I had seen for a long time. Tho[ugh] accustomed to their painful sight in the South I never meet with a drove of slaves without pain. There is usually an old one horse waggon made in N[ew] England with battered curtains. The women and young children who are unable to walk ride in it [and] their baggage is also carried with their provisions. In this that I met the other day the children were barefoot [and] miserably clad[;] their driver rode a horse near them. They went on slowly[;] melancholly and despair was pictured in their countenances. They had been torn from their families and friends and [were] going like bullocks to the slaughter into the hands of some blood hound they know not who. To a boy of about sixteen that lingered on behind I said where are you from my good boy. Old V[irgini]a Sir. Where are you going. To Ala[bama], Sir. Have you been there Master. I had. Is it a good country master. I told him a very good country. He said is it master. This poor fellows countenance brightened up at the little consolation my reply afforded him while he quickened his pace to overtake his fellows. Mr Johnstone told me that a few days before I was at his house a drove of twelve passed chained together. They were on the way to Louisiana. I had hoped this trade was at an end but it seems not to be. On the old worn out plantations they find it necessary to sell off a part of their laborers to buy food and rainment for the idle and dissolute. I hope the good cause is prosperous in the Northern states. That is the great field for the contest. When slavery is universally viewed [as] ruinous then it will soon be so viewed here.

I fear that my letters hastily written and this one commenced at a late hour will be hardly worth the trouble that the decyphering will cost. There is much of it that would be improper to publish. But if any part of it can be of service after being revised you may publish it or loan it to your friends. It may interest them to learn that they have some friends at the South, while I hear but few censures. Should my friend Birney be with you I would tender him my best wishes. With the assurances of kind regards to your wife, I am

Sincerely Yours
E. Birdseye

Notes

1. The Hiwassee Railroad, so near completion as Birdseye describes it, nevertheless was a victim of the depression following the Panic of 1837, when both state funding and private investment collapsed. Not until 1855 would a successor company complete this railroad, but recriminations over the failure of the Hiwassee Railroad, which finally succumbed to bankruptcy in 1842, continued to exacerbate intrastate sectional hostility and antagonism. Stanley John Folmsbee, *Sectionalism and Internal Improvements in Tennessee, 1796–1845* (Knoxville: East Tennessee Historical Society, 1939), 119–235.
2. James Chamberlain Jones (1809–1859) was a Whig candidate who twice defeated the Democratic incumbent, James K. Polk, for governor, in 1841 and 1843. *BDTGA,* 1:415–16.
3. Josiah K. Johnston was postmaster at Sweetwater, Monroe County, Tenn., Nov. 1838–Aug. 1845. Frazier, *Tennessee Post Offices,* 592.
4. Madison should be Madisonville.
5. Col. James F. Bradford (1801–1852), prominent member of the early bar in Athens, began practicing law in McMinn County in 1823. Birdseye mistakenly gives his first name as "John." Reba Bayless Boyer, comp., *Wills and Estate Records of McMinn County, Tennessee, 1820–1870* (Athens, Tenn.: Privately printed, 1966), 14–15; *History of Tennessee, Containing Historical and Biographical Sketches,* 812.
6. Nathan Sullins, born in Virginia, moved to McMinn County at an early age and became a prosperous farmer. Both Nathan and his wife, Rebecca Mitchell Sullins, were devoted Christians, and their home was long a preaching place for Methodist ministers; the lower part of their house was designed for this purpose and was furnished with a plain pulpit. Two of their sons, David and Timothy, later became highly regarded ministers in the Holston Conference. David Sullins was president of both Sullins College and Emory and Henry College, and founded Centenary College in Cleveland, Tenn. *History of Tennessee, Containing Historical and Biographical Sketches,* 982; Isaac Patton Martin, *Methodism in Holston* (Nashville: Methodist Historical Society of the Holston Conference, 1945), 427–28.

13. To Gerrit Smith, November 27, 1841

Newport Cocke Co[unty] E[ast] Ten[nessee]
Nov[ember] 27 1841

My Dear Sir—

I re[ceive]d a paper from you The Friend of Man of Oct[ober] 5th, by which I learn that you have purchased the freedom of those colored persons in Mississippi of whose residence you inquired of me some time last spring, or I suppose them to be the same. Samuel and his family will I have no doubt feel grateful to you for your act of kindness to them and will I would hope make a good improvement of their freedom.

I returned to this town from Athens two days since. During my sojourn many incidents came to my knowledge which may interest the philanthropist—much that gives us additional ground to hope that the cause which interests us is making progress in East Tennessee.

You will probably recollect that I suggested the possibility some three years since that East Tennessee might be detached from the other part of the state and made a separate and free state. I had hopes even then that such might be the result. Afterwards I was in so much doubt that I almost despaired to seeing it accomplished soon if ever. From my first arrival in this state I have endeavored to convince those with whom I became aquainted that such a division would contribute to the well being of East Ten[nessee,] that the natural resources of the country were its mineral agricultural and manufacturing resources[,] that with free labor [and] with well directed industry—a home market for the farmer [and] such legislation as would encourage improvements in the useful arts and with all protect the virtuous[,] would insure its wealth and prosperity. During the year past this has been a good deal discussed in private circles and appeared to meet with favorable consideration by influential good citizens. It is now popular in all parts of East Tennessee. On Monday and Tuesday of this week I attended the internal improvement convention of E[ast] Ten[nessee] at Knoxville.[1] This was discussed in the convention on both days. Not a single opponent appeared. The convention adjourned to meet again on Monday the 13th day of Dec[ember] when a more full attendance is expected. There are three political newspapers in Knoxville all of which will now advocate the policy of separating E[ast] from W[est] Ten[nessee]. The other papers in East Ten[nessee] will so far as I am informed give their support of the measure. Mr Williams[2] the member of Congress from Knox County is with us. I am disposed to believe that our delegation in Congress will unitedly favor it.

Those who hope by this means to exterminate slavery in East Tennessee think it will be prudent to say but little on that subject or publickly on it untill the act of separation is determined then to make a united effort to carry that measure. I should suppose there could be no doubt but a very large majority of our people would vote for the termination of slavery without delay. The surrounding slave states would take the alarm and no doubt make strenuous efforts to counteract a policy which they deem destructive to their interests.

The friends of the slave would have an open field and an opportunity to meet the advocates of slavery in debate. In this, native citizens would have one advantage over those from the free states. They would be among their acquaintances, would be well acquainted with the modes of reasoning among their fellow citizens. Enough of these could be found ready to engage in the cause. With these there should be some from the Northern states who could explain to them the superior advantages of free over slave labor.

As to the mode of conducting the very important measures now in contemplation there are men better qualified than myself to judge, among the number my worthy friend John Caldwell. He is known in all parts of East Tennessee. Altho[ugh] a self taught man he has talents is honest in the cause is a man who beyond most others has the esteem and good will of the community. He expects to leave next month for Talahasse Florida to return in the spring. Quite recently the colonization society requested him to use his influence in procuring the liberation of slaves to go to Liberia. He has consented to do so not because he has confidence that that is much to advance the cause of emancipation. But some will liberate their slaves for that purpose who would not consent to do so to have them remain here. In the first place they are objects of persecution; in the next the laws of the state make it difficult to liberate them to remain here. Mr C[aldwell] thinks he shall obtain the liberation of a number who will be of great use in civilizing and Christianizing Africa. It is true that many slaves in E[ast] Ten[nessee] maintain very excellent characters as professing Christians, I should hope would be very useful in Africa. Mr. Caldwell stated to me that he fully united in opinion with the abolitionists and was ready to give the cause his most efficient support.

On my return I spent a night with Robert Bogle in Blount County. I met at his house Rev[erend] Mr Craig[3] a professor in the Maryville Colledge. They with a young friend were met to concert measures to advance the cause. When I was at his house on my way down Mr. B[ogle] informed me that they had a meeting appointed at one of the churches to discuss the subject of the abolition of slavery. He informed me that their meeting was well attended no disorder or disturbance took place. Another meeting was appointed in the county for next month. The prospects there are very encouraging. I met with the P[ost] Master of Unita[4] P[ost] O[ffice] Blount Co[unty] (I have his name but not convenient at this time). He is a man of ardent feelings, a good deal animated in the cause and will I have no doubt make a good use of any thing sent him on the subject.

Mr Fife[5] P[ost] Master Athens Ten[nessee] with whom I became acquainted is in favor of a separation of the state and for the total abolition of slavery. Through him much good may be done. He is a man of influence both in and out of the Church.

I called to see the venerable Samuel Johnstone.[6] I had a wish to see him. His son requested me to visit his Father. I found him at work near his house clearing some new ground with a colored man that he had made free many years ago. He is now about 80 years of age active and industrious. His white locks and venerable appearance much reminded me of the Venerable Dr Johnson whom I used to see at Stratford in Conn[ecticut] when a youth myself. Mr Johnstone conversed much on the subject of slavery. He said the children of Israel were a long time in bondage but their oppressors had to let them go and were visited with severe judgments. The slaves in our country would be liberated and he believed their oppressors visited with the severe displeasure of the Almighty. He said much on the cruelties he had witnessed and of those transpiring now. Some years ago he saw 300 in Knoxville a large proportion chained. There was now near him a slave dealer by the name of Upton who had collected about 30 which he had in a private prison awaiting their removal to Louisiana. Among them was one from the neighborhood of Knoxville who had been taken from his family—he escaped with the intention of going back to see his family again. They pursued him and in taking him struck him with a club across the loins so as to disable him. He was then lying in a dangerous state with but little prospect of recovering. My aged friend is a member of the Seceders Church. Their clergyman lives in Blount Co[unty]. Something like a year ago he was in S[outh] C[arolina]. Duty led him to express his sentiments on the subject of slavery. They tarred and feathered him and gave him much rough usage.

Mr. Johnstone has a large farm, I think the best cultivated that I saw in the county. In his supplications for mercy he does not forget the poor slave. He said he was happy to hear that the Abolitionists were increasing in number and influence. He hoped that their labors might be crowned with success. The good man does not conceal his opinions but expresses them with an open undisguised frankness which testified how much he loved the cause. He spoke with ardent feelings of those who had been active in the cause. I inquired if he should not like to correspond with them. He raised his hand to show me that it was palsied. He said he wrote with difficulty but if there is any who wish I will try. I told him I thought they would send him some pamphlets and papers. He said he should receive them with pleasure. He would wish them addressed to Madisonville Monroe County E[ast] Ten[nessee].

Judge Peck with myself have determined to try the entire exclusion of slave labor in our lands here. At his plantation he has some 4 or 5. They are a family who enjoy much freedom. He would gladly make them entirely free but would wish to have all free. He will give his influence to effect the separation of E[ast] Ten[nessee] and then to make it a free state. The situation is of such that if the object can be accomplished, the early downfall of slavery in all the slave states may be confidently anticipated. Our information is continually more favorable from Kentucky and North Carolina. It is favorable even from Middle and West Tennessee. I meet with men frequently from there who express their abhorrence of the institution, more who admit that it is an evil and slave labor unprofitable. I have requested Judge Peck to assist me in making an estimate of the extent and resources of E[ast] Ten[nessee]. I have the following estimate which is principally his.

East Tenn[essee] contains 18000 square miles, 11,450,000 acres. One half 5,728,000 may be profitably applied to agricultural purposes or arable lands. 3,000,000 acres limestone land. 3,000 square miles produce bituminous coal none better. Some Anthrocite is found but none extensively explored. Navigable streams, Tennessee Holston F[rench] Broad Nolichucky Clinch Hiwassee Lesser Rivers Powel Emory Tellico Wattauga. With more than a 1000 streams suitable for driving machinery of every description with any power. Iron ore of every quality found everywhere Lead Zinc Copper Manganese Marble Gypsum Gold Silver Salt Petre in caves. Allum Copper as Epsom Nickel. We have specimens of all the above and can readily give further information as to their localities. The mines are but little wrought. Those of gold and silver are in the Ocoe district. Gold has been found to some profit; some silver but none has been extensively worked. Further up the mountain range specimens of silver ore have been found, united with lead and antimony. The iron coal marble and lime are the most useful and so abundant that they add nothing to the market value of lands or very little.

To all the motives the philanthropist should urge for the abolition of slavery that of religious and moral obligation will have great influence, but with those who are most influenced by such motives but few own slaves and as a general rule they are not slaveholders from principle but either hold them by descent or have purchased to save them from a worse fate. Many have done so who believe they were doing an act of humanity. Whether mistaken or not in that opinion they will give aid in abolishing the institution. To those who own slaves as a matter of gain a candid argument to prove to them that it is not profitable will be listened to with attention. Now in the extreme depression that prevails at the South particularly in this state is a favorable time to bring this to their attention. Every movement made to introduce manufacturers will be received with encouragement and appreciation. I commenced this letter after nine oclock after much fatigue and must ask you to make allowance for errors and a want of method. It would not be expedient to say much about the object of separating E[ast] from W[est] Tenn[essee] but I will advise you from time to time.

With great Respect I am
yours Most Ob[edientl]y
E. Birdseye

Notes

1. Two conventions were held in Knoxville, on Nov. 22–23 and Dec. 12–14, 1841, to consider internal improvements for East Tennessee, attended by delegates from Bradley, Cocke, Hamilton, Jefferson, Knox, McMinn, and Washington counties. Birdseye was present at both meetings. The last convention petitioned the state legislature to award East Tennessee $650,000 previously appropriated in 1838 for the construction of the now defunct Louisville, Cincinnati, and Charleston Railroad. These funds were to be used to construct a graded, macadamized turnpike from the Virginia line near Abingdon to Knoxville; to complete construction of the Hiwassee Railroad; and for various improvements to aid navigation on the Tennessee River. The legislature's failure to respond positively to these requests led, in 1842, to the movement for separate statehood for East Tennessee. Folmsbee, *Sectionalism*, 222–67.
2. Joseph Lanier Williams (1810–1865) was elected as a Whig from Tennessee to the 25th, 26th, and 27th Congresses (1837–43). *BDAC*, 1930.
3. John Sawyers Craig, D.D. (18?–1893), graduated from Maryville College in 1836. He became a tutor in 1837 and was elected professor of languages in 1840, in which capacity he served until the outbreak of the Civil War in 1861. Craig was the most outspoken abolitionist on the faculty. Samuel Tyndale Wilson, *Isaac Anderson*, 89.

4. James Jones was the postmaster at Unitia, Blount County, from 1825 until 1845. He was a Quaker especially active in promoting antislavery memorials through correspondence. Burns, *History of Blount County*, 59, 270.
5. James H. Fyffe was postmaster at Athens from 1829 until 1842. Frazier, *Tennessee Post Offices*, 566.
6. Samuel Johnston, father of Josiah K. Johnston, Birdseye's friend who was postmaster at Sweetwater, died intestate on Aug. 11, 1846, in Monroe County, Tenn. Reba Bayless Boyer, comp., *Monroe County, Tennessee: Chancery Court Records, 1832–1887* (Athens, Tenn.: Privately printed, 1988), 48.

14. To Gerrit Smith, December 14, 1841

KNOXVILLE E[AST] TENN[ESSEE]
DEC[EMBER] 14TH 1841

My Dear Sir

I am now in this city attending a convention as a delegate from Cocke County. The object of our meeting is to take into consideration necessary internal improvements in E[ast] T[ennessee] and asking some further aid from the state to complete the Hiwassee Rail Road. I have here met a respectable delegation from the counties of E[ast] Ten[nessee] on the business of the convention. There is as much harmony as could have been expected.

There has also been much discussion in private circles of the projected division of the State. It is now popular in all parts of E[ast] Ten[nessee]. While here I have not heard an individual opinion against it. All appear to be ardently in favor of the measures. So far as I know every paper in E[ast] Ten[nessee] is in favor of it. We are informed that a member of the State Senate has introduced a Bill into the Senate for the purpose of carrying the measure into effect. We hope it will meet with no serious obstacle anywhere. If we can succeed in accomplishing this and I believe we can, with reasonable efforts we can make it a free state. It is not our intention to say much on the subject of making it a free state untill we effect the separation unless in private circles where it will not have a tendency to awaken the opposition of the slave holders. In all cases where it will be prudent we intend to prepare the public mind and especially the minds of individuals for the measure so that as soon as one is effected we can be ready for the other.

You will probably have received a letter from my venerable friend Judge Peck before this reaches you.[1] He appears to be fairly satisfied in both of these important measures and anxious for a continued correspondence with you. Some time since when your letter to Mr. Clay came to my address at Mossy Creek the P[ost] M[aster] discovered what it was and took it to Judge Peck and consulted him about delivering it to me. I believe similar opinions were asked from Newmarket. At both offices they are slave holding. They know your handwriting and would be apt to intercept any communication from you, for this reason we have thought it best to have your letters to him come through me at Newport. I have thought on these considerations that that was expedient as those men are in practice and principle slaveholding. Individually they profess friendship for me as they do for my friend Caldwell while in the narrow circle of slaveholding they privately express opinions in the terms familiar here that we are "ugly customers." From all I can learn our prospects are beyond my most sanguine expectations and not the least flattering is the acquisition of our influential and talented friend Judge Peck. He was as you are probably aware the senior Justice of the Supreme Court of Ten[nessee]. No man understands the people better or can exercise an influence over them with his pen beyond him. He has now commenced a series of essays on the resources of E[ast] Ten[nessee], the exped[i]ency of a separation from the western parts of the state and the great advantages to be derived from the separation and organization as an independent state.

To carry these important measures it is possible that we may need some aid and if so I hope our antislavery friends will consider our case. We will get on without if possible if not do with as little as possible and for that little make an equivalent in land if that would be acceptable.

We have for some time projected a free labor community or settlement on our land. That is yet a favorite measure with us. We shall have to purchase one additional tract of land to make a necessary improvement. When that is done we will send you a map of our land or a metrical post of them. They will have great natural advantages and we have the confident hope that here where we exclude slavery wholly we can exhibit the advantages of free labor in a light so favorable that it will do much good. This is popular. Slaveholders and those who are not tell us they hope we shall succeed in our undertaking so that in this we have to dread no annoyance that we are aware of.

With this I send you one of our locofoco papers. I have directed the Editor of the Register to mail you his paper untill further notice. You will in that have the essays of Judge Peck and much that may interest you. I am sorry to say that the Editor[2] tho[ugh] a native of Newhampshire is quite too timid and often inserts advertisements and articles which are against his better feelings.

When at Athens last month I met with the Rev[erend] Mr. White[3] of the Presbyterian Church. He is located about 11 miles from this city. I was coming on and was pleased to have his company. He had been to Cassville in Georgia to attend a meeting of ministers and delegates at that place in part for the purpose of locating a Southern Theological Seminary. It appeared that there were delegates and clergymen from South Carolina Geo[rgia] Ala[bama] and all of the three divisions of Tennessee. Mr White urged on the convention to locate at Maryville. The South Carolina delegation stated that they now considered themselves as measurably separated from the northern church, that the Presbytery of Kingston had taken decided antislavery ground and for that reason Maryville was objectionable. Mr. White endeavored to satisfy them that these acts were not such as should be considered a decided expression of the whole church and I very much fear that he endeavored to prove to them that if they would locate their institution at Maryville that the Presbyterian church would become orthodox in the slaveholding faith.

In this he did not succeed. The matter was postponed untill another time and for further consideration. I shall suggest this to some of my friends in the church and I hope effectual measures will be adopted to prevent such a calamity to the Presbyterian Church in this section of the South. An attempt now to enlist it in the cause of slavery would distract it as certainly as it would with you. The measure must be hid to be successful. I think it was unfortunate that Mr. White attended the association alone. He is the only clergy man in the church that I am acquainted with that is pro slavery. During the past three years I have been acquainted with Mr White but could never engage him in a conversation on the subject of slavery. When it was introduced he was always silent. While riding together he inquired if Mr Allen son of Rev[erend] Allen of Huntsville[4] had visited his father. I told him I had inquired of Mr. Potter who assured me that he could not. The slaveholders there would kill him if he did. He thought the young man had acted very foolishly and inquired as to what right the people of one state had to interfere with the institutions of another state. I asked him if he had not advocated missions to India where widows were burned on the funeral piles of their husbands. He said he had but that was a very different matter from slavery. I replied different to be sure but not a greater sin. There but few widows were burned. Those submitted to their fate voluntarily—while here husbands and their wives were separated without any crime or voluntary action on their part and taken off in chains—if not to endure so keen an agony as the burning widow was yet a more protracted one. With this the subject was dropped. I have since been pained to learn that there had been much disorder in his church and that there was a probability that it would be broken up. Some of it was of so very extraordinary a character that I may notice it more particularly in another letter. Mr White is a man of strong sectarian feelings; but with none but kind feelings to the man I fear that he has a mistaken view of his duty and that he exhibits feelings which should not enter the pulpit—and that place where the robes of those who have the awful charge of a messenger of grace to guilty men should be unspotted. I fear he may have done much to produce unchristian feelings in his flock. This letter is a hasty one commenced after 10 oclock PM. No part of it I should think ought to be published.

Sincerely Yours
E. Birdseye

WRITTEN ACROSS PAGE 1:
When at Doctor Andersons in Maryville on my way down to Athens his only son was taken sick. He was his only child. He died a few days before my return. Doct[or] A[nderson] preached on the day I was there to a large congregation. He was quiet under the very great affliction but appeared more awakened to his duty. I had a wish to have conversed with him on the subject of their Theological Seminary but the painful circumstance in which he was providentially placed seemed to make it an unpropitious time. It is certainly a very important time with the Presbyterian Church in this state in all the South. I will endeavor to ascertain how far this proslavery influence is to be feared and see if countervailing influence cannot be used to save the church at least of E[ast] Ten[nessee] from such a contaminating influence. Should some of our pious antislavery clergymen correspond with Doctor Anderson on this and other important interests of the church it might do good. The people are poor the churches poor. I am not free from fear that a corrupting proslavery influence may be get[ting] into the church or the theological seminary. On the other hand a little aid may by being timely furnished save them from these dangerous influences. Some of Dr. Greenes[5] writings may be especially calculated to do good if sent to Dr. Anderson or the Rev[erend] Mr Craig a professor in the colledge at Maryville.

Blount County is in a very interesting situation. There is a lively antislavery influence—and that unmolested. It is more important as it is the site of a colledge where youth from all parts of the south may imbibe the healing influences—one of the professors being an active abolitionist. If some of our good abolitionists would correspond with Robert Bogle and Mr Craig and furnish them with such papers as would be useful that county would in a little time become so thoroughly abolitionized that no dread could be entertained from these active influences and a little field well cultivated. In this[,] humanity[']s solicitude (I speak of the whole South) must be of very great importance and I hope will be considered so at the north. If these men could have papers paid for by the friends of the cause at the North the cost would be but small. They would spread them over the field now white for the harvest.

You will be occasionally advised of such incidents and matters as may interest you. We hope the means used may be blessed if clouds and darkness should be round about us. I trust we shall be constant in our duty. The blessing if long withheld may be granted at last.

NOTES

1. Judge Jacob Peck did write to Gerrit Smith on Nov. 30, 1841, explaining his friendship with Ezekiel Birdseye and their plans to establish a free labor colony on lands they had purchased for that purpose in Cocke County. He solicited financial help from Smith for this project and talked about the possibility of East Tennessee becoming a free state in the near future. Jacob Peck to Gerrit Smith, Nov. 30, 1841, Smith Papers.
2. James C. Moses (1818–1870), a native of Exeter, N.H., printer, editor, and merchant, came to Knoxville in 1839 as a printer of the *Times*, a semiweekly newspaper. In 1841, he became both publisher and editor of the *Knoxville Register*. Rothrock, *French Broad–Holston Country*, 460–61.
3. Gideon Stebbins White (1803–1863), Presbyterian minister born at Granville, N.Y., was educated at Maryville College. In 1835 he took charge of the Shunem Presbyterian Church at Strawberry Plains, Jefferson County, and about the same time became pastor of the Washington Presbyterian Church in Knox County, preaching part-time in both these churches. He was frequently a commissioner to the Presbyterian General Assembly. Ibid., 500–501.
4. William T. Allan (1810–1882), son of a distinguished Presbyterian minister in Huntsville, Ala., who owned slaves, was a graduate of Centre College who studied under Theodore Dwight Weld at Lane Theological Seminary and subsequently became converted to the antislavery cause. One of the famous Lane rebels, in 1835 he became an agent of the American Anti-Slavery Society. He was regarded in the South as an apostate, and the rumor among slaveholders was that he could not return home to Alabama. Dumond, *Antislavery*, 162–63; Benjamin P.

Thomas, *Theodore Weld, Crusader for Freedom* (New Brunswick, N.J.: Rutgers Univ. Press, 1950), 41, 70–72, 77, 84, 93, 98.

5. Beriah Green (1795–1874), Congregational minister and leader in the antislavery cause, wrote some 35 pamphlets denouncing slavery, which were widely used by abolitionists. In 1833 he accepted the presidency of the Oneida Institute at Whitesboro, N.Y., which he attempted to maintain as a school devoted to manual labor and abolitionism as well as academic studies, and which was open to students of every color and nationality. *DAB*, 7:539–40.

15. To Gerrit Smith, February 7, 1842

Newport E[ast] Ten[nessee]
Feb[ruary] 7th 1842

Dear Sir

Your letter in reply to mine of Nov[ember] 27 is rec[eive]d and today two numbers of the friend of man is reviewing the letter published in one of them. I notice a word or two that does not exactly convey my meaning. My remark that we do not intend saying much about slavery untill a division of the state was (is) effected was only meant so far as to declare that the motive. On all suitable occasions I endeavour to convince the people with whom I have intercourse that slavery is destructive to their best interests. On this subject I speak freely and with as little fear as I should in the Northern states. In E[ast] T[ennessee] there appears to be a freedom of discussion on this subject that does them much honor. A few days since I had a conversation with Maj[or] William Robertson[1] one of the magistrates of this county and a year ago last Dec[ember] one of the purchasers of the slaves sold as the property of a Mr Jones. He has some 7 or 8 I believe. He told me he was fully convinced that it was the most destructive thing that could be to the happiness and prosperity of a community. He declares that he will set all of his free readily if others will do the same. At other times he openly declares himself an abolitionist. Of all the slaveholders in this county that I know which is near all[,] there is but two who do not offer their lands for sale. Slaveholding agriculture is so miserable that it appears to be dying of natural weakness.

There was a few incidents in my late tour that I omitted to notice. On the

2nd week in Nov[ember] I went down to Calhoun on Hiwassee. This is on the northeast bank of the river where the R[ail] R[oad] crosses the river. On the opposite side is Charleston. It was there that the Cherokees were quartered before removing to the West. I went out among the frail tenements where they were sheltered now silent and falling to ruins. The dram shop too is deserted where they were tempted to drunkenness. They were kept idle, their living different from what they had been accustomed to. Their despondency under the injustice with which they were robbed of their country—all together hurried them to their graves—they died in great numbers. I saw some who were guarding them. Others who went with them to the West. Some said the detachments which they accompanied lost more than one tenth on the journey by death. At night I stopped at the house of an aged widow on the road to Athens. The good lady was acquainted with many affecting incidents that occurred with these oppressed people. She said our country had much to answer for for their treatment of the poor Indians.[2]

When about 5 miles below Athens on passing the house of a Mr. Rice I was surprised to see his slave a man of about 25 years of age tied to a locust tree in the yard nearby in front of his house. The poor fellow was stripped to his waist. The cords were roped round his legs so as to confine them closely to the tree, his hands crossed and tied together bro[ugh]t up next to the tree and lashed fast to it.

He appeared to have been prepared for one of those terrible scourgings so common with unrestrained despotism. Mr R[ice] was not in sight. Some two weeks before I had been introduced to him and had had one or two friendly conversations with him. I determined to call and see if I could not dissuade him from such barbarity. I stepped immediately before the door. He came out took me by the hand but so much excited by passion that he spoke with difficulty. I continued a friendly conversation with him for some 10 or 15 minutes without at all alluding to his slave, when his passion appeared to become calmed. Then turning to the slave I inquired of him if his "boy" gave him trouble. He said yes that the night before he went out without leave—he did not say whether from bad motives or to visit a friend—that he had determined on whipping him and went with a whip for the purpose and that the slave ran down the road. He followed with his horse and caught him in about a half mile. He had then tied him to give him a very severe whipping.

I inquired if he had generally been obedient. He said he had. I asked him if he would not be safe to take a fair promise and try him again adding that where mild measures would answer I thought them best. He said he would—that he had been very angry—was glad he had not whipped him—for he had intended to have been very severe. It was the first time he had allowed himself to get in such a passion with him. He appeared a little mortified that he had indulged such violent passions. As I bid him good morning he went to untie the poor fellow who I have no doubt was as much obliged to me for my call as his master was. Mr Rice in his usual intercourse with society had nothing of the appearance of the tyrant about him. He is a man of ardent but I should think when not in a passion, of tender feelings. Accustomed to indulge unrestrained passions from youth they will when angry lacerate the poor slaves and often express their sorrow for it when their passions have subsided.

At Athens the community were thrown into a high excitement by the murder of a Mrs McMahan[3] and her little daughter of about 12 or 13 years of age by their slave. The family lived about 4 miles from Athens. The husband had gone with his wagon and another slave some miles from home that morning when a person calling at his house discovered his wife lying dead with her daughter. They had been killed by an axe, what could have prompted the deed no one knew. She was said to be kind to him, a woman of amiable character and pious.

They followed and soon overtook the waggon and informed the husband of the melancholly fate of his wife and daughter. They took the slave with him, tied him and whipped him to make him own that he was an accomplice, that the murder was a concocted plan between them, that he was to have murdered his master before he came home. The poor fellow like the unfortunate soldier in the siege of Montgar would swear to anything. They made him own so much that they had little confidence in anything he confessed. He was bro[ugh]t to jail after some 9 or 10 days. The murderer was caught severely scoured by the mob tried by the court and hung. He fully acquited his fellow slave of any knowledge or participation in his crime. He said it was a momentary resolution that he did not like his mistress. I do not learn that he gave any other reasons for killing her and her daughter. He was something about 22 extremely ignorant and said to be ill tempered. The other slave was I heard taken off to be sold. This I believe to be the fifth case of a slave killing his owner within the last three years in E[ast] Ten[nessee] that I have learned of—but in any instance before it was the master who was killed and for cruelty to their wives or children.

When at the house of Robert Bogle a few days after I mentioned this murder of Mrs McMahan. He said she was his own cousin. He told me that her brother living in Mississippi some two or three years since followed a slave who had committed some misdemeanor and run away. They caught him chained him to a tree and burnt him alive. Mr Caldwell told me that a short time before passing his house in Nov[ember] that a slave had been dangerously wounded by Adam Meek.[4] Meek was a member of Mr Whites church. The slave was owned by a Mr. McBee.[5] A year or more before the slave of McBee was at Meeks when two of Meeks slaves assaulted him. He defended himself and went home. Soon after they crossed the Holston River and again assaulted him in the field of McBee and were again repulsed. Meek sent word to McBee to either whip him or send him over to him to be whipped. McBee said that in the affair his slave had only defended himself, that in his view he was not to blame. In the first instance he should refuse to do either but cautioned his slave to avoid Meek. After a year had passed Mrs McBee took him with her. As she forded the river on the sabeth after crossing gave him leave to make a call but to avoid Meek to pass round through fields. Unfortunately he met with Meek in one of his fields who ordered him to stand. He declined. He then called some of his associates to help him and to bring a bull dog. The dog caught him and tore his legs. He had a club and could keep off the dog when standing but if he attempted to run the dog caught and tore him. Meek threw stones at him they had sharp angles and cut him badly. A vein in his neck was so cut that the blood ran profusely from it. He surrendered and was taken to the house of Meek who became alarmed fearing he would bleed to death sent for Mrs McBee who was his sister to come and stop the blood. She came but told him as he had opened his veins he might close them; she should not interfere. Near evening McBee came home. Learning what had happened he went for his slave. He met him all covered with blood supported by one on each side who were conducting him home. McBee only inquired of him if he thought he should recover. He said he hoped so. Then passed on to Meeks—inquired of him why he had so abused his slave. Meek said sit down I will tell you. McBee said you will tell me so many lies that I shall not know what to believe—which excited Meek. McBee said had you not better get your gun and shoot me. Meek said he would, went into the other room and took down his gun. Two young men I believe his sons seized it took it from him and discharged it. McBee who is usually a cool quiet man next attacked him with his cane—which he used without mercy and left him for home. Meek seized the rifle charged it and pursued. In taking it from his son he used his knife but before he overtook McBee fainted with the loss of blood and fell and was carried home. McBee has sued him for injuring his slave and indited him for an assault with intent to kill. Meek has indighted McBee for an assault and sued for damages. This I know must be painful to you perhaps offensive. Meek is a member of a Presbyterian Church that has a proslavery clergyman. The slave is living and now able to work but a brother of McBee told me he feared he would never entirely recover.

Tho[ugh] we have slavery in a mitigated form in E[ast] Ten[nessee] it has horrors enough here. A few days since[,] 127 slaves passed in a drove. They were going from a worn out plantation in N[orth] C[arolina] to a fresh one in the western district of this state. When they have made that sterile they may go next to Texas. They were furnished with corn meal and bacon enough for their necessary food. They were camped by the side of the road around fires. They are owned by a Mr Polk. Some time since tis said their owner passed in his coach and four. The brothers I suppose them to be removed through some year or two since. They were of the aristocracy of N[orth] C[arolina], drove their coach and four going with their slaves in quest of new lands. One thing has always struck me as remarkable. A slaveholder appears to have no attachment for his place of nativity or ancestral farm. When worn out he abandons it without care or regret goes to some new one soon spreads desolation and sterility around him and removes again.

But with all slavery is growing unpopular. The price of produce is low cotton so depressed that it pays but poorly for raising. If it keeps at what it now is or falls lower the conclusion will soon be that slavery is not worth quarrelling about.

Since my last I believe I have not seen either Judge Peck or Mr. Caldwell. Mr C[aldwell] I believe has gone to Florida. When at his house in Dec[ember] he told me he had made up his mind to sell his farm. He was offered $4000, had asked 4500. I asked him if he could not avoid it. He said no he was obliged to have $300 dollars. If he could get that sum he could go to Florida and avoid the sale but the banks would not lend it. There was no man in E[ast] Ten[nessee] who could. I told him I knew of two who could lend him that am[oun]t and would assist him in obtaining the loan. As he did not apply to both I hope he was accommodated.

Sincerely your friend
E. Birdseye

Notes

1. William Robinson was one of the trustees of Cocke County and one of the commissioners appointed by the Tennessee General Assembly in 1835 to lay off the county into districts of convenient size. Since no Robertson can be located in the 1839 Cocke County tax list, Birdseye must have been referring to this man. *History of Tennessee, Containing Historical and Biographical Sketches*, 867; Creekmore, "East Tennessee Taxpayers," 124, 127, 133, 140.
2. Birdseye's response to the removal of the Cherokees from East Tennes-

see was similar to that of most missionaries from various Protestant denominations. See McLoughlin, *Cherokees and Missionaries,* 266–334.
3. A jury of inquest found that Peter, a slave of John McMahan's, murdered Ester and Mary Jane McMahan on Nov. 15, 1841. Boyer, *Wills and Estate Records of McMinn County,* 107.
4. Adam R. Meek was the son of Adam Meek, Sr. (1746–1828), the first white settler, surveyor, and farmer in Strawberry Plains, Tenn. He was a native of the County of Derry in Ireland, came to America in 1763, and arrived in Tennessee in 1780. In his will, Adam Meek, Sr., left several slaves to his son, Adam R. Meek, the man involved in the episode Birdseye relates. Wood, *Hitch Hiking,* 18, 22, 23.
5. Sarah Meek, daughter of Adam Meek, Sr., and sister of Adam R. Meek, married Lemuel McBee and lived in Grainger County, just across the Holston River from her home. Ibid., 18.

16. To Gerrit Smith, March 14, 1842

KNOXVILLE TEN[NESSEE]
MARCH 14TH 1842

Dear Sir

With this I send you the Post a paper published here weekly. Edited by a Mr. Williams[1]—more distinguished as a tolerably fair specimen of a southern swaggerer than for literary merit. It is a custom with him to vent his spleen against Northern men and the Northern states more especially such as he supposes to be unfriendly to the patriarchial institution of the South. As my sentiments on the subject are no secret here he has thought proper to thunder forth some anathemas for my special benefit. Soon after my arrival in town on Saturday he gave me one of his papers, I suppose to be certain that his labors did not escape my attention. I have become so accustomed to southern blustering that I put a very low estimate on it. These effeminates of the south are seldom dangerous where they would have reason to apprehend substantial opposition to their threats. They vent their spleen; we either let it pass in silence as unworthy of notice or treat it with contempt. They make here but a small part of our community and have a limited influence. This man I do not believe could influence a dozen men to openly abet his causes in town. He established his paper with a view of aiding some of his aristocratic friends into office. The result showed that they had mistaken their strength. The opinion he expresses of Northern laborers they are supposed to entertain for laborers here. Our honest hearted yeomanry refuse them their votes. With all of this I would not have troubled you but for the opinion of our Northern laboring people. As this man expresses not only his own opinions but those of the despotic slaveholders generally I have thought it not improper that it should be laid before them.

Slavery in principle is not confined to color at the South. Many who are slaves are as white as I am—where the offspring has been for generations from a white father untill all traces of African blood has disappeared. Yet while they are the descendants of a slave they are bought and sold like cattle and of females often at a much higher price for being white. Had these despots the power they would just as soon sell our Northern laborers as slaves as the negroes. The man or body of men whom they can bully most they dispise just in proportion to the concessions made. If our Northern states take high ground and maintain it firmly they will be treated with respect and courtesy by the South. If they yield to their insolent and unjust demands they will be treated with the scorn and contempt of vassals. Since New York took a firm stand in resisting the unjust claim of V[irgini]a the north has been spoken of with more respect. The south thought the customary gasconade would bring her to terms. As she appeared refractory Geo[rgia] & S[outh] Ca[rolina] thought by uniting with V[irgini]a the object would soon be accomplished. I do most sincerely hope that not only N[ew] York but all the North will be united in maintaining their rights and resisting the unwarantable demands of the South. It is I hope too late for the North to be told that slavery at the south has any power. It is tottering to its fall. One year of free discussion would overthrow it. Those who do not own them (slaves) and many who do most earnestly wish its downfall. Slavery will never venture into the field. These despots know that they are powerless but they hope to maintain an ascendancy by blustering and threatening. During the time that nullification was rife I was in S[outh] C[arolina]. I was fully aware that the object was not dissolution it was simply to bully the North into terms.

But little is said here about the affair of the Creole.[2] No interest is manifested to have the blacks restored to their masters—with the intel[l]igent there is no belief that they will be restored. I speak of E[ast] Tennessee but this would apply to much of the South. In the late contest with Mr Adams the public sentiment here was generally with him. I hope these occurrences have done good at the North.

I met here my worthy young friend W[illia]m W Dunn[3] of Blount County who married the adopted daughter of Robert Bogle. He informed me that about two weeks since Rev[erend] Thomas Kendall[4] the clergyman of the seceder church[5] (the same who was tarred and feathered by a mob in S[outh] Carolina some time since) gave an antislavery address at Louisville Blount County. Some men who live in this county hearing of the appointment sent word that they would come down and mob him if he attempted to speak. The people sent word to them that they might come they should be well prepared for them. They met well armed and what may appear very extraordinary was a number of slaveholders there with their rifles ready to defend the liberty of speech. No attack was made and had one been attempted it would have proved disastrous to the aggressors. It is true that a very considerable proportion of our slaveholders most sincerely desire its abolition. The laws do not permit them to emancipate them to remain here. If it did they are objects of persecution to such men as the editor of this paper. They want the whole fabric overthrown so that the prosperity of the South may be placed on a durable basis.

In Cocke County there are two societies of the young men recently formed for the public discussion of slavery and other subjects. Last week and the week before[,] the debate was whether slavery or intemperance were the greatest national evils. The debate is to be continued. There is there no sign of opposition that I have heard of. I am candid in the opinion that if there was an antislavery press there[,] that the public sentiment would sustain it. Tho[ough] in the present state of the question it would not be expedient to attempt to establish one there.

A few days since I met with an intelligent young man from Laurens district S[outh] Ca[rolina] who told me that there was much dissatisfaction there among the non slaveholding part of the community. But he said almost the only intelligence they get on the subject was what appeared in the National Intelligencer.[6] The low price of cotton is doing much. Slave labor at the present prices is worthless or nearly so for growing cotton. Sales I am credibly informed range in Augusta from 4 to 6¢ some extra lots a little higher. They are now becoming excessively alarmed about the culture of cotton in India. I have much wished that our Northern people would petition congress to repeal the duty on foreign cotton as it adds but little or nothing to the revenue. The South claim to be opposed to protective duties. If the petition should state the prospect of getting a supply of cotton from the free laborers of India cheaper than it could be grown by slave labor in the U[nited] S[tates] in as strong language as the facts would justify[,] all the better. The petition would cause great excitement at the South and would run through their papers. The cotton growers have been willing to prostrate the North and refuse their industry all protection. I should like to see what they would say in pleading for the protection of cotton. If the North would bring the South to terms on the subject of protection it could be best done by showing them that they need it and unless they would consent for the industry of the North to be protected they had no favors to expect.

The friend of whom I speak Mr Dunn is laboring under a slight affection of the lungs. His physician advises him to go to the North and spend the summer. He wishes to ride on horseback and when there be able by his industry to maintain himself and his horse untill he should return. He is a printer now working here at the Journals of the Legislature is a good workman of industrious temperate habits and an ornament in the church of which he is a member. He wishes me to inquire whether he could obtain employment in the office of the Friend of Man or some other office so as to sustain himself while there. He is an intelligent man has lived in Nashville and would hope to do something for the good cause. His object would be to regain his health. His expectations as to reward would be moderate. I should hope that these and the further commendation of his being a member of the Antislavery society of Blount County would recommend him to favorable consideration. A letter would find him at Maryville T[ennessee] or a communication thro[ugh] me would reach him.

Sincerely Your Friend
Ezekiel Birdseye

WRITTEN ACROSS PAGE 1:
Mr. J. F. Clairborne[7] of Nashville recently rejected by the US Senate was one of the leaders of the mob that lynched Amos Dresser. If England would modify his corn laws and add a duty on American cotton[,] that would hasten the downfall of slavery.

Notes

1. James Williams (ca. 1814–1869) served in the Tennessee house of representatives in 1843–45, representing Knox County as a Whig. In 1841 he edited the *Knoxville Post*; in 1852 he was among the organizers in Knox County of the Knoxville and Charleston Railroad Company. Appointed U.S. minister to Turkey by President James Buchanan in 1857, he resigned when the Civil War broke out in 1861 and went to London, where he wrote articles for London newspapers on behalf of the Confederate cause. Indicted for treason after the war, he remained in Europe until his death. *BDTGA,* 1:793–94.
2. On Oct. 27, 1841, the ship *Creole* sailed from Hampton Roads for New

Orleans with a cargo of 135 slaves. These slaves overpowered the crew and seized the ship, killing one passenger. Unable to sustain a voyage to Africa, the slaves put into the British port of Nassau. British officials held 19 of them for trial on a charge of murder but allowed the remaining slaves to go free. President John Tyler, Secretary of State Daniel Webster, and others demanded the return of these slaves. James G. Birney wrote an article in the *New York American,* in which he argued that the slave states did not have the constitutional right to demand the return of these slaves on behalf of all the states, including the free states in the North. The *Creole* case thus became a *cause célèbre* among abolitionist and proslavery forces alike. Dumond, *Antislavery,* 268–70.

3. William W. Dunn was a member of the Clover Hill Presbyterian Church, organized by John S. Craig, the outspoken abolitionist professor at Maryville College in 1841. During the Civil War, Dunn's daughter Cynthia was a captain in the "Loyal Ladies Home Guard" of Blount County. Burns, *History of Blount County,* 63, 101.

4. Thomas S. Kendall, an ardent abolitionist, was minister at the Big Springs Seceder Church in Blount County and in 1841 served as superintendent of the Louisville Academy. Ibid., 59, 105, 146.

5. The Associate, or Seceder, Church is a descendant of the first secession from the established Church of Scotland. The Blount County Sessions records indicate that this sect was by far the strictest church group in the county. Ibid., 104–5.

6. The *National Intelligencer* (1800–1869) was a leading political newspaper, published in Washington, D.C. It carried full and accurate reports of Congressional proceedings which were reprinted widely in newspapers throughout the U.S. Generally moderate in its editorial policies, it advocated compromise on the issue of slavery, urged gradualism, and argued that slavery should be abolished but not through political means. William E. Ames, *A History of the National Intelligencer* (Chapel Hill: Univ. of North Carolina Press, 1972), 17–376.

7. Thomas Claiborne (1780–1856), Nashville lawyer, served in the Tennessee house of representatives (1811–15, 1831–33), representing Davidson County. He was elected to the U.S. House of Representatives, 15th Congress (1817–19), after serving as mayor of Nashville. His name is listed by Amos Dresser as among those who tried and punished him by whipping in 1835 for the charge of distributing abolitionist literature in the state. *BDTGA,* 1:145–46; Dresser, *Narrative of Amos Dresser,* 3.

17. To Gerrit Smith, April 16, 1842

Newport Cocke County E[ast] Ten[nessee]
April 16th 1842

Dear Sir

I rec[eive]d yesterday the friend of man March 22 which is the first I have rec[eive]d since the no. of Jan[uary] 11th. I have from my brother 11 numbers of the New York American of late dates all of which indicate a favorable change in public sentiment in the Northern states. The good people of the free states appear to [have] become alarmed at the despotic pretentions of the slaveholding states. I hope too that they will prepare to resist the further unwarrantable pretentions of Southern despots.

It appears probable that a crisis will soon arrive when these claims will have to be met and decided. The slave holding part of the South with a power wholly contemptible appear determined to lose no opportunity to hurry on measures which must decide the momentous question whether the liberty of the North or the slavery of the South is to rule the nation.

For a time war on the creole case was confidently predicted. They said the nation was committed and could not retreat—that Mr Websters instructions had committed the North. England must surrender the slaves liberated from the creole or pay for them, or war was inevitable. Fortunately a few members of Congress have had the moral courage to convince them of their error. The tone of the Northern press has been such as to lower the hostile pretentions of the Southerners.

An impression is becoming general at the South that abolitionists are increasing very fast at the North. Some seem to suppose that most of the intelligent and influential men of the North are already abolitionists or at least giving them countenance and aid. A man of intelligence who was conversing with me recently on the subject said that he believed Mr Birney would be elected president of the US at the second election for that office. This impression which I would hope the facts were such as to justify is having a favorable effect in various ways on the South. Those opposed to slavery are more bold and openly so. As the North became united, the friends of the slave at the South will act more openly and more efficiently. In a late letter I informed you that the subject was debated by two societies in this county. The societies are formed for the purpose of diffusing useful knowledge by debating all subjects calculated to promote the design of the founders. The question before them was whether slavery or intemperance were the greatest national evil. At Newport Rev[erend] Spencer Henry[1] and John F. Stansberry[2] took the affirmative as to slavery. Mr. Henry is a clergyman in the Methodist Church. Mr S[tanberry] clerk of the county court both reputable for talents. The decission was that slavery was the greatest of the two evils. Next morning a slaveholder called on Mr. H[enry] somewhat excited. "Said" I understand you have decided that intemperance is no national evil at all—Mr. H[enry] "No Sir only that slavery is a greater evil"—the slaveholder— "I think such decisions very improper Sir." H[enry]—"Well Sir if you are dissatisfied we will have the matter tried over again when you can have an opportunity of arguing the question"—S[laveholder]—"No Sir I am no orator Sir"—

Yesterday I met with a man who was a few years since a slaveholder. He said Mr. B[irdseye] I understand you employ no slaves, that you are much opposed to slavery. You are correct Sir. I employ no slaves and think slavery a great evil—ruinous to the country, injurious to both master and slave. "You are right Sir. I respect you for your opinions & a few years since I had 22. It has ruined me and injured my family. It fostered habits which have made me completely insolvent. I am now going to apply for the benefit of the Bankrupt law." Instances of this kind are not unfrequent. Bankruptcy is very frequent among slaveholders—with them it is a calamity for slavery has unfitted them for business by which they might hope to recover.

On the first week of this month the circuit-court was held at Newport. I met there William Thompson[3] Esq[uire] a very worthy man from Blount County. I had a conversation with him about the antislavery society there. He said it was prosperous that they had frequent meetings and apprehended no difficulty. The indications of public sentiment were so favorable in this county that I had thought of proposing to my friends to form one and should have done so but for an occurrence on Wednesday morning of the court week. News came in town that a slave owned by John Thomas had killed a man by the name of Benson dangerously wounded Thomas & wife and burnt all his buildings. The excitement was high. A number went out armed to take him. We soon learned that he was taken and near town, soon after that the mob had determined to hang him on the opposite bank of the river. This was suggested to a member of the bar and by him to the court. His Hon[or] Judge Lucky[4] at once ordered the civil authority to arrest anything of the kind and to bring the prisoner to town. He was bro[ugh]t in and placed in jail. The mob appeared anxious to hang him but a little afraid unless they could obtain the countenance of the leading men. One came to see the states att[orne]y Mr Garrett,[5] and inquired if he should notice it if they took him out of the jail and hung him. He replied he would indict everyone aiding or abetting for murder. Another spoke to Judge Peck—and inquired if there would be any harm in taking him out of jail and hanging him. He said none only the court will order the sheriff to hang you—Will he? Yes every one of you. Not satisfied—one of them got a drum and beat up for volunteers—to go and hang him. The grand jury found a bill ag[ain]st him instanter. The She[ri]ff arrested him while beating his drum and bro[ugh]t him into court. He was bound over for trial next term, with this all symptoms of violence ceased. The slave was bro[ugh]t into court on Saturday morning. A member of the Bar rose and stated to the court that he had known him for years that he was a well known maniac he killed a negro in Blount County washed his hands and face in his blood stuck his head on a pole then told another negro to tell his master to call the Doctor. He was then confined in jail three years and discharged as a maniac—sold for a trifle as a maniac, bro[ugh]t into this county and sold to Thomas as a maniac, he knowing all the facts. He has been worse at times than others, but supposed to be dangerous at all times. During this excitement our good citizens manifested a determination to sustain the laws and preserve order. The disorderly have been taught some respect for the laws at the last three terms of the circuit court which has three sessions annually. There were over 100 convictions for gambling a conviction in every case tried but one—about 20 convictions for retailing ardent spirits. The fines for gambling were from 10 to 50 dollars with costs from 40 to 75 dollars each. For retailing spirits, fines from 10 to 30 dollars costs about the same as in gambling cases.

 The Temperance cause is making some progress. In the adjoining county of Greene over 1000 signatures were obtained to the total abstinence pledge in one week during the spring court term. In most of the counties of E[ast] T[ennessee] special efforts in the good cause are about to be made or are in progress. Last month when about to go to Knoxville our late county surveyor a worthy man met with me and requested me to do him a favor. He said his colored man had run away about the Christmas holidays and had since been lying out in the woods—that he had a wife in Jefferson Co[unty] and a mother 15 miles above Knoxville. He wished me to call as he tho[ugh]t it would be on my road and see his mother and if I could the slave and ask her if I could meet with him that if he would return he should have as kind treatment as before; as a further inducement that it was his intention to buy his wife if circumstances should make it possible for him to do so, that he could live with his family. He added you may assure him on your own responsibility that he can rely on my promise and if he has these assurances from you he will I think return. I inquired as to the cause of his leaving. He said he was himself from home that the slave became much intoxicated in the morning. His wife requested him to take care of the cattle. There was some disorder among them which required immediate attention. He gave her a flat contradiction and went immediately off he supposed through fear of punishment. During the few years he had owned him he had never punished him. As this was the first offense he and his wife would both forgive it. They supposed it owing to his intoxication and that I think he said was the first instance of that. Soon after coming into this state I formed an acquaintance with his master. He is a man of an amiable disposition kind to his slaves—I think he owns three strictly regarding his word at all times. I told my friend that knowing his uniform kindness to his slaves—and as there was so much benevolence in his request I would call and see the slave's mother—and communicate the whole to her to the slave if I saw him but that I could form no coercive measures. He did not wish any. Then on my way 10 miles above Knoxville I inquired for Smith the owner of his (the slave's) mother. I was told that he was a slave dealer then gone to the S[outh] West with slaves. I determined to call. As I came to his house I introduced myself to his wife told her the nature of my errand. She called the mother a woman of about 50 years of age to the front of the house. She had the appearance of being an intelligent well bred old lady. I told her I was authorized to assure her son of the pardon of his master and kind treatment if he would return that he had pledged himself to me that he should not be punished but as a further inducement he would endeavor to buy his wife for him. She said she had not seen him for more than two years. If she should see him she would advise him to return. She had no doubt Mr. Fowler[6] would keep his word as he had stated to me. She said she had another son whose name was Jess. He was about to be sold with all his family—that it almost distracted him—he had left about the same time. She supposed they had met and gone together to the *free states*. This conjecture of the old lady is probably the true one. I dismissed the old lady and took a seat in the house. The inquiry if I could learn anything of him. I told the lady that his mother tho[ugh]t he had gone to a free state. She said she supposed so that there would be no use in following them, that her husband had two who had gone to Indiana that he had heard where they were. "Does your husband intend going after them"— "O God bless you no, it would be more than his life is worth to go there after them—" Here was our neighbor Mr McBee who went to P[ennsylvani]a after one and they had to call out a regiment of soldiers to protect his life. The lawyers called him a southern blood hound that had come after his pound of flesh. The jury gave the case against him and he thought himself well off to get away alive. Once when they are there they are safe. My husband will never go there to risque his life after them. One of them went to the river & pretended to be very drunk and took the canoe to cross in the evening. Next morning, he was missing. They found the canoe down stream with his hat and bottle and supposed him to be drowned searched the river for his body. I had heard of McBee['s] tour to P[ennsylvani]a before; there is no doubt that he came away much frightened.

Almost in the same neighborhood 7 or 8 miles in Jefferson Co[unty] there were two men by the name of Hodges—who went to Indiana after a runaway slave. They went to Wayne Co[unty] I think it was—and introduced themselves to a man by the name of Hoover as abolitionists and by that means found the runaway slave and attempted to bring him off. What occurred afterwards we do not know only that they came off without him and are glad that they are alive. The impression is becoming common with the slave catchers that they take their lives in their hands when they go into the free states after slaves.

Sincerely y[ou]rs
E Birdseye

WRITTEN ACROSS PAGE 1:
Some one is attacking me in the Register at Knoxville as the colonizationist in the Mountains. I shall probably be there soon and inquire more about it of the Editor. They will venture no open attack on me but may try to employ some assassin. I shall give myself no trouble about it. I would only say that should you extract anything from this for the press—I would have you be cautious about names and places.

WRITTEN ACROSS PAGE 2:
I shall confer with my friends about a further organization in this county. I think that we may now form a confidential association. The great contest is to be in the North. When they are firm and united we shall act efficiently.

Notes

1. Spencer Henry (1805–1883) was a member of the Blount County Court from 1834, having been elected justice of the peace for the 15th Civil District. He was ordained by the Holston Conference of the Methodist

Episcopal Church in 1840 and served as a Methodist circuit rider until his death in 1883. He was clerk of the Blount County Court in 1853–54 and a delegate to the Union Convention in Knoxville on May 30, 1861, representing Blount County. He remained a staunch Unionist throughout the Civil War. Aurelia Cate Dawson, *Our East Tennessee Kinsmen: Cate, Henry, and Related Families* (Seaford, Del.: Privately printed, 1962), 47–48; *History of Tennessee, Containing Historical and Biographical Sketches*, 833; Thomas William Humes, *The Loyal Mountaineers of Tennessee* (Knoxville: Ogden Brothers and Co., 1888), 348; Oliver P. Temple, *Notable Men of Tennessee, from 1833 to 1875: Their Times and Their Contemporaries* (New York: Cosmopolitan Press, 1912), 53.
2. John F. Stanberry was clerk of the Cocke County Court between 1839 and 1844. *History of Tennessee, Containing Historical and Biographical Sketches*, 867.
3. William Thompson was a Blount County attorney whose daughter, Martha Wallace Thompson, married Dr. Calvin Post, an abolitionist and entrepreneur searching for minerals in Cades Cove before the Civil War. Thompson's other daughter married the only son of Dr. Isaac Anderson of Maryville College. Burns, *History of Blount County*, 209; Durwood Dunn, *Cades Cove: The Life and Death of a Southern Appalachian Community, 1818–1937* (Knoxville: Univ. of Tennessee Press, 1988), 86, 270–71.
4. Judge Seth J. W. Lucky was an antislavery advocate who earlier had freed all his own slaves. Temple, *East Tennessee*, 107, 109.
5. Gray Garrett (1800–1848) was admitted to the bar in Cocke County in 1821 and served as attorney general in 1838–43. He also served in the Tennessee senate in 1827–29, representing Claiborne, Grainger, and Jefferson counties. Gray Garrett also served as a delegate to the constitutional convention of 1834. His father, William Garrett, had served as attorney general of his circuit, too, and as clerk of the Cocke County Circuit Court (1798–1828). *BDTGA*, 1:277–78; O'Dell, *Over the Misty Blue Hills*, 263–64.
6. John F. Fowler, who is listed in an 1839 Cocke County tax list as owning three slaves and who in 1835 had been appointed one of the commissioners to lay off the civil districts of Cocke County, is probably this person, since Birdseye identifies him as a former surveyor. Creekmore, "Early East Tennessee Taxpayers," 124, 132.

18. To Gerrit Smith, May 21, 1842

NEWPORT COCKE COUNTY E[AST] TEN[NESSEE]
MAY 21, 1842

My dear Sir

I returned to this town last evening from a journey as far down the river as Chattanooga. I found the stores closed and our little village having the appearance of the sabath. Our people were at church where a meeting of the different denominations were holding a union meeting accompanied by one of the most remarkable revivals I have ever known in this part of the country.

We have reason to hope that it is real[l]y a work of divine grace. The meeting is to be continued on the sabath tomorrow and may be continued even longer while our town has a large concourse of people from the adjacent county.

There are other towns where more than ordinary attention is paid to religion and in some places special revivals. I am at the house of Rev[erend] Spencer Henry of the Methodist Church. This morning there were some 5 or 6 ministers of this church all assembled after breakfast when he read them the resolutions of the Baptist Church of Vermont on the subject of slavery. This brought opinions from all present but one adverse to slavery. Some of them were ardent and expressed to make it a subject of investigation. One very intelligent young man told me he had Clarkson[1] on slavery but he wanted other works. I suggested to him that Theodore Weld's Bible argument[2] might be of service to him and gave him the address of my friend J C Lewis—Terryville Conn[ecticut] who I ventured to engage would procure it for him.

But the one who thought he could defend slavery from the Bible requested a conversation with me on the subject. In our chamber we took the Bible and after much discussion he said he wished to have his mind satisfied and would be glad to obtain further light. I must do him the justice to say that he treated me courteously even kindly. I told him I hoped we should make honest and earnest endeavours to learn our duty and implore the divine aid in following it. He said he would endeavour to do so. I gave him the address of my friend Lewis a man honest and ardent in the cause and one who will I doubt not attend promptly to his request.

The argument of this man was substantially this[:] that in Africa they were idolaters that God might justly punish them for their idolatry by permitting them to be taken away and sold into slavery. I replied that before we ventured to execute the judgments of an offended God on them we should be certain that we have the warrant for it. That they often gave evidence while here of sincere piety—that then the punishment if even authorized by God himself for idolatry became unwarrantable and should cease—so far from that we saw them sold taken from their families in chains to a distant part of the country to market—that if the professed Christian did it or countenanced it in others—Christ had said in the latter part of the 25 of Matthew that they did it unto him. He said servants were spoken of in the Bible a recognition of the relation master & slave—that was never intended to justify our Am[erican] slavery as it bore no relation to it etc.

I have but faint hopes of this man. Possibly before I leave here I may give him your address. Should he inquire for the truth with an honest heart I hope all the avenues may be opened to him. With the others I shall have further intercourse and may also give them your address. It is now an interesting time in East Ten[nessee]. The Temperance cause has been advancing with renewed vigor. The discussions about slavery are more open. Bankruptcy is sweeping our state—the South like a tornado.

God in his righteous providence may overrule all for the best. There is one view I have often taken on this subject that we see in the temperance cause how soon a correct public sentiment at the North operates on the South. Would the North make slavery a test of membership in the churches[,] it would soon be done in the South. Would they even exhort the South not to contribute the wages of rob[b]ery to the support of the missions a sum much larger than they now obtain would be contributed by those at the South with the more confident hope that the Lord would bless their offering to the spreading of his Gospel.

As I went down by water but little opportunity for intercourse occurred with the citizens. Still I met with a few abolitionists one by the name of Williams some 20 miles above Knoxville. I was at Knoxville 4 days and visited Rev[erend] Mr. Mack. His heart is engaged in the good cause. In reply to my inquiry whether he did not think the South would see it to be their true interest to give up slavery he said they had been so much accustomed to have them and to exercise that kind of despotic authority and be waited *on by them* that he did not think they would. He thought it would terminate but in some way by violence. In this opinion I must differ with him. My intercourse with society for many years has led me to the opinion that a very large proportion of the slaveholders would rejoice if all could be emancipated. More would if their duty could be laid open before them. The few despotic slaveholders— would be too weak and powerless to oppose with effect the united wishes of the liberal slaveholders—and a vast majority of the free men who do not own slaves.

The few individuals whom I had been led to suppose hostile to me for my opinions on this subject treated me with politeness.

I arrived at Chattanooga on Saturday I think the 7th inst[ant]. The town appeared noisy with the drum and fife which I found to be from a company of volunteers for Texas. They were young men generally[;] many of them mere boys—very coarsely clad in hunting shirts most of them made of ticking. They appeared to be intemperate ignorant and whatever good or ill they might cause in Texas they would do our state but little injury by leaving it. Among them I saw one fine looking young man by the name of Brown who I understood to be their commissary. I convened with him some time on the hazardous nature of their enterprize [and] the little prospect of honor still less of reward. He said he could do but little at home. If he worked the compensation was low *not* exceeding $8 per month. I told true but with industry frugality & temperance he would obtain a competency and with that he was sick. He replied that he believed he had been acting in the dark. I was glad to hear that this young [man] succeeded in getting out his baggage about 20 miles below and left them. Some 5 or 6 others left who reported that more would desert. There were said to be 4. They had kept several under guard for fear of desertion.

Chattanooga is pleasantly situated on the S[outh] bank of the Ten[nessee River] and at the termination of the Georgia R[ailroad] from Savannah and Augusta on the Tennessee R[iver]. The graded road is made into the town. It was said that all but about six miles was partially graded most of it in a state of forwardness. The rails was expected to be laid this year so as to bring the coast within about 100 miles—but the state of Georgia is so depressed that but little more can be done soon if the stocks of the state 6 p[e]rc[en]ts 50¢. The town is said to contain about 800 inhabitants is in plain view of the Cumberland M[ountain]. The lookout mountain being about one mile distant which is to be occupied for a summer residence. The town has had the reputation of being unhealthy. The town is on high land with a small pond on the hill back of it which if drained and filled up would probably remove the cause.

It was here that I learned that on the day or two before that the records of McMinn Co[ounty] at Athens had been burnt with all the papers of the office. A lawyer by the name of Montgomery told me that such was the desperation that a few days before a man shot another in a distant county for bidding on his property at sh[eri]ffs sale killing him instantly. My worthy friend Mr Fife of whom I spoke to you as P[ost] M[aster] of Athens had become involved in Bankruptcy—liabilities for other is said to have been the cause. During my stay which was one week I heard frequent discussions on slavery. Some young [men] manifested some of the Georgia blustering. One of the most candid that I met with was a Mr Standifer[3] a member of the Legislature of this state[, reacting] to an article in the N[ew] Y[ork] Am[erican] on constitutional law much in accordance with the resolutions of Mr Giddings.[4] He read it attentively. He said the idea was new to him but he must say that he was unable to answer the argument. Near the R[iver] I saw an old negro said to be near 100 blind but active for his age. Old William as he is called—I was told by one of the citizens[—]was taken down the river some time ago and taken out into a very desolate place and left supposed to be for the purpose of relieving his owner of the further charge of him but he wandered about untill he found inhabitants who befriended him and had him sent home. My informant told me he saw him tended and told [him] that he was in Chattanooga. He exclaimed Bless God is dis Chattanooga. It attracted attention. The crowd gathered round him and learning his story became so much excited that they gave him many presents and expressed much sorrow for his sufferings. His extreme sufferings appear still to recommend him to their favorable consideration—he is fed wherever he goes the boat men give [him] food whenever he appears on the bank of the river. "Bless God I tank you masser." After my short stay in this town I left some interesting acquaintances and came up the river on board the S[team] B[oat] Harkaway. This is now the only S[team] B[oat] running in E[ast] Ten[nessee] and such has been the decline of business that she makes only an occasional trip from Knoxville to Decatur Ala[bama]. I found boat neat well manned with polite attentive persons with scientific good engineer. It was also a temperance S[team] B[oat] on the total abstinance plan. There were two Bibles in the Cabin & other useful books. Among the few passingers I found a Mr John Cooke[5] ardent in the cause of the slave. He said he would cheerfully give one half of all he was worth if slavery could be abolished. He is making efforts to sell his place in view [of] removing to Iowa territory. By some means he had got hold of Gurneys letters of Henry Clay on the W[est] India emancipation. He inquired if this publication was continued and how he could obtain it. I could [not] tell whether that paper was yet published. He is anxious to procure antislavery publications. Their minister Rev[erend] Anderson Trim[6] had preached much on the subject untill it was made a penitentiary offense. He said Mr Trim often declared his intention of preaching again for the slave and if taken into the Penitentiary to preach all the way untill he got there. This man requests you to send them antislavery papers and documents. He says they [k]no[w] where to use them. He will engage that [they] shall be circulated where they will do great good. I gave him your address promised to request you to send him publications. The address of both is Sulphur Spring Rhea County E[ast] Tennessee. Since writing the above Rev[erend] William H. Rogers[7] whose P[ost] O[ffice] is now at Dandridge E[ast] Ten[nessee] most respectfully requests you to send him papers and documents. If you could add Weld's Bible argument you could not put it in better hands. He is a learned young man ardent in the cause. He says his father Rev[erend] Doswell Rogers Delphi Marion County E[ast] Tennessee is enlisted in the same grand cause and hopes you will remember him.

The way is opening to the good people of the South. I hope the northern philanthropists will send a few ni[c]kles. The laborers are here and the harvests are growing white. While passing up the River in the lower part of Blount County a reputable farmer by the name of Bustle came on board of the S[team] B[oat]. He inquired of me what would probably be done with the negro—in jail here—as he was from that neighborhood. I told him it depended on the opinion of the court as to his being insane. He did not believe him crazy but said his mind was not right and had not been since his sister was hung. His sister was sold to slave dealer run away and come back was punished later on and ran away again. She was missing and found hung from that time he was crazed.

Sincerely y[our] friend
E Birdseye

WRITTEN ACROSS PAGE 1:

Upton the slave dealer of whom the venerable Samuel Johnston spoke to me is missing. He was known to be on the way home from the S[outh] W[est] in Ala[bama] with money. His friends suppose him murdered. This is noticed in the papers.

Notes

1. Thomas Clarkson (1760–1846) was a famous British abolitionist and writer, who, along with other British abolitionists, finally succeeded in persuading Parliament to abolish slavery throughout the British Empire in 1833. His writings were widely used by American abolitionists. *DAB*, 4:454–57.
2. Theodore Dwight Weld (1803–1895) was a famous American abolitionist whose *The Bible Against Slavery* (1837) abolitionists used widely as propaganda. *DAB*, 19:625–27.

3. William I. Standifer (1801–?), a Whig, represented Hamilton County in the 23rd General Assembly, and Hamilton and Marion counties in the 24th (1839–43). *BDTGA*, 1:692–93.
4. Joshua R. Giddings (1795–1864), an Ohio representative in the U.S. House, took a radical position in the 1842 *Creole* case, largely based on arguments presented by James G. Birney in the *New York American*. Basically, he said slavery could not exist outside the limits of a slave state; therefore Congress, as the agent of all the states, could not enforce returning slaves who had mutinied to secure their freedom, nor could Congress protect the coastal slave trade. This argument led to his being formally censured by his colleagues in the House of Representatives. He resigned and promptly was overwhelmingly voted back into office by his constituents. Dumond, *Antislavery*, 368; *DAB*, 7:260–61.
5. John Cook was a Rhea County trustee (1842–44). *History of Tennessee, Containing Historical and Biographical Sketches*, 819. I also found John Cook's name or signature on an 1837 petition to the state legislature from Rhea County protesting the "too bloody" and tyrannical law passed by the Tennessee General Assembly on Feb. 13, 1836, curtailing the right to free speech by making circulation of antislavery materials a criminal offense. Petitions, 1837.
6. Anderson Trim is listed in the 1860 census of Rhea County, Tenn., as being 63 years old. Bettye J. Broyles, *Rhea County, Tennessee, Census, Marriage, and Tax Records, 1850–1900* (Rhea County, Tenn.: Privately printed, 1982), 521.
7. William H. Rogers, son of Rev. Daswell Rogers, was born in Sequatchee Valley, 20 miles east of Jasper, Tenn. Both he and his father were Methodist preachers. The chief historian of Methodism during this period, R. N. Price, does not speak highly of him: "He was brainy but eccentric. His principal faults were vanity and affectation. He had an affected style of delivery—a mock solemnity that greatly impaired the usefulness of his sermons, exhortations, and conversations. But he was well read, and his mind was stored with general information. He was robust in body, above the average in size and strength, though not corpulent. He had a strong voice, a ready utterance, some imagination, and sometimes preached a sermon of real eloquence. He was not wanting in wit and sarcasm." Richard N. Price, *Holston Methodism*, 4:350.

19. To Gerrit Smith, June 18, 1842

> Greeneville E[ast] Ten[nessee]
> June 18th 1842

Dear Sir

When I wrote you last at Newport there was a very considerable revival of religion there. Tho[ugh] attended with some excitement peculiar to the southern population, there was apparently much sincerity and sincere devotion. This awakening continues so that in the county something over 150 have been added to the churches. All this for a time appeared well. Among those who had joined the church was Mr R W Pulliam merchant of Newport. I had a conversation with him in which he expressed his firm belief that it was a real work—the outpourings of the Holy Spirit.

In a letter of last year you may recollect that I mentioned this same man as one who sold his colored woman to a man from North Carolina followed him and reclaimed her.

In dealing in slaves he appeared to have no remorse of conscience. In punishing he was said to be cruel. I hoped as he had now become a member of the church he would most sincerely and heartily repent of these enormous sins.

On Thursday last in the afternoon I was in Newport. Mrs. Henry the lady of the Methodist clergyman in town (her husband was absent) told me that in the morning he (Pulliam) had tied up a colored woman the property of his father in law Maj[or] Roadman stripped her to the waist and whipped her with a heavy cow skin they supposed about 200 stripes. She said her back was cut to pieces. The blood ran freely down her person and was on him. Her screams were heard all over the village. Her only crime was for having made some severe remarks because of the whipping of her husband a few days before by the same man[,] who was cut equally bad[,] in the upper part of his ware house. It was supposed he inflicted more than 200 stripes on him. Mr Roadman the father in law of Pulliam and owner of the slaves did not interfere to prevent it. Yet he too has been a long time a leading member of the Methodist church. There was a large meeting a few miles out so that there were probably but few men in the village at the time. Why they did not interfere I do not know. The matter occasioned excitement and will come before the Church. Either he must be expelled from it or many will withdraw. This good lady whose piety seems to be beyond doubt laments these deplorable evils by which the church is distracted. Such instances of cruelty occur in the church too often. Sometimes the member is expelled. At others he is able to silence all interference, the matter is hushed up. Those who are wounded withdraw. In this way the southern church is distracted. The more enlightened who mourn over these evils say there is no hope for them to maintain the peace and purity of the church but to separate it from slavery entirely, unless this should be done the prospects of the Southern church is deplorable indeed.[1]

In a late letter I mentioned the case of a runaway slave belonging to a Mr Fowler. A few days since I met with Mr Fowler and inquired if his slave had returned. He said no that he was still lying out that he had sent word to him both to his wife and mother since he had sent by me to his mother that if he would return he should not be punished in the least that he thought him extremely unreasonable that when he had sent him word so often that he would still refuse to return that he took him from a hard place that he had never struck him has always endeavoured to treat him kindly—that he was now ungrateful for it all and he had no doubt suffered more than he would at work.

Of all the slaveholders I have known this man was one of the most kind—I may say conscientious humane and mild—he thought they would be unwilling to leave him. The slave too was a man of good sense. He reasoned no doubt differently. He was living with a man of frail constitution liable to be taken away at any time. He would then be sold. No part of his earnings would accrue to him. That by going off he might have his own earnings and possibly be able ultimately to buy his wife and children and then live fearless of being sold as chattels.

It was about the third week in Nov[ember] when three men came from N[ew] Y[ork] to my lands. The night before the[y] reached me they lodged with my friend Fowler. They were in the evening husking out a large pile of corn. They proffered their assistance. The negro sat on one side of one of those men a young man of the country on the other who inquired minutely about their journey. They had come on by way of the Ohio to Maysville K[entuck]y. He inquired about the freedom of colored persons in the states from which he came their rights there and in Canada—to all of which the negro gave the best attention and a few days after was off. The affected intoxication the insolent language to his mistress was probably all affected to give an impression that he left on that account and would soon return. I have no doubt he went direct to the free states tho[ugh] from the peculiar circumstances have not tho[ugh]t proper to suggest it.

With the deplorable influences of slavery we have some cause for rejoicing. The great reformation now in progress in the South. The temperance cause is doing wonders in this county. More have signed the pledge of total abstinance than there are legal voters in Cocke. The reformation is in progress. I should think that 9/10ths of the whole population of the county would sign the pledge. I believe we have no distiller there in prison and at this time I know of no distiller. Some of our good people think that this is one of the great reformations expected at the approach of the Millenium.[2] I hope great good may result from it. Years since this great work began at the North by and bye it came South. We have indications that our antislavery reformation is coming too.

During the last fall and winter 84 are said to have been liberated to go to Africa from E[ast] Tenn[essee]. There are more who are promised their freedom to go another year. For years my impressions have been against the colonization society. Perhaps their movements may be overruled for good. By giving their slaves their freedom a change is manifested in the public sentiment. There was in this county an old gentleman by the name of Gass[3] who gave his slaves their freedom at his death about thirty. His will was contested on the ground of his being in an unsound state of mind at the time he made it. The trial occupied this court a whole term. The jury decided on sustaining the will, but slaves to be sent to a free state with some property. I will try to procure you a printed copy of his will and send you for in a case somewhat doubtful the jury leaned to the claims of justice. On my way up from Chattanooga I rhode in company a few miles with John Martin a son of a Mr Martin that died some 3 or 4 years since at Dandridge. His Father gave his slaves their freedom if they would go to Africa. As they were about to depart—one of them was charged with setting fire to a stable in Dandridge. It was an out stable and worth but little [and] the fire was soon extinguished. But the man was committed to prison. John Martin now of Chattanooga supposed it to be a malicious prosecution that the testimony was circumstantial and procured by a man by the name of Roper of no immaculate fame. Yet he feared that with the influence of this man they would convict him. He tried the influence of his purse to procure terms from the prosecutors. He paid them $180 principally to Roper and got him off. A little before I met with him he had fitted him out for Liberia. He went near Dandridge to take leave of his friends and when going quietly thro[ugh] the town was arrested by a young man and thrown into jail. This soon reached Martin who was on his way up 140 miles to procure his liberation. He heard before he got there that he was liberated on his way up the state for the Potomac. He told me that his Father charged him when on his death bed to see that his will in respect to his slaves was carried into effect and expressed the deepest sorrow that he had ever owned a slave. Probably this excellent young man will never own a slave.

At a leisure moment I drop you an occasional line in giving you some hasty sketches of the lights and shades of slavery. I may not always select such incidents as would be the best but I have endeavoured to be accurate and impartial. If any good comes from it I shall be glad. If you select anything from this hasty letter for the press be careful about names and places and omit to send me the paper for fear that it might fall into the wrong hands.

Accept my best wishes
my Dear Sir
E. Birdseye

NOTES

1. The Methodist Church did indeed split in 1844 over the issue of slavery. For the best discussion of this division, see Donald G. Mathews, *Slavery and Methodism: A Chapter in American Morality, 1780–1845* (Princeton, N.J.: Princeton Univ. Press, 1965), 62–290.
2. For the interrelationships among abolitionism, millennialism, and the temperance crusade during the 19th century, see Alice Felt Tyler, *Freedom's Ferment: Phases of American Social History from the Colonial Period to the Outbreak of the Civil War* (Minneapolis: Univ. of Minnesota Press, 1944), 68–85, 308–50, 463–547.
3. John Gass died on Mar. 1, 1837, and provided in his will that at the death or marriage of his widow, his slaves should be set free, and the sum of $100 given to each family, to enable them to remove to a free state. Gass's children appealed the will, and a jury found in favor of it, as Birdseye correctly reported. The heirs then appealed this verdict to the Tennessee Supreme Court, which overruled the original trial decision on the basis that one of the witnesses testifying to John Gass's sanity at the time he made a codicil to his will, David Gass, was an interested party, since he was a legatee under the will. *Gass' Heirs v. Gass' Executors*, 22 Tenn. 266–75 (1842).

20. To Gerrit Smith, July 2, 1842

NEWPORT E[AST] TENNESSEE
JULY 2, 1842

My Dear Sir

I rec[eive]d of late the Abolitionist[1] of Cazenovia June 7th, your letter addressed to public support of Missions and the address to slaves and its vindication. I have taken another copy from the P[ost] O[ffice] for Judge Peck which I may have the opportunity of handing to him next week. Everything of this kind is important. In the sentiments expressed in both pamphlets I fully concur. I am much gratified to see so fine a paper from Cazenovia. It says much for the public spirit of the good people there and would seem very shiny proof that the cause of the oppressed was flourishing.

A few weeks since I met with Mr. Caldwell just returned from Florida where he had spent several months. On the whole his report is gratifying. He says there is growing dissatisfaction with slavery all the way. In Tallahassee the pressure was so great that he thought the master was the greatest sufferer. This pecuniary suffering continues general through the South. The jail was there filled with slaves and the court house too, taken to be sold under execution. During the day they were out under guard at night locked up. The master was not permitted to speak to his slave unless in the presence of an officer. Mr. Caldwell said he found them more disposed to converse on the subject of emancipation. He said one large slave holder told him he might apprise his Northern friends that they need have no anxiety about abolition it would soon come there itself. He was endeavoring to procure payment from the Union Bank of Florida for deposits he had there a long time due but I believe with little success. There was a man from K[entuck]y who had sold horses mules etc there and taken part notes on N[ew] York which with his deposits amounted to $20,000. He was with him at the Bank when he applied for payment. They told him they could not pay him unless he would take it in slaves. He replied that he was conscientiously opposed to dealing in slaves. They requested him to call again at the Bank in the morning which he did in company with Mr Caldwell. In the meantime the presiding elder of the Methodist Church had called on him on behalf of the Bank and endeavored to persuade him to take the slaves. He told him that he probably might sell them in K[entuck]y so as to save himself from loss, that the slaves would be in a better condition in K[entuck]y than they would be in Florida. The Gent[leman] from K[entuck]y belonged to the Methodist Church. Mr C[aldwell] accompanied him to the bank in the morning. The directors were in attendance. The cashier stated to the gent[leman] that they could make him payment in no other way unless he took the slaves. He rose and replied that he had considered their proposition that while he had a consciousness of his duty to his fellow men and a proper sense of his accountability to his God He could not deal in slaves. It was true that at home he had slaves—whom he had bro[ugh]t up that he had instructed them and sent them to the Sabath school that he had always assured them he would never sell them. If the debt due him from the Bank was lost it was not improbable the sh[eri]ff might sell them but his farm and other property might pay his debts and all that should be first sold. He left them without pay[men]t.

On Monday last I returned from a journey in S[outh] Carolina. My route led me by the Warm Springs[,] Asheville. Soon after leaving we began to ascend the mountain. There was some good land in a tolerable state of cultivation on the road. We crossed the mountain and began our descent over a very rough rocky road about noon. There were small patches of cultivated land mostly in corn generally on the hill sides and much impoverished by washing. On our right as we were near the base of the M[ountain] we saw a stupenouous rock with a large creek falling about 300 feet nearby perpendicular. The country wore a melancholly aspect a large proportion of the cultivated land was worn out more washed in deep gullies the soil appeared to be a red loam with white sand. The rocks were primary—granite quartz—talcose, slate, etc. At evening we arrived at the village of Rutherfordton, the C[ourt] H[ouse] Village of the county of Rutherford. The village appeared to contain some 8[00] or 900 inhabitants and has some appearance of being slightly improving or "holding its own." There is considerable gold found in the county by some said to average $1000 per week coined there by a German into Bulion pieces worth 5 dollars. We next passed on in Spartanburgh Dist[rict] near the old Cow Pens Battle ground to the Cowpens Furnace. This is one of the Furnaces owned by a large company some of them Northern men. They are supplied with bacon, horses hogs mules etc. from E[ast] Ten[nessee]—and then send us iron and nails to pay for it, while iron could be made for about one half of the expense in E[ast] Ten[nessee]. The company owns a large number of slaves and employs many white persons. Different opinions were expressed as to their proffits and prosperity. Early in the morning we rhode a few miles to the Lime stone springs where we stopped to spend the sabath. This is a large establishment erected a few years since when slaveholders had more disposable means than at present. It cost $110,000—and was sold to the Bank of the state to pay a debt of $23,000. Last year it rented to a company for 1500 dollars. They claimed to have lost $1300. This year the Bank rents it at $500. When we arrived there were three boarders—which equalled the number of partners in the firm. We had found no public house the night before. Our host was leaving home in the morning. I had travelled through our route from Rutherford 22 years before. Then there was much cotton cultivated[,] now but very little. The old presses had fallen to decay—the land then in cultivation barren old fields now. Our principal Landlord Mr. Gurnay who also holds the office of

P[ost] M[aster] is a gentleman of intelligence—assured me that he would not take a plantation and the slaves as a gift to cultivate cotton even lower down where the soil and climate are more favorable.

On Monday I rhode to Union C[ourt] H[ouse] the shire town in Union District. I was first in this village in 1818. There was then about 30 dwelling houses. I should suppose there was now probably 50 or 60 some of them built in good style. The court house and jail were built by a man from Conn[ecticut] of hammered granite said to be the first instance when that was used as a building material in the western part of the state. In about 1822 this village had 13 places for retailing spiritous liquors. Now the number is reduced to three or 4. I saw but little drinking while the Temperance cause is doing much in all parts of the state. There was an old man by the name of Davis now tottering over the grave who had his servant boy tried and hanged for raising the back door latch of a grog shop and taking a piece of gingerbread. The boy had but one arm. The same court that tried him (2 magistrates and 5 freeholders) appraised his value and drew an order on the state treasury for payment. The motive was to get a higher price of the state than he would otherwise bring.

I had an interview with Mr Colton of the firm of Brooks & Wlton. Mr C[olton] was from Springfield Mass[achusetts]. He said slavery had ruined the country. He was confident in the opinion that the measures now in progress would abolish it in ten years. He deemed it unsafe to say much on the subject there. There were individuals well known to be opposed to slavery, but no active measures were taken by any of them that he was aware of. I called on A. W. Thompson[2] Esq[uire] att[orne]y at law with whom I had left business. We had been acquainted from my first arrival in the place in 1818. He had the two first numbers of the Southern quarterly review[3] published at Charleston with the avowed intention of sustaining their "peculiar institutions." I took a hasty glance on an article in the 2 No. on the culture of cotton in India. It was apparent that the writer was much alarmed at this competition but I thought that the language was more respectful of the abolitionists than most of their writings have been. This work will be noticed by the abolitionists of the North. Several southern periodicals have been before commenced for the same purpose and soon died of natural weakness. Mr T[hompson] inquired if I owned slaves. I told him by no means I was opposed to slavery both from principle and interest & that its injurious effects on their state in the most striking form ruined plantations idleness and misery among the white inhabitants. He thought it cheaper than free labor. We made a calculation

average cost 5400 int[erest] 10 per[cent]	$50
clothing—$15—insurance on life 25	40
Physicians bill and taxes	_5_
	95

These were his estimates—the clothing too low no man can there give them a p[ai]r of shoes hat a warm suit and shirts twice a year for 15—With a blanket. Yet this man said he clothed his for that, but even at that a white man could be hired for less in E[ast] Ten[nessee]. In Union village I saw none at work. I inquired if they were raising as much cotton as usual. They generally said yes but I noticed that they were clearing the more undulating lands. Frequently the fields were washed barren and abandoned to[o] while the old trees were standing. Mr T[hompson] was digging some gold by slave labor. Others dig a little in the District generally it is reported unprofitable.

Tuesday evening 12 inst[ant] I stopped with Col[onel] Robert Martin 13 miles from Union near the cross Keys. I was acquainted with this gentleman some 20 years before. At the cross his Father in law lived and packed about 1000 bags annually. Little cotton is now produced on the plantation. A brother of Mr M[artin] has fallen in a personal contest in 1835.

At Laurens I found the village to have slightly improved in the dwellings a few good dwelling houses but like Union the business has fallen off. I called on J H Irby[4] Esq[uire] also an att[orne]y. I boarded with his Father in 1818. We were near in age and intimate. He has now over 100 slaves and a plantation about 4 miles square. He told me that he sold his crop of cotton last year for $7000. This year he has over 500 a[cres] in cotton. I spent a part of the day at his house. We conversed freely about slavery. He said that of late years a great improvement has taken place in their treatment. They were better fed better clad and cruel treatment not countenanced by public sentiment. This was a place of much cruelty when I was there in by gone years. This man censured cruelty tho[ugh] he dealt in slaves then as now. He once when I was there threatened his brother in law who had whipped a woman so as to endanger her life. Even in S[outh] Ca[rolina] the abolitionists have made them ashamed of their cruelty. Pecuniary pressure is crushing this state everywhere. The cotton growers are in debt and have no way to get out.

WRITTEN ACROSS PAGE 1:
Irby remarked that the slaves were better fed than the poor whites for the slave owners now bought bacon at 4¢ and would feed the slaves well for his own interest. Whites the poor whites had to labor as they could find employment

at low wages and buy bacon at 12¢ at retail. There is much truth in this. The poor slaves fares hard enough but the poor white is more depressed in S[outh] C[arolina] than in any part of the world where I have travelled. They say much in their publications about the poor laborers of England. They suffer but their distress is public and generally meets with attention. In S[outh] C[arolina] they live retired[,] their distress unknown and uncared for. I left Laurens for Greenville where I arrived the next day. This is one of the most pleasant villages in the state and a summer retreat for the planters and aristocracy of the low country. It has now the appearance of decline; the spacious hotels that used to be filled with the careless spendthrift[s] of the low country are now empty. The cotton planter has no funds to gratify his taste for extravagance and show. After staying a few hours in Greenville I rhode 10 miles to the house of a Mr Lynch a neat well kept house. The good people were from Charleston inteligent industrious and agreeable. Mr Lynch remarked that many plantations in the district had been mortgaged for loans, that no instance had come to his knowledge where one had been redeemed. From thence I came to the Flat Rock the mountain ridge between the east and west. Here is a small village where a few of the aristocracy of Charleston have houses for a summer residence. It is favored to[o] by the engineers of the R[ail] R[oad] Co[mpany], 2000 feet above tide water on Brit Mountain Gap near the village and nearly as high. The air is cool; next morning the thermometer stood at 54. They have some good meadows cultivate oats potatoes buckwheat and some corn. For 12 miles the land of the county is nearly level, the land of but mid[d]ling quality or a little below, yet not worn out. There was a gent[leman] from Connecticut who lives in Augusta Mr Waterman a director in the bank of Augusta. In remarking on the condition of the Southern planters he said when one got into the Bank he seldom ever got out. There is an expensive hotel here built to accommodate the low country people doing little. Asheville was 25 miles. I stopped for two hours. This town has given up on "low country custom" as it is termed the large hotels empty. Near here are several large buildings at springs where much capital has been invested— as also at the Warm Springs now useless. This falling off of such custom will bankrupt many. At Greenville I met with a man from England. I asked a woolgrower who had been induced to come to S[outh] C[arolina] for a grazing farm. He said he should [have] expected to have found a better state of agriculture among the Indians. He had hired a waggon to take him to the state of Ohio. I endeavored to get him to examine our lands in E[ast] Ten[nessee]. He said he had no doubt they were fertile but he wished to get his children out of the slave states as quickly as possible. I found that Woodfin had sold the slave he bought of Franklin for 550 dollars to a man in this county 250 less than he held him at last year. Next year he will probably be as much lower. He had to give me notice in case he offered him for sale. I suppose pressure to have been the cause.

With this I sent you some papers.

Sincerely Your friend
E Birdseye

Notes

1. The *Madison County Abolitionist* of Cazenovia, N.Y., was started in September 1841 and continued until 1842. Published by Luther Myrick and edited by James Caleb Jackson (1811–1895), an abolitionist and physician, it received considerable financial backing from Gerrit Smith. Selling this newspaper in 1842, Jackson moved to Utica, N.Y., where he edited the *Liberty Press* for two years. He then went to Albany and purchased the *Albany Patriot,* which he edited until 1846, when poor health forced him to sell the paper to William L. Chaplin. *DAB,* 9:547; Henderson, "History of the New York Anti-Slavery Society," 336–37.
2. Andrew Wallace Thomson (1789–1868), wealthy lawyer and gold-mine owner, also possessed a large mill. He represented the Union District in ten South Carolina General Assemblies between 1824 and 1863. In 1860 he owned 186 slaves. Alexander Moore, *Biographical Directory of the South Carolina House of Representatives* (Columbia, S.C.: South Carolina Department of Archives and History, 1992), 5:268–69.
3. The *Southern Quarterly Review,* founded in January 1832, was Charleston's second attempt to publish a dignified, scholarly quarterly review. A void had been left by the demise of the city's distinguished *Southern Review,* edited from 1828 to 1832 by Stephen Elliott, Sr.; Stephen Elliott, Jr.; and Hugh Legaré. Edited by transplanted northerner Daniel K. Whitaker, the *Southern Quarterly Review,* from beginning to end, espoused the cause of slavery and free trade. Later, between 1849 and 1855, it was edited by the famous South Carolina author, William Gilmore Simms. Sam G. Riley, *Magazines of the American South* (Westport, Conn.: Greenwood, 1986), 258–62.
4. James Henderson Irby (1793–1860), son of wealthy South Carolina planter William Irby, graduated from South Carolina College in 1816, studied law, and was admitted to the bar in 1817. He represented Laurens District in the South Carolina house of representatives in

1826–51. He served as lieutenant governor of South Carolina between 1852 and 1854. Accumulating a large estate, at the time of his death in 1860 his property was worth nearly half a million dollars. An advocate of internal improvements, he was president of the Laurens Railroad Company between 1853 and 1855. As a delegate to the 1851 South Carolina convention to consider secession, he was a strong Unionist. N. Louise Bailey, Mary L. Morgan, and Carolyn R. Taylor, comps., *Biographical Directory of the South Carolina Senate, 1776–1985* (Columbia, S.C.: Univ. of South Carolina Press, 1986), 2:792–93; *Cyclopedia of Eminent and Representative Men of the Carolinas of the Nineteenth Century* (Madison, Wis.: Brant and Fuller, 1892), 1:219–20.

21. To Gerrit Smith, September 1, 1842

Newport East Ten[nessee]
Sept[ember] 1, 1842

My dear Sir

I am yet in this county. Occasionally I find a leisure hour when I can write you. Should I be able to communicate anything interesting or anything that will encourage you in the good cause I shall be more than paid. There are some indications of a favorable change in public sentiment on the subject of slavery. Slaveholders inquire more and appear more willing to examine the subject. Continued calamities appear to have softened the hearts of many.

One of the late pleasing indications of a change was some ten days since. A paper was handed me by Rev[erend] Spencer Henry of this place given him by our postmaster W[illia]m C. Roadman for circulation. It was the 2nd number of the Bondmans Advocate published at Great Falls by John Wood, New Hampshire a small sheet but a very able one well calculated to make an impression on the mind of any man where feelings of humanity are to be found. I returned it after giving it a circulation in our neighborhood. It will go into other hands and this little sheet may do more for the poor slave in this country than Mr Wood had a distant hope of. I have loaned out my papers and pamphlets on the subject even the little address to the slaves I have loaned out where it circulates and will I hope do good.

It has been an object with us to try if possible to effect a separation of E[ast]

Ten[nessee] from the other part of the state. Our prosperity would be much promoted by it we think in all respects. We could then put an end to slavery in a little time in E[ast] T[ennessee].

The most intelligent men that I have found in the state are clearly of the opinion that we can effect it so far as Tennessee is concerned. There are county meetings held on the subject in a number of counties. On Monday next there is one to be held in this county for the purpose of taking the subject into consideration. Resolutions will doubtless pass in favor of the measure.

Some months since a Mr Fowler of this county requested me to call at the house where the mother of his slave Chamberlain lived on my return from Knoxville for the purpose of assuring her that if her son would return he should receive kind treatment. I had doubts as to the propriety of even lending my aid in so remote a degree to the recovery of a slave but on reflection a moment I thought it could do him no injury. I though[t] Chamberlain safe in her Majesties dominions. If I was mistaken in this and Chamberlain be still lying out in the woods suffering with cold and hunger as Mr F[owler] anticipated anxious to return but afraid to do so the pledge through me to his mother would insure him the kind treatment. From an intimate acquaintance with his master I could hardly suppose that a pledge of this kind to me would in any case be violated.

This is the same slave that I spoke of in a former letter. Months have passed on but no word from him. Some two weeks since I happened to be at the home of Mr F[owler] when he requested me to have a conversation with his other slave Simon. He said both his slaves had much friendship for me and would rely on a pledge from me that he supposed Chamberlain to be in the woods that the two had intercourse that he believed that Chamberlain would come in if he had a pledge from me that he should not be sold and should be treated kindly. I was a little surprised at this singular and unexpected request, I had supposed that the pledge from himself direct would be all that would be required in case he should want any assurances of kind treatment and should not be sold from his family. From my first entrance into this state I had been acquainted with Mr F[owler]. I had never heard him speak harshly to his slaves. He appeared to feed them well clothe them comfortably and not overwork them. Chamberlain had been owned by a man by the name of Davis[,] an intemperate man who used to be harsh to him when drinking. About 4 years since Davis shot his wife with his rifle in a spell of drunkenness and is yet in prison sentenced for life. A year since C[hamberlain] went with me to Jefferson County on business for his master. Passing an old stillhouse near the road he told me that in that house he was required to attend the still night and day, that the whiskey he made there was the cause of the death of his mistress and the cause of the death of several other persons. He reasoned well was a man of good natural talents and from one half to three fourths white. Simon the other slave is quite black but a man of superior talents. Could he have been educated he would have made one of the first men of the country. Slavery has never broken his manly spirit. Some years since he was sold to a slave dealer but eloped and lay out in the woods. He declared he would die before he would go with him. Mr F[owler] told me that he viewed it as a case of great hardship and found the claimant or his agent and bought him, he told other slaves to tell him he had bought him and where he could meet him. Simon came with a large club and asked him if it was true that he had bought him. Otherwise he was not to be taken. He required the bill of sale to be produced and read before he would surrender. Since that time Mr F[owler] says he has been a faithful efficient hand. No difficulty has occurred with either that I heard of. I had often thought that if slavery could be tolerable anywhere it was here with Mr F[owler].

I told Mr F[owler] I was willing to converse with Simon on the subject if he was willing that I should invite him to my house on a pledge of protection and assurance that he might depart in safety that I should give him food and rainment. He said he was not only willing but wished me to do so that my word should protect him from capture from any other persons.

One of the most difficult things in the slave states is a confidential conversation with a slave. The master is jealous if anything happens it is easy to raise a popular tumult against the individual who attempts it. Should the slave report the conversation and it should happen to be of an "incendiary" character he would be in danger of his life in most of the South. I find that most of the slaves have a tolerably correct idea of the free states. This they get by hearing conversation between citizens and communicate with each other. I found Simon and had half an hours conversation with him. He readily expressed his confidence in my friendship. He said it was understood by the colored people that I was opposed to slavery. I inquired if he had seen Chamberlain since he left home. He said no he had no positive information of him. I told him that his master had authorized me to invite him to my house to furnish him food and clothing and allow him to depart again in peace—that if he should meet him he might assure him that he could come safely to my house and depart that I would not permit any person to lay violent hands on him. If it was his wish to return I would procure a pledge for his kind treatment and that he should not be sold. I asked him if Mr F[owler] should send me his word to that if he thought there would be danger of his disregarding it. He said no—

if master promises you that[,] he is not going to break his word. But when a promise is made to a black man he never knows when to rely on it, sometimes they will promise to keep them and not sell them and perhaps keep them for a few months and then in the night the first the poor slave knows he is handcuffed and taken right off from his wife and children never to see them again. We poor slaves are always in dread of this. The white men have no idea how much we suffer. When we see our wives and children we never know but it is the last time. Before we see them again we may be harnessed up and taken off to New Orleans or Mississippi. If the white people would let us be free and live in peace it would be better for them. They would get along better in this world and have less to answer for in the next.

I told him that I had understood that he was once sold to a slave dealer and lay out for some time to avoid going off. He said he did and several times came nigh being taken. Did you not suffer much while lying out? "I did some Sir— but it was not much compared to being taken off." Did Chamberlain think he was about to be sold? "I think so Sir or he would not have gone off and left his family. The poor slave has a hard life do you think there will be a change?" "We do, we think we have friends." I told him substantially what had been done and what was doing for the slaves in our country. I thought the time coming when all would be free. Some how they find out much that is doing for them. Mr F[owler] thinks some persons who wished to do him an injury induced Chamberlain to believe he was about to be sold to Franklin. His circumstances are easy. I have no doubt the report of such reached his slave was false. His object is now to try to reassure him that he shall stay with him and meet with kind treatment. The poor slave is probably beyond the reach of his kindness. He has been gone over 8 m[onths] and might have been taken for a white man even in a slave state.

I think the time soon coming when men will engage openly in the cause here risking all that the slaveholder can do should even lead them to the stakes. I should not be surprised if Henry leads the cause.

I meet with abolitionists here frequently, Dr Hunt[1] of Newport an ardent one, had a conversation a few since with Maj[or] Roadman. Mr R[oadman] said he would freely liberate his slaves and wished them all free. The feelings of this man have changed—a year since he expressed surprise that so much freedom of debate on this subject was permitted in congress.

Franklin is now gone to Illinois after a runaway slave. He was taken up there and imprisoned and a letter of message sent. There is much to do in the Northern states to change the public sentiment so that acts like this will not be permitted. In my attempts at leisure moments to give you the lights & shades of slavery I fear I may be tiresome in my attempts. If any good is done I shall rejoice.

Sincerely y[ou]rs
Ezekiel Birdseye

Note

1. Dr. William Hunt, one of Cocke County's earliest physicians, was born in Washington County, near Johnson City, in 1810. He graduated from Transylvania University, Lexington, Ky., in 1839 and subsequently began to practice medicine in Cocke County, until he removed to Bradley County in 1854. In 1862 he was arrested by the Confederate authorities, and, without trial, sent to prison in Tuscaloosa, Ala., where he died from prison life. He was a peaceable, amiable man, according to contemporaries, and was guilty of no offense other than being an outspoken Union man. Dr. Hunt was the brother-in-law of William G. Brownlow. O'Dell, *Over the Misty Blue Hills,* 270; Temple, *East Tennessee,* 406, 409, 419.

22. To Gerrit Smith, September 24, 1842

NEWPORT COCKE COUNTY E[AST] TEN[NESSEE]
SEPTEMBER 24, 1842

Dear Sir

Some time since I wrote you that I should be glad to contribute something in aid of the Abolition Society. I am now situated much as I was then with regard to money. I intimated a willingness to contribute a mite in another way. I am ready and willing to do so. I will give one thousand acres of land. If that that is well supplied with timber water power and iron ore of good quality is preferred I will give that. If such as is well adapted to grazing farms is preferred I will give that. Could you use it to advance the good cause do not fail to let me know it. I will make the conveyance at anytime when it may suit you to receive it.

I have land in the state[s] of Ohio New York and Connecticut. If I could borrow on real estate in either of those states I would make a contribution in money but I should want to borrow so as to meet some other liabilities. Should you know where a loan could be had by giving sufficient security on real estate in New York if preferred, I would pay such a rate of interest as loans on productive real estate command and pay a comission for the negotiation. I would then pay a contribution to aid you in the good cause in money.

Bankruptcy and ruin has spread over the South untill it seems difficult to say where it is to end. To collect debts or sell property for cash is here impossible. I have reduced my liabilities to less than 1000 dollars here but with property and debts enough due me to meet the remainder is apparently impossible. I have supposed that at this time at the North loans might be negotiated on productive real estate. If so I could give security for what I need untill we might hope for a change for the better. I am sorry to again trouble you with my private affairs but such is our condition in this state that I must ask my friends to lend me their good offices so far as to advise me whether such a loan could be negotiated and on what terms. I will furnish securities and I believe satisfactory assurances that I would meet the debt and interest promptly.

A very small debt often ruins those here who have thought themselves quite well off for property. Good may and I hope will grow up out of it to the South.

On the first Monday in this month our meeting was held at Newport to take into consideration the expediency of dividing the state so as to constitute East Tennessee a separate and independent state. The vote in the affirmative passed unanimously. Our people appear well disposed towards the measure but such is the general depression and despondency that they appear discouraged and at a loss what to do.

Amidst the gloom which surrounds us in our pecuniary affairs we have much cause for rejoicing for the great Temperance reformation. It has been so general in our county that I do not know of a distillery in operation or a man engaged in the vile trafic. So too our drunkards appear to have all reformed. I could not name one in the county who can be said now to be an habitual drunkard. The progress has been onward for some years in E[ast] Ten[nessee] but this year has been the most distinguished of all. The reformation appears to be general. It has been a year too of extensive religious revivals. The church I hope has in her great increase in numbers many who are the sincere worshippers of our savior. Yet while the church has cause for rejoicing it has much for mourning. Slavery comes in to spoil it. In the same church where we hope there are sincere worshippers—there are those who buy and sell their own brethren. There are many who hope and pray for the cleansing of the sanctuary and who prophesy that the time is near at hand when it will be done—that these great movements will be followed by others of no less magnitude.

My worthy friend Rev[erend] Spencer Henry of the Methodist Church told me the last time I saw him a few days since that he had reflected much on his duty to preach openly against slavery. He said he had a family of small children with but limited means that by the state laws he should be liable to a fine and imprisonment. He said he had a wish to correspond with you on the subject. I told him I would venture to say that his letter would be kindly received and answered. I have hoped that our churches in the North would lead in this great reformation. If they would I am confident that in the South a reformation in the church would soon follow.

On Monday of this week I met with Mr Fowler who told me his slave Chamberlain had returned. He came to him the morning before and told him that he left him in consequence of an intimation that he was to be sold to a slavedealer that he had wandered about in forests and after suffering much had come back to submit to his fate whatever it might be. I told him I felt sure he would treat him kindly. He said he had done so but how much that poor man must have endured with hunger cold and wet while out in the mountains and caves from the last of Dec[ember] untill his return. Yet this is slavery in its most mitigated form.

Should I give you a brief relation of a case in the other extreme it would I know pain you but may be important that you should fully informed of the despotism under which the slave groans in the South. In the adjoining county of Greene there is a despotic slaveholder by the name of Daniel Allen.[1] A slave of his who visited his wife some miles distant came in the morning later than usual. He took him into his cellar made his slaves hold him or assist in tying him. When he emasculated him, he died soon after was thrown into the river Nolichucky floated down and lodged in a fish trap from which his body was taken and buried. The wounds were apparent, and the report which went out from his slaves not doubted. One of them the father of Jeremiah owned by Mr. J. Huff stated that to be the facts to his son who related them to Mr Huff from whom I had them. I have heard the same from others and have no doubt of the truth of the story. This last summer he killed one of his slaves with a pitchfork a fact which I had from Mr. Huff. These facts are well known in E[ast] Ten[nessee] no man doubts their correctness but there is no legal proof as a slave cannot testify against a white man and none but slaves saw him commit the murders. The law does not restrain a despot in the treatment of his slaves unless he kills them then slaves are not admitted to testify against him, so that the protection that the law affords is very little.

So far as I can judge there is a favorable change in the public mind which might be turned to good account if we had the means to spread light before them. Many suppose that the slave will be persecuted while here or if free that they will still be persecuted with none to protect them and look to Africa as the only asylum for them. Less is known here of the Colonization society than at the North particularly of its faults. The good people who ask that the slave may be free on condition that he will go to Africa suppose that by procuring his liberation they do him a very essential service and by this means carry civilization into Africa [and] send the Bible to Africa. If pious as many of them are that by them they send a missionary into Africa well qualified by constitutional habits for the climate. Patton Howel[2] a very worthy man on Mossy Creek is learning one the trade of a blacksmith and axemaker. His owner I understand gives him his freedom that he may go to the land of his Fathers and carry a very useful art with him. I have heard that the Rev[erend] Mr. Harrison[3] of the Presbyterian Church was instructing a young colored man in divinity that he might preach in Africa. I think he came to Mr Harrison by a relative.

The excitement on the part of the slaveholders has in a measure subsided. Papers and documents sent out probably have a better prospect of meeting with attention than at any time the last 5 or 6 years. Such as I have rec[eive]d I have given circulation and shall continue to do so. On my return to the North which I hope may not be long I intend subscribing for Antislavery periodicals. Our worthy friend Mr Caldwell is much injured by losses in Florida. His ardent antislavery feelings have exposed him to suffer from combinations of slaveholders.

With great respect
my Dear Sir I am
Sincerely yours
E Birdseye

Notes

1. Daniel Allen (1791–1857) owned a farm of 1,300 acres, a first-rate roller grain mill, and an ore bank in Greene County, in addition to holding numerous notes for money loaned and many slaves. *Historical Greene County, Tennessee, and Its People, 1783–1992* (Waynesville, N.C.: Greene County History Book Committee and Don Mills, Inc., 1992), 4.
2. Patton Howell was one of the early blacksmiths at New Market, Jefferson County, who later opened an ax-handle factory there. *History of Tennessee, Containing Historical and Biographical Sketches*, 861–62.
3. Rev. William Harrison was a Presbyterian minister who had studied

under Isaac Anderson at Maryville College. He was minister at the New Market Presbyterian Church in 1842–46. Wilson, *Isaac Anderson*, 161; *History of Tennessee, Containing Historical and Biographical Sketches*, 862.

23. To Gerrit Smith, October 17, 1842

Newport E[ast] Ten[nessee]
Oct[ober] 17th 1842

My Dear Sir

I have again cause to thank you for a kind letter of the 17th Sept[ember] and the Emancipator of the 15th. They came last week in safety. Though your letter notices some things which may seem discouraging I think we have abundant cause for gratitude that we are blessed with so many indications of the smiles of a kind and ever watchful Providence. It is not to be expected that our friends will at all times exhibit the same zeal in the good cause. Violent party contests in which they think their whole temporal interests to be involved will draw them off for a little while. These things are to be expected are temporary in their nature and a change of the scene will call them back to renewed and redoubled efforts. That the great cause is making steady progress at the North I have abundant testimony in the altered tone of many of the political papers [and] in the increased attention to it in private correspondence that reaches this region through a great many avenues—in the altered tone of the slaveholders themselves for they now speak of the Antislavery movement as no temporary excitement but one that endangers the "craft." There is here a subdued feeling among the slaveholders. The loss of property the unprecedented embarrassment and corroding cares have brought them to consider. I have never seen the time when they were so much disposed to listen to reason. Almost every day I have conversations with slaveholders on the subject of slavery. I give them papers and documents on the subject to read. It has not procured me an unkind word and when done in a spirit of kindness I have little fear that it will. This is a great change from what it was three or four years since.

The Temperance reformation and the religious revivals we hope are preparing them for other great changes and improvements in Christian morals. One great enquiry is here now will the Church at the North do her duty on this momentous question. They seem to think that in the Providence of God for the liberation of the oppressed—that is the most important of all—will she come up to the help of the Lord against the mighty or will she remain neutral. Will she pour oil into the wounds of the poor slave or go by on the other side. Should she pass such resolutions as the church in Providence lately passed, pray for the slave expostulate kindly with the Southern church but earnestly and faithfully would every member feel as though he had a duty to perform in carrying the cause of the oppressed to the throne of his heavenly father, the heart of the Southern church would be softened. She would begin the glorious work of letting the oppressed go free. Her example would be followed by all good men then the work would soon be done. When only bad men held slaves they would not hold them long. This is a cause where every Christian should pray that he might be guided in the path of duty or that God would turn the heart of the slaveholder and dispose him to be merciful to the poor slave. He should seriously examine himself as to his fitness for heaven while he neglects this duty.

On Saturday last I met with an aged slaveholder a member of the Methodist Church. He introduced the subject himself by inquiring about the situation of the Northern free states. Much about the effect produced on the people when labor is wholly free. He said to be free from slavery is a great blessing. Had I my life to live over again I should do very differently from what I have done.

On Wednesday last I met with my friend Fowler of whom I have spoken before. An interesting man tho[ugh] not a member of a church I had felt much interested in his two slaves for they too were my friends. Mr F[owler] told me that his slave Cambridge[1] told him that he left in fear of being sold to a slavedealer. He had had such intimations from others that he thought there was no doubt. He assured him that he would not sell him but would treat him kindly. Cambridge was incredulous but at length became satisfied that his fears were groundless for the present [and] probably during the life of his master. Should he die without a will he would then find it too true that he was to be sold and in the little crowd around him some commiserating his fate and disposed to buy him even at a pecuniary sacrifice. There would be the slave dealer probably out bidding them all and taking him where he could no more see his wife and little ones.

A few days since Simon the other slave of Mr Fowler called at my house on business of his master. I had some more conversation with him about his winters residence in the mountains when lying out to avoid being carried off from his family and friends by a slavedealer who had purchased him. I inquired how he managed to elude pursuit. He said in cold weather he made his fire of oak bark in the night burnt them to a coal so that there was no smoke by daylight and sat over the coals. During some of the coldest weather he said he found a cave that was dry and comfortable. I said I suppose your colored friends gave you some provisions. He said I found some blacks who gave me provisions and some white folks that did. I think more white persons who were my friends than black ones. I said notwithstanding I suppose you must have suffered much. He said I did some Sir but it was but a trifle to the idea of being sold and carried off by a slave trader. It struck me forcibly how light he made of his physical sufferings compared with the mental agony of being fettered and carried off from his friends and family. Also his other remark that he found more friends who gave him provisions among the whites than he did among the blacks—no doubt true we have here a heroic yeomenry who detest slavery as an enormous cruelty. They will often feed the poor slave while exiled in the forests and mountains if they have but a scanty supply for their own table—while a large reward has no influence with them. There are exceptions to this rule but I am clear in the opinion that it will apply to the largest part.

Some months ago there was a planter in the near part of the county of Greene 8 miles distant by the name of James McMurtry[2] who died leaving some 45 slaves. A few weeks since the sale of his effects and slaves took place at his plantation. One of my neighbors Mr Jefferson R attended. He told me that of the slaves about 20 were the children of white fathers most of them had colored or light mothers. 15 of them he supposes were the children of McMurtry himself. This is common report. Mr R states that the resemblence is so striking to the other children of McMurtry as to leave no doubt of the fact in the mind of any one who will observe them. Whether he had any intention to provide for their freedom is unknown to me. He died leaving his estate endebted so as to render a sale legally necessary. I do not know that he had any will. Here were parents and children bound together by all those ties which could be supposed to exist in that relation then to be separated forever. Mr R says it was the most distressing sight he ever saw. All those poor slaves were in tears. The women embraced their husbands in the anguish of their hearts. The husband in quiet grief sustained his weeping wife—the child frantic with screams clung to the bosom of its mother.

I did not attend the sale. It is sufficiently distressing to me to hear of it from one who did. Slavery in its best estate is a bitter cup but who can describe a scene like this—of such unutterable woe. Would our good Christians and Christian ministers in the North if they had witnessed this scene of distress have turned coldly away and said it was a matter with which they had nothing to do. I hope and believe not. It is because they do not realize the distress of the downtrodden that they do not interest themselves more for him. If those who are quietly surrounded with their wives and children in the family circles of the North loving and being loved could immagine what would be their feelings if suddenly they were to be put up on a stand to be sold to the highest bidder in a slave market and then taken to parts of the world where they would see each other no more. If they can immagine their distress in such a calamity they can pity the slave. If they have no feelings of compassion for him no pity—or so little that they do not like to offend the slaveholder by making it known will they not be distressed to hear—inasmuch as ye did it not to one of the least of these ye did it not to me.

If the lovely Dr Nelson[3] was here with his lamb like temper he could preach plainly to our people on this important subject. No one would hurt him. E[ast] Ten[nessee] would be a safer place for him than many of the free states. The subject of a separation will be kept before the people. If we of E[ast] Ten[nessee] can only effect a separation we shall then hope to carry this important change into our constitution. If there can be free discussion there can be no doubt.

Some weeks probably a month since Franklin returned from Illinois where he went for a runaway slave. It appears that he was taken up by the sheriff of Washington County who wrote to Franklin that he had his slave in custody. For this he was to have one hundred dollars. Before Franklin arrived he escaped from the custody of the sh[eri]ff of Washington County. When Franklin caught him and brought him off without paying the sh[eri]ff of Washington one cent. I heard F[ranklin] make the statement that hard hearted man the sh[eri]ff of Washington has been rightly served. He deserves no pay but the scorn and contempt of all good men.

Oct[ober] 20th 1842 Slave labor is unprofitable. Mr Irby of whom I spoke in S[outh] C[arolina] had over 100. He was the most energetic planter in Laurens District that I was acquainted with. He stated that he sold his last crop of cotton for $7000. He bought horses mules farming tools hogs bacon etc for the subsistence of his slaves and means of employment. There would be clothing and taxes, physicians bill etc—and interest on them as capital invested—all enough to make a very loosing concern were it not for a profitable practice at the Bar.

I write from Greeneville. Mr R McKinney[4] who was a member of the convention to reverse the constitution of this state and a man of talents well understood to be opposed to slavery approves the formation of a new state of East Tennessee. He says that surrounded as we are by slaveholding states we should find their influences too strong for us to counteract, that congress would object to the measure especially the North which would view with jealousy any increase of slaveholding states. He rather prefers our influence on the South tending to gradual manumission and the deportation of colored persons to Africa by the public funds—the vain experiment of colonization. Mr McKinney says it would be difficult to immagine the excitement produced in the convention when he presented the petitions for the gradual abolition of slavery says it was unfortunate that they were presented at all as it led to restrictions in the constitution that would not have been thought of.

y[ours]
E Birdseye

Notes

1. Birdseye called this slave Chamberlain in his earlier letters to Gerrit Smith.
2. The settlement of James McMurtrey's estate dragged on into 1847. Some of the slaves were returned after they had been bid off, and the administrators had to sell them again. Goldene Fillers Burgner, comp., *Chancery Court Minutes, Greene County, Tennessee, November 1825–May 1876* (Easley, S.C.: Southern Historical Press, 1987), 85, 88, 144, 150, 151, 153, 155, 169, 174, 175, 181.
3. David Nelson (1793–1844), Presbyterian clergyman, educator, abolitionist, was born near Jonesboro, in East Tennessee, and educated by Rev. Samuel Doak at Washington College. After studying medicine in Philadelphia, he entered the ministry and founded Marion College near Palmyra, Mo. In 1836 he was mobbed by slaveholders in his congregation at Palmyra for preaching the antislavery gospel, and subsequently he was forced to flee Missouri. He became an agent for the American Anti-Slavery Society and lectured extensively in western Illinois on behalf of the abolitionist cause. *DAB*, 8:414–15.
4. Robert J. McKinney (1803–1875) later would serve on the Tennessee Supreme Court (1847–61), where his opinions invariably betrayed deep sympathy for the plight of the slaves. He was a well-known opponent of slavery who earlier had freed all his own slaves. Temple, *East Tennessee*, 113; Caldwell, *Sketches of the Bench and Bar*, 155–59.

24. To the *Christian Freeman*,[1] April 14, 1843

LETTER FROM TENNESSEE.
DOMESTIC AFFLICTIONS: NATIONAL GUILT
AND NATIONAL JUDGMENTS. THE TENDER
MERCY OF SLAVERY. A SLAVE SENTENCED
TO DEATH FOR KILLING HIS MASTER IN
SELF DEFENSE.

We cannot forebear to give our readers the whole of the following letter from East Tennessee. There is something so touching—so true to nature and so much the fruit of Divine grace, that we could not content ourselves with merely its important and deeply interesting Antislavery intelligence.—ED.

EAST TENNESSEE,
FEB[RUARY] 15, 1843

My Dear Friend:

Your esteemed favor reached me at ——— on Monday of last week.

It was with no ordinary feelings, that I read your letter, and learned the severe trials you are called upon to pass through—a most affectionate and amiable wife taken from you, and now your lovely daughter, in all probability, soon to follow. I am grieved to hear the visitation, and while I sympathise with you for your loss, my mind recurs to the trying time when my heart bled from the same stroke. Oh, how trying to think of parting with an affectionate partner, when all those ties—those tender cords are to be severed—we are to bid adieu to them until we meet them in the mansions of the blessed, where there are no more tears, and no more scenes of distress to pass through. All those afflictions appear to me, as though they were of yesterday. My lovely and beloved L.[2] was taken away—How severe the trial, none can tell, who are not called to endure such bereavement. But, my Dear Friend, there is a joy in grief—We should call to our minds, that 'smitten friends, are angels sent on errands full of love'—that while our Father in Heaven does not willingly afflict us, he takes the treasure to himself. While we are mourning here below, they adore and praise Him.

On myself, the lot has been heavy. Trials of no ordinary character have attended me since I saw you. I have been placed in difficulties from which I hoped to escape, yet could not without absolute destruction to my pecuniary affairs, and until quite recently, would have injured my friends here, at a time when they could not bear it. I hope to be able to leave this spring, and see my wife and daughter.³—The hand that has fallen heavily on our country has touched us both. I see that it is ordered by a wise providence, for wise reasons. God is angry with us as a nation. A slaveholder, whose all has been taken from him, said to me last week; 'We are a guilty nation and I fear there are judgments in store for us.' I fear so too. The dreadful crimes of our nation! Who can tell how much we are to suffer. Should God be just, he might cast us off, and punish us till our land so highly favored, become a barren waste. The North has not been guiltless in this matter. They have looked calmly on, and not even entreated the South to be merciful and just to the injured and oppressed slave.

When I got your letter, I saw a crowd at the door of the Court House, as I walked by. It was a sale of a little girl, about seven or eight years old; one of the most pleasant little children you ever saw. Her mother was by her side—a good looking well dressed woman.—She was the slave of a man with whom I was well acquainted, who died some two years ago. He was kind to her, and would have tried to keep the family together, but died in debt. The mother had five children; one had to be sold to pay a part of the debts; another—and then another, until the last. *All to different persons,* to be separated and sold again and again. Yet this is the operation of slavery in its mildest form.

Last evening I came here on business—a few moments' leisure were improved to go into the Court House, to hear the trial of a slave, about twenty-one or twenty-two years of age. Some weeks since he killed his master, who was a cruel hard-hearted man; who frequently scourged the poor fellow so cruelly, that he had told his friends for eighteen months, that he could not live so, and would take his own life.—This was, no doubt, his intention; but while covering a coal pit near this town, his master assaulted him with a heavy club. The slave whose name is Hannibal, struck him with his spade and killed him unintentionally. He then sat down until some person came and made the discovery, and took him. He admitted all the facts, and no one doubts but he told them correctly. Two able counsellors defended him, and tried to get the crime reduced to manslaughter. One of them the moment I stepped in said; Gentlemen of the jury; I know the feelings which you are accustomed to indulge towards slaves from your youth in this country. But on the bench and in this court you should divest yourself of them, and regard him as a man, a fellow-man, entitled to all the justice that one of you are—that the supreme court of the State had decided that when a master approached his slave with a dangerous weapon, the slave had a right to resist—that in this case the slave had this right, for his master had a club that was dangerous—that he was known to the community to be severe—to be cruel—That the slave in resisting went too far—he admitted; but it was in self-defense, and in the heat of passion, and he should only be regarded as guilty of manslaughter or murder in the second degree. The jury found him guilty; and on rendering their verdict, Hannibal rose as undaunted as Hannibal of old, and said; 'Gentlemen, I thank you all.'— Tomorrow the judge will pass the sentence on him to be hanged—a judge too, who is one of the most amiable men living, who has freed his own slaves, and whose opinion of slavery corresponds with ours. Since I have been in the State I have heard of some eight or ten cases of the same kind, where the slave killed his master, because the cruelty was so intolerable that they preferred death. This evening I had a conversation with one of his counsel, who said the slave expected the result, and was now well satisfied to die, he did not want to live.

Feb[ruary] 16.

Early this morning on the opening of the court, the slave Hannibal was brought into court to receive sentence of death. The Judge made a most impressive address to him, and was himself so much overcome by his feelings, that he found it difficult to conclude his sentence. The slave for the first time wept. I should think that more than one half of the audience wept. He was sentenced to be hanged on the second day of March.

You ask me how many of our people would be willing to abolish slavery. In E[ast] Tennessee nine-tenths at least. In N[orth] Carolina a majority—in fact a majority of the legal voters of the whole South. All that is wanting is energy and concert of action. *The abolitionists have not retarded the emancipation of the slave, but ameliorated his condition,* and laid the axe at the root of the tree. By persevering industry, with God's blessing, they will triumph. The light gets into the South; so much so that a late paper at Nashville said, that nothing but the election of Mr. Clay could sustain slavery.

Slavery is a great evil. The South are coming to be sensible of it. Nothing but the culture of cotton has sustained it so long. Slave labor in that business is now worthless. Cotton has sold in S[outh] Carolina, in the country, at from 3 to 5 cents per lb. The culture of cotton in Brittish India by free labor can be done for less than it can be done here with slave labor. The planters are deeply in debt; slave and land encumbered and hopeless so. Forced sales constantly reduce the prices. Farms which a few years since cost some five or six thousand dollars, are now sold for less than the buildings cost in many instances. Eli Whitney was the innocent cause of the continuance of slavery by the invention of the cotton gin, and how did they reward him for his invention, which they said, more than three folded in value all the property of the South. Free labor in India has broken the spell; they can use Whitney's cotton gin too, and will continue to do it.—Slaveholders are becoming desperate. They will, if they can, hold on to their slaves for a while, but in a few short years they will find they cannot hold slaves and lands too, for the free laborer with the intelligence of the European farmer or the Northern man, will be able to out-bid them for the land, while the slaves he would not want. I have heard to day the frequent remark from the most intelligent citizens, that slavery could not exist long, should cotton continue at the present rates. The hope is openly expressed by such persons, that it will fall, and that speedily.

The improved communications have had much effect at the North. *They brought southern influence to operate on the cities,* much to discourage the good cause. But at the South they were the means of letting the light in and diffusing a salutary influence. I would rejoice to see the communications improved, that will carry light into the South. *Persevere! Persevere!! PERSEVERE!!!*

The abolitionists have made an impression on the South, beyond their estimation. A few years of perseverance and the system will fall. Our worthy judge told me in a conversation this evening, that he rejoiced at the success of the culture of cotton in India. Although it caused much distress in our country, ultimately the effect would be beneficial. We have in East Tennessee, some 220,000 whites and 20,000 slaves. Most of the non-slaveholders and two thirds who are slaveholders, wish the evil abolished. You would hear the system spoken of with as much severity as at the North. The slaveholders hope to keep out the light, but hope in vain. It comes in, in the correspondence and by papers.—Many an abolition paper gets in and circulates until worn out—and by travellers returning from the free States.

Efforts have been made to separate E[ast] Tennessee from the other divisions of the State, and will be continued. If successful, this would then be a free State in six months.—Slave labor is worth nothing here. Slaveholders at the South are in debt. More of them will be sold out this year than in any previous one since the foundation of our government. In this and the adjoining county above, there are some farmers from P[ennsylvani]a, who own no slaves, who have fine farms, and who would not own a slave for all 'the wealth that sinews bought and sold have ever earned.' The same change is going on in V[irgini]a; the same in K[entuck]y. Should slaveholders hold on to the poor victims of their service, they will have to part with their land, or the sheriff will do the business for them.—CARRY YOUR PRINCIPLES TO THE POLLS. Show your faith there by your works. I have seen too much suffering brought on the country by elevating a murderer—a slaveholder and duelist[4] to the first office in the gift of the people, to feel any anxiety to have another there.

Affectionately yours,

I am sorry to see such communications as Gov[ernor] Bouck's[5] Message to the Legislature of N[ew] Y[ork]. Not a Southern paper that I have seen, says any thing good about it. It only serves to make His Excellency appear ridiculous, both at the North and South.

NOTES

1. In 1843, William Henry Burleigh became editor of the *Christian Freeman*, the official publication of the Connecticut Anti-Slavery Society. Dumond, *Antislavery*, 266.
2. On Oct. 5, 1826, Ezekiel Birdseye married Lucinda Pierce in the First Congregational Church in Cornwall, Conn. She died on May 27, 1828, in Limestone County, Ala. Will and Inventory of Estate of Lucinda Pierce Birdseye, Court of Probate for the District of Litchfield, Conn., 14:112; Cornwall Vital Records, 2:65, in Barbour Collection of Connecticut Vital Records Prior to 1850, Connecticut Historical Society, Hartford; Jean Waldrop Smith, *Limestone County, Alabama, Orphan's Court Minutes*, 99, 114, 212, 162.
3. In 1834, Birdseye married Mary M. Stone, the daughter of the Reverend Timothy Stone of the First Congregational Church of Cornwall. Reverend Stone had performed the ceremony when he married his first wife, Lucinda Pierce. While Birdseye traveled, Mary M. Stone remained at the home of her father. In 1838, their only daughter, Irene Lucinda, was born. She became a schoolteacher but died on Feb. 25, 1858, just before she was to have been married. Cornwall Vital Records, 3:32, in Barbour Collection; George F. H. Birdseye, comp., and Lucien H. Birdseye, ed., "Outline of the Birdseye Family in America," 1951, typescript in the Connecticut State Library, Hartford, Conn., p. 62.
4. Birdseye here refers to U.S. President Andrew Jackson.
5. William C. Bouck (1786–1859) was Democratic governor of New York in 1842–44 and a leader of the conservative faction of the Democratic party in his state. From the outset, his administration was a stormy one, despite his efforts to achieve reconciliation between the warring factions within his own party. *DAB*, 2:476–77.

25. To Gerrit Smith, June 18, 1845

SALISBURY N[ORTH] CAROLINA
JUNE 18TH 1845

Dear Sir

I have been near six months in the Southern states but so much occupied that I found it difficult to pay that attention to my friends that would have been desirable.

Near three months were spent in K[entuck]y where less transpired that would interest you. I arrived in Greenup County in Jun[e]. One of the first things that attracted my attention was a slave dealer who had purchased a colored woman who was taking leave of her friends. In a few minutes a Steam Boat came down the river in which the poor woman was a passenger with her purchaser. She left 3 children and appeared broken down with grief. She was placed in one corner of the gentlemans cabin where she remained untill we reached Maysville where she was taken on shore. These slave dealers appear afraid to trust a slave out of their sight while passing up or down the river bordering the free states.

I witnessed no other instance of cruelty in K[entuck]y and heard of but few. A slave dealer by the name of Heady whipped one of his slaves to death near Natchez. He was from Louisville indicted there—Natchez—and on trial while I was at Louisville. I had not heard the result of his trial. It was spoken of at Louisville as a case of great cruelty. The poor fellow was said to have lived untill he received from the inhuman monster 1700 stripes from a heavy cowskin. There is a restraining public sentiment in K[entuck]y and much liberality of sentiment on the subject of slavery; predictions that it will terminate soon are heard constantly. Everything indicates its overthrow in a few years. Much has been done to ameliorate their condition. Which may be said of this state Ten[nessee] and I believe most of the Southern states. It is often asserted in the Northern states that the condition of the slave is made worse by the influence of the abolitionists. Such assertions are not correct. The abolition excitement has had a beneficial influence on the condition of the slave. The improvements in K[entuck]y which has increased their intercourse with the free states has had a good influence. Their mc'adamed roads and river improvements give them greater facilities of intercommunication. Particularly the railroad & river improvement. There is a R[ail] Road from Lexington to Frankfort, from thence to the Ohio by 4 locks and dams on the K[entuck]y river. A steam boat leaves daily for Cincinnati from Frankfort carrying a great many there who see people much more prosperous than themselves and see as well as hear that slavery has a withering influence.

In East Tennessee there appears to be but little change but little improvement in the state of society agriculture or the arts. It is thought by many that the schools and seminaries of learning if not on the decline are not improving. If there is any improvement in the public sentiment on the subject of slavery it is difficult to perceive it. The country is insulated and must be opened to the world by thoroughfares before great improvements can be expected.

On my way through Buncombe County last week I called on David Davis who owns the slave William or as he is usually called the captain. I introduced myself to him & inquired if he was disposed to part with him telling him frankly that the motive was to make him free in case his purchase was effected. He said if the capt[ain] would consent to go he would sell him. I inquired if he was willing I should converse with him on the subject. He called him at once. I explained the motive I have in proposing his purchase by telling him that I had a friend at the North in a free state who had heard of him and the cruel treatment he had re[ceive]d who proposed to purchase his freedom with the intention [of] making him free and securing him a good home and kind treatment. He inquired if I was the gentleman who spoke to Mr Woodfin about buying him some 3 or 4 years since. I told him I was and asked if Woodfin told him. He said no that Woodfin was advised by Patton & others not to sell him as my motive must be to show him and make a speculation out of him in that way as he had been badly cut up. I assured him that no such speculation was intended that he would not be shown for money to anyone. I made no disclosure to anyone but Woodfin & Mr McAnally a Methodist clergyman. It is possible that they thought that was the motive. They were doubtless unwilling that he should be exhibited in any manner in the Northern states.

He said I dont understand it. That a man so far off who never saw me should be willing to pay so much money to give me my freedom. Could I do anything for him that he could afford to pay it. I told him that my friend had heard that he was an honest man and industrious. He had also heard of his sufferings and that was what induced him to make the proposal that he might have a good home and kind treatment. He said he would willingly go and make himself as useful as possible. He was evidently much pleased with the idea. During the conversation Mr D[avis] was present. He owns no other slaves and is in apparently moderate circumstances. He would need the money as he has several sons grown up ready to be provided for in whatever he can give. The colored man is supposed to be about 30 years of age. I should think he might be 31 or 32. He will weigh about 175 has a firm constitution strong athletic a first rate laborer and well accustomed to taking care of a carriage & horses sensible and manly in his deportment, and evidently a man of firmness and good natural talents fluent in conversation.

Mr. Davis asks $525 for him. He says he paid $503 in specie for him. I should think that he would not take much if any less. He has no wife or family. I should think he had kind treatment and a comfortable home for a slave. How far the objects of benevolence may be promoted by his purchase you will be best able to judge. Should you think the motive sufficient to justify the expense I will try to conclude the contract. I told Mr Davis his price was over my limits that I could not make the purchase without new authority and could give him no opinion whether the requisite sum would be paid or not. I could only ascertain by writing. I wish it was in my power to join in the purchase but I cannot. I have land and owe money.

Y[ou]rs
E Birdseye

WRITTEN ACROSS PAGE 1:
Should you find it convenient to write me address your letter to Newport Cocke County E[ast] Tenn[essee]. I should be happy to hear that the good cause is prosperous. Please accept for yourself & Mrs. Smith the assurance of my best wishes.

E Birdseye

26. To Gerrit Smith, November 28, 1845

NEWPORT E[AST] TENNESSEE
Nov[EMBER] 28, 1845

My Dear Sir

I arrived in this town five days since from Connecticut and found in the P[ost] Office your two letters July 8th & Aug[ust] 10, 1845 with the Albany Patriot[1] dated in June with all of which I am deeply interested.

I left this county in June. It was on my way that I called on Mr Davis to inquire about the slave William. I have a large body of land in this county and in Greene County next adjoining between 50 & 60,000 acres generally new and unproductive. On my way out I came through K[entuck]y and undertook some business there as agent for my friend Lewis Tappan.[2] On my way back I went through Aug[ust] the state of S[outh] C[arolina] Eastern V[irgini]a Maryland & Delaware arriving in Conn[ecticut] about the 10th of Oct[ober]. When I left this county in June I expected to have been back at the first in July but a temporary illness prevented. I then wrote to have my letters forwarded to Conn[ecticut] but by some carelessness that was omitted. So that I was not apprised of your letters until Mr Tappan mentioned it to me in his office. I requested him to say that I should be here soon and would then write you. I came in the stage by way of Asheville but under the necessity of coming directly on so that I could not stop to see Mr Davis. I heard from him and the slave William on the day I had the interview with Mr Tappan in N[ew] J[ersey]. I wrote Mr Davis and informed him of my intention of seeing him soon after the court in this term. I will probably see him next week and learn definitely what can be done. I shall also endeavor to renew my acquaintance with William and should I have any doubts as to the expediency of concluding the contract shall await you for an opinion or further instructions. I feel confident that he will be an acquisition to the good cause that he has firmness talents and the evidences of barbarities of the system on his person which will do much to influence our Northern people. So fully has this been impressed on my mind that I would have advanced the money to buy his freedom had it been in my power but it was not and is now not in my power but I will bind myself to pay one half of any pecuniary loss you may incur as soon as I can make it convenient do so. I am now negotiating with the hope of selling a part or an interest in my land here. If successful that would give me the means. I have a valuable tract of 1417 acres of land in Marion County Ohio worth about $10 per acre but the man of whom I took a deed of trust to receive $2292 in 1833 sold it 4 days after in Lexington K[entuck]y. My deed was recorded first but a question is raised whether it has any validity untill recorded and that depends on whether it is a mortgage or an instrument for the encumbrance of lands. If the latter I am safe. This title has been with the courts of law and Chancery in Ohio 11 years, and may be determined in one or two more. I have some money invested in Steuben & Chemung counties N[ew] York and some land in Conn[ecticut] but have had severe losses. I hope to escape bankruptcy and am more encouraged now but can only promise you to do my full share if able. If unfortunate, you will have to take my good will in discharge of this obligation.

During my journey this year past I had an opportunity to watch the signs of the times in those states where I have travelled. At a more leisure moment I may write you some few brief remarks on my tour. While travelling I could not for two reasons. My time was necessarily occupied in the business of others, and that business would have been injured by any publication from me as it would have been recognized and resulted in injury to Mr. T[appan]. In K[entuck]y Ten[nessee] N[orth] C[arolina] V[irgini]a Maryland & D[elaware] the sighns are favorable. Slavery is on the wane in all. If our Northern people are faithful its overthrow cannot be distant. A more general knowledge is spreading of the blighting effects and a dread of public sentiment to such deters many from the cruelties and enormities of the system. The casual observer can see that the condition of the slave is ameliorated.

I shall advise you soon of my success in this matter. If I purchase him I should deem it unsafe to send him unless under the protection of some man of well known integrity & responsibility. There would be now frequent opportunities to send him through K[entuck]y by the stage driver returning from the Carolinas. I will endeavour to see that he is well provided with necessary clothing and money.

You will please present my best respects to Mrs. Smith and accept my kind regards. A letter would find me at this office.

Ezekiel Birdseye

Notes

1. The *Albany Patriot* was a weekly antislavery newspaper published from Oct. 15, 1843, to 1848 in Albany, N.Y.; it was edited by James Caleb Jackson until 1846 and by William L. Chaplin from 1846 to 1848. Henderson, "History of the New York State Anti-Slavery Society," 408; *DAB*, 9:547.
2. Lewis Tappan (1788–1873), merchant and famous abolitionist, repudiated William Lloyd Garrison when the latter proposed to attach other reforms to the cause of abolitionism. With the resulting split in the American Anti-Slavery Society in 1840, he assumed a leading role in forming the American and Foreign Anti-Slavery Society, of which he was the first treasurer. *DAB*, 17:303–4.

27. To Gerrit Smith, December 9, 1845

Dandridge Jefferson Co[unty] E[ast] Ten[nessee]
December 9th 1845

My Dear Sir

I arrived in this county yesterday to attend to business in the Chancery Court. On Friday last I was at the house of David Davis near Lapland P[ost] O[ffice] Buncombe County N[orth] C[arolina] for the purpose of purchasing William, the slave but as yet my success is uncertain.

I had a conversation with Mrs Davis before I saw her husband. She expressed a wish to have the contract made. She said that William once ran away and in attempting to get to the free states was taken up and imprisoned in Harlan County K[entuck]y making them an expense of $50 or more, that owing to the uncertainty of his staying she thought he had better be sold to me for fear that he would be traded off and sent to Mississippi.

I then went to the field where I saw Mr Davis at work with William. I inquired of him whether he was disposed to make the sale. He said it would depend much on the feelings of William, that some persons had been talking to him and had got him much alarmed about going, that he would talk to him and write me in a few days. That if he sold him to anyone he would sell him to me.

Before seeing Mr Davis I went to the house of Benjamin Peake who sold him to Mr Davis. Peake lives about 4 miles distant is an intelligent man. He is a friend of mine and readily tendered me his best services in the matter should I need them. He says that Davis is a very eccentric man of limited information and expressed his doubts of my success with him. He says he is so variable in his feelings that within the three years he has owned him that he has declared his readiness to sell him for $400 and in a few days would declare with equal vehemence that he would not take $1000. There are slaveholders who would use their influence to dissuade William from going well knowing that he has talents to expose the system and a scarrified body which would show how true his statements must be.

Mr Peake tells me that if I can trade with Davis I shall probably have to pay him *specie*. Mr Davis intimated the same. Bank notes are here now on a par with specie or nearly so. A Bill on N[ew] York will command but one percent from the Bank at Asheville sell at 3/4 at prem[ium] buy at par to —

perc[ent] prem[ium]. If I am informed by Davis or Mr Peake that the purchase can be effected I can probably sell the check for 1 per[cent] at prem[ium] for them. If then disap[p]ointed can change the specie to Am[erican] gold or for a check at the Bank near the same % as to make no considerable loss. For the present it will remain as it is untill I am further advised in the matter.

I shall write Mr Peake if the matter rests with William. Mr P[eake] will satisfy him, but if with Davis himself it is more uncertain. Produce has advanced near 50 percent here, this without causing any apparent advance in lands or slaves, make the holders more firm.

Mr Peake says William is now 41 years old, an excellent laborer one of the most able bodied industrious willing men he ever knew. Strictly honest and very intelligent. That if the trade is made he will give him that character in writing a matter which I shall be careful not to neglect. I requested Mr Davis to let me converse with William. He declined by saying he thought he could do better with him than I could. My acquaintance with him is very limited. He probably feared I should say something which might induce him to run away. It is not surprising that William should be distrustful as it is so common for all who deal in slaves in the South to state any falsehood to them in order to accomplish their objects.

I shall probably have to pay the full amount of $525 if I can make the purchase. He will then need some clothing to make him comfortable and decent for a journey North. Should you deem it expedient to authorize me to draw on you for that purpose in case I make the purchase for any am[ount] not exceeding $100 I will forward my note and pay it within one year from date with interest. I am now negotiating a sale of an interest in my lands in Ten[nessee]. Untill I do that or return North advances will be made with difficulty. I am applying for a Charter for a manufacturing company, principally with a view to make iron which I shall probably obtain.

With this I send you a paper which I hope will arrive safe. My worthy friend Rev[erend] Spencer Henry of Newport always the friend of the slave wishes to be remembered to you. Present my kind regards to Mrs. Smith. Address me at Newport Cocke Co[unty] E[ast] Tenn[essee].

Very truly yours
My Dear Sir
Ezekiel Birdseye

28. To Gerrit Smith, January 20, 1846

Long Creek Mills Cocke Co[unty]
Jan[uary] 20th 1846

My Dear Sir

Yours of [last] date came safe to my hands 2 days since. It might have been a few days in the P[ost] Office at Newport. Nothing new has transpired in regard to William. No letter has come from either Mr Peake or Davis. I am somewhat at a loss as to what the real difficulty is. I have concluded to go up and spend a night with Davis. Then I can learn fully. He has some sons living with and near him. All will have to be consulted with his good lady and daughters. They are an illiterate superstitious family. A mere suggestion from a slave holder that some mischief was hidden in the proposition would render any negotiation with him impossible for me. Should it be an unwillingness on the part of William it will be owing to the same influence. They would be unwilling that a man of his natural talents, covered with wounds and bruises should go to the North. Another cause may be that he will not think it advantageous in a pecuniary way. There are few laborers able to do as much as he is. He is also industrious. Corn the principal production of his farm is much higher this year than usual owing to the great scarcity in North & S[outh] Carolina particularly the latter. It is there selling in the western part of the state for from 100 to 150 per bushel. Much has been taken from corn here and all that could be purchased in the adjoining counties of N[orth] Carolina. This approach to a famine in S[outh] C[arolina] has caused a rapid decline in the price of slaves. Many are brought here to be kept through the winter, and droves of horses and mules. The failure of the crop there has increased the pressure on all classes particularly slave owners. There are frequent public sales and as constant private ones and at prices much reduced. Should Davis wish to invest his money in slaves he might do it to advantage much better than to keep William. Under all the circumstances I concluded to go up again and see him and spend as much time at his house as might be necessary to learn the real cause if any which prevents the purchase. I have consulted my worthy friend Rev[erend] Spencer Henry of N[e]wport, who expresses a readiness to aid us in this matter. He is well acquainted with William and could at once convince him that he had better go. He says that after seeing him and explaining to him that the object is to make him free he will be worth nothing to Davis should he refuse to sell him.

I shall first go up this week and then get Mr Henry to go up if necessary or expedient, and I still flatter myself that I can effect the purchase. If I fail I shall have your remittance returned. Last week I was at Dandridge and made a contract with a merchant by the name of William Harris,[1] a man of whose responsibility and integrity of character I am well informed, to sell him the draft should I make the purchase. I can have specie or paper at a premium of 1 percent. One half of one percent will change it into specie should that be necessary gold if preferred. I agreed with him to take $100 and see if I could effect the purchase if not with liberty to return without any charge. If I should not see him in time to return the $100, he will be directed to place the $400 on deposite for you in N[ew] Y[ork]. I shall then get the $100 changed into gold bring it on and deposit it or pay to you personally. Mr Harris intends leaving for N[ew] Y[ork] on the 1st week in Feb[ruary]. I have to go to Knoxville on the 2nd week in Feb[ruary] and from there North through the valley of V[irgini]a where I shall do some business for Mr Tappan on my way which will not detain me long. I shall expect to be in the western part of the state of N[ew] Y[ork] soon after my return and hope to make you a call. By the last of this week I hope to be able to learn what the probability is of buying William and should it be necessary for Mr Henry to go up that it may be done in time for me to see Mr Harris before he goes East.

This has been a very hard year for some parts of the South particularly South Carolina. Their crops were short all over the state but more particularly in the western districts. There the approach is near to a famine. The people are poor with small accumulated means of buying from abroad. A large majority of the new slaveholders have none unless in the sale of articles of necessity or their land. To escape this calamity they have tried to sell at some prices and move to the West. About 100 families have come into this county. Some of them with small means to render them comfortable, others with little if anything but have procured a passage in some waggon coming out after corn and have made a tent aside of the road wherever the journey of the waggoner terminated. Other roads have a like proportion and the routes through Georgia, making in all a great diminution of the population. Many who came here tell me that there are large numbers who cannot get away and have no visible means of living there. I have inquired of many how they sold their property. None have stated the price of their land at more than $2.50 per acre and some at less. Others have left their land to be sold should there ultimately be a price for it. Cows horses mules etc have sold at nominal prices. Slaves are going off in almost equal numbers. Some emigrate from their worn out lands to the West and even Texas. The planters were generally in debt having failed to make a crop or but a poor one and that at a low price so far as it consisted of cotton, their debts have to be paid by a sale of their slaves. Probably no part of the United States at this time has this desolate appearance or is so much apparently under the curse of Heaven as South Carolina. Yet their calamities appear to produce no contrition. They denounce the abolitionists with equal vehemence and as if intent on blotting out all humane feelings towards these poor persecuted Africans. They circulate Governour Hammonds[2] letters to Mr Clarkson in pamphlet form. There is one now lying before me handed me by a member of the Baptist church, given him by another member of the same church in South Carolina for gratuitous distribution. When these letters first appeared I saw them in a N[ew] Y[ork] paper. I took but a cursory glance at them. They now appear in a new dress carefully done up for the South and have a deleterious influence. Many men who were conscientious on this subject and appeared anxious to know their duty have become so far poisoned with these deleterious influences and not permitted to see any of a counteracting tendency that they appear to have arrived at the conclusion that the Bible sanctions slavery, that it is to be perpetual and that it is the duty of the church to take this as the standard of their faith and practice. These influences appear to originate more in S[outh] C[arolina] and to prevail more there and in the same place are they suffering the vengeance of Heaven.

I write in haste and send my letter by a private conveyance to the P[ost] Office. You may expect to hear from me again before many days. Present my kind regards to Mrs Smith and accept the assurances of my best wishes.

E Birdseye

Notes

1. William Harris was a prominent merchant at Dandridge, Tenn. *History of Tennessee, Containing Historical and Biographical Sketches*, 1272.
2. James Henry Hammond (1807–1864), radical outspoken proslavery governor of South Carolina and U.S. senator, in 1830 established a newspaper, the *Southern Times*, to advance his fiery advocacy of nullification and secession. By 1834, he was an advocate of the death penalty for abolitionists. *DAB*, 8:207–8.

29. To Gerrit Smith, March 2, 1846

Newport E[ast] Ten[nessee]
March 2nd 1846

My Dear Sir

I had unavoidable detention untill Friday of the 1st week in last month. I then passed Dandridge on my way to Knoxville where I was required to attend court as a witness. Mr Harris had left for New York two days before my arrival. I requested his clerk to direct him to deposite the amount of that cheque in Bank and send you the certificate after deducting his advance and have no doubt it will be correctly done. I shall leave in a few days for New York and pay you the balance in my hands on my return.

I regret the failure to accomplish your very benevolent purpose but should it be deemed expedient it can yet be accomplished by purchasing the wife of William. If not advisable you will be happy to know that for a slave his situation is good.

Nothing very important appears to be taking place in regard to slavery more than has been stated that has come to my knowledge. The marks of decline are apparent the decreasing population in S[outh] C[arolina] and probably decrease in the slave population are matters of importance. The tone of the South Carolinians is less haughty while some say they must have a change of policy or they are ruined. This is apparent to those who have been attentive observers of that state for a considerable time, land is selling for less where it will sell at all than it was 30 years since. A great number of plantations are so worn out that they will not sell for anything and are abandoned. The proportion of worn out land is increasing every year with it a decline of their staple production cotton both in price and quantity. Their dependence on the west for provisions is annually increasing with decreasing means of payment. Very large quantities of pork are stored up there by western drovers but such is the poverty of the country that they are unable to buy to pay in cash while the dealers refuse to credit—but are under the necessity of offering low for cash. Over 15000 emigrants have passed this county from the N[orth] & S[outh] Carolinas since last harvest. It is said that the emigration will continue through the spring.

Expressions of confidence in the decline of slavery and a wish that it should terminate by the most considerate citizens are more frequent. There appears to be a decreasing feeling of hostility towards the abolitionists which may be owing in part to a belief that their number is on the decline.

While in N[orth] C[arolina] some weeks since I heard a conversation between a gentleman from K[entuck]y and one from S[outh] C[arolina], the subject of slavery made one of their topics. The one from S[outh] C[arolina] said there had been no instance in that state where a white man had been punished with death for killing a black one. A case had occurred at Newberry, where a man narrowly escaped. He had sold his slave and forbid his return to his plantation. Sometime after he caught him there and whipped him with extreme severity and left him over night in the stocks. In the morning he was dead. On trial at the court he narrowly escaped conviction. He remarked what I had long known to be true that if a man stole a slave it was the most certain crime of any to bring him to the gallows. Both expressed to each other confidence in the continuance of their favorite institution notwithstanding all the efforts of the abolitionists.

The pamphlet you had the goodness to send me arrived on the 1st Monday of Feb[ruary]. It had been circulated in the neighborhood for some time as I have reason to believe. I read it with satisfaction and at the request of Mr Caldwell gave it to him. His ardor in the cause is not abated. For a year or two he has been mining for silver but I am sorry to say I fear his efforts will prove fruitless. He had mistaken (probably) black slate called by the french Geologists Protegene having pyrites of iron for silver or an ore of silver. He went to a mine in N[orth] C[arolina] at Davidson Co[unty] and obtained the opinion of a man there who was but imperfectly acquainted with the ores of silver but who confirmed Mr C[aldwell] in his opinions. He dug several shafts at great labor and erected a furnace with a blowing aparatus. He has found a vein of copper running through his land in Jefferson County which may prove more valuable. He is an excellent man and exerts a good influence in Tennessee. You will please present my best respects to Mrs Smith and accept the assurances of my

             Kind Regards
             Ezekiel Birdseye

30. To Gerrit Smith, March 25, 1846

NEWPORT MARCH 25TH 1846
(E[AST] TEN[NESSEE])

My Dear Sir

Enclosed you will find a certificate of deposite in the Union Bank N[ew] York for four hundred & ten ($410) dollars made payable to the order of Greenway Henry & Smith and by them endorsed payable to your order.

I am disappointed and dissatisfied with the way this business has been done. I was detained on very urgent business for a friend of mine in superintending the taking of depositions in a cause of great importance and then summoned to attend court myself in Knoxville. When I passed Dandridge Mr Harris had been gone two days. I made a memorandum and requested his clerk to forward it immediately, directing him to deposit the amount in his hands to your credit and send you the certificate of deposite to your address in Peterboro Madison Co[unty] N[ew] York.

I had no doubt the business would be correctly done, and expected to follow in a few days myself. Business detained me. I thought for abundant caution I would inquire and see if the business had been done as directed. Yesterday to my surprise I found that Harris had brought the certificate on with him. I regret it much but sent it by the first mail.

I expect to leave in 3 or 4 days and on my arrival in New York will pay you the balance $90 dollars without delay. Probably I shall be soon at your house as I have business in Chemung & Steuben, and wish to visit my brother Victory,[1] as I am detained unexpectedly I have no late advices as to his health.

My business of late has been such that I have no additional particulars of much interest on the subject of slavery. I see by the papers that a man was recently convicted for killing his slave in S[outh] C[arolina] but if so he will be in no danger of punishment. The emigration from that state continues. A great many emigrants are going to the west. Many of them to Texas. A large proportion of them are extremely poor and miserably clad. Very few of them ever stop for meals or lodging at a public house. They buy or beg their provisions and at night erect a small tent by the road build a fire and cook their meals by their tents. No matter what the season or weather they expect no other accommodations. The opinion of all who travel in S[outh] C[arolina] seems to be that it is poor and in a fair way to be soon the poorest part of the whole country. If they do not abolish slavery slavery will abolish them.

My time does not permit me to write more at this time as the mail will close soon.

I hope I may have the pleasure of seeing you in a few weeks. I shall be happy to learn that the good cause is making progress generally. I think the indications are favorable here.

Probably I shall mail you a number of the Southern Review in which you will find an article on the state of South Carolina (by the next mail). You will find some candid statements honestly made as home truths.

Present my kind regards to Mrs Smith and accept the assurances of my best wishes.

Very Truly Yours
Ezekiel Birdseye

Note

1. Victory Birdseye (1782–1853) was Ezekiel's half-brother. He graduated from Williams College in 1804, and after studying law practiced in Pompey Hill, Onondaga County, N.Y. He was elected to the 14th Congress (1815–17); served as postmaster of Pompey Hill in 1817–38; was district attorney of Onondaga County in 1818–33; and served in both the New York senate (1827) and New York assembly (1823, 1838–40). He ended his political career as a Whig representative to the 27th Congress (1841–43) and afterward resumed the practice of law in Onondaga County, N.Y., until his death in 1853. *BDAC*, 595.

31. To Andrew Johnson, February 20, 1861

KNOXVILLE TEN[NESSEE]
FEB[RUARY] 20TH 1861

Hon[orable] Andrew Johnson
My dear Sir

I congratulate you on the result of the late election in this state. Since I wrote you some weeks since, I have been in sev[e]ral counties of East Tennessee. I hardly heard but one opinion as to your course, all with a very rare exception approved it in the warmest terms. Not only in this state but in others particularly the Northern states speak of you with great respect as a statesman. We hope your efforts to reconcile these difficulties may be successful. Your enemies here are very quiet. I am confident that not one of them has been heard to denounce you since the 9th inst[ant].[1]

I accidentally mentioned to one of my friends that you had done me the honor to send me your speech. He inquired if I could use my influence with you to obtain the Post Office here for him. If I had I should be happy to serve him. He is my friend Mr Lee Rogers whom I regard as a very worthy young gentleman—any service you can render him will be a favor conferred on merit.

I am Sir with great respect

truly yours
E Birdseye

Note

1. Andrew Johnson had given two rousing pro-Union speeches in the U.S. Senate on Dec. 18–19, 1860, and Feb. 5–6, 1861, which caused a sensation in both sections of the country and solidified support for the Union in Tennessee. He received many requests for copies of these speeches, and undoubtedly when Birdseye mentions writing Johnson "some weeks since," it would have been for the speech of Dec. 18–19. Johnson's "course" was praised by unionists and roundly condemned by secessionists. The "late election" refers to the Tennessee referendum of Feb. 9 on a call for a convention, or no convention, to consider the state's relation to the Union, and if there were a convention whether Union candidates or seceders would serve. Voters defeated the call by 68,282 to 59,449, and unionist delegates were selected by 91,803 to 24,749. Hans L. Trefousse, *Andrew Johnson: A Biography* (New York and London: W. W. Norton, 1989), 130–37.

Bibliography

I. Primary Sources

A. Manuscripts

Barbour Collection of Connecticut Vital Records Prior to 1850. Connecticut Historical Society, Hartford.
Birdseye, Ebenezer, Store Account Book, Cornwall, 1789–1828. Connecticut Historical Society Library, Hartford.
Birdseye, George F. H., comp., and Lucien H. Birdseye, ed. "Outline of the Birdseye Family in America," 1951. Typescript in the Connecticut State Library, Hartford.
Court of Probate for the District of Litchfield, Connecticut; Cornwall Deeds, Litchfield County. Connecticut Historical Society Library, Hartford.
Knox County, Tennessee, Administrative Settlements. Knox County Archives, Knoxville.
Pactolus Iron Works Account Book, 1811–1815. Southern Historical Collection, Wilson Library, Univ. of North Carolina, Chapel Hill.
Peck's Notes. McClung Historical Collection, Knox County Public Library, Knoxville, Tenn.
Smith Papers. Letters and Papers of Gerrit Smith. George Arents Research Library for Special Collections, Syracuse Univ. Many of the letters in this

collection which were addressed to Smith are listed in *Calendar of the Gerrit Smith Papers in the Syracuse University Library, 1819–1854.* 2 vols. Syracuse, N.Y.: Historical Records Survey, 1941.

Tennessee County Records: Wills, County Court Minutes, Circuit Court Minutes, Chancery Court Minutes, and Deeds for the following counties in East Tennessee: Anderson, Blount, Bradley, Carter, Claiborne, Grainger, Greene,, Hawkins, Jefferson, Knox, McMinn, Marion, Meigs, Monroe, Rhea, Roane, Sevier, Sullivan, and Washington. Available on microfilm from the Tennessee State Library and Archives, Nashville.

Tennessee General Assembly. *Public and Private Acts,* 1796–1861.

B. Published

Axford, Faye A., ed. *Limestone County Alabama Cemeteries: Athens City and Additions.* 3 vols. Athens, Ala.: Limestone County Historical Society, 1979.

Boyer, Reba Bayless, comp. *Monroe County, Tennessee: Chancery Court Records, 1832–1887.* Athens, Tenn.: Privately printed, 1988.

———. *Wills and Estate Records of McMinn County, Tennessee, 1820–1870.* Athens, Tenn.: Privately printed, 1966.

Burgner, Goldene Fillers, comp. *Chancery Court Minutes, Greene County, Tennessee, November 1825–May 1876.* Easley, S.C.: Southern Historical Press, 1987.

———. *Greene County, Tennessee, Wills, 1783–1890.* Easley, S.C.: Southern Historical Press, 1981.

Caruthers, R. L., and A. O. P. Nicholson, comps. *A Compilation of the Statutes of Tennessee, of a General and Permanent Nature, from the Commencement of the Government to the Present Time. With References to Judicial Decisions, in Notes, to Which Is Appended a New Collection of Forms.* Nashville: Steam Press of James Smith, 1836.

Catterall, Helen Tunnicliff, ed. *Judicial Cases Concerning American Slavery and the Negro.* Vol. 2: *Cases from the Courts of North Carolina, South Carolina, and Tennessee.* Washington, D.C.: Carnegie Institution of Washington, 1929.

Currey, Richard Owen. *A Sketch of the Geology of Tennessee: Embracing a Description of Its Minerals and Ores, Their Variety and Quality, Modes of Assaying and Value; with a Description of Its Soils and Productiveness, and Palaeontology.* Knoxville: Kinsloe and Rice, 1857.

Drake, Daniel. *Dr. Daniel Drake's Letters on Slavery to Dr. John C. Warren, of Boston, Reprinted from the National Intelligencer, Washington, April 3, 5, and 7, 1851.* New York: Schuman's, 1940.

Dresser, Amos. *The Narrative of Amos Dresser, with Stone's Letters from Natchez, an Obituary Notice of the Writer, and Two Letters from Tallahassee, Relating to the Treatment of Slaves.* New York: American Anti-Slavery Society, 1836.
Featherstonhaugh, George W. *Excursion through the Slave States, from Washington on the Potomac to the Frontier of Mexico; with Sketches of Popular Manners and Geological Notices.* 2 vols. London: John Murray, 1844.
Frazier, D. R., comp. *Tennessee Post Offices and Postmaster Appointments, 1789–1984.* Dover, Tenn.: Privately printed, 1984.
Gold, Theodore S., comp. *Historical Records of the Town of Cornwall, Litchfield County, Connecticut.* 2d ed. Hartford, Conn.: Hartford Press, 1904.
Gurney, Joseph John. *A Winter in the West Indies, Described in Familiar Letters to Henry Clay, of Kentucky.* London: John Murray, 1840.
Haywood, John, ed. *A Revisal of All the Public Acts of the State of North Carolina and of the State of Tennessee Now in Force in the State of Tennessee.* Nashville: Thomas G. Bradford, 1809.
Journal of the Constitutional Convention of 1834. Nashville: W. H. Hunt, 1834.
Kain, W. C. *The Constable's Guide: Being a Practical Treatise on the Powers, Duties, and Liabilities of Constables in the State of Tennessee, Both in Criminal and Civil Proceedings. With Approved Forms, Adapted to Every Service and Duty Required. To Which Is Added, an Appendix, Containing the Laws of Tennessee Respecting Partnerships, Assignments, Wills, Etc., with a Variety of Reliable Business Forms.* Knoxville, Tenn.: Jesse A. Rayl, 1859.
Meats, Stephen, and Edwin T. Arnold, eds. *The Writings of Benjamin F. Perry: Essays, Public Letters, and Speeches.* 3 vols. Spartanburg, S.C.: Reprint Co. for the Southern Studies Program, Univ. of South Carolina, 1980.
Meigs, Return J., and William F. Cooper, eds. *The Code of Tennessee, Enacted by the General Assembly of 1857–1858.* Nashville: E. G. Eastman and Co., State Publishers, 1858.
Mims, Anna Roe, comp. *Tennessee Records of Cocke County: Scrap Book of W. J. McSween.* Nashville: Works Progress Administration, 1936.
Olmsted, Frederick Law. *A Journey Through the Back Country in the Winter of 1853–54.* New York: Mason Brothers, 1860.
O'Neall, John Belton. *Biographical Sketches of the Bench and Bar of South Carolina.* 2 vols. Charleston, S.C.: S. G. Courtenay, 1859.
———. *The Negro Law of South Carolina.* Columbia, S.C.: J. G. Bowman, 1848.
Osborn, Charles. *Journal of that Faithful Servant of Christ, Charles Osborn, Containing an Account of Many of his Travels and Labors in the Work of the Ministry, and His Trials and Exercises in the Service of the Lord, and in Defense of the Truth, as It Is in Jesus.* Cincinnati, Ohio: Achilles Pugh, 1854.

Parker, Anthony E., comp. *A Guide to Moore County Cemeteries.* Carthage, N.C.: Moore County Historical Association, 1975.

Pearson, Abel. *An Analysis of the Principles of the Divine Government.* Athens, Tenn.: William P. Reid, 1833.

Peck, Jacob. "Geological and Mineralogical Account of the Mining Districts in the State of Georgia—Western Part of North Carolina and East Tennessee, with a Map." *American Journal of Science and Arts* 23 (1833): 1–10.

Rankin, A. T. *Truth Vindicated and Slander Repelled.* Ironton, Ohio: Privately printed, 1883.

Rankin, John. *Letters on American Slavery, Addressed to Mr. Thomas Rankin, Merchant at Middlebrook, Augusta County, Virginia.* Boston: Garrison and Knapp, 1833.

Robinson, John Joseph. *Memoir of Rev. Isaac Anderson, D.D.* Knoxville: J. A. Rayl, 1860.

Ross, Frederick Augustus. *The Doctrine of the Direct Witness of the Spirit as Taught by the Rev. John Wesley Shown to be Unscriptural, False, Fanatical, and of Mischievous Tendency.* Philadelphia: Published for the Author by Perkins and Purves, 1846.

———. *Position of the Southern Church in Relation to Slavery: As Illustrated in a Letter of Dr. F. A. Ross to Rev. Albert Barnes.* New York: J. A. Gray, printer, 1857.

———. *A Sermon on Intemperance, Delivered in the First Presbyterian Church in Knoxville, Tenn., on the Evening of Twelfth of October, 1829.* Rogersville, Tenn.: Printed at the *Calvinistic Magazine* Office, 1830.

———. *Slavery Ordained of God.* Philadelphia: J. B. Lippincott, 1857.

Safford, James Merrill. *A Geological Reconnaissance of the State of Tennessee; Being the Author's First Biennial Report, Presented to the 31st General Assembly of Tennessee, December, 1855.* Nashville: G. C. Torbett and Co., State Printers, 1856.

———. *Geology of Tennessee.* Nashville: S. C. Mercer, 1869.

Scott, Edward. *Laws of the State of Tennessee, Including Those of North Carolina Now in Force in This State: From the Year 1715 to the Year 1820, Inclusive.* 2 vols. Knoxville: Heiskell and Brown, 1821.

Shick, Tom W. *Emigrants to Liberia, 1820–1843: An Alphabetical Listing.* Newark, Del.: Liberian Studies Association in America, 1971.

Smith, J. Gray. *A Brief Historical, Statistical and Descriptive Review of East Tennessee, United States of America: Developing Its Immense Agricultural, Mining, and Manufacturing Advantages with Remarks to Emigrants.* London: J. Leath, 1842.

Smith, Jean Waldrop, comp. *Limestone County, Alabama, Orphan's Court Minutes, 1822–30*. Athens, Ala.: Privately printed, 1950.

Tennessee. Supreme Court. *Reports*. Second Edition of Cooper's Edition. Vols. 1–41. Louisville, Ky.: Fetter Law Book Co., 1908.

Troost, Gerard. *Fifth Geological Report to the Twenty-third General Assembly of Tennessee, Made November, 1839*. Nashville: J. Geo. Harris, Public Printer, 1840.

Wagstaff, H. M., ed. *Minutes of the North Carolina Manumission Society, 1816–1834*. Chapel Hill: Univ. of North Carolina Press, 1934.

White, Robert H., ed. *The Emancipator (Complete), Published by Elihu Embree, Jonesborough, Tennessee, 1820: A Reprint of* The Emancipator, *to Which Are Added a Biographical Sketch of Elihu Embree, Author and Publisher of* The Emancipator, *and Two Hitherto Unpublished Anti-Slavery Memorials Bearing the Signature of Elihu Embree*. Nashville: B. H. Murphy, 1932.

Wiley, Bell I., ed. *Slaves No More: Letters from Liberia, 1833–1869*. Lexington: Univ. Press of Kentucky, 1980.

C. Newspapers and Journals

African Repository and Colonial Journal, 1825–36.
Agriculturalist, and Journal of the State and County Societies, 1840–45.
Albany Patriot, 1843–48.
American and Foreign Anti-Slavery Reporter, 1844–46.
Christian Freeman, 1843.
Emancipator, 1833–50. Also called *Emancipator and Free American, Emancipator and Republican*, and *Emancipator and Weekly Chronicle*.
Friend of Man, 1836–42.
Genius of Universal Emancipation, 1821–36.
Knoxville Gazette, 1797.
Knoxville Post, 1841.
Knoxville Register, 1816–63.
Knoxville Whig, 1839–61.
Liberator, 1831–60.
Liberty Press, 1842–49.
Maryville Record, 1904.
Nashville Daily Press and Times, 1868.
Nashville Gazette, 1820.
Nashville Republican and State Gazette, 1834.
Nashville Republican Banner, 1841–55.

National Banner and Nashville Whig, 1833.
New England Anti-Slavery Almanac for 1841
Niles' Weekly Register, 1818–46.
Philanthropist, 1838–43.

II. Secondary Sources

A. Books

Abel, Annie Heloise, and Frank J. Klingberg, eds. *A Side-Light on Anglo-American Relations, 1839–1858, Furnished by the Correspondence of Lewis Tappan and Others with the British and Foreign Anti-Slavery Society.* Lancaster, Pa.: Lancaster Press of the Association for the Study of Negro Life and History, 1927.

Alexander, Thomas B. *Thomas A. R. Nelson of East Tennessee.* Nashville: Tennessee Historical Commission, 1956.

Allison, John. *Dropped Stitches in Tennessee History.* Nashville: Marshall and Bruce Co., 1897.

Ames, William E. *A History of the National Intelligencer.* Chapel Hill: Univ. of North Carolina Press, 1972.

Andrew, John A. *From Revivals to Removal: Jeremiah Evarts, the Cherokee Nation, and the Search for the Soul of America.* Athens: Univ. of Georgia Press, 1992.

Aptheker, Herbert. *Abolitionism: A Revolutionary Movement.* Boston: Twayne, 1989.

Armstrong, Zella. *The History of Hamilton County and Chattanooga, Tennessee.* 2 vols. Chattanooga: Lookout Publishing Co., 1931.

Arthur, John Preston. *Western North Carolina: A History from 1730 to 1913.* Raleigh, N.C.: Edwards and Broughton, 1914.

Ayers, Edward L. *Vengeance and Justice: Crime and Punishment in the Nineteenth-Century American South.* New York: Oxford Univ. Press, 1984.

Bailey, N. Louise; Mary L. Morgan; and Carolyn Taylor. *Biographical Directory of the South Carolina Senate, 1776–1985.* 2 vols. Columbia: Univ. of South Carolina Press, 1986.

Barclay, R. E. *Ducktown Back in Raht's Time.* Chapel Hill: Univ. of North Carolina Press, 1946.

Barnes, Gilbert H. *The Antislavery Impulse, 1830–1844.* New York: D. Appleton-Century Company, 1933.

Bateman, Fred, and Thomas Weiss. *A Deplorable Scarcity: The Failure of*

Industrialization in the Slave Economy. Chapel Hill: Univ. of North Carolina Press, 1981.

Beck, Hari von. *Chronicles of the Peck Family.* Jefferson City, Tenn.: Privately printed, 1956.

Bell, Getha Gina. *The Bells in U.S.A. and Allied Families, 1650–1977.* Buford, Ga.: Privately printed, 1977.

Bender, Thomas, ed. *The Antislavery Debate: Capitalism and Abolitionism as a Problem in Historical Interpretation.* Berkeley: Univ. of California Press, 1992.

Bennett, Lerone. *Pioneers in Protest.* Chicago: Johnson Publishing Co., 1968.

Bergeron, Paul H. *Antebellum Politics in Tennessee.* Lexington: Univ. Press of Kentucky, 1982.

Berlin, Ira. *Slaves Without Masters: The Free Negro in the Antebellum South.* New York: Random House, 1974.

Biographical Directory of the American Congress, 1774–1971. Washington, D.C.: U.S. Government Printing Office, 1971.

Birney, William. *James G. Birney and His Times.* New York: Appleton, 1890.

Blassingame, John W. *The Slave Community: Plantation Life in the Antebellum South.* New York: Oxford Univ. Press, 1972.

Blassingame, John W., and Mae G. Henderson. *Antislavery Newspapers and Periodicals.* 5 vols. Boston: G. K. Hall and Co., 1980.

Bodenhamer, David J., and James W. Ely, Jr., eds. *Ambivalent Legacy: A Legal History of the South.* Jackson: Univ. Press of Mississippi, 1984.

Boles, John B., ed. *Masters and Slaves in the House of the Lord: Race and Religion in the American South, 1740–1870.* Lexington: Univ. Press of Kentucky, 1988.

Boles, John B. *The Great Revival, 1787–1805.* Lexington: Univ. Press of Kentucky, 1972.

Bowen, David Warren. *Andrew Johnson and the Negro.* Knoxville: Univ. of Tennessee Press, 1989.

Briscoe, W. Russell, and Katherine Boies Buehler. *Her Walls Before Thee Stand: History of the Second Presbyterian Church, 1818–1968.* Knoxville, Tenn.: Privately printed, 1968.

Broyles, Bettye J. *Rhea County, Tennessee, Census, Marriage, and Tax Records, 1850–1900.* Rhea County, Tenn.: Privately printed, 1982.

Bruce, Dickson D. *Violence and Culture in the Antebellum South.* Austin: Univ. of Texas Press, 1979.

Burnett, James J. *Sketches of Tennessee's Pioneer Baptist Preachers.* Nashville: Marshall and Bruce, 1919.

Burns, Inez E. *History of Blount County, Tennessee, from War Trail to Landing Strip, 1795–1955*. Nashville: Tennessee Historical Commission, 1957.

Caldwell, Joshua W. *A Memorial Volume Containing His Biography, Writings, and Addresses: Prepared and Edited by a Committee of the Irving Club of Knoxville, Tennessee.* Nashville: Brandon Printing Co., 1909.

———. *Sketches of the Bench and Bar of Tennessee*. Knoxville: Ogden Brothers and Co., 1898.

———. *Studies in the Constitutional History of Tennessee*. Cincinnati, Ohio: Robert Clarke Co., 1907.

Campbell, Mary Emily Robertson. *The Attitude of Tennesseans Toward the Union, 1847–1861*. New York: Vantage Press, 1961.

Cheney, John L., Jr. *North Carolina Government, 1585–1979: A Narrative and Statistical History*. Raleigh: North Carolina Department of the Secretary of State, 1981.

Cimprich, John. *Slavery's End in Tennessee, 1861–1865*. Tuscaloosa: Univ. of Alabama Press, 1985.

Coleman, J. Winston, Jr. *Slavery Times in Kentucky*. Chapel Hill: Univ. of North Carolina Press, 1940.

Conrad, Alfred H., and John R. Meyer. *The Economics of Slavery and Other Studies in Econometric History*. Chicago: Aldine, 1964.

Cooper, William J., Jr. *Liberty and Slavery: Southern Politics to 1860*. New York: Alfred A. Knopf, 1983.

Corgan, James X., ed. *The Geological Sciences in the Antebellum South*. Tuscaloosa: Univ. of Alabama Press, 1982.

Coulter, E. Merton. *William G. Brownlow: Fighting Parson of the Southern Highlands*. Chapel Hill: Univ. of North Carolina Press, 1937.

Council, R. Bruce; Nicholas Honerkamp; and M. Elizabeth Will. *Industry and Technology in Antebellum Tennessee: The Archaeology of Bluff Furnace*. Knoxville: Univ. of Tennessee Press, 1992.

Cover, Robert M. *Justice Accused: Antislavery and the Judicial Process*. New Haven, Conn.: Yale Univ. Press, 1975.

Crofts, Daniel W. *Reluctant Confederates: Upper South Unionists in the Secession Crisis*. Chapel Hill: Univ. of North Carolina Press, 1989.

Cross, Whitney R. *The Burned-Over District: The Social and Intellectual History of Enthusiastic Religion in Western New York, 1800–1850*. Ithaca, N.Y.: Cornell Univ. Press, 1950.

Current, Richard N. *Northernizing the South*. Athens: Univ. of Georgia Press, 1983.

Cyclopedia of Eminent and Representative Men of the Carolinas of the Nineteenth Century. 2 vols. Madison, Wis.: Brant and Fuller, 1892.

David, Paul A., et. al. *Reckoning with Slavery: A Critical Study in the Quantitative History of American Negro Slavery.* New York: Oxford Univ. Press, 1976.

Davis, David Brion. *The Problem of Slavery in the Age of Revolution, 1770–1823.* Ithaca, N.Y.: Cornell Univ. Press, 1975.

———. *The Problem of Slavery in Western Culture.* Ithaca, N.Y.: Cornell Univ. Press, 1966.

———. *The Slave Power Conspiracy and the Paranoid Style.* Baton Rouge: Louisiana State Univ. Press, 1969.

Davis, Hugh. *Joshua Leavitt: Evangelical Abolitionist.* Baton Rouge: Louisiana State Univ. Press, 1990.

Dawson, Aurelia Cate. *Our East Tennessee Kinsmen: Cate, Henry, and Related Families.* Seaford, Del.: Privately printed, 1962.

Degler, Carl N. *The Other South: Southern Dissenters in the Nineteenth Century.* New York: Harper and Row, 1974.

Dillon, Merton L. *The Abolitionists: The Growth of a Dissenting Minority.* DeKalb: Northern Illinois Univ. Press, 1974.

———. *Benjamin Lundy and the Struggle for Negro Freedom.* Urbana: Univ. of Illinois Press, 1966.

———. *Elijah P. Lovejoy, Abolitionist Editor.* Urbana: Univ. of Illinois Press, 1961.

———. *Slavery Attacked: Southern Slaves and Their Allies, 1619–1865.* Baton Rouge: Louisiana State Univ. Press, 1990.

Duberman, Martin B., ed. *The Antislavery Vanguard: New Essays on the Abolitionists.* Princeton, N.J.: Princeton Univ. Press, 1965.

Dumond, Dwight L. *Antislavery: The Crusade for Freedom in America.* Ann Arbor: Univ. of Michigan Press, 1961.

———. *Antislavery Origins of the Civil War in the United States.* Ann Arbor: Univ. of Michigan Press, 1939.

Dunn, Durwood. *Cades Cove: The Life and Death of a Southern Appalachian Community, 1818–1937.* Knoxville: Univ. of Tennessee Press, 1988.

Eaton, Clement. *A History of the Southern Confederacy.* New York: Macmillan, 1954.

Eaton, Clement. *Freedom of Thought in the Old South.* New York: Peter Smith, 1951.

Elkins, Stanley M. *Slavery: A Problem in American Institutional Life.* Chicago: Univ. of Chicago Press, 1959.

Eller, Ronald D. *Miners, Millhands, and Mountaineers: Industrialization of the Appalachian South, 1880–1930.* Knoxville: Univ. of Tennessee Press, 1982.

Fields, Barbara Jeanne. *Slavery and Freedom on the Middle Ground: Maryland During the Nineteenth Century.* New Haven, Conn.: Yale Univ. Press, 1985.

Filler, Louis. *The Crusade Against Slavery, 1830–1860.* New York: Harper, 1960.

Fink, Paul M. *Jonesborough: The First Century of Tennessee's First Town, 1776–1876.* Johnson City, Tenn.: Overmountain Press, 1972.

Fladeland, Betty. *James Gillespie Birney: Slaveholder to Abolitionist.* Ithaca, N.Y.: Cornell Univ. Press, 1955.

Fogel, Robert William. *Without Consent or Contract: The Rise and Fall of American Slavery.* New York: W. W. Norton, 1989.

Fogel, Robert William, and Stanley L. Engerman. *Time on the Cross: The Economics of American Negro Slavery.* Boston: Little, Brown, 1974.

Folmsbee, Stanley J. *Sectionalism and Internal Improvements in Tennessee, 1796–1845.* Knoxville: East Tennessee Historical Society, 1939.

Foner, Eric. *Politics and Ideology in the Age of the Civil War.* New York: Oxford Univ. Press, 1980.

Foner, Philip S. *Business and Slavery: The New York Merchants and the Irrepressible Conflict.* Chapel Hill: Univ. of North Carolina Press, 1941.

Ford, Lacy K., Jr. *Origins of Southern Radicalism: The South Carolina Upcountry, 1800–1860.* New York: Oxford Univ. Press, 1988.

Foster, Charles I. *An Errand of Mercy: The Evangelical United Front, 1790–1837.* Chapel Hill: Univ. of North Carolina Press, 1960.

Fox, Early Lee. *The American Colonization Society, 1817–1840.* Baltimore, Md.: Johns Hopkins Univ. Press, 1919.

Freehling, William W. *The Road to Disunion.* Vol. 1: *Secessionists at Bay, 1776–1854.* New York: Oxford Univ. Press, 1990.

Friedman, Lawrence J. *Gregarious Saints: Self and Community in American Abolitionism, 1830–1870.* Cambridge, England: Cambridge Univ. Press, 1982.

Friedman, Lawrence M. *A History of American Law.* New York: Simon and Schuster, 1973.

Frothingham, Octavius Brooks. *Gerrit Smith: A Biography.* New York: G. P. Putnam's Sons, 1878.

Genovese, Eugene D. *The Political Economy of Slavery: Studies in the Economy and Society of the Slave South.* New York: Pantheon, 1965.

———. *Roll, Jordan, Roll: The World the Slaves Made.* New York: Pantheon, 1974.

———. *The Slaveholders' Dilemma: Freedom and Progress in Southern Conservative Thought, 1820–1860.* Columbia: Univ. of South Carolina Press, 1992.

Gerteis, Louis S. *Morality and Utility in American Antislavery Reform.* Chapel Hill: Univ. of North Carolina Press, 1987.

Goen, C. C. *Broken Churches, Broken Nation: Denominational Schisms and the Coming of the American Civil War.* Macon, Ga.: Mercer Univ. Press, 1985.

Goodheart, Lawrence B. *Abolitionist, Actuary, Atheist: Elizur Wright and the Reform Impulse.* Kent, Ohio: Kent State Univ. Press, 1990.

Gordon, Donald. *The Diary of Ellen Birdseye Wheaton.* Boston: Privately printed, 1923.

Green, Fletcher M. *The Role of the Yankee in the Old South.* Athens, Ohio: Univ. of Georgia Press, 1972.

Green, John W. *Lives of the Judges of the Supreme Court of Tennessee, 1796–1947.* Knoxville: Archer and Smith, 1947.

Greene, Mott T. *Geology in the Nineteenth Century: Changing Views of a Changing World.* Ithaca, N.Y.: Cornell Univ. Press, 1982.

Gutman, Herbert G. *The Black Family in Slavery and Freedom, 1750–1925.* New York: Pantheon, 1976.

———. *Slavery and the Numbers Game: A Critique of* Time on the Cross. Urbana: Univ. of Illinois Press, 1975.

Hahn, Steven, and Jonathan Prude, eds. *The Countryside in the Age of Capitalist Transformation: Essays in the Social History of Rural America.* Chapel Hill: Univ. of North Carolina Press, 1985.

Hamer, Philip M., ed. *Tennessee: A History, 1673–1932.* 4 vols. New York: American Historical Society, 1933.

Harlow, Ralph Volney. *Gerrit Smith: Philanthropist and Reformer.* New York: Henry Holt, 1939.

Harrold, Stanley. *The Abolitionists and the South, 1831–1861.* Lexington: Univ. Press of Kentucky, 1995.

———. *Gamaliel Bailey and Antislavery Union.* Kent, Ohio: Kent State Univ. Press, 1986.

Hawkins, Hugh. *The Abolitionists: Immediatism and the Question of Means.* Boston: Heath, 1964.

Haywood, John. *The Civil and Political History of the State of Tennessee from Its Earliest Settlement Up to the Year 1796, Including the Boundaries of the State.* Knoxville: Heiskell and Brown, 1823.

Henderson, W. A. *Life and Character of Judge McKinney: A Paper Read Before the Bar Association of Tennessee, Thursday, July 3rd, 1884.* Nashville: Privately printed, 1884.

Hesseltine, William B., ed. *Dr. J. G. M. Ramsey: Autobiography and Letters.* Nashville: Tennessee Historical Commission, 1954.

History of Tennessee, Containing Historical and Biographical Sketches of Thirty East Tennessee Counties. Chicago and Nashville: Goodspeed Publishing Co., 1887; reprinted Greenville, S.C.: Southern Historical Press, 1991.

Horine, Emmet Field. *Daniel Drake, 1785–1852: Pioneer Physician of the Midwest.* Philadelphia: Univ. of Pennsylvania Press, 1961.

Hoss, Elijah Embree. *Elihu Embree: Abolitionist.* Nashville: Univ. Press Co., 1897.

Howard, Victor B. *Conscience and Slavery: The Evangelistic Calvinist Domestic Missions, 1837–1861.* Kent, Ohio: Kent State Univ. Press, 1990.

Howe, Daniel Walker. *The Political Culture of the American Whigs.* Chicago: Univ. of Chicago Press, 1979.

Howington, Arthur F. *What Sayeth the Law: The Treatment of Slaves and Free Blacks in the State and Local Courts of Tennessee.* New York: Garland, 1986.

Humes, Thomas William. *The Loyal Mountaineers of Tennessee.* Knoxville: Ogden Brothers and Co., 1888.

Humphrey, Steve. *"That D——d Brownlow"*... Boone, N.C.: Appalachian Consortium Press, 1978.

Inscoe, John C. *Mountain Masters, Slavery, and the Sectional Crisis in Western North Carolina.* Knoxville: Univ. of Tennessee Press, 1989.

Jacoway, Elizabeth; Dan T. Carter; Lester C. Lamon; and Robert C. McMath, Jr., eds. *The Adaptable South: Essays in Honor of George Brown Tindall.* Baton Rouge: Louisiana State Univ. Press, 1991.

Jennings, Thelma. *The Nashville Convention: Southern Movement for Unity, 1848–1850.* Memphis: Memphis State Univ. Press, 1980.

Jones, Howard. *Mutiny on the "Amistad": The Saga of a Slave Revolt and Its Impact on American Abolition, Law, and Diplomacy.* New York: Oxford Univ. Press, 1986.

Ketring, Ruth Anna. *Charles Osborn in the Anti-Slavery Movement.* Columbus: Ohio State Archaeological and Historical Society, 1937.

Kolchin, Peter. *American Slavery, 1619–1877.* New York: Hill and Wang, 1993.

Konkle, Burton Alva. *John Motley Morehead and the Development of North Carolina, 1796–1866.* Philadelphia: William J. Campbell, 1922.

Kraditor, Aileen S. *Means and Ends in American Abolitionism: Garrison and His Critics on Strategy and Tactics, 1834–1850.* New York: Pantheon, 1967.

Kraut, Alan M., ed. *Crusaders and Compromisers: Essays on the Relationship of the Antislavery Struggle to the Antebellum Party System.* Westport, Conn.: Greenwood, 1983.

Kulikoff, Allan. *The Agrarian Origins of American Capitalism.* Charlottesville: Univ. of Virginia Press, 1992.

Lamon, Lester C. *Blacks in Tennessee, 1791–1970.* Knoxville: Univ. of Tennessee Press, 1981.
Levine, Lawrence W. *Black Culture and Black Consciousness: Afro-American Folk Thought from Slavery to Freedom.* New York: Oxford Univ. Press, 1977.
Locke, Mary Stoughton. *Anti-Slavery in America from the Introduction of African Slaves to the Prohibition of the Slave Trade, 1619–1808.* Gloucester, Mass.: Peter Smith, 1901.
Lutz, Alma. *Crusade for Freedom: Women of the Antislavery Movement.* Boston: Beacon Press, 1968.
Mabee, Carleton. *Black Freedom: The Nonviolent Abolitionists from 1830 through the Civil War.* London: Macmillan, 1970.
Magdol, Edward. *The Antislavery Rank and File: A Social Profile of the Abolitionists' Constituency.* Westport, Conn.: Greenwood, 1986.
———. *Owen Lovejoy: Abolitionist in Congress.* New Brunswick, N.J.: Rutgers Univ. Press, 1967.
Martin, Isaac Patton. *Methodism in Holston.* Knoxville, Tenn.: Methodist Historical Society of the Holston Conference, 1945.
Mathews, Donald G. *Religion in the Old South.* Chicago: Univ. of Chicago Press, 1977.
———. *Slavery and Methodism: A Chapter in American Morality, 1780–1845.* Princeton, N.J.: Princeton Univ. Press, 1965.
Merrit, Frank. *Early History of Carter County, 1760–1861.* Knoxville: East Tennessee Historical Society, 1950.
McBride, Robert M., and Dan M. Robison, eds. *Biographical Directory of the Tennessee General Assembly, 1796–1861.* Vol. 1. Nashville: Tennessee Historical Commission, 1975.
McFerrin, John Berry. *History of Methodism in Tennessee.* 3 vols. Nashville: Southern Methodist Publishing House, 1869–73.
McLoughlin, William G. *Champions of the Cherokees: Evan and John B. Jones.* Princeton, N.J.: Princeton Univ. Press, 1990.
———. *Cherokees and Missionaries, 1789–1839.* New Haven, Conn.: Yale Univ. Press, 1984.
McKinney, Gordon B. *Southern Mountain Republicans, 1865–1900: Politics and the Appalachian Community.* Chapel Hill: Univ. of North Carolina Press, 1978.
McKivigan, John R. *The War Against Proslavery Religion: Abolitionism and the Northern Churches, 1830–1865.* Ithaca, N.Y.: Cornell Univ. Press, 1984.
McTeer, Will A. *History of New Providence Presbyterian Church, Maryville, Tennessee, 1786–1921.* Maryville, Tenn.: New Providence Church, 1921.

Mooney, Chase C. *Slavery in Tennessee*. Bloomington: Indiana Univ. Press, 1957.
Moore, Winfred B., Jr., and Joseph F. Tripp, eds. *Looking South: Chapters in the Story of an American Region*. Westport, Conn.: Greenwood, 1989.
Netherland, Frank. *A History of the Ross Silk Factory and Other Events of Rotherwood, Tennessee*. Rogersville, Tenn.: East Tennessee Printing Co., 1988.
Noe, Kenneth W. *Southwest Virginia's Railroad: Modernization and the Sectional Crisis*. Urbana: Univ. of Illinois Press, 1994.
Nye, Russel B. *William Lloyd Garrison and the Humanitarian Reformers*. Boston: Little, Brown, 1955.
Oakes, James. *Slavery and Freedom: An Interpretation of the Old South*. New York: Alfred A. Knopf, 1990.
O'Dell, Ruth Webb. *Over the Misty Blue Hills: The Story of Cocke County, Tennessee*. Newport, Tenn.: Privately printed, 1951.
Orcutt, Samuel. *A History of the Old Town of Stratford and the City of Bridgeport, Connecticut*. 2 vols. New Haven, Conn.: Press of Tuttle, Morehouse and Taylor, 1886.
Patterson, Caleb P. *The Negro in Tennessee, 1790–1865: A Study in Southern Politics*. Austin: Univ. of Texas Press, 1922.
Patterson, Orlando. *Slavery and Social Death: A Comparative Study*. Cambridge, Mass.: Harvard Univ. Press, 1982.
Pease, Jane H., and William H. Pease. *Bound with Them in Chains: A Biographical History of the Antislavery Movement*. Westport, Conn.: Greenwood, 1972.
Perdue, Theda. *Slavery and the Evolution of Cherokee Society, 1540–1866*. Knoxville: Univ. of Tennessee Press, 1979.
Perry, Lewis. *Radical Abolitionism: Anarchy and the Government of God in Antislavery Thought*. Ithaca, N.Y.: Cornell Univ. Press, 1973.
Perry, Lewis, and Michael Fellman, eds. *Antislavery Reconsidered: New Perspectives on the Abolitionists*. Baton Rouge: Louisiana State Univ. Press, 1979.
Phillips, Ulrich Bonnell. *American Negro Slavery: A Survey of the Supply, Employment and Control of Negro Labor as Determined by the Plantation Regime*. New York: D. Appleton, 1918.
Powell, William S., ed. *Dictionary of North Carolina Biography*. 5 vols. Chapel Hill: Univ. of North Carolina Press, 1979–94.
Price, Richard N. *Holston Methodism from Its Origin to the Present Time*. 5 vols. Nashville: Methodist Publishing House, 1903–13.

Reynolds, Emily Bellinger, and Joan Reynolds Faunt. *Biographical Directory of the Senate of South Carolina, 1776–1964.* Columbia: South Carolina Archives Department, 1964.

Riley, Sam G. *Index to Southern Periodicals.* Westport, Conn.: Greenwood, 1986.

———. *Magazines of the American South.* Westport, Conn.: Greenwood, 1986.

Roberts, George Braden. *Genealogy of Joseph Peck and Some Related Families.* Washington, D.C.: Privately printed, 1955.

Ross, Charles C., ed. *Story of Rotherwood, from the Autobiography of Rev. Frederick A. Ross, D.D.* Knoxville: Bean, Warters, 1923.

Rothrock, Mary U., ed. *The French Broad–Holston Country: A History of Knox County, Tennessee.* Knoxville: East Tennessee Historical Society, 1946.

Ruchames, Louis. *The Abolitionists: A Collection of Their Writings.* New York: Putnam's, 1963.

Savage, W. Sherman. *The Controversy over the Distribution of Abolition Literature, 1830–1860.* New York: Negro Univ. Press, 1938.

Sellers, Charles. *The Market Revolution: Jacksonian America, 1815–1846.* New York: Oxford Univ. Press, 1991.

Sellers, James Benson. *Slavery in Alabama.* University, Ala.: Univ. of Alabama Press, 1950.

Shapiro, Henry D. *Appalachia on Our Mind: The Southern Mountains and Mountaineers in the American Consciousness, 1870–1920.* Chapel Hill: Univ. of North Carolina Press, 1978.

Shore, Laurence. *Southern Capitalists: The Ideological Leadership of an Elite, 1832–1885.* Chapel Hill: Univ. of North Carolina Press, 1986.

Siebert, Wilbur H. *The Underground Railroad from Slavery to Freedom.* New York: Macmillan, 1898.

Smith, Timothy L. *Revivalism and Social Reform in Mid-Nineteenth Century America.* New York and Nashville: Abingdon Press, 1957.

Sonderlund, Jean R. *Quakers and Slavery: A Divided Spirit.* Princeton, N.J.: Princeton Univ. Press, 1985.

Sorin, Gerald. *Abolitionism: A New Perspective.* New York: Praeger, 1972.

———. *The New York Abolitionists: A Case Study of Political Radicalism.* Westport, Conn.: Greenwood, 1971.

Stampp, Kenneth M. *The Peculiar Institution: Slavery in the Ante-Bellum South.* New York: Knopf, 1956.

Stange, Douglas C. *Patterns of Antislavery among American Unitarians, 1831–1860.* Rutherford, N.J.: Fairleigh Dickinson Univ. Press, 1977.

Starr, Edward C. *A History of Cornwall, Connecticut: A Typical New England Town.* New Haven, Conn.: Tuttle, Morehouse and Taylor, 1926.

Stephenson, Wendell Holmes. *Isaac Franklin: Slave Trader and Planter of the Old South.* Baton Rouge: Louisiana State Univ. Press, 1938.

Stewart, James Brewer. *Holy Warriors: The Abolitionists and American Slavery.* New York: Hill and Wang, 1976.

———. *Wendell Phillips: Liberty's Hero.* Baton Rouge: Louisiana Univ. Press, 1986.

———. *William Lloyd Garrison and the Challenge of Emancipation.* Arlington Heights, Ill.: Harlan Davidson, 1992.

Tappan, Lewis. *The Life of Arthur Tappan.* Cambridge, Mass.: Riverside Press, 1870.

Taylor, Alrutheus Ambush. *The Negro in Tennessee, 1865–1880.* Washington, D.C.: Associated Publishers, 1941.

Taylor, Rosser H. *Ante-Bellum South Carolina: A Social and Cultural History.* Chapel Hill: Univ. of North Carolina Press, 1942.

Temple, Oliver P. *East Tennessee and the Civil War.* Cincinnati, Ohio: Robert Clarke Co., 1899.

———. *Notable Men of Tennessee, from 1833 to 1875: Their Times and Their Contemporaries.* New York: Cosmopolitan Press, 1912.

Thomas, Benjamin P. *Theodore Weld, Crusader for Freedom.* New Brunswick, N.J.: Rutgers Univ. Press, 1950.

Trefousse, Hans. *Andrew Johnson: A Biography.* New York and London: W. W. Norton, 1989.

Tushnet, Mark V. *The American Law of Slavery, 1810–1860: Considerations of Humanity and Interest.* Princeton, N.J.: Princeton Univ. Press, 1981.

Tyler, Alice Felt. *Freedom's Ferment: Phases of American Social History from the Colonial Period to the Outbreak of the Civil War.* Minneapolis: Univ. of Minnesota Press, 1944.

Van Deusen, Glyndon G. *William Henry Seward.* New York: Oxford Univ. Press, 1967.

Vandiver, Frank E. *Ploughshares into Swords: Josiah Gorgas and the Confederate Ordinance.* Austin: Univ. of Texas Press, 1952.

Wade, Richard C. *The Urban Frontier: Pioneer Life in Early Pittsburgh, Cincinnati, Lexington, Louisville, and St. Louis.* Chicago: Univ. of Chicago Press, 1959.

Walker, Peter F. *Moral Choices: Memory, Desire, and Imagination in Nineteenth-Century American Abolitionism.* Baton Rouge: Louisiana State Univ. Press, 1978.

Walker, Robert Sparks. *Torchlights to the Cherokees: The Brainerd Mission.* New York: Macmillan, 1931.
Walters, Ronald G. *The Antislavery Appeal: American Abolitionism after 1830.* Baltimore, Md.: Johns Hopkins Univ. Press, 1976.
Warner, Ezra J. *Generals in Gray: Lives of the Confederate Commanders.* Baton Rouge: Louisiana State Univ. Press, 1959.
Watson, Alan. *Slave Law in the Americas.* Athens: Univ. of Georgia Press, 1989.
Weeks, Stephen B. *Southern Quakers and Slavery: A Study in Institutional History.* Baltimore, Md.: Johns Hopkins Univ. Press, 1896.
Williams, David. *The Georgia Gold Rush: Twenty-Niners, Cherokees, and Gold Fever.* Columbia: Univ. of South Carolina Press, 1993.
Williams, Eric. *Capitalism and Slavery.* Chapel Hill: Univ. of North Carolina Press, 1944.
Williams, Samuel Cole. *History of the Lost State of Franklin.* Johnson City, Tenn.: Watauga Press, 1924.
Wilson, Charles Reagan, ed. *Religion in the South.* Jackson: Univ. Press of Mississippi, 1985.
Wilson, Samuel Tyndale. *A Century of Maryville College, 1819–1919: A Story of Altruism.* Maryville, Tenn.: Maryville College, 1919.
———. *Isaac Anderson, Founder and First President of Maryville College: A Memorial Sketch.* Maryville, Tenn.: Privately printed, 1932.
Wood, Mayme Parrott. *Drifting Down Holston River Way, 1756–1966.* Maryville, Tenn.: Privately printed, 1966.
———. *Hitch Hiking along the Holston River, 1792–1962.* Gatlinburg, Tenn.: Brazos Printing Co., 1964.
Woodward, C. Vann, ed. *Mary Chesnut's Civil War.* New Haven, Conn.: Yale Univ. Press, 1981.
Wooster, Ralph A. *The Secession Conventions of the South.* Princeton, N.J.: Princeton Univ. Press, 1962.
Wright, Gavin. *The Political Economy of the Cotton South: Households, Markets, and Wealth in the Nineteenth Century.* New York: W. W. Norton, 1978.
Wyatt-Brown, Bertram. *Lewis Tappan and the Evangelical War Against Slavery.* Cleveland, Ohio: Press of Case Western Reserve Univ., 1969.
———. *Southern Honor: Ethics and Behavior in the Old South.* New York: Oxford Univ. Press, 1982.

B. Articles

Ahern, L. R., Jr., and R. F. Hunt, Jr. "The Boatyard Store, 1814–1825." *Tennessee Historical Quarterly* 14 (Sept. 1955): 257–77.

Conklin, Forrest. "Parson Brownlow Joins the Sons of Temperance," pt. 1. *Tennessee Historical Quarterly* 39 (Summer 1980): 178–94.

———. "Parson Brownlow—Temperance Advocate," pt. 2. *Tennessee Historical Quarterly* 39 (Fall 1980): 292–309.

Conklin, Forrest, and John W. Wittig. "Religious Warfare in the Southern Highlands: Brownlow versus Ross." *Journal of East Tennessee History* 63 (1991): 33–50.

Creekmore, Pollyanna, comp. "Early East Tennessee Taxpayers: XIII. Cocke County, 1839." *East Tennessee Historical Society's Publications* 37 (1965): 122–51.

Dillon, Merton L. "The Abolitionists: A Decade of Historiography, 1959–1969." *Journal of Southern History* 35 (Nov. 1969): 500–522.

———. "Three Southern Antislavery Editors: The Myth of the Southern Antislavery Movement." *East Tennessee Historical Society's Publications* 42 (1970): 47–56.

Fede, Andrew. "Legitimized Violent Slave Abuse in the American South, 1619–1865: A Case Study of Law and Social Change in Six Southern States." *American Journal of Legal History* 29 (Apr. 1985): 93–150.

———. "Toward a Solution of the Slave Law Dilemma: A Critique of Tushnet's *The American Law of Slavery*." *Law and History Review* 2 (Fall 1984): 301–20.

Fink, Paul M. "The Bumpass Cove Mines and Embreeville." *East Tennessee Historical Society's Publications* 16 (1944): 48–64.

Finnie, Gordon E. "The Antislavery Movement in the Upper South Before 1840." *Journal of Southern History* 35 (Aug. 1969): 319–42.

Flanigan, Daniel J. "Criminal Procedure in Slave Trials in the Antebellum South." *Journal of Southern History* 40 (Nov. 1974): 537–64.

Folmsbee, Stanley J. "Blount College and East Tennessee College, 1794–1840: The First Predecessors of the University of Tennessee." *East Tennessee Historical Society's Publications* 17 (1945): 22–50.

Foster, Gaines M. "Guilt Over Slavery: A Historiographical Analysis." *Journal of Southern History* 56 (Nov. 1990): 665–94.

Friedman, Lawrence J. "The Gerrit Smith Circle: Abolitionism in the Burned-Over District." *Civil War History* 26 (Mar. 1980): 18–38.

Galpin, W. Freeman, ed. "Letters of an East Tennessee Abolitionist." *East Tennessee Historical Society's Publications* 3 (1931): 134–49.

Glenn, L. C. "Gerald Troost." *American Geologist* 35 (Feb. 1905): 72–94.

Goodman, Paul. "The Manual Labor Movement and the Origins of Abolitionism." *Journal of the Early Republic* 13 (Fall 1993): 355–88.

Grimm, Paul R. "The Rev. John Rankin, Early Abolitionist." *Ohio State Archaeological and Historical Quarterly* 46 (1937): 215–56.

Harrold, Stanley. "Violence and Nonviolence in Kentucky Abolitionism." *Journal of Southern History* 57 (Feb. 1991): 15–38.

Hoss, Elijah Embree. "Elihu Embree, Abolitionist." *American Historical Magazine* 2 (1897): 113–38.

Howington, Arthur F. "'Not in the Condition of a Horse or an Ox': *Ford v. Ford*, the Law of Testamentary Manumission, and the Tennessee Courts' Recognition of Slave Humanity." *Tennessee Historical Quarterly* 34 (Fall 1975): 249–63.

———. "'A Property of Special and Peculiar Value': The Tennessee Supreme Court and the Law of Manumission." *Tennessee Historical Quarterly* 44 (Fall 1985): 302–17.

Hunt, Raymond F., Jr. "The Pactolus Ironworks." *Tennessee Historical Quarterly* 25 (Summer 1966): 176–96.

Huston, James L. "The Experiential Basis of the Northern Antislavery Impulse." *Journal of Southern History* 56 (Nov. 1990): 609–40.

Imes, William Lloyd. "The Legal Status of Free Negroes and Slaves in Tennessee." *Journal of Negro History* 4 (1919): 254–72.

Inscoe, John C. "Olmsted in Appalachia: A Connecticut Yankee Encounters Slavery and Racism in the Southern Highlands." *Slavery and Abolition* 9 (Sept. 1988): 171–82.

Kolchin, Peter. "More *Time on the Cross*? An Evaluation of Robert William Fogel's *Without Consent or Contract*." *Journal of Southern History* 58 (Aug. 1992): 491–502.

Lewit, Robert T. "Indian Missions and Antislavery Sentiment: A Conflict of Evangelical and Humanitarian Ideals." *Mississippi Valley Historical Review* 50 (June 1963): 39–55.

Martin, Asa Earl. "Anti-Slavery Activities of the Methodist Episcopal Church in Tennessee." *Tennessee Historical Magazine* 2 (June 1916): 98–109.

———. "The Anti-Slavery Societies of Tennessee." *Tennessee Historical Magazine* 1 (Dec. 1915): 261–81.

———. "Pioneer Anti-Slavery Press." *Mississippi Valley Historical Review* 2 (Mar. 1916): 509–28.

Mooney, Chase C. "The Question of Slavery and the Free Negro in the Tennessee Constitutional Convention of 1834." *Journal of Southern History* 12 (Nov. 1946): 487–509.

Nash, A. E. Keir. "Negro Rights, Unionism, and Greatness of the South Carolina Court of Appeals: The Extraordinary Chief Justice John Belton O'Neall." *South Carolina Law Review* 21 (1969): 141–90.

Patton, James W. "The Progress of Emancipation in Tennessee, 1796–1860." *Journal of Negro History* 17 (1932): 67–102.

Pearson, Alden B., Jr. "The Tragic Dilemma of a Border-State Moderate: The Rev. George E. Eagleton's Views on Slavery and Secession." *Tennessee Historical Quarterly* 32 (Winter 1973): 360–73.

Parks, Edd Winfield. "Zollicoffer: Southern Whig." *Tennessee Historical Quarterly* 11 (Dec. 1952): 346–55.

Queener, Verton M. "East Tennessee Sentiment and the Secession Movement, November 1860–June 1861." *East Tennessee Historical Society's Publications* 20 (1948): 59–83.

Rooker, Henry Grady. "A Sketch of the Life and Work of Dr. Gerard Troost." *Tennessee Historical Magazine*, 2d ser., 3 (1935 for 1933): 3–19.

Sheeler, J. Reuben. "The Development of Unionism in East Tennessee, 1860–1866." *Journal of Negro History* 29 (Apr. 1944): 166–203.

Stamper, James C. "Felix K. Zollicoffer: Tennessee Editor and Politician." *Tennessee Historical Quarterly* 28 (Winter 1969): 356–76.

Stewart, James Brewer. "Evangelicalism and the Radical Strain in Southern Antislavery Thought During the 1820s." *Journal of Southern History* 39 (Aug. 1973): 379–96.

Swint, Henry Lee. "Ezekiel Birdseye and the Free State of Frankland." *Tennessee Historical Quarterly* 3 (Sept. 1944): 226–36.

———. "Higher Education in the Tennessee-Kentucky Region a Century Ago." *Tennessee Historical Quarterly* 2 (July 1943): 129–43.

Trabue, Charles C. "The Voluntary Emancipation of Slaves in Tennessee as Reflected in the State's Legislation and Judicial Decisions." *Tennessee Historical Magazine* 4 (Mar. 1918): 50–68.

Tushnet, Mark. "Approaches to the Study of the Law of Slavery." *Civil War History* 25 (Dec. 1979): 329–38.

Williams, Samuel Cole, ed. "Journal of Events (1825–1873) of David Anderson Deaderick." *East Tennessee Historical Society's Publications* 8 (1936): 121–37 and 9 (1937): 93–110.

Woodman, Harold D. "The Profitability of Slavery: A Historical Perennial." *Journal of Southern History* 29 (Aug. 1963): 303–25.

C. Theses and Dissertations

Atkins, Jonathan M. "'A Combat for Liberty': Politics and Parties in Jackson's Tennessee, 1832–1851." Ph.D. diss., Univ. of Michigan, 1991.

Bryan, Charles Faulkner. "The Civil War in East Tennessee: A Social, Political, and Economic Study." Ph.D. diss., Univ. of Tennessee, Knoxville, 1978.

Dillon, Merton L. "The Antislavery Movement in Illinois, 1809–1844." Ph.D. diss., Univ. of Michigan, 1951.

England, James Merton. "The Free Negro in Ante-Bellum Tennessee." Ph.D. diss., Vanderbilt Univ., 1941.

Finnie, Gordon E. "The Antislavery Movement in the South, 1787–1836: Its Rise and Decline and Its Contribution to Abolitionism in the West." Ph.D. diss., Duke Univ., 1962.

Groce, W. Todd. "Mountain Rebels: East Tennessee Confederates and the Civil War." Ph.D. diss., Univ. of Tennessee, Knoxville, 1992.

Henderson, Alice Hatcher. "The History of the New York State Anti-Slavery Society." Ph.D. diss., Univ. of Michigan, 1963.

Ledford, Allen James. "Methodism in Tennessee, 1783–1866." M.A. thesis, Univ. of Tennessee, Knoxville, 1941.

Moody, David Whitaker. "Legal Phases of Emancipation in Tennessee." M.A. thesis, George Peabody College for Teachers, Nashville, 1934.

Nave, Robert T. "A History of the Iron Industry in Carter County to 1860." M.A. thesis, East Tennessee State Univ., 1953.

Purifoy, Lewis McCarroll, Jr. "The Methodist Episcopal Church, South, and Slavery, 1844–1865." Ph.D. diss., Univ. of North Carolina, Chapel Hill, 1965.

Shay, John Michael. "The Antislavery Movement in North Carolina." Ph.D. diss., Princeton Univ., 1971.

Tallant, Harold Donald. "The Slavery Controversy in Kentucky, 1829–1859." Ph.D. diss., Duke Univ., 1986.

Van Dyke, Roger R. "The Free Negro in Tennessee." Ph.D. diss., Florida State Univ., 1972.

Index

abolitionism: EB's gradual conversion to, 32; as form of extremism, ix, 22; and gradualism, 11, 12, 16, 41, 251; linked with entrepreneurial capitalism, xi, 44–46, 47, 54–55, 58–61, 65; and manual labor movement, 56, 113n, 174–75, 180n; as moral obligation, 200–201; *see also* abolitionists; antislavery movement

abolitionists: attacks on, 6, 19, 35; attempts by, to purchase slaves, 33, 149, 152, 262; clergy as, 39, 186; in East Tenn., 46–47, 91n, 144, 194, 199, 207; historiography, 7, 67–68, 71; influence of, in South, 102n, 136, 137, 154, 169, 236, 254, 255, 257; motives of, 45, 47, 48, 55, 56, 68; as political activists, 13–14, 144, 155, 255; southern attitudes toward, 29, 68–69, 175, 183–84, 235, 268; *see also* abolitionism; antislavery movement

Adams, John Quincy, 172, 174n, 213

African Americans. *See* blacks; free blacks; slaves

Agriculturalist, 172, 174, 184

agriculture, 172; improvements in, 193–94; in S.C., 237; in Tenn., 167, 168, 176–78, 181, 186

Alabama: droves of slaves to, 195; EB's residence in, 30–31; impunity for slaveholders in, 132; proslavery clergy in, 175, 204; treatment of slaves for theft in, 132

Albany Patriot, 259, 261n

Allan, William T., 204, 206n

Allen, Daniel, 84, 245, 246n

American & Foreign Antislavery Reporter, 189n

American Anti-Slavery Society, 6, 133n, 191n, 261n

American Colonization Society, 7, 10, 41, 160n, 246

Amistad (ship), 174n

Anderson, Alexander Outlaw, 159n

Anderson, Isaac, 6, 37, 38, 65, 109n, 160n, 180n, 190n; antislavery interest of, 11, 20, 47; death of son of, 205; educates blacks and Indians for ministry, 33–34, 46, 48, 103n, 159n; interest of, in African missions, 187, 188

Anderson, Joseph, 159n

Anderson, Thomas A., 38, 118n, 156–57, 159n

antislavery movement: changing attitudes toward, 19, 20; in East Tenn., 4–8, 11,

antislavery movement *(cont.)*
  14, 16, 17, 166, 226; influence of, on South, 144, 160, 189; literature circulated, 9–10, 16–17, 118n, 136, 154, 169, 172, 205–6, 239, 255, 268; memorials and petitions, 4–5, 8–9, 11–14, 21, 92n, 97n, 161; and northern churches, 223, 245, 247–48; publications, 5, 6, 7, 16–17, 45, 133n, 160, 164n, 189, 226–27, 238n, 239, 246, 247, 256n; Tenn. clergy involved in, 37–38, 46–47, 214; *see also* abolitionism; abolitionists
Appalachian region: impoverished by outside control, 61–62
Aptheker, Herbert, 91n
Arnold, Thomas, 21–22
Asheville, N.C., 237; description of, 151; EB visits, 37, 260, 262
Athens, Tenn.: description of, 191
Axley, James, 8

Badger, Willard, 156
banking: condition of, in East Tenn., 96n, 171, 192; depressed state of, 167, 168, 170–71; and exchange of slaves, 233–34; at premium rates, 262–63, 265
bankruptcy, 192, 218, 224, 225, 244
Baptists: and slavery, 38–39, 175–76, 184, 223
Beckley, Guy, 164n
Bell, Samuel, 183, 184n
Benson (of Cocke County): killed by slave, 83, 218
Bible: used to defend slavery, 223–24, 266
Birdsey, John, 26
Birdseye, Ebenezer, 28
Birdseye, Ezekiel: as agent for mineral leases, 62–63, 64, 87; ancestry, 26–27; attempts to purchase and free slave, 33, 81, 149, 262, 264; character of, 26–27, 35, 37, 68; as Cherokee rights defender, 39–40, 208; death of, 27, 64, 88; as delegate to Internal Improvement Convention, 18, 115n, 197, 201n, 202; as entrepreneur, 27, 37, 45, 60, 62–63, 64, 87, 114n, 263; estate of, 35, 59–60, 63–65, 116n; family of, 27, 28, 253, 256n; finances of, 63, 135, 139, 244, 259, 260–61, 269; free labor colony proposed by, 55–56, 179; as friend to blacks, 69, 79, 80, 118n, 208, 219–20, 240–41; gradual espousal of abolition, 32; as impartial observer, 42, 79, 122n, 231–32; importance of observations of, 23, 42–43, 68, 70, 78–79, 129n, 232; land holdings of, 19, 31, 54, 63, 64, 87, 116n, 138, 244, 260; mill owned by, 37, 48, 63, 87; mineral property of, 54, 60, 112n–13n; missing letters of, 106n; offers land for abolition cause, 243–44; political affiliation of, 37; property of, sold for taxes, 64; rapport with slaveholders, 29, 30, 33, 34, 35, 69, 224–25, 230; residences of, 28, 30, 31, 100n, 236; sheep raising by, 102n, 193; on southern editors, 38, 156, 203–4, 212, 221; threats against, 113n, 221; travels of, 31, 37, 151, 234–38, 260, 261, 265; will of, 32, 102n
Birdseye, Ezra, 32
Birdseye, Irene Lucinda, 31, 88, 256n
Birdseye, Lucinda Pierce, xi, 30–31, 101n, 252, 256n
Birdseye, Mary M. Stone, 31, 100n, 253, 256n
Birdseye, Nathan, 26–27
Birdseye, Victory, 28, 37, 139, 269, 270n
Birney, James G., 37, 40, 68, 158n, 164n, 196, 217; and colonization, 11; on *Creole* affair, 216n, 228n; rumored plot to murder, 31, 32, 155
Blackburn, Gideon, 48, 91n
blacks, 143, 187, 230, 249; *see also* free blacks, slaves
Blount County, Tenn.: abolitionist sentiment in, 17, 21, 39, 198–99, 205; antislavery society in, 218; secession vote in, 22; slavery debates in, 17, 189
Bogle, Robert, 189, 191n, 198, 205, 209, 214
Bolton, Ellen, 76
Bondmans Advocate, 239
Bouck, William C., 256, 256n
Bradford, James F., 17, 194, 196n

Index 297

Bradshaw, Richard, 94n
Branner, George, 170, 173n
Brazelton, William, 20, 58, 90n, 145, 170, 172n
Brown (Nashville lawyer), 162–63
Brown, John, 41
Brownlow, William G., 15, 22, 97n, 148n, 156, 159n; newspaper of, 172; as proslavery advocate, 15, 19, 20, 38, 145; and temperance movement, 38, 104n
Bulloch, James S., 173n
Buncombe County, N.C., 258, 262
Burleigh, William, 256n
Bustle (of Blount County), 227
Butler, Elizur, 176, 180n

Cahal, Terry H., 12
Caldwell, John, 19, 22, 35, 140n; antislavery advocate, 4, 14, 55–57, 166, 186; and colonization, 11, 198; on developing resources, 57–60, 60–61, 65, 114n, 268; EB's friendship with, 19, 35, 80, 87, 137, 157–58, 203; as EB's partner in mining interests, 59–60; farm of, 167, 186; financial difficulties of, 57–58, 167–68, 170–71, 172, 173n, 211, 233, 246, 248; in Florida, 198, 211, 233; horse trading by, 166–67, 170–71; prepares slaveowners' wills for emancipation, 154–55; quoted on self-sufficiency, 60–61; unionist, 21; as witness to slave abuses, 80, 209–10
Caldwell, Joshua W., 57
Calhoun, John C., 136
Calhoun, Tenn., 192, 208
Capers, Rev. (of S.C.), 136
Carter, Alfred M., 107n
Caruthers, R. L., 23
Catron, John, 122n, 123n
Catterall, Helen Tunnicliff, 78
Chaffee, Eben, 32
Chaffee, Hannah, 32
Channing, William Ellery, 55, 67, 117n–18n, 159n; pamphlet of, 157
Chaplin, William L., 238n, 261n
Charleston, S.C.: slave market in, 136–37

Charleston, Tenn.: site of Cherokee removal camp, 208
Chattanooga, Tenn., 37, 225
Chemung County, N.Y.: EB's property in, 260, 269
Cherokee Indians: EB on removal of, 39, 208, 211n–12n; educated for the ministry, 48; missionaries to, 176, 180n; as road builders, 48, 59
Christian Freeman, 256n; EB's letters in, 83, 252–56
Chunn, J., 176–77
Cincinnati, Ohio, 129, 186
Claiborne, Thomas, 215, 216n
Clark, Aaron R., 135, 140n, 150, 152, 153
Clark, L. F., 17, 95n–96n, 186–87, 190n
Clarkson, Thomas, 223, 227n, 266
Clay, Henry, 57, 254; Gerrit Smith's letter to, 136, 144, 155, 203: Gurney letters to, 154, 158n, 169, 188–89, 226
Cocke County, Tenn., 22, 44, 214; EB's land holdings in, 54, 63, 64, 116n, 138, 260; EB's mill in, 37, 48, 63, 87; EB's residence in, 100n; revival in, 223; slavery debates in, 17, 214; temperance in, 230–31, 244
colonization: of free blacks, 10–12, 33–34, 73, 93n–94n, 198; loss of confidence in, 47, 193, 231, 246; opposition to, 160n; with public funds, 10–11, 72, 251; as task of the benevolent, 14–16
Colton (of Union Court House, S.C.), 235
Confederate Ordnance Bureau, 60
Confederates: confiscation by, 64, 115n
Congress, U.S.: antislavery petitions in, 174n; *Creole* incident in, 228n
Connecticut, 194; EB's land in, 244, 260; judicial ruling on slaves in, 171, 173n
Cook, John, 226, 228n
copper mines, 53, 58–60, 192, 200, 268
corn, 264; cultivated in East Tenn., 177, 181, 186
Cornwall, Conn.: EB's home in, 27, 100n
cotton: decline of growth in East Tenn., 186, 192; depressed sales of, 211, 214, 250, 254, 266; grown in India, 214, 235, 254, 255; grown in S.C., 234–35, 236; southern dependence

cotton *(cont.)*
 on, 194, 215, 254, 255; and tariff, 214–15
Courtney (of Cocke County, Tenn.), 52, 178–79
Cowpens Furnace (S.C.), 234
Craig, John Sawyers, 47, 198, 201n, 205
Creek Path: in Cherokee territory, 187, 191n
Creole, 171, 213, 215n–16n, 217, 228n

Daby, Augustine W., 62
Davis, David, 33, 81, 154, 240, 258–59, 260, 262
Davis, Mrs. David, 262–65
Davis, Samuel, 133
Deaderick, David A., 22, 147n
Deaderick, James A., 144
Delaware, 260; slavery on wane in, 261
Denison, Charles, 133n
Dillon, Merton L., 7, 71, 106n
distilleries, 231, 240–41, 244
District of Columbia: slavery in, 161, 171–72
Divitt, Dr. (of S.C.), 130
Doak, Samuel, 5–6, 91n
Doan, John, 155, 158n
dogs: used to capture fugitives, 152–53, 210
Drake, Daniel, 129, 133n, 134
Draper (Knoxville silversmith), 183
Dresser, Amos, 16–17, 163, 165n, 215, 216n
Ducktown copper mines, 53, 58, 59–60; confiscated by Confederates, 115n; sale of, 62
dueling, 38, 145, 162–63
Dunn, Cynthia, 216n
Dunn, William W., 213, 215, 216n

East Tennessee: agriculture in, 169, 176–77, 181, 191–94; attitudes on slavery in, 11, 24, 69, 84–85, 142–43, 194, 198, 207, 224, 254, 258; banking in, 18, 96n, 167, 171; bankruptcies in, 192, 225; clergy views on slavery in, 37–39, 226; described by F. L. Olmsted, 23; dissenters from, in 1834 Constitutional Convention, 11–16; distinctiveness of, 24–25; early antislavery crusaders in, 4–8; EB's arrival in, 31, 32, 102n; economic ties with South, 19, 21, 65–66; industry in, 25, 45–46, 58–60, 61–62, 115n, 138, 234; internal improvements for, 18, 19, 115n, 201n, 202; manumission societies in, x, 4–8, 10, 17, 45, 46, 47, 90n, 137; mineral resources in, 47, 53–55, 58, 61–62, 112n–13n, 192, 200, 268; population in, 25, 255; separate statehood proposed for, ix, 17, 18–19, 21, 23, 55, 115n, 197, 198, 200, 202, 207, 239–40, 244, 250, 251, 255; slave population in, 23, 78, 99n; slavery as cause of migration from, 8, 17, 91n, 137, 194; temperance reform in, 155–56, 166, 219, 224, 230–31, 244; treatment of slaves in, 23, 80, 84–85, 86, 195, 209, 211; Union sentiments in, 21, 22, 23, 24, 270–71
Edmunds (overseer), 176, 177, 178
Elkins, Stanley, 70
Eller, Ronald D, 61–62
Elliott, Stephen, 238n
emancipation: disadvantages of, 193, 198; and gradualism, 4, 8, 11, 12, 160n, 251; laws regulating, 50–51, 71–75, 119n–20n; petitions for, 4–5, 8–9, 92n–93n, 119n; by voluntary action, 16, 20, 73, 107n, 141n, 144, 156; by wills of slaveholders, 50–51, 57, 72, 120n, 154–55, 179, 231
Emancipator (New York), 45, 47, 133n, 136, 189, 247; EB's letters in, 42, 129–33
Embree, Elihu, 3, 56, 65, 108n; antislavery publications of, 6–7, 45; author of antislavery memorial, 4–5, 21, 90n; ironworks of, 60, 107n; as slaveholder, 107n, 108n
Embree, Elijah, 45, 46, 96n
Embree, Thomas, 4
Embreeville Iron Works, 60, 62
England, James Merton, 70, 119n
Erskine, George M., 33, 46, 104n, 159n

Featherstonhaugh, George W., 23, 24

Fellenberg schools, 56, 113n, 174, 180
Fields, William, 51
Flat Rock, N.C.: planters' summer homes in, 237
Florida: financial distress in, 166–67, 170–71, 233–34; as market for slaves and horses, 166, 183
Foster, Ephraim Hubbard, 162, 165n–66n
Foster, Theodore, 164n
Foute, Jacob Fauble, 10, 93n
Fowler, John F., 36, 69–70, 220, 222n, 230, 240–42, 245, 248
Frankland, 18, 88
Franklin, Isaac, Sr., 33, 146n, 153; sells slave, 135, 142, 149, 238, 242; travels North to capture slave, 242, 250
free blacks, 36, 178, 193, 260; befriended by EB, 36; and colonization, 10–11, 33–34, 231; enforced removal of, 10, 72, 73, 120n, 163, 246; enfranchised, 4, 89n; historiography, 70–71; in judicial system, 22–23, 52; laws regulating movement of, 73, 120n; legal status of, 70–71, 73; living conditions of, 12, 14, 193; as missionaries, 33–34, 46; re-enslavement of, 50, 82, 163, 164; and Tenn. Constitution (1834), 14–15; trained in a trade, 246; *see also* blacks; slaves
free labor, 169, 175, 255; advantages of, 138, 172, 197, 198; colony proposed, 55–56, 145, 156, 169, 179, 203; compared with slave labor, 174, 176, 177, 235–36; immigrants as, 115n–16n; as moral example, 56; *see also* slave labor
Free Labor Advocate and Anti-Slavery Chronicle, 5
Free Masonry, 194
Friend of Man, 151, 197, 217; circulation of, 172; EB's letters published in, 42, 67, 142–46, 207
Fyffe, James H., 199, 202n, 225

gambling: fines for, 219
Garrett, Gray, 13, 95n, 218–19, 222n
Garrison, William Lloyd, 7, 40, 45, 191n, 261n
Gass, John, 231, 232n

Genius of Universal Emancipation, 7
Georgia, 53, 180n, 265; EB's residence in, 31, 129; proslavery clergy in, 175, 176, 204; railroads, 19, 225
Giddings, Joshua R., 226, 228n
Gillespy, James Houston, 94n–95n
Gloucester, John, 46
gold mining: in East Tenn., 200; in Georgia, 53
Goodell, William, 133n, 146n
Gordon, Charles, 133
Gould, David, 156
Great Britain, 130, 215; abolishes slavery, 227n; and *Creole* case, 215n–16n, 217; poor laborers in, 237
Green, Beriah, 41, 205, 207n
Green, Nathan, 23, 74, 77, 123n, 124n
Greene County, Tenn., 21, 22, 23, 75; early abolition movement in, 4, 11; EB's property in, 63, 64, 260; slave auction in, 33, 82, 249, 251n
Greenville, S.C.: description of, 237
Greenway Henry & Smith, 269
Groce, W. Todd, 21, 65
Gurnay (of Limestone Springs, S.C.): innkeeper/postmaster, 234–35
Gurney, John G. *See* Gurney, Joseph John
Gurney, Joseph John, 154, 158n, 172; letters to Clay, 169, 188, 226

Hadley, Joshua, 50
Haiti, 10
Hale, John, 53
Hammond, James Henry, 266
Harkaway (steamboat): EB describes trip on, 226
Harris, Jeremiah George, 162, 165n
Harris, Martha Erskine, 33
Harris, Sion, 11, 33, 46, 57, 186, 187–88, 189, 190n
Harris, William, 265, 266n, 267, 269
Harrison, William, 246, 246n–47n
Harrison, William Henry, 150–51, 151n
Harrold, Stanley, 7, 91n
Haynes, Landon Carter, 38, 159n
Haynes, Rev. (Presbyterian minister), 57, 168
Heady (slave dealer), 257

Heddington, Liberia: attack on, 188, 191n
Heiskell, Fred, 21–22
Henry, Spencer, 21, 37, 87, 218, 221n–22n, 239, 242, 245; EB boards with, 100n, 223; as friend of blacks, 263, 264–65
Henry, Mrs. Spencer, 79, 100n, 185, 229
Hiwassee Railroad, 18, 115n, 202; bankruptcy of, 196n; construction of, 19, 97n, 192
Hodge, Calloway, 80, 143, 147n, 170, 221
horses: traded in Florida, 166, 170, 183, 233
Houston, Sam, 91n
Howell, Patton (free black), 246
Howington, Arthur F., xi, 23, 76, 77–78, 83–84
Huff, J., 84, 245
Hunt, William, 242, 243n
Huston, James L., 67–68

Illinois, 3; slave catchers in, 242, 250
India: cotton grown in, 214, 235, 254, 255; sacrifice of widows in, 38, 204
Indiana: antislavery leaders migrate to, 3, 5; EB's land holdings in, 31, 64; slave catchers in, 221
individual slaves: Chamberlain, 35, 69–70, 152–53, 230, 240–42, 245, 248; Daniel, 183; Ephraim, 52; Hannibal, 83, 253–54; Isaac, 75; Jeremiah, 245; Josiah, 124n; Moses, 83–84; Peter, 212n; Samuel, 197; Simon, 36, 70, 81, 240, 248–49; Tom, 85; William, 226; *see also* William ("Captain")
industry: in East Tenn., 25, 45–46, 58–60, 61–62, 138, 234; with free labor, 55, 138; with immigrant labor, 115n–16n
Inscoe, John C., 23
internal improvements, 129; conventions on, 18, 201n; and sectionalism in Tenn., 17–19, 115n, 201n, 202
Irby, James Henderson, 29, 236, 238n–39n, 250
Irby, William, 29, 132, 134n
iron, 112n–13n, 138, 192, 200
ironworks, 129, 192: in East Tenn., 45–46, 263; loan sought for, 60; northern investment in, 234

Isaac (free black), 178

Jack (black physician), 74
Jackson, Andrew, 10, 37, 155, 171, 173n, 255
Jackson, James Caleb, 238n, 261n
Jackson, Nancy (black): freed by court order, 173n
Jacksoniana, 19
Jefferson County, Tenn., 22, 24, 170; antislavery petitions from, 14–15, 15–16, 20–21; Manumission Society, 17, 137
Johnson, Andrew, x, 18, 22, 88; EB's letter to, 270–71
Johnston, Josiah K., 194, 195, 196n
Johnston, Samuel, 194, 199–200, 202n, 227
Jones (of Cocke County): slaves of, auctioned, 81, 153, 207
Jones, Agnes, 133, 134n
Jones, George, Sr., 64
Jones, James, 7, 64, 90n, 92n, 202n
Jones, James Chamberlain, 194, 196n
Jonesboro Sentinel, 38
Jonesboro Whig, 38
judicial system: blacks in, 131–33, 166n, 171, 173n; *see also* Tennessee courts

Kendall, Thomas S., 39, 213, 216n
Kentucky, 233; attitudes toward slavery in, 144, 255, 257, 261; compared with Ohio, 44, 129; EB travels to, 257, 260; internal improvements in, 44, 257
Kincaid, Joseph, 12
Kirkpatrick, Jacob, 53
Kirkpatrick, William M., 138, 141n
Knight, Tristam Day, 144, 147n
Knoxville, 265, 267; description of, 23; EB's death in, 27, 64, 88; internal improvement conventions in (1841), 18, 115n, 197, 201n, 202; Union convention in, 21
Knoxville Gazette, 4
Knoxville Post, 35; EB on editor of, 212–13
Knoxville Register: attacks EB, 35, 56, 221; EB on editor of, 203–4
Knoxville Whig: proslavery defender, 19
Kolchin, Peter, 65

Index

Kyle, W. C., 21–22

Lane, Thomas, 139
Lane Theological Seminary, 6, 16, 206n
Latimore, George S., 50
Lauderdale, John, 84
Laurens, S.C.: description of, 236
Lea, Robert H., 135, 136, 139n, 193
Leavitt, Joshua, 133n
Letters on American Slavery, Addressed to Thomas Rankin, 6
Lewis, J. C., 223
Lewis, J. H., 163
Liberia: black missionaries in, 34, 46, 57, 104n, 159n, 198, 246; colonization of free blacks in, 10, 11, 15, 33–34, 47, 72, 73, 187–88, 231; Heddington in, attacked, 188, 191n
Liberty Party, 37, 40, 106n, 133n
Limestone Springs, S.C., 234
liquor: fines for sales of, 155, 219
livestock: raised in East Tenn., 192, 234; sales of, 186, 266
Lockhart, Jesse, 6, 91n
Locofocos, 145, 148n
Lotspeich, Samuel, 85
Louisiana, 184; removal of slaves to, 195, 199
Louisville, Ky.: trial of slave dealer in, 257
Lovejoy, Elijah P., 6
Lucky, Seth J. W., 21–22, 139, 141n, 218, 222n
Lundy, Benjamin, 6–7
Lyell, Sir Charles, 52
Lynch (innkeeper), 237

Mack, William, 39, 186–87, 190n, 224
Macy, Barachia, 90n
Madison County Abolitionist, 232, 238n
Mann, R. D., 115n
Manning, Joseph, 39, 105n, 184n
Mansfield (of Jefferson County): reports on slave abuse, 80–81, 143
Manumission Intelligencer, 45
manumission societies, x, 4–8, 10, 17, 45, 46, 47, 90n, 137
Marion County, Ohio: EB's land holdings in, 63
Marshall, John, 172

Marshall, Thomas F., 144, 147n
Martin, John, 231
Martin, Robert, 236
Maryland, 260; slavery on wane in, 261
Maryville College, 103n, 187; abolitionists in, 47, 201n, 205; seminary proposed for, 204, 205
Maynard, Horace, 3
McAnally, David Rice, 135, 139n, 142, 146, 149–50, 258
McBee, Lemuel, 80, 210, 212n, 220–21
McCampbell, John, 157, 160n
McCampbell, Robert, 59
McDowell, James P., 21
McDuffie, George, 136
McGaughey, John, 94n
McKinney, John A., 12, 16, 94n, 95n; report of, 12–13, 14–16
McKinney, Robert J., 14, 16, 22–23, 75, 250–51, 251n
McMahan, Ester, x, 82–83, 209, 212n
McMinn County, Tenn.: description of, 191–92; records burned, 225
McMurtrey, James, 33, 82, 249, 251n
medicine: slave practice, 74
Meek, Adam, Sr., 212n
Meek, Adam R., 80, 210, 212n
Meek, Sarah, 212n
Meigs County, Tenn., 9
Methodists, 139n; and antislavery movement, 8, 229–30; and clergy opposed to slavery, 37–38, 145, 165, 245; churches split over slavery, 8, 79–80, 232n
Middle Tennessee: attitudes toward slavery in, 11, 17; compared with East Tenn., 25, 78; and sectionalism, 17–18, 115n; slave acquittals in, 23, 78
Milligan, Samuel, 18
mineral resources, 156, 192; commercial value of, xi, 47, 54, 59–60, 62–63, 138; description of, 53–54, 112n–13n, 200
miscegenation, 33, 102n, 213, 249; result of, 82
Mississippi, 153, 197; cruelty toward slaves in, 184
Missouri, 139n; slaveholders in, 6
Montgomery (attorney), 225
Mooney, Chase, 75

Moore, Elisha, 85
Moore, William, 24, 80, 143, 147n
Morehead, John Motley, 34, 103n, 161, 165n
Moses, James C., 204, 206n
Myrick, Luther, 238n

Nashville: antislavery materials in, 166n; Dresser incident in, 16–17, 163; EB on violence in, 37
Nashville Daily Press and Times: Caldwell's letter in, 60
Nashville Gazette, 46
National Intelligencer, 214, 216n
Negro Law of South Carolina, The (1848), 30
Nelson, David, 6, 20, 91n, 250, 251n
Nelson, David Deaderick, 91n
Nelson, Samuel Kelsey, 91n
Nelson, T. A. R., 21–22
Netherland, John, 21
New York: antislavery society in, 146n; banking in, 168, 171, 262, 269; EB's property in, 31, 64, 244, 260; fugitive in, 213
New York American, 217, 226, 228n
Newman, Benjamin F., 162, 165n
Newport, Tenn. *See* Cocke County, Tenn.
Nicholson, A. O. P., 119n
Niles' Weekly Register, 46, 49
nonslaveholders: attitude of, toward slavery, 255; as jurors, 75; in S.C., 214; and Tenn. constitution (1834), 14, 15
North: antislavery attitudes in, 154, 217, 224, 247; churches and antislavery cause, 34, 188, 224, 247–48; compared with South, 160–61, 186; resists southern demands, 164, 213; runaway slaves protected in, 221
North Carolina, 23, 161, 264, 267, 268; attitudes toward slavery in, 34, 103n, 144, 151, 183–84, 254, 261; description of, 234; EB's landholdings in, 31, 64, 138; slavery on wane in, 261; statute on emancipation, 71
northern capitalists, 115n; benefited by Tenn. investments, 59, 61–63; invest in South Carolina, 234

Ohio, 154, 230; antislavery leaders migrate to, 3, 5, 237; EB's land in, 244, 260; prosperity in, 44, 129
Olmsted, Frederick Law: visits East Tenn., 23
O'Neall, John Belton, 30, 51, 162, 165n
Oneida Institute, 6
Osborn, Charles, 4, 5, 6
overseers, 143, 178

Parham, Marcellus B., 63
Patterson (of Jefferson County), 17, 137
Patton (of Ashville, N.C.), 258
Peake, Benjamin, 262–63, 264
Pearson, Abel, 37, 104n, 157, 159n
Peck, Adam, 49
Peck, Isham T., 142, 179
Peck, Jacob, xi, 17, 22, 65, 142, 153, 155, 211, 233; description of, 48–49, 146n; EB's friendship with, 41, 48, 87; as EB's partner, 49, 63, 113n, 138, 156; essays of, 203, 204; free labor promoted by, 55, 145, 156, 168–69, 200, 206n; as friend of blacks, 49–52, 77, 110n, 178, 219; as Gerrit Smith correspondent, 144, 179; land holdings of, 49, 54, 138, 167; mining interests of, 52–53, 112n, 114n; opinion on court jurisdiction, 72, 110n–11n; sons of, 22, 41, 142, 179
Peck, William Raine, 22
Pennsylvania, 156, 167, 192, 255; fugitive in, 220
Philanthropist, 5
Phillips (of Mooresille, Ala.): reports on slave abuse, 132
Phillips, Ulrich B., 65, 70, 75
Polk (N.C. planter): moves to Tenn., 211
Polk, James K., 163
poor whites: condition of, 192, 236–37; employment for, 156; slavery's effect on, 45, 61, 107n, 171
Porter, George M., 178, 180n
Position of the Southern Church in Relation to Slavery, 20
Post, Calvin, 47, 222n
postmasters: and abolitionist mail, 17, 35, 139, 203

Index

Potter, William, 40, 48, 105n, 187, 188, 190n–91n
Presbyterians: antislavery attitudes of, 6, 8, 37, 91n; antislavery clergy, 5–6, 37–38, 39, 46–47, 145, 186, 214; educate black missionaries, 33–34, 104n; establish Cherokee missions, 48, 180n; proslavery clergy, 20, 38, 156, 210; revivals, 187; Seceders, 39, 214, 216n; seminaries of, 48, 204, 205; split over slavery, 204, 205; and temperance, 188
Pulliam, Robert W., 79, 185, 229, 190n

Quakers: as antislavery leaders, 4, 6–7, 8; antislavery petitions of, 103n, 161, 165n

railroads: in East Tenn., 18, 19, 21, 25, 62, 115n, 117n, 192, 201n; in Ga., 225; in Ky., 257–58
Randolph, Robert B., 171, 173n
Rankin, John, 5–6, 16–17, 91n
Rayner, Kenneth, 179, 180n
Reese, James, 141n
Reese, Joseph B. M., 125n, 138, 141n, 193
Reese, William B., 22–23, 121n, 125n, 139, 141n
revivals, 34, 187, 223, 229, 244; as morality builders, 37, 247
Rhea County, Tenn.: antislavery attitudes in, 9, 226–27
Rhoton, Josiah, 138, 141n
Rice, Mr. (near Athens, Tenn.), 36, 79, 208–9
Roadman, William Chesley, 14, 17, 95n, 140n; postmaster of Newport, 136, 239; on slavery, 242; slaves of, whipped, 229
Robertson, William, 207
Robinson, John J., 47
Robinson, William, 211n
Rogers (of Jefferson County), 182
Rogers, Daswell, 227, 228n
Rogers, Lee, 271
Rogers, William H., 227, 228n
Roper, John, 170, 173n, 231
Ross, Frederick Augustus, 20, 97n, 156, 158n–59n, 169

Rutherfordton, N.C.: description of, 234

Safford, James M., 58, 60
Saint-Domingue: slave revolt, 71
Saunders, Romulus Mitchell, 34, 161, 164n
Sevier, Valentine, 146, 148n
Seward, William H., 154, 158n, 171
sheep raising: in East Tenn., 102n, 186, 192–93
Shelby, John, 174, 179n
Signal of Liberty, 160
silk culture: in East Tenn., 20, 156, 169
silver mining, 268
slave labor: compared to free labor, 166, 184, 198; distorted labor market, 61; inefficiency of, 23, 174; in Kentucky 129; unprofitability of, 55, 177, 214, 235–36, 250, 254; *see also* free labor
slave trade, 82, 195, 199
slaveholders: abandon worn-out lands, 153, 211, 266, 267; anti-slavery attitudes of, 34–35, 142, 150, 151, 154, 194, 207, 239, 247; considered kind masters, 36, 69, 149, 151n, 152, 182, 194, 220, 230, 240, 253; cruelty of (*see* slaves: physical punishment of); debts of, 153, 182, 254, 255, 266; dissipated sons of, 27, 130–31, 175, 176; EB's rapport with, x, 34, 35–36, 41, 69, 208–9; emancipating by will, 50–51, 57, 72, 120n, 154–55, 179, 231; to face God's judgment, 199, 253; and impunity for killing slaves, 76, 82, 84, 124n, 132, 269; interest of, in free labor system, 175, 203; keep slaves for humanity reasons, 49, 193, 200–201, 214; killed by slaves, 82, 83–84, 124n; and miscegenation, 33, 82, 213, 249; slavery's effect on, 79, 233; and support for emancipation, 193, 207, 214, 224–25, 226, 248, 255
slavery: Biblical arguments on, 223–24, 266; as cause of migration, 5, 8, 17, 39, 91n, 137, 194; church splits caused by, 8, 79–80, 204, 205, 232n, 244; clergy as defenders of, 20, 35, 38, 156, 175, 210; clergy opposed to, 5–6, 20, 37–38, 39,

slavery *(cont.)*
46–47, 145, 186, 214, 223; compared with wife burning in India, 204; in D.C., 161, 171–72; economic effects of, 23, 35, 61, 130, 158n, 172, 174, 186, 218, 269; effect of, on southern whites, 24, 37, 107n, 130, 207, 218, 235; end of, predicted, 39, 71, 136, 145, 157, 189, 200, 213, 224, 235, 240, 257, 261, 267; growing dissatisfaction with, 186, 194, 211, 233, 248, 267; historiography, 65, 67–68, 70–71, 75–78, 83–84, 91n; and miscegenation, 213, 249; and morality of, 5, 32, 34, 108n, 130–31, 200–201; petitions to abolish, 11–12, 14–16, 46, 47; planters opposed to, 29, 142, 150, 153, 194, 207; profitability of, 65, 66, 129, 207, 269; as protection for blacks, 12, 193; retarded growth of industry, 44, 46, 61, 66; southern opinion on, 20, 68, 125n, 136, 151, 183, 211, 235, 239; sustained by cotton culture, 194, 215, 254, 255

Slavery Ordained of God, 20

slaves: auctions of, 33, 74, 81, 123n, 153, 207; barter of, 233–34; burning alive of, 84, 85, 131, 136, 209; as children of white masters, 82, 213, 241, 249; conditional freedom for, 73, 120n, 246; costs of keeping, 235–36, 250; dealers in, 146n, 182, 199, 257; EB as friend of, 36, 208, 241; EB tries to purchase, 135, 142, 149, 152, 258–59; families separated by sale, 32, 81, 82, 123n, 153–54, 178, 181–83, 204, 230, 242, 248, 249, 253, 257; fear of being sold, 36, 69, 81, 154, 230, 242, 245, 248, 249; freed by owner's will, 50–51, 57, 72, 154, 179, 231; fugitives captured, 162, 172, 187, 194, 210, 220–21, 242, 250; humanity of, recognized by courts, 51, 77, 124n, 125n; improving conditions for, 134n, 257; in the judicial system, 22–23, 30, 49–50, 72, 74, 75–78, 83–84, 121n–25n passim, 173n, 253–54; killed by owners, 51, 75, 76, 82, 84, 133, 227, 235, 245, 269; laws protecting, 122n–23n, 124n, 245; legal status of, 10, 71–75, 104n, 110n, 119n–20n, 121n; liberated to go to Africa, 198, 231, 246; manslaughter committed by, 49, 76, 82–83, 85, 121n, 124n, 131, 209, 212n, 218, 253–54; physical punishment of, 3, 74, 76–81 passim, 132, 143–44, 152, 188, 209, 253; as property, 121n, 123n, 185, 268; prosecution for maiming or murder of, 76, 124n; public executions of, 29, 32, 83, 131, 136; purchase price of, 149–50, 151n, 152, 153, 178, 238, 259, 263, 264; purchased by abolitionists, 41, 81, 146n; revolts and threats of insurrection by, 71, 72, 104n, 161; runaways, 35, 36, 74, 81, 136, 152–53, 163, 171, 219–21, 230, 240–42, 249, 250, 262; sold for owner's debts, 82, 153, 182, 266; sold south, 81–82, 195, 199, 211, 242, 266; voluntary emancipation of, 16, 20, 107n, 141n, 144, 156, 199 *(see also* emancipation); whipped to death, 132, 257, 268; *see also* blacks; free blacks; individual slaves

Smith, Gerrit, 17, 19, 32, 35, 37, 40, 49, 65, 133n; buys slave's freedom, 33, 41, 81, 135, 146n, 197; and colonization, 11, 160n; and compensated emancipation, 106n; on Cultural Voluntarism, 41; EB as business agent for, 41–42; EB's correspondence with, 25, 33, 42, 67, 87; EB's letters to, 135–39, 142–46, 149–51, 151–58, 160–64, 166–69, 170–72, 174–79, 180–84, 185–90, 191–96, 197–201, 202–6, 207–11, 212–15, 217–21, 223–27, 229–30, 231–38, 243–46, 239–43, 247–51, 257–59, 259–61, 262–63, 264–66, 267–68, 269–70; financial support sought from, 55, 57–58, 147n, 173n, 206n; as gradualist, 41; and Liberty Party, 37, 40, 106n, 133n

Smith, Henry, 26
Smith, John, 143
Smith, Phillipa, 26
South: antislavery influence in, 7, 34, 136, 137, 144, 172, 183–84, 206, 254; antislavery sentiment in, 183, 189, 194,

199; bankruptcies in, 224, 244; beneficial climate in, 175; census comparison with North, 160–61; depression in, 35, 186, 201; dissipated youth of, 56, 175, 176; East Tenn. economic ties with, 19, 21; historians on the economy of, 65; immorality in, 130–31; industry needed in, 138, 213; northern influence on, 39, 154, 160, 169, 195–96, 217, 224, 245, 255; northern tutors in, 161; proneness to violence in, 37, 162; treatment of free blacks in, 163; women's responsibilities in, 131, 134n

South Carolina, 270; abuse of slaves in, 29, 84, 131–33, 136, 143, 236, 268; agriculture in, 237; attitudes toward slavery in, 29–30, 214, 235; Baptist clergy in, 175; condition of poor whites in, 162, 236–37; EB describes visit to, 235–37; EB's residence in, 28, 129, 130, 213, 236; economic distress in, 235, 236, 264, 265–66, 267; migration from, 265, 267, 269; nonslaveholders dissatisfaction in, 214; northern capitalists invest in, 234; observations on society in, 161–62, 181; Presbyterian clergy in, 199, 204

Southern Quarterly Review, 235, 238n, 270

Southern Rights Convention (1851), 29

Stampp, Kenneth, 70

Stanberry, John F., 218, 222n

Standifer, William I., 226, 228n

Stearnes and Sturges Mining Company, 62

Stephenson, Matthew, 13, 16, 94n

Steuben County, N.Y.: EB's property in, 260, 269

Stewart, Alvan, 41

Stone, Timothy D. P., 31, 32, 64, 65, 256n

Sullins, David, 196n

Sullins, Nathan, 194, 196n

Sullins, Timothy, 196n

Tappan, Lewis, 63, 191n, 261n, 265; EB as agent for, 41, 260

tariff: and cotton question, 214–15

Taylor, Rev. (of Lee County, Va.), 187

temperance movement, 9, 160, 175; as issue in slavery debate, 17, 214, 218; literature, 172; as morality builder, 37, 247; progress of, in Tenn., 155–56, 166, 187, 188, 219, 224, 230–31, 244; in S.C., 30, 235

Temple, Oliver P., 16, 21, 22, 57

Tennessee: antislavery attitudes in, 4, 144, 166, 261; geologic surveys in, 54; laws regulating blacks in, 9–10, 71–74, 104n, 110n, 120n; proneness to violence in, 162–63; secession vote in, 22; sectionalism in, 17–19, 24–25, 96n, 115n, 202; slave population in, 25; temperance reform in, 155–56, 230–31, 244; *see also* East Tennessee; Middle Tennessee; West Tennessee

Tennessee Colonization Society, 72, 93n–94n

Tennessee Constitutional Convention (1796): abolition attempts in, 3–4; enfranchised free blacks, 4, 89n

Tennessee Constitutional Convention (1834): slavery issue in, 8, 11–14

Tennessee courts: and emancipation, 119n; and slave defendants, 22–23, 49–52, 72, 74–78, 83, 110n, 121n, 123n, 124n, 232n; sympathetic jurists in, xi, 22–23, 49–50, 51–52, 123n; whites punished for murder in, 76; *see also* judicial system; Tennessee Supreme Court cases

Tennessee legislature: antislavery petitions in, 4–5, 8–9, 42n, 92n–93n, 97n; and circulation of antislavery materials, 9–10, 228n; and East Tenn. statehood, 18, 21, 202; and legislation relating to blacks, 10–11, 50–51, 72–74, 104n, 120n

Tennessee Manumission Society, 4, 5, 7, 10, 45, 46, 47, 90n

Tennessee Mining Company: northern interests in, 59

Tennessee Supreme Court cases: *Abraham Vaughan v. Phebe, a Woman of Color,* 52, 111n; *Blakemore and Hadley v. Negro Phill,* 110n; *Bob, a Slave v. The State,*

Tennessee Supreme Court cases *(cont.)* 77, 110n, 121n; *Fisher's Negroes v. Dabbs,* 50–51, 110n–11n; *Jacob v. The State,* 83–84, 124n; *Moses, a Slave v. The State,* 83–84, 124n; *W. E. Jones v. John S. Allen,* 75, 121n; *William Fields v. State of Tennessee,* 51; *see also* Tennessee Courts

Texas: migration to, 266, 269; slaves removed to, 82, 211; Tenn. volunteers bound for, 225

Thomas, John, 83, 218, 219

Thompson, William, 218, 222n

Thomson, Andrew Wallace, 235–36, 238n

Totten, A. W. O., 124n

Trim, Anderson, 226, 228n

Troost, Gerard, 53–54, 58, 138, 174, 179n–80n; geology reports of, 54, 112n

Turner, Nat, 10, 71, 72

turnpikes, 18, 138, 201n

Underhill, John, 90n

Union Court House, S.C.: description of, 235

Upton (slave dealer), 199, 227

Van Dyke, Roger R., 70

Vesey, Denmark, 71

Vicksburg, Miss.: violence in, 163

Virginia, 265; changing attitudes toward slavery in, 255, 261; EB in, 260; and fugitive slave, 171–72, 213; progress in, held back by slavery, 147n; treatment of slaves in, 195

Wadsworth, William, 34, 144, 148n, 161

Walter, William, Jr., 52

Warm Springs, N.C., 234, 237

Washington County, Tenn.: antislavery attitudes in, 4, 11; iron industry in, 45–46

Waterman (of Augusta, Ga.), 237

Waters (of S.C.): killed by slaves, 131

Webster, Daniel, 216n, 217

Webster, Thomas, 115n

Weld, Theodore Dwight, 206n, 223, 227n

Werner, Abraham Gottlob, 52, 54

West Tennessee, 11, 19, 23, 25; and sectionalism, 18, 96n; slave acquittals in, 78

Whitaker, Daniel, 238n

White, Gideon Stebbins, 38, 210, 204–5, 206n

Whitney, Eli, 254

William ("Captain"): EB tries to buy, 33, 81, 135–36, 149–50, 237–38, 258–59, 260, 262–65, 267; life story of, 152–53

Williams, James, 212, 215n

Williams, Joseph Lanier, 197, 201n

Willis, Jesse, 6

Wilson, Samuel Tyndale, 47

Wood, John, 239

Woodfin, Archibald, 135, 140n

Woodfin, Nicholas W., 142, 153; EB's dealings with, 33, 81, 135, 146, 149–50, 258–59; as kind master, 103n, 152; as large slaveholder, 139n–40n; as owner of William ("Captain"), 149–50, 151n, 237–38

Worcester, Samuel A., 176, 180n

Worcester v. Georgia: U.S. Supreme Court rules on, 180n

Worley, Gabriel, 124n

Worthington (slaveholder of Mississippi), 41, 138, 142, 146n

Wright, Isaac, 187, 190n

Wyatt-Brown, Bertram, 124n

Zollicoffer, Felix Kirk, 174, 180n